Decolonizing Psychology

Explorations in Narrative Psychology

Mark Freeman
Series Editor

Books in the Series

Speaking of Violence
Sara Cobb

Narrative Imagination and Everyday Life
Molly Andrews

Narratives of Positive Aging: Seaside Stories
Amia Lieblich

Beyond the Archive: Memory, Narrative, and the Autobiographical Process
Jens Brockmeier

The Narrative Complexity of Ordinary Life: Tales from the Coffee Shop
William L. Randall

Rethinking Thought: Inside the Minds of Creative Scientists and Artists
Laura Otis

Life and Narrative: The Risks and Responsibilities of Storying Experience
Edited by Brian Schiff, A. Elizabeth McKim, and Sylvie Patron

Not in My Family: German Memory and Responsibility After the Holocaust
Roger Frie

A New Narrative for Psychology
Brian Schiff

Decolonizing Psychology: Globalization, Social Justice, and Indian Youth Identities
Sunil Bhatia

DECOLONIZING PSYCHOLOGY

Globalization, Social Justice, and Indian Youth Identities

Sunil Bhatia

OXFORD
UNIVERSITY PRESS

Oxford University Press is a department of the University of Oxford. It furthers
the University's objective of excellence in research, scholarship, and education
by publishing worldwide. Oxford is a registered trade mark of Oxford University
Press in the UK and certain other countries.

Published in the United States of America by Oxford University Press
198 Madison Avenue, New York, NY 10016, United States of America.

© Oxford University Press 2018

CIP data is on file at the Library of Congress
ISBN 978-0-19-996472-7

9 8 7 6 5 4 3 2 1
Printed by Webcom, Inc., Canada

I dedicate this book to my father, Satpal Bakshiram Bhatia, and to my mother, Sabita Satpal Bhatia.

I am here because they were there for me when I took my first steps and many leaps of faith along the way.

CONTENTS

ACKNOWLEDGMENTS

There are many people who have supported the remarkable journey of this book. I am especially indebted to Mark Freeman, the series editor for explorations in narrative psychology. He showed great faith in the book project and his unwavering support, brilliance, and keen editorial insights made the book stronger and authentic. I am particularly grateful for his wise mentoring and the advice that I should give more space to the stories of participants in the book.

Abby Gross, the senior editor, played a vital role in overseeing the project. My special thanks to her for having confidence in the project right from the beginning and providing crucial input during various phases of the manuscript. It has been an absolute delight to work with the assistant editor, Courtney MCCaroll—who very smoothly shepherded the various stages of the production of the book. I also want to thank the four anonymous reviewers who provided thoughtful, extensive, and constructive feedback on the book proposal and manuscript.

Notwithstanding their contributions, any errors in the book are mine alone.

The heart and soul of this book is anchored in the study of lives and without my participants' willingness to share their life stories and perspectives, this book would have lost its moorings. I am forever indebted to the youth, families, parents, professionals, and many other people from various cultural and class backgrounds in India who embraced this project, gave me their time and spent many hours talking to me about their lives.

I am grateful to Nisha Kagal and Pushpa Darekar for doing such a thorough job with transcribing all the interviews.

Michelle Fine and the faculty and students at the critical social-personality psychology program at CUNY have provided an intellectual home to me for exploring many of the key ideas that found their way in the book. The four colloquium talks that I gave at the critical psychology program eventually became woven in the threads of the different chapters. In particular, Michelle's steadfast support has been extremely valuable to my growth as a scholar. I owe her a debt of gratitude for inspiring me to imagine a more humane and social justice oriented psychology.

The American Psychological Association's Division 24, Society for Theoretical and Philosophical Psychology, Dialogical Self Conference, Narrative Study of Lives and Personology group, and Society for Qualitative Inquiry in Psychology have served as important generative spaces for my scholarship. The numerous colleagues I have met in these spaces have contributed immensely to my growth as a theorist and scholar.

The seeds of this project were born out of many conversations I had with Ram Mahalingam. He encouraged me to write this book even before I had written a single chapter. My sincere thanks for his rock-solid backing over the years and giving critical feedback on the manuscript and just being there for me.

Michelle Mamberg's compassionate and vigorous reading of the manuscript was such a gift especially when I was stuck in my writing. Her unfaltering encouragement and warmth was an important source of reassurance and motivation for me to plod along. My heartfelt thanks to her for taking on the role of being one of the trusted outside readers.

I feel very fortunate to have a circle of supportive and amazing colleagues in the Department of Human Development and Education at Bolles House at Connecticut College. I owe a special thanks to Michelle Dunlap, Jenny Fredericks, Mike James, Loren Marulis, Donna Graham, Sandy Grande, Lauren Anderson, Dana Wright and Charlie Cocores. It has been a joy to work with such a special group of people who have fostered an excellent spirit of inquiry, collaboration, and reflection in the work space. My conversations with colleagues at Bolles House have served as a graceful reminder to me that the work of social justice and decolonization is a long struggle that is composed of many moments of resistance, collaboration, and re-imagination. Their commitment to social justice, human development and education is awe-inspiring.

The Center for the Comparative Study of Race and Ethnicity (CCSRE) at Connecticut College has also given me a community to critically engage with issues of social justice, racial inequality, and social difference. I am especially thankful to Sandy Grande for her solidarity, radical vision of justice, and for introducing me to the history of decolonization from indigenous perspectives.

I want to specially thank Jefferson Singer for his continuous support and for inviting me to be a part of the broader community of scholars in the personology and narrative group.

I am grateful to Donna Graham for her exceptional service to the department and for assistance with this project. There are times when I have given her an assignment and she has completed it quickly and asked, "Is there anything else I can help with." Her positive demeanor, generous and caring attitude and a thoroughly professional outlook has made Bolles House such an inviting place to work.

This research project was partially funded from Peggy Sheridan Community Learning Grants from the Holleran Center of Public Policy and Community Action and R.F. Johnson Grants. Specifically, the Sheridan Community Learning Grants have been very valuable in allowing me to conduct ethnographic field work in India. I want to thank Jennifer Fredericks, Tracee Reiser and Rebecca McCue for providing the structural support for undertaking community based research.

This book was a result of transnational relationships and connections. There were key people in Pune who had my back and they went out of their way to make sure my project moved forward.

Meenakshi Iyer played a pivotal role in assisting me in launching the pilot project and connecting me to her network of friends and colleagues in the Pune IT sector. My special thanks to Reena Bonagiri for introducing me to her dozens of families and friends who were willing and eager to engage in conversations about globalization and identity. Suparna Karpe was my gatekeeper to Meridian College who helped me in setting up interviews with faculty and staff and and the students. Rahul Bajaj, Poonam Mercandante, and Poonam Aurora opened up the world of call centers for me taught me important lessons about about the culture of outsourcing and business processing offices.

My friends, Nagraj Vedadri, Shankar Gaonkar, and Ravi Jathar were important interlocutors for me as they were able to narrate complicated and varied stories of cultural change and identity formation in India. The India of their youth was in the distant past and they had lived through two decades of neoliberalization that had profoundly impacted their lives. Their perspective on neoliberal globalization in India was tremendously useful in formulating the arguments in the book.

My friendship with Rohidas Shetty has been a source of fulfilment and personal transformation. Over the years, his generosity, equanimity, and wisdom have brought immense joy. Unbeknownst to him, many of our conversations over our evening walks on Dhole Patil Road have found a place in the book.

Pratima Joshi has also profoundly influenced my thinking about social inequality and urban poverty in India. Her leadership on providing sanitation to the urban working- class residents in India through her non-profit, Shelter Associates, is nothing short of a local revolution. Her message and commitment to this cause has inspired to me to follow in her footsteps. Pratima's dedicated colleagues and social workers were very helpful in connecting me to the youth and families in Panchsheel Basti. I thank them for trusting me with their legacy.

I am thankful to the National Academy of Psychology in India for inviting me to give a keynote talk that was based on this book at their conference at IIT in Chennai. In particular, I am grateful to Kumar Ravi Priya and Sadhana Natu for their incisive feedback and their affirmation that a decolonizing perspective is much needed in psychology. My visits to the non-profit organizations Pukar in Mumbai and Toxiclinks in Delhi taught me about the significance of local resistance and how people who are marginalized fight back against structures of oppression.

Many of the ideas in the book were first tested out and discussed in my courses HMD: 416: Globalization and Cultural Identity and HMD 306: Language, Narrative and Self. I am grateful for the students in these courses for enthusiastically engaging and debating the preliminary ideas that were presented to them.

I am very grateful to Ruma Sen for always being willing to engage in conversation related to India. Over the years, she has served as important conversational partner and a reliable source of validating and challenging my reading of social phenomena back home. She has been a good friend and an ideal godmother to my kids—her presence has been a precious gift to me and my family.

My mother-in-law, Radha Gopal Ram, has been source of strength and love for me and my family. Her watchful eye and loving presence has given my children a life time of well-being and serenity.

Finally, I want to acknowledge my wife, Anjali Ram, whose unshakeable confidence in the project and in my vision of psychology made this book possible. Her critical reading of the chapters transformed the overall quality of the arguments. Above all, her love and companionship has sustained me in immeasurable ways and given me the strength to forge ahead.

My children, Amit and Anusha, have given me much love and happiness. I wrote much of this book at home around the presence of my children. I thank them for their smiles, moods, laughter, playfulness as it has often lifted my spirts and infused my writing.

I have dedicated this book to my parents, Satpal Bhatia and Sabita Bhatia, without whom I would not have take the first steps in my journey of life. I am grateful for their love, childhood memories in Ambernath, and sacrifices. In dedicating this book to them, I honor my ancestors and the struggles they have embodied.

I am because they were there.

INTRODUCTION

I have been an eyewitness to a changing India ever since 1990 when I left to pursue my doctorate in psychology at Clark University in Worcester, Massachusetts. Every other year, I would return home to Pune city in the state of Maharashtra in India—a city that was changing beyond recognition. The cumulative effect of these changes is difficult to describe because, to a large extent, I was revisiting the familiarity of home. I usually felt I was returning to a recognizable cultural space, but in 2003, I recall being struck by the steady onslaught of globalization on the local spaces in Pune. The buildings and landmarks from my college days were slowly giving way to new office buildings, sprawling residential apartments, and shopping malls. At that time, I could see cultural fissures and breaks in patterns that previously seemed familiar and ordinary. With every visit to Pune, I realized that "my story" was not just solely born out of my first-hand experiences with globalization as a social phenomenon, but it was part of a larger story of identity and cultural change that was unfolding in India. My narrative was embedded in a host of other stories about colonization, postcolonial India, social class inequality, excessive wealth, and consumption—none of which I fully understood. I heard numerous accounts from my family and friends about how they were reconstructing their identities in the face of enormous change.

During the past decade, the most significant transformation I witnessed in India was not the outrageous surge of new malls or the increase in the number of cars on the road. Rather, what I witnessed was a shift in how segments of middle- and upper-class urban Indians were imagining and reimagining their identities. I also noticed that the jarring juxtaposition of desperate poverty growing steadily alongside affluent malls did not seem to rankle their sensibilities. The young and old repeatedly affirmed this to me in a fusion of Hindi and English that colloquially is characterized as *Hinglish*: "*Abhi*, there is future here, *na?* ("Now, there is future here, no?"), "*Zyada* opportunities *hai*" ("There are more opportunities here"), and "*Nai baaba*, there are openings here now so why go abroad?" A popular Pepsi commercial launched in India in the late 1990s, "*Yeh Dil Maange More!*" ("The Heart Wants More!"), captured the mood of the times. Middle-class families were rushing to buy apartments, cars, and motorcycles on bank loans as their purchasing power was exponentially increasing due to their higher salaries. The sites of self-making were everywhere.

MAKEOVERS AND THE DRESSING UP OF A NEW INDIA: THE LAUNCH OF *VOGUE*

In 2008, I purchased a copy of the first issue of *Vogue* magazine that was launched in India for the emerging middle- and upper-class segments of urban Indians who were brand conscious and had the money to consume expensive luxuries. The first 50 pages of the Indian *Vogue* magazine were not different from those of the American *Vogue*. There were slick and glossy advertisements for Gucci, Lancôme, Tudor, Chanel, Dolce & Gabbana, Audi, Salvatore Ferragano, Ganjam Jewelers, and Tommy Hilfiger. What was different about this inaugural issue was that the editor of *Vogue* had asked each of the Indian and foreign contributors to answer the following question: "If India were a woman, how would you dress her?" Shobha De (2007), a well-known chronicler of gossip and the social lives of celebrities in India, answered the question, "I would dress her in a sari . . . of course! But give her a look, a more contemporary spin, using accessories that say 'today'" (p. 50). What did "today" or the "contemporary spin" mean in this context? "Contemporary" and "today" referred to an India that was viewed as becoming modern, advanced, and global. Lucinda Chambers (2007), the fashion director of the British *Vogue*, was more detailed in her answer as it incorporated many of the old tropes of Orientalist language. She wrote,

> I see India as a woman who perhaps is the first generation of her family to go to university. She has a job; she is earning money that she can spend on herself. She is newly confident and happy. She is international but hasn't lost touch with what is wonderful in her background. She would dress in an individual, charming and quirky way, mixing the modern, such as Miu Miu, Westwood, with Sabyasachi Mukherjee and Comme, with some pieces from her grandmother's wardrobe. Nothing mannered or studied about her; she is spontaneous and spirited and that is reflected in her clothes. (p. 53)

In this excerpt, Chambers describes India as coming of age, as she transforms herself from being an uneducated, village woman to someone who is getting a university education and has arrived in the global 21st century. The message is not subtle but, rather, quite direct. She compares contemporary India to a first-generation university student, implying that the older India was largely poor, uneducated, and illiterate. As a first-generation student, India will mingle with the league of highly educated and advanced countries. India is traditional and international, but there is nothing sophisticated or "mannered" about her. However, having come into money, she is showing off her confidence. Prabuddha Dasgupta (2007), an Indian fashion photographer, writes,

> Figuratively speaking, I think India needs to "undress" before anything else, to rid herself of the heavy layers of accumulated baggage, colonial and otherwise. That has contributed to her confused and schizophrenic notion about body and sexuality. Then I would drape her in a Kanjeevaram sari, worn dangerously low, with a sliver anklet on her foot, kaajal [eyeliner] in her eyes, and crown it all with a glorious bouquet of jasmine in her hair. (p. 52)

Dasgupta wants to transform India into a blank slate so her colonial history could be erased and she could overcome her traditional views about sexual identity. Once India had been undressed, stripped of her historical baggage, Dasgupta would then portray India as someone who is not afraid to display her sexuality. In their answers, other contributors described India as a woman who is exotic, colorful, independent, vibrant, multicultural, and as someone who would be wearing a "Kingfisher blue *sari*, with threads of gold . . . with Manolo Blahnik shoes . . . Chanel leather bag and Jackie O black sunglasses" (Haddi, 2007, p. 53).

These contributors were capturing the desires of upper-class urban, educated, English-speaking wealthy Indians, who in the first place had the financial background and the cultural capital to afford the luxuries and objects that were displayed in the magazine. These descriptions also reflected their individual fantasies of India and the desires of a certain class of people to see India as being on the world stage. They wanted to "undress" India so her excess baggage of tradition, poverty, and colonial history could be obliterated, and India could then be given a makeover as though it were a lifeless mannequin, devoid of people, history, politics, and culture.

In 2007, a single copy of *Vogue* cost approximately Rs. 100 or $2—a sum that approximately 200 million Indians earn daily by mostly engaging in work that requires physical labor. The *Vogue* India edition includes another article, titled "The Burden of Wealth," that gives tips to Indians on how to spend and invest their money. The author of the article, Alex Kuruvilla (2007), states that whether you "love it or loathe it, this is the new India" (p. 148). Everywhere you go in this new India, he writes, people are talking about their increasing wealth and extraordinary spending. Kuruvilla observes that since liberalization reforms in 1991, India has added 25,000 millionaires and 36 billionaires. He further states that the post-liberalization, educated, Indian youth have come into new money and are uncertain about how to spend their wealth.

Furthermore, he elaborates that those Indians who have become rich should not hesitate to publicly flaunt their newly acquired wealth by having lavish dinner parties and "intimate gatherings in boutique hotels along the Turkish Rivera" (p. 150).

Kuruvilla (2007) also writes that India is living in a gilded age, and the newly rich should learn from philanthropists in the United States (e.g., Warren Buffett and Bill Gates) and should champion social causes and make government largely irrelevant during times of prosperity. *Vogue* was unabashedly pushing for the handing over of large portions of the Indian government to privatization and corporate power. How to undress India and give her a polished corporate makeover had become one of the preoccupations of the elite, and they were using their financial and cultural clout to construct and display new forms of Indianness.

The series of comments in *Vogue* reveal that the Indian nation was problematically imagined through the pathology of schizophrenia, tropes of Orientalism, elitism, and through a gendered, objectified, and sexualized discourse. In addition, the contributors were also reinforcing the point that globalization and the new accumulation of wealth had made India modern, brand-conscious, and ready for a Western makeover. The views of the contributors who highlighted the arrival of a global India in the 21st century were not some isolated and exclusive opinions expressed only by international and Indian writers of the Indian fashion magazine world. Rather, several urban Indian youth from middle- and upper-class families to whom I spoke expressed similar sentiments about India that echoed those of the *Vogue* writers. The English-speaking youth that I spoke to expressed an ambition to become rich, powerful, and make India a "world-class" nation.

There were many complex and varied stories of globalization that were circulating around in the public imagination. Several of the people I interviewed in Pune viewed their encounters with globalization through their respective social class locations. The middle-class families may not have had the financial capacity to celebrate their birthdays in the hotels along the Turkish Rivera, but they were reimagining the nation as a global player, a superpower, and a modern country of vast talents, and they wanted to make India like Singapore and London.

NARRATIVES OF NOSTALGIA: MY STORY AND THE "SWEET REVENGE OF TIME"

The representations of self were etched in multiple urban signs—the semiotics of the affluent class were in exhibition all around the city and in new cultural sites. These manifestations could be seen in the ostentatious display of wealth possessed by this new affluent class; in the restlessness of youth in pubs, bars, and cafés; in the indiscriminate growth of glass-encased shopping and office complexes; in the rise of luxury apartments that bespoke opulence and unlimited comforts; and in the creation of colossal information technology (IT) parks. The collective rise of rapacious ambition in the upper and middle classes and the wealthy and elite stood out in contrast to the plight of the disadvantaged youth with their never-ending struggles with poverty and unemployment.

The India in which I had grown up was gradually vanishing from my sight. Growing up in India in the 1970s and 1980s, I used to listen to Hindi music that was played on a government-owned radio station, Vivid Bharti, which was my family's only media-based source of entertainment.[1] My parents would turn on a Phillips radio in the morning and evening, playing old and new Hindi songs. One of my favorite songs from that time was a melancholic song about the painful effects of time on unreciprocated love titled "*Waqt Ne Kiya Kya Haseen Sitam*" from the movie *Kagaz Ke Phool* (Guru Dutt, 1959). This song, translated in English, emphasizes how it was time for the hero of the movie to let go of his unrequited love. In the movie, the hero sings that time had crafted a beautiful tragedy that had altered his life and the life of the woman whom he desired. But the passage of time had made sure that both their lives had transformed. Their restless hearts had joined each other as if they had never gone astray. But both the lover and the object of his love were betrayed by time. They searched for solutions. They took two steps on one path, but then their lives diverged. They did not know where they were going.

I remembered this song when I would visit India through the years and witnessed the transformation of my hometown in Pune. I felt time had taken sweet revenge on my relationship with India. My migration to the United States began to feel like a betrayal, as the familiar city of Pune that I once called home was being replaced with new buildings, infrastructure, and attitudes. There were many occasions when I felt I was an outsider in a place I had known so well and that had shaped much of my youth. Time had played both India and me differently. Pune had moved on—time had cast a die, and globalization had taken hold of the city and its imagination—whereas I felt myself unchanged, still a citizen of the old Pune.

What was once a vast patch of green farmland, and a nest of small villages near my home, was replaced by two large malls, two five-star hotels, and thousands of residential buildings. New condominiums and buildings had gobbled up the open spaces where I use to play cricket on Sundays. The old Café Naaz, where I had spent many hours chatting with friends over *Irani chai* and *maska pao* (butter and bread), was replaced by an Adidas showroom.

I knew Pune was undergoing a radical change when, during every visit, I was confronted with the erasure of recognizable old landmarks—bungalows, shops, sites, playgrounds, theaters, and cafés. These landmarks evoked powerful memories of the past. Café Delite near my college, where I spent many hours *laagoing adda* (hanging out) with friends and doing *time-pass*, was now replaced with a residential and commercial building.[2] Empire Theatre, where I saw many English and Hindi matinees while skipping school and college, was now a three-star hotel. The *Chowpatty* food stalls, where my friends and I use to go for late-night street food—for butter-laden *Pav-Bhaji* (spicy mashed vegetable mix eaten with toasted hamburger buns sautéed in butter) and for cold sugar cane juice on sweaty summer afternoons—was now a small mall called Shoppers Stop.

Many of the young participants whom I interviewed for the material for this book were witness to these remarkable changes, yet unlike me, they seemed defiantly buoyant and did not grumble much about the changes around them. To them and many others, Pune was bubbling with future prospects, brilliantly glowing in the aftermath of new call centers, multinational offshore business processing offices (BPOs), and IT parks, as well as the many high-class restaurants, bars, and multiplex theaters that showed slick Bollywood films. The urban middle- and upper-class youth would complain about the traffic, overpopulation, crowds, and interruptions to electricity, but the cultural changes were interpreted as ushering in a new India that was perceived as shedding its old traditional garb and stepping into a new cultural attire. Their positive outlook was reflected in the idea that globalization and modernity had come to *them*. They did not have to go anywhere to feel modern. These participants told me "we don't have to go abroad, we have opportunities here." One of the most common statements I heard from friends and family members was *"idhar, sab milta hai"* ("we get everything here now"). Prior to the economic reforms of 1991, the market for foreign products and brands was highly regulated in India. Foreign products/goods or, in local slang, "imported *maal*" were now available to everyone—provided one had the financial means to buy them. Foreign jeans, electronics, liquor, perfume, cars, wine, gourmet cheese, and other foods were now available in malls and American-style grocery stores. For many young, educated urban Indians, these commodities signified the arrival of a global India.

I was lamenting the fact that my list of familiar signposts and landmarks that were torn down had grown longer with every return trip. My friends who had stayed in Pune and were living through the sociocultural changes that globalization had wrought also seemed despondent about the rapid pace of urban development. They had become the voice of the older generation that they had once derided. One of my college friends, Raj,[3] sounded alarmed: "You know, in Bangalore, you won't believe . . . in the call center in the morning, they have found condoms! This is the new India. The India of condoms."

The local bookstore, Manney's Bookseller, where I bought my first set of books and comics, was shut down to make way for a corporate-run franchise. The landmark Manney's Bookseller was gone—almost run out of business— by the new avatar of corporate globalization, and this new store was interestingly called Landmark. This mega bookstore, which I visited frequently, had many levels and was similar to the American franchise Borders, selling books, music CDs, video games, stationery, luggage, dolls, and other paraphernalia of branded goods. There were dozens of books on the new India and Indian fiction—a list too long to reiterate here. I was gratified to read these books because they captured what I had observed, and I was struck by how many of these books gave compelling, evocative, and edifying accounts of societal change and seismic cultural shifts in India in graceful, vibrant, and nuanced prose.[4]

The youth, adults, teenagers, and families whom I met in India were grappling with sociocultural change, and everywhere I went people had a story to share about globalization. I heard stories about chaotic urban expansion, traffic jams, India's economic rise, and many tales about increasing social mobility. Dinesh Sharma (2003), a cultural psychologist, writes that "in the midst of the push-and-pull of tradition and modernity, a new type of childhood and family environment is being reconstructed in India, along with a new conception of motherhood and fatherhood" (p. 1). The cultural negotiations between the forces of modernity and tradition and globalization and localization that Sharma describes were a significant facet of the changing Indian society. Over the years, I heard how newly minted graduates were making Rs. 15,000 (~$200) in their entry-level call center and BPO jobs, and software engineers were making more than Rs. 2 lakhs (~$3,200) a month. These salaries were considered unprecedented for entry-level jobs. The media regularly printed stories of youth embracing a new lifestyle that involved an emphasis on materialism, indulging in smoking, drinking alcohol, and having premarital sex. It appeared that everyone had an "unconscious" narrative about globalization that needed to be told, and upon some prodding and probing, their personal story would emerge with "those culturally rooted aspects of one's history" (Freeman, 2010, p. 139).

I wanted to make sense of the stories that were being told and those not yet told by urban Indian youth, as well as those stories that appeared both "small" and "big" within the context of a global India. I wanted to learn about the lives of urban Indian youth. What were the cultural paradoxes and tensions that surfaced in their stories and how did they imagine their future selves? What did globalization mean to them? How did their class and gender locations intersect with their stories of globalization and identity formation? How were concepts such as *global, Western, modern,* and *traditional* being imagined and deployed in their narratives? How was globalization used as a discourse to construct narrative meaning about *Indianness*?

As I was searching for answers to the questions posed previously, I was simultaneously forced to confront another series of questions. I wondered why 356 million Indian youth (United Nations Population Fund, 2014), who make up the world's largest youth population, remain so utterly invisible in the discipline of psychology. Why were their stories not considered worth telling? Why was there almost no research in the field of psychology on understanding of Indian identity in contexts of globalization? How is it that mainstream Western or Euro-American psychology or psychological science[5] emerges out of a local history and geography but yet it positions itself as "The Psychology" that represents the entire world? How does Euro-American psychological science acquire the power to universally speak for all psychologies and cultures? How has psychological science been able to colonize the production and exportation of psychological knowledge? What would a "decolonized psychology" look like? Can the intersecting and fluid cultural dynamics of globalization give us a new psychological perspective that goes beyond Euro-American psychological science?

DECOLONIZING PSYCHOLOGY: THE SPECTER OF EURO-AMERICAN PSYCHOLOGICAL SCIENCE

One of the main objectives of this book is to invite readers to imagine a different psychology—an alternative psychology that goes beyond the mechanistic, universalizing, essentializing, and ethnocentric dimensions that make up the hegemony of Euro-American psychological science. Following Gramsci (1971), I use the term *hegemony* to explain (1) how Euro-American psychological science has become dominant and imperial to the extent that it speaks for and represents the majority of humanity; and (2) the way in which psychological science subordinates, limits, and marginalizes other psychological perspectives that fall out of its canon. Although Gramsci used the term hegemony to describe the economic and cultural domination of the ruling classes, it can be also used to understand the general processes of domination, social control, and subordination (Williams, 1977). The act of decolonization compels us to think about how disciplines, territories, nations, and empires acquire a colonizing stance—a stance that creates a power structure in which other views, perspectives, and ways of thinking become undermined, made invisible, and eviscerated. Ultimately, a decolonizing perspective shows how the production of psychology is deeply governed by and connected to the academic centers of the North.

Decolonizing psychology entails examining both how Euro-American scientific psychology becomes the standard-bearer of psychology throughout the world and how specific local cultural flows and ideas play an important role in shaping identities across the world. The turn to understanding Indian youth stories or Asian counternarratives, however, is not an exercise in replacing an essentialized Euro-American psychological science with an equally reified Asian or Indian psychology. Rather, I articulate a vision of a "decolonized psychology" that takes into account how the co-mingling of colonial, modern, traditional, postcolonial, local, and global creates new narratives of identity that go beyond the binary logic of East versus West, collectivistic versus individualist, and autonomy versus relatedness.

The move to decolonize Euro-American psychology is part of a small but growing movement that brings attention to the "colonial" mentality of psychological science and the "psychological imperialism" that is embedded within the power structures of Euro-American disciplinary knowledge systems (Smith, 2012). Psychological imperialism, according to Maori indigenous scholar Linda Tuhiwai Smith (2012), is enacted even in present times through (1) economic expansion in other sovereign states; (2) subjugating or undermining knowledge of indigenous, non-Western, and marginalized populations; (3) maintaining the spirit of imperialism through varied forms and means; and (4) privileging particular language, symbols, and stories that make up the discursive field of the disciplines. To decolonize, as Segalo, Manoff, and Fine (2015) note, is "to look within and undo/rework the colonizing oppressive structures from the inside-out and then look again from the outside-in" (p. 324). Thus, calling into question the dominance and the oppressive structures of Euro-American psychology is not an attempt to reject its legacy but, rather, an effort to "provincialize" (Chakrabarty, 2000) its historical origins, identify its power structures, and resituate it as a local discipline. Decolonizing psychology also means using the lens of intersectionality and social justice to study how identity is positioned within and across structures of power. Crenshaw (1994) coined the term *intersectionality* to articulate how multiple categories of identities interact with difference, privilege, and disadvantage and are further shaped by varied axes of oppression, social inequality, and power. The intersectional articulation of multiple social categories, Cole (2009) argues, must be embedded in three basic questions: "Who is included within this category? What role does inequality play? Where are there similarities?" (p. 176). Psychology anchored in questions of social justice and equality needs to theorize these distant slivers of inequities as a set of interwoven issues that cut across class, race, caste, nations, sexualities, and diverse locations. Decolonizing psychology understands the morphology of injustice that gets inscribed when the conditions of "here" and "there" are seen as connected by two ends of a long interwoven arch. It is hoped that a psychology that focuses on structures and processes that bind diverse and distant local instances of injustice will reveal what Frantz Fanon (1963) has called the silent "atmosphere of violence" that "sits below the skin" (p. 71).

What I am proposing in this book can be construed as offering another critical voice to the current scholarship that has made calls to move beyond the Eurocentric bias of American psychology (Arnett, 2008; Bhatia, 2007; Gergen, Gulerce, Lock, & Misra, 1996; Sundararjan, 2015). Arnett questions the status of American psychology and where is it headed. He asks, "Is it mainly an enterprise of, by, and for Americans, with an occasional contribution from another voice among the most privileged in the Western world. If this is what American psychology is, is it enough for American psychologists?" (p. 613) Arnett concludes that American psychology produces research findings about social, emotional, and cognitive function that are based on 5% of the population of the world, but these American findings are posited as having universal applicability and relevance for 95% of the world. He further writes that there is a need to

> broaden American psychological research so that it encompasses not only Americans and other Westerners but people around the world. Research on fundamental processes and principles should be balanced by more research that recognizes the extraordinary diversity in the lives of the world's human population and the resulting diversity in psychology. (p. 612)

We also know from a much-cited study by Henrich, Heine, and Norenzayan (2010) that 97% of the population that American psychological research represents tends to come from what they have famously characterized as WEIRD societies—that is, Western, Educated, Industrialized, Rich, and Democratic. One of the points made by the WEIRD study is that an American undergraduate student is 4,000 times more likely to be randomly selected as a subject for research compared to a random non-Westerner. What caught my attention in their study was not merely the disquieting fact that our psychological model of "human nature" is based on American undergraduate students. Rather, I felt compelled to ask the question of what would happen if Indonesia or India and many other societies that usually do not indulge in such universalizing discourse in psychology begin to acquire the power to universalize their own psychologies?

THE GLOBALIZATION OF PSYCHOLOGY VERSUS THE PSYCHOLOGY OF GLOBALIZATION

For too long, American psychology has been consumed with how to globalize and internationalize psychology rather than thinking about the *psychology of globalization*. The globalization of psychology occurs through exporting American psychological science as a dominant framework to the world. In their book, *Psychology Beyond Western Perspectives*, British psychologists Owusu-Bempah and Howitt (2000) argue that the "game" of psychology is played between "unequal players" because Western psychology is located within the "historical, intellectual, organizational roots of the Western nations and North America in particular" (p. 5). They etch out the various sites in psychology where such inequality is manifested, and they foreground how Western psychology continues to operate within a culturally imperialistic framework although it professes to be culturally relevant in diverse societies.

Owusu-Bempah and Howitt (2000) note that Western or Euro-American psychology is not a global or a universal psychology but, rather, an indigenous psychology created out of a set of local cultural assumptions and values about the Western, individual self. They argue that both Western and many non-Western psychologists continue to hold the mirror of Western psychology as they endeavor to understand the psychic self/image of non-Western, non-European people. Owusu-Bempah and Howitt explain such a phenomenon by posing the following question: "Is it racism again?" (p. 9). It is no surprise that the authors do, indeed, believe that there is a "covert" racist framework operating in much of Western psychology at the institutional, professional, and personal levels. Thus, they argue that "racism remains, only the framework within which racist thoughts are expressed and deeds carried out has changed" (p. 10). Cross-cultural psychology's growth in the United States and around the world illustrates this preoccupation with globalizing American psychology.

Today, the imperialism of cross-cultural and American psychology takes many forms. One of the forms that it takes is clearly visible in the direct circulation of Euro-American psychological knowledge and products that contribute to the ideology of a neoliberal self. What is the neoliberal conception of self or personhood? Sugarman (2015) explains that a neoliberal conception of a self is anchored in the idea that

> people own themselves as if they are entrepreneurs of a business. They conceive of themselves as a set of assets—skills and attributes—to be managed, maintained, developed, and treated as ventures in which to invest. As enterprising subjects, we think of ourselves as individuals who establish and add value to ourselves through personal investment (in education or insurance), who administer ourselves as an economic interest with vocabularies of management and performativity (satisfaction, worth, productivity, initiative, effectiveness, skills, goals, risk, networking, and so forth), who invest in our aspirations by adopting expert advice (of psychotherapists, personal trainers, dieticians, life coaches, financial planners, genetic counselors), and who maximize and express our autonomy through choice (mostly in consumerism). (p. 104)

Neoliberal discourses about happiness, optimism, well-being, and creativity are increasingly being used by global corporations to encourage their employees to maximize their productivity and efficiency (Binkley, 2014; Sathaye, 2008). This process has also been described by Jan De Vos (2012) as "psychologization," where the "double figure of psychology and psychologization, not only permeates but actually defines and structures the field of modern science, modern culture and modern politics" (p. 9).

In this book, I illustrate that it is through the application of neoliberalism that *corporate cross-cultural psychology* is increasingly being consumed and used by the Indian IT industry and call centers and that its deployment is creating new narratives of self in the social life of Indian urban society. This type of cross-cultural psychology is grounded in "science" and continues to espouse reified notions of cultures as collectivistic and individualistic and equates cultures with nations. The IT industry and call centers increasingly rely on cross-cultural psychology's highly essentialized notions of "culture" to manage and regulate discourses of cultural difference. Thus, breakdowns in communication between Indian tech workers and their European and American clients, for example, are largely attributed to deficiencies in the collectivistic orientation of "Indian culture" rather than to deeper structural inequalities and asymmetrical contexts of power (Upadhya, 2008). Cross-cultural psychology personality tests and other exercises were similarly used to exhort the Indian call center and IT worker to adapt and assimilate to global cultural practices, which were explicitly described as Euro-American. This global cross-cultural psychology as a manifestation of Euro-American psychological science now reworks the old forms of imperialism and domination that I discussed previously through neoliberal contexts of globalization.

The aim of "decolonizing psychology" is to shift the focus from creating structures that enable the globalization of American psychology to the goal of understanding the processes that underpin the psychology of globalization. This shift is not just a play of words, but instead it marks an epistemological shift in our understanding of how we can refashion the discipline of psychology through two broad goals: (1) Understanding the cultural dynamics of neoliberal globalization and (2) articulating how Euro-American psychological science continues to impose itself on the world by being complicit in promoting a neoliberal narrative of self and identity in non-Western nations. The psychology of globalization then requires us to shift our focus from the center to the margins, the hierarchy within the margins, and the complex ways in which the center and margins are now related and inescapably tied to each other. It compels us to ask how global flows of Euro-American psychological science are being incorporated in everyday narratives and stories of people living in developing or postcolonial nations. We should be wary of how these "colonizing" instruments are reinserting themselves in the postcolonial nation as naturalized and normative psychologies. Psychology is now implicated in creating and promoting a neoliberal self and, as Sugarman (2015) states, "there is ample evidence that many psychologists are operating in ways that sustain and promote the globally dominant neoliberal agenda" (p. 115).

TOWARD A TRANSNATIONAL CULTURAL PSYCHOLOGY: NARRATIVES OF URBAN YOUTH IN PUNE

The turn toward understanding creating new cultural psychologies is not intended to "reproduce or reverse the binaries of West/non-West. Nor is it to mindlessly reify an Asian centrism (or African centrism or South American centrism, as the case may be)" (Shome, 2012, p. 200). Rather, it is to show that the cultural psychology of groups and individuals in places such as Lagos, Pune, Mumbai, and Jakarta is being shaped by uneasy encounters between the incommensurable cultures of North and South, modern and traditional, East and West, as well as colonial and postcolonial spaces and sensibilities. The project of decolonizing psychology is a constructive and positive project that aims to study interconnected histories, asymmetrical cultural flows, and intersecting cultural stories.

In this book, I invite readers to understand how globalization is creating new narratives of self and identity in cultural contexts that are undergoing rapid transformations. In particular, I argue that the growing field of narrative psychology is well suited to understand the identity formation of urban Indian youth within the contexts of transnational connections and globalization. I discuss stories of Indian urban youth from three different social classes to show how the study of these fractured, shifting, and hybridized identities provides a valuable site from which narrative psychology has an opportunity to remake itself as a subdiscipline that becomes relevant in a world that is rapidly becoming transnational, diverse, and riddled with conflicts of ideology. The stories of urban Indian youth unsettle the taken-for-granted assumptions about human development and identity within American psychology. For youth who are growing up with exposure to globalization, multiple cultures, and multiple reference points, the process of identity formation involves different types of psychological challenges and experiments (Jensen, 2003).

One question that is central to this book is how India's urban youth, who are described as "liberalization's children" (Lukose, 2009), are engaging with practices and discourses of globalization. By discourses, I mean the varied ways in which adults, youth, and families in urban India use narrative and the language of globalization to make sense of the cultural changes that surround them. These discourses, as Gee (1992, 1999) argues, involve socially situated actors who use language, symbols, stories, gestures, and vocabulary to share, negotiate, contest, and construct meaning about their cultural practices. I also use discourse to exemplify how society "interpellates" (Hall, 1996) or places individuals in particular sociocultural conditions as "subjects."

The term "liberalization's children" (Lukose, 2009) is a nod to Nehru's famous speech made in August 1947 and Rushdie's (1981) evocative novel, *Midnight's Children*. The midnight's generation refers to those born during the first hour of the year 1947, when India gained independence from British rule. The liberalization generation, on the other hand, indicates those born after 1991 as the Indian economy started opening up. Paying special attention to the narratives of "liberalization's children," I argue that their narratives are organized around the dissonances between notions of autonomy and relatedness, ambivalence and belonging, tensions between family and self, and imagined ideas about Indianness and Americanness.

The project of decolonizing psychology through the dynamics of globalization provides us with the conceptual framework for reimagining the discipline. It gives us the epistemological tools to undertake the important work of building new theories and perspectives. It compels us to ask whose stories get told, what knowledge is considered as legitimate, and whose lives are considered central to the future of psychology. Reflecting on these questions is critical because it has implications for how psychology can contribute to a deeper understanding of how individuals living in the "Global South" cope with their survival, their anxiety, uncertainty, and the possibilities that emerge from the contact between local and global forces.

I draw a nuanced narrative portrait of how urban youth in Pune, who belong to the transnational elite, middle, and working classes, reimagine their identities within the new cultural contexts of globalization and neoliberalization. We often hear of the intersection of global and local cultures, but psychologists have seldom explained how *individuals* who experience the global–local dynamic are reframing and reworking these intersections. I examine how particular class identities shape narratives about globalization generally, as well as specific stories about family, relationships, work, marriage, and practices of consumption. It is my intention to show how narrative psychology can contribute to an understanding of the identities and new subjectivities of urban Indian youth. The task of understanding urban "Indian youth" is quite daunting given the complexity of unpacking the intersecting categories of caste, class, religion, linguistic diversity, and regional cultural variation.

A NARRATIVE APPROACH TO GLOBALIZATION: THE "REAL" BARBIE DOLL ARRIVES IN PUNE

While its content is specifically located in an urban Indian setting, this book contributes to the larger debates that examine the relationship between narrative, culture, and identity. I use the particular example of the urban Indian context to explain the power of narratives in shaping cultural meanings about self and identity. The Indian urban cultural context serves as an example to illuminate the complex interactions between new forms of cultural identity and global flows of media, images, brands and commodities, and outsourcing. Narrative psychology has been a fertile ground to study how memory, history, and culture shape individual and collective meanings about identity (Bruner, 1990; Freeman, 2010; Polkinghorne, 1988; Sarbin, 1986). Narrative is central to the architecture of the book, and the actual and imagined realities of youth identities come alive as I combine both the "big story" and the "small story" approach to understand cultural change in contemporary India.

In July 2015, I interviewed Kareena, a 22-year-old woman who described herself as being from a low-income, Punjabi family. She was one of Pune's upcoming "anchors" known for launching brand-name products such as motorcycles, clothes, and cars in local malls and franchise stores.[6] Her boyfriend, Akhil Raj, had groomed her and taught her what in Indian cities is called "personality development skills." These skills are taught in many institutes that give many non-English-speaking youth training in basic conversational English, speaking with "correct pronunciation," and "voice modulation."

Kareena's father, who owned a small business selling tubes and tires for two wheelers such as mopeds and motorcycles, had fallen on hard times. Her cousin Geeta, who was 25 years old and lived in the same house, was doing reasonably well as a college lecturer, and she also contributed to the running of the household. These two young women had become the major earning members in a family that was fairly conservative and patriarchal. After obtaining her Bachelor of Arts degree in commerce, Kareena wanted to become a Chartered Accountant, but she gave up that goal in favor of pursuing a career in launching branded products at malls and choreographing Bollywood dances at local weddings. The path to becoming a Chartered Accountant required studying 12 hours a day, and she was not sure whether she had the ability to pass this competitive test. Kareena had tried working as a call center agent, but she found it too monotonous and dull and thus left her job after a week. Her first major breakthrough came when she was asked to be an "anchor" in a mall for the launch of the American product, Barbie doll, in one of Pune's new malls. She explained[7]:

> I had to go through a very competitive process to get the Barbie doll event, which 14 other contestants were vying for. The launch of Barbie spanned over 10 days. It was a big break for me because as a girl I loved Barbie dolls. There are only 7 Barbie dolls worldwide and one of the dolls was going to be launched live. These were not fake imitation dolls that you get in India, but proper American dolls. I passed the audition and interview to be a part of the crew that conducted

games and distributed expensive 1,500 Rupee Barbie dolls to children. The only Barbie store is in the Inorbit Mall and they wanted to create brand awareness of their doll in Pune and in India so this was a mega event. A woman dressed as an American Barbie doll was going to come to Pune on December 24th in 2014 and the event was widely advertised in newspapers and local radio stations. The event was advertised for young girls in Pune as an opportunity to get a Barbie makeover and the kids here are quite crazy about Barbie, so we were expecting a big crowd.

Kareena had persuaded her father to buy her a Barbie doll when she was in elementary school; given that these dolls were very expensive in India, she had treasured her first Barbie doll. She also expressed being grateful to be one of the few young women in Pune to be selected to be a part of hosting the Barbie launch in India.

Being an avid "fan" of American Barbie dolls, Kareena was quite proud to be a part of a Barbie event that was considered an "all India" event. A woman dressed as a Barbie doll was going to appear at various cities in India, and the Inorbit Mall in Pune was one of the locations:

I would like to tell you this incident when Barbie was supposed to come to the Mall on December 24th, 2014. The Barbie doll was supposed to represent an American White girl. I think the young girl that came dressed as a Barbie doll was an Iranian girl. I am not fully sure, but my friends told me that she was an Iranian girl dressed as an American Barbie. I think she was wearing a blond wig. This lady was running late by 2 hours and there were over 1,500 people at the mall who were getting angry and impatient. Barbie was supposed to come at 7:00 p.m. and take pictures with kids and she was going to participate in distributing the Barbie dolls. She got stuck in Viman Nagar as December 24th was a big party day at Penthouze nightclub and at the Westin Hotel at Kalyani Nagar. There was a huge traffic jam in that area. The kids had gathered there since 6:00 p.m., so I was recruited last-minute by the management to represent Barbie because of my beautiful hair. I then took over the stage and started amusing the kids by creating games for them. I was asked to go in and represent the Barbie doll to calm down the angry parents. It was 9:30 p.m. and the real Barbie still had not shown up. I was given a nice gown and then I took the mike and I just entertained the kids for over 2 hours.

Kareena continued narrating this story by telling me that "the Iranian lady" dressed as Barbie arrived at 9:30 p.m. The parents were furious, and because there was no mall management and adequate security, the parents started hurling abuses at the crew that was hosting this event. The woman who was dressed up as Barbie then came and took pictures with the kids, but later the families were still agitated and some of them came in the mall and stole many of the Barbie dolls that were outside the store. The situation, according to Kareena, had completely spun out of control as the security guards and the management crew fled the scene. Because this was a 10-day Barbie event at the mall, Kareena went to work the next day, and the promoters of the Barbie event praised her ability to calm the crowd and keep the kids engaged for more than 2 hours. Kareena was offered the position as "anchor" for the remainder of the Barbie event, which proved to be a major breakthrough for her career.

The launch of Barbie dolls across India not only reflected the movement of cultural products and images that were Americanized but also revealed the creation of local practices that gave new meaning to these Westernized symbols, light-skinned dolls, and holidays such as Christmas and Valentine's Day. The primary market for Barbie dolls was for upper- and middle-class young Indian girls of preschool age, and they were told that if they wore pink or if their hair was styled like Barbie, they could participate in events without prior registration. Kareena also reminded me several times during the interview that there is an entire "Barbie" doll imitation industry for those families that cannot afford to purchase the real "original" doll. These working-class families often bought cheap, fake look-alikes from the street vendors or in the old marketplaces.

Kareena told me that Barbie was a desirable commodity across all classes, and her success in launching the Barbie doll in India secured her career as a mall anchor. Subsequently, she became sought-after for launching other products across Pune and was given contracts for running team-building workshops for corporations. She received 50,000 rupees ($850) for her job at the Barbie doll event, and in just the month of December 2014, she made more than 200,000 rupees ($3,200)—a sum she described as record breaking for a young woman from her social class background.

Kareena used the surplus money she had earned to buy a brand new Honda scooter for her father, who had been driving an old and broken scooter that often needed repairs. This was an important moment for Kareena because she wanted to show her father and her uncle that she could earn as much as the son the family always wished they had. Her uncle had two daughters, and she had another sister; all the children had grown up in the joint family with the clear, if unspoken, message that both her father and her uncle had always wanted a son who could look after them in their old age.

Kareena's self-narrative emerges out of the intersections between the larger transnational global flows and the local culture and history. The money earned through her Barbie doll gig at a local mall was a result of the presence of transnational global product (Barbie doll); her fluency in English; a growing set of middle-class parents with Barbie doll fetishes; the rise of the mall industry;

the restructuring of gender relations in her patriarchal home; and the rearrangement of arranged marriages, dating, and romance in urban India.

Kareena was using her English language skills and her vibrant personality to acquire social mobility in a market that was driven by multinational companies, a new mall culture, and the growing aspirations in the Indian middle class for acquiring brand-name goods. She had upended the patriarchal norms of her family by contributing to the household income by working as an anchor in a mall; breaking further norms, she went on to open a production company with her boyfriend whom she was going to marry in the future, even if her parents did not give their consent. Kareena drove a scooter and stated that one of her main challenges was facing men on the street who commented on her "looks" and made catcalls when she drove to the various events dressed in fancy clothes, wearing full stage make-up.

Kareena's story is shaped by her class identity, and the inflection of neoliberal globalization in all its cultural avatars played a vital role in how she reconstructed her identity as a young professional urban Indian woman whose career was launched in part due to a Barbie doll campaign. Kareena's narrative is linked to decades of economic neoliberalization; gender politics; and a rise in narratives of neoliberal selves that are connected to consumption, enterprise, creativity, social status, and a preoccupation with branded goods. Decolonizing psychology also shows that there are millions of youth in India who are battling their future horizons within the conditions of scarcity—lack of education, unemployment, lack of permanent housing, corrupt politicians, and lack of sanitation—and dealing with eviction, hardship, sickness, and disease. Their stories need to be told. Their stories need to be heard within and made sense of by any psychology true to its name.

This book includes stories of people who are the most visible populations in the world, but at the same time they are an invisible and powerless part of the urban poor class. Class status in India is not just a reflection of one's socioeconomic standing but also deeply connected to practices of consumption, marriage, sexuality, family values, education, work, and lifestyle. Class identities are constructed and formed by their interaction with other cultural categories of caste, religion, and gender. Malls, marketplaces, restaurants, theaters, residential areas, and bazaars are public spaces that are predetermined in their class orientation—they are already carved out with segregated histories, hierarchies, and practices.

Class in the contemporary Indian urban context is essentially rooted in social and economic hierarchies, but it also signifies politics of inclusion and exclusion, and it creates a social imagination in which some people are viewed as central and others are framed as outsiders in the globalization process. Kareena's narrative shows that she "was made" by her class status, but she was creatively asserting her agency and remaking herself in a neoliberal urban

India. Throughout my fieldwork, I heard many stories that were both similar to and different from Kareena's story, and it is this corpus of complex stories centered around "personal experience" and told "from the ground" that make up some of the important features of the project of decolonizing psychological science.

This book is essentially a narrative and cultural study of lives—I examine how youth and families imagine, re-fashion, create, and re-create their stories of self and other against the backdrop of cultural change. Decolonizing psychology through the lens of globalization also means that we need to move beyond seeing psychological research solely through the mirror metaphor. The "captivating gaze" of the mirror metaphor fosters the idea that scholars mirror social phenomenon in their research and shed light on "what is the case" or "what is the object" of study (Gergen, 2014b, p. 9). Such a view is helpful and gives us insight into the current state of affairs, but such research is not "future forming" and does not fully capture psychology's creative potential for enacting social change. The cultural context of a new urban India provides a rich and compelling example of a "future-forming psychology" that also attempts to map out the possibility of what psychology can become. A future-forming psychology with a social justice orientation would then ask the following questions: What kind of a world could we create? How can principles of social justice shed light on identities that are messy, multilayered, marginalized, excluded, and highly class bound? The story of globalization and neoliberalization can be analyzed and mapped through statistics and numbers, but narratives of social class differences illuminate Indian urban youth's daily experiences with practices of globalization. I analyze Indian youth's definition of globalization; their fashioning and refashioning of their identity as "Indians"; and their stories of aspirations, ambition, failure, family expectations, and their larger struggles with social inequality in a new India. Narrative psychology provides a very powerful theoretical frame to answer questions about self and identity in contemporary urban India.

PLAN OF THE BOOK

In Chapter 1, "Decolonizing Moves: Beyond Eurocentric Culture, Narrative, and Identity," I discuss how globalization through the mechanism of neoliberalization shapes spaces, places, and identities. I contextualize and clarify the larger aims of the book by embedding them within the interrelated theoretical frameworks of culture, narrative, and identity. In particular, I explain in detail how globalization as a discourse creates new identity narratives among urban Indian youth culture. I specifically show how discourses of culture, self, and identity that are associated with Euro-American cross-cultural psychology and personality theories are being incorporated within the Indian work culture.

In Chapter 2, "The Cultural Psychology of Globalization: Constructing Desirable Identities and Spaces," I use an interdisciplinary lens to examine the contested and multiple meanings, references, and definitions of globalization that vary across the different disciplines of political science, geography, cultural studies, economics, and sociology. I show how contemporary forms of globalization practices, structures, and discourses occur through neoliberalism and the ways in which new urban spaces and identities are being reconfigured. I specifically examine how global and transnational Indianness is constructed in the semiotics and spaces of urban malls and through Indo-German cultural exchange programs.

Chapter 3, "Psychology and the Neoliberal Self: Global Culture and the 'New Colonial Subjects,'" investigates how neoliberal globalization is not just an economic concept or an economic condition; rather, it brings with it shifts in the spheres of culture psychology and identity. I specifically analyze how personality and assessment tests and cross-cultural workshops on identity and difference that are primarily developed form Euro-American psychology are utilized in the Indian IT and call center industry. This chapter reveals how neoliberal psychological discourses of self, identity, and happiness are becoming a mainstay of Indian culture and society.

In Chapter 4, "Stories and Theories: Globalization, Narrative, and Meaning-Making," I make a case for why narrative inquiry is particularly suited to capture how individuals make meaning of their identities as they engage with mutually shifting global–local cultural interactions. I provide a brief history of the concept of identity in psychology to show how culture and identity are analyzed as depoliticized variables in mainstream psychology. I lay out the conceptual framework that examines how globalization shapes the narrative imagination and how it gives us insights into understanding the psychology of globalization in urban India.

Chapter 5, "Traveling Transnational Identities: Imagining Stories of 'Ultimate' Indianness," describes how the transnationally oriented elite and upper-class urban Indian youth are negotiating their everyday experiences with globalization. I show how the college-age elite youth psychologically imagine themselves as being world-class citizens not just by going abroad but also by reimagining new forms of Indianness through their active participation in specific cultural practices of watching American media, shopping at exclusive malls, and constructing emancipatory narratives of globalization. In particular, I show that the transnational urban youth's narratives are hybrid and are organized Indianness that is mobile, multicultural, connected to consumption practices, and crosses borders easily.

In Chapter 6, "Outsourcing the Self: Work, Love, and Money in the Call Center Culture," I analyze how call center workers, who are mostly middle- and working-class youth, create narratives that I describe as expressing modern forms of "individualized Indianness." I demonstrate how call center workers produce narratives of individualized Indianness by engaging in practices of mimicry, accent training, and consumption; by going to public spaces such as bars and pubs; and by having romantic relationships that are largely hidden from their families.

In Chapter 7, "Identities Left Behind: Globalization, Social Inequality, and the Search for Dignity," I analyze stories of young men and women who live in *basti* (slum settlements) near one of the most affluent neighborhoods in Pune. In particular, I analyze the stories that youth narrate about engaging with uneven benefits of globalization. I argue that the *basti* youth's "capacity to aspire" is not just an individual trait or a psychological ability. Rather, their aspirations are shaped by their caste identities, structural conditions of poverty, their schooling in vernacular language, and the prestige accorded to speakers of English language in urban India.

In Chapter 8, "Toward a Transnational Cultural Psychology: Narrative and Social Justice in the Age of Unequal Globalization," I use a decolonizing perspective to show how urban Indian youth identities across the different classes unsettle long-held beliefs about Eurocentric understandings of youth culture, identity, and subjectivities. I also show how *narrative psychology* can be useful in providing a counterpoint to the depoliticized, individualistic, universal, and scientific views of culture. In particular, I articulate a vision of psychology that locates the psychological understanding of identity, cultural difference, power, and practices in neoliberal transnational contexts and reimagines the discipline of psychology in which concepts of indigenous psychology, social justice, and equity are central.

In Chapter 9, "Studying Globalization at Home: Reflections on Method, Self-Reflexivity, and Narrative Inquiry," I document the ethnographic context in which the interviews and participant observation were conducted. I examine how the current class formations and social hierarchies in urban India are deeply tied to India's colonial and postcolonial history and I contextualize the social class locations of young people in Pune so their stories can be better understood. I also situate my study within the contexts of narrative inquiry and develop arguments about the role of self-reflexivity in doing ethnography at "home" and producing qualitative forms of knowledge that are based on personal, experiential, and cultural narratives.

NOTES

1. Hindi songs played on Vividh Bharti were a service of the All India Radio, and they were mostly Hindi songs from Hindi films. These songs and their lyrics also played an important role in shaping our imagination about romance, unrequited

love, and social and family roles. They also gave an entire generation of Indians a vocabulary to express their moods, desires, and emotions.

2. Chakrabarty (2000) writes that *adda* was a form of social practice that was dominant in the first half of the 20th century in Calcutta. It symbolized a place where predominantly middle-class male friends typically met in tea shops or clubs or in private spaces for indulging in idle talk. Chakrabarty defines *adda* as "roughly speaking, it is the practice of friends getting together for long, informal, and rigorous conversation" (p. 181). *Adda* as social get-together was practiced in many cities in India, and when I was growing up in Pune, *adda lagana* meant engaging in idle talk at local tea shops owned by Parsis or Iranians. We also used the phrase "time-pass" as a substitute for *adda*, and it meant getting together with friends to "kill time" or to pass time in order to get over our boredom or lack of engagement with our academics. Craig Jeffrey (2010) has done an in-depth analysis of how unemployed youth in Meerut in northern India participate in the "politics of waiting" or "time-pass." This type of waiting reflected purposelessness of *adda* meetings and also gave opportunities to youth to acquire new skills and experiment with new fashions and cultural styles.

3. All the names of the participants have been changed in order to protect their identities. Furthermore, in some cases, their professional occupations, place of residence, and the names of their businesses or firms and companies have also been altered.

4. The large bookshelf in the center of the store that displayed the bestseller list was mainly composed of management books written by Indian authors with titles such as *Corporate Chanakya*, *Jugaad Innovation*, and *The Wining Habit*. On one of the display shelves were the old favorites or classics on India by Jawaharlal Nehru, Anita Desai, V. S. Naipual, Nirad Chaudhary, Vikram Seth, Shashi Tharoor, Suketu Mehta, Amitav Ghosh, Jumpha Lahiri, and Salman Rushdie. However, I noticed that there were two or three rows of shelves of books on contemporary India or books that were trying to capture some aspect of India that was rapidly undergoing cultural transformations. The following is a partial list that were considered popular bestsellers: *India Becoming: A Journey Through a Changing Landscape* by Akash Kapur; *India's Unending Journey* by Mark Tully; *In Spite of the Gods: The Rise of Modern India* by Edward Luce; *India: A Portrait* by Patrick French; *The Great Indian Middle Class* by Pavan Varma; *Imagining India* by Nandan Nilekani; *The Argumentative Indian* by Amartya Sen; *The Idea of India* by Sunil Khilnani; *The Beautiful and the Damned: A Portrait of the New India* by Siddarth Deb; *What Young India Wants?* by Chetan Bhagat; *The Indians: Portrait of a People* by Sudhir and Kathrina Kakar; *Beautiful Thing: Inside the Secret World of Bombay's Dance Bars* by Sonia Faleiro; *India Grows at Night: A Liberal Case for a Strong State* by Gurcharan Das; *India Calling: An Intimate Portrait of a Nations Remaking* Anand Giridhardas; and *Behind the Beautiful Forevers: Life, Death, and Hope in Mumbai Under City* by Katherine Boo.

5. I use the term *Euro-American psychological science* to refer to the mainstream production of scientific psychology that is mainly shaped by modern European cultural, political, economic, and scientific practices. These frameworks have produced widely circulated and dominant conceptions about normative methods and definitions about what constitutes the larger field of psychology. The terms *Euro-American* and *Western* are frequently used interchangeably in the field.

6. Young male and female "anchors" constituted a new profession in India that had come into being with the rise of malls and consumption of branded goods.

"Anchor" jobs were given mostly to young women who were slim, attractive, and had good public-speaking skills and polished English. "Anchoring" an event involved being a master of ceremonies at corporate events, weddings, birthdays, or parties and being "on stage" in front of small or large audiences.

7. Most of the interviews for this study were primarily conducted in English. Because most of the participants were fluent in English, I have used their own "original" language—words, phrases, and sentences. Although the participants in this study were fluent in English, many of these excerpts had to be edited for clarity, grammar, and coherence. During this editing process, I have tried to keep the language structure and syntax as close to the participant's own language as possible. I also conducted several interviews in Hindi and Marathi and translated them into English.

CHAPTER 1

Decolonizing Moves

Beyond Eurocentric Culture, Narrative, and Identity

The move to decolonize psychology is a political move and part of the larger "decolonial epistemic turn" (Grosfoguel, 2007) that entails calling attention to the discipline's colonizing effects in the past and the present contexts of globalization. The power to represent the non-Western "Other" has always resided, and still continues to reside, primarily with psychologists working in Europe and America. The idea that Euro-American psychological science is being exported by First World psychologists for the consumption of indigenous populations in Third World societies points to a different kind of Orientalism that Said (1993) described as cultural imperialism. He explained:

> The term "imperialism" means the practice, the theory, and the attitudes of a dominating metropolitan center ruling a distant territory . . . In our time, direct colonialism has largely ended; imperialism, as we shall see, lingers where it has always been, in a kind of general cultural sphere as well as in specific political, ideological, economic and social practices. (Said, 1993, p. 9)

Euro-American psychology lingers on in the cultural sphere of non-Western, postcolonial contexts in varied forms. Although Euro-American psychology has come a long way from describing the non-Western "Other" in 19th-century Orientalist terms, the core theoretical and conceptual frameworks that are used to represent and study the non-Western "Other" continue to emerge from the bastions of Euro-American psychology (Bhatia, 2002). Thus, it is important to delineate the historical role of psychology in creating Orientalistic representations of non-Western others to show how contemporary concepts such as adolescence and youth identity are inextricably linked to the legacy of colonialism, Orientalism, and Eurocentric assumptions.

I consider the move to decolonize psychology as part of a larger project of critical psychology (Teo, 2015); my attempt to rethink the contours of psychology is obviously not new. There are growing numbers of psychologists, located in various subfields of psychology throughout the world, who have employed a critical lens to emancipate psychology from its universal, scientific, and Eurocentric tenets. The critical rethinking of psychology has occurred in various disciplines and from different areas of the world (Fine & Sirin, 2007; Fox & Prilleltensky, 1997; Gough, McFadden, & McDonald, 2013; Morwaski, 1994; Parker, 2005; Teo, 2015). There are a large number of subfields in psychology that have not just provided a critique of Euro-American psychology but also made efforts to reconstruct and reimagine the discipline through varied theories, methods, and vocabularies (Marsella, 1985, 1998).

Such critical efforts have been undertaken in developmental psychology (Burman, 1994; Nsamenang & Dawes, 1998), social psychology (Fine, 2006; Hammack, 2011; Walkerdine, 2002), social constructionism (Danzinger, 1990; Gergen, 1999), subjectivity and identity theories (Hook, 2012; Parker, 2005), hermeneutic-oriented psychology (Christopher, Wendt, Marecek, & Goodman, 2014; Cushman, 1990; Martin, Sugarman, & Hickinbottom, 2010), feminist psychology (Lykes & Moane, 2009; Macleod, 2011; Swartz, 2005), and globalization and international studies (Arnett, 2008; Brock, 2006; De Vos, 2012; Pickren & Rutherford, 2010).

Those who use a critical psychology approach employ diverse theories and concepts in their intellectual inquires, but what unites most of the critical psychologists is

> an understanding of society based on intersectionalized societal power differences with consequences for human subjectivity in the conduct of one's life. . . . Critical psychologists intend to challenge societal structures of injustice, ideologies, psychological control, and the adjustment of the individual. Instead of making individuals and groups into problems, CP attempts to work on problems that individuals and groups encounter in a given society. (Teo, 2015, pp. 3–4)

Critical psychology is committed to undertaking a critique of psychology, but it also provides robust frames for the reconstruction of psychological categories through history, theory, narrative, action research, and political action.

The movement to redefine psychology is embedded in several distinct but related critical and cultural theories, perspectives, and methods: liberation theology (Martín-Baró, 1994), indigenous psychology perspectives (Bulhan, 1985; Enriquez, 1992; Sinha, 1984; Tripathi, 2011), narrative psychology (Brockmeier, 2014; Clandinin & Rosiek, 2007; McAdams, 2006; Freeman,

2014; Schiff, 2013), and dialogical psychology (Hermans & Kempen, 1993). The cultural psychology movement now consists of a wide variety of theoretical perspectives that represent many areas of the world (Bruner, 1986; Chaudhary, 2004; Gregg, 2005; Mahalingam, 2012; Paranjape, 1984; Rogoff, 2003; Shweder, 1990; Sinha, 1986; Stetsenko, 2015; Wertsch, 1991).

The previously mentioned psychologists may not use the term "decolonize" to describe their efforts to remap and reinterpret psychology, but in essence what these theorists have done is given us alternative ways to reimagine the discipline of psychology. A "decolonial perspective" on psychology is part of a broader critical psychology movement as it draws on several perspectives to rethink the substance, relevance, and future of psychology. However, what is different or distinct about using a postcolonial or decolonizing perspective on Euro-American psychology is that it gives us specific conceptual frameworks to excavate its cultural origins; allows us to analyze the colonial and postcolonial structure of the discipline through the lens of history, identity, power, and culture; and highlights the ways in which the Euro-American version of psychology is exported, reiterated, and reproduced in the era of neoliberal and global capitalism.

The field of postcolonial or decolonial psychology is rather new, but it has taken steps to unsettle and interrupt the Eurocentric narratives about culture, self, and identity inherent in psychological science. There have been several relatively recent contributions to the postcolonial psychology literature, mainly under the critical psychology perspectives (Bhatia, 2002; Hook, 2012; Painter, 2015; Staeuble, 2005). Also, in the past decade, a growing number of books have analyzed the construction of the psychological realm in relation to postcolonial theory (Bhatia, 2007; David, 2011; Desai, 2013; Hook, 2012; Macleod, 2011; Moane & Sonn, 2015). Despite these contributions, postcolonial or decolonial psychology is far from being an established or significant subdiscipline of psychology. The growing interest and positive reaction to this scholarly work (Desai, 2013; Parker, 2012) must, however, be viewed as an important step in illustrating the promising potential of applying postcolonial approaches to psychology, especially given the social and political conditions in the 21st century (Macleod & Bhatia, 2008). Let me cite another example of a collective effort undertaken by psychologists to decolonize psychology. Recently, the *Journal of Social and Political Psychology* devoted a special issue to the theme of "decolonizing psychological science." Writing in the introduction to this special issue, Adams, Dobles, Gómez, Kurtis, and Molina (2015) state that they draw on postcolonial theory of Fanon and the liberation and cultural psychology of decolonial theorists such as Walter Mignolo, Anibal Quijan, and Martin-Baro to counter the hegemony of Euro-American psychological science. Adams et al. argue for the creation of a "decolonial psychology" (p. 230) that speaks to not only the lives and concerns of the privileged minority who reside in Western, educated, industrialized, rich, and democratic (WEIRD) societies but also the lives of the global majority of the world—especially those who live in marginalized cultures of the Global South. The larger goal of decolonizing psychology becomes clear in the following explanation offered by Adams et al.:

> In contrast to the idea of the modern global order as the leading edge of intellectual progress and pinnacle of human development, references to coloniality emphasize the extent to which the modern global order—and the ways of being or habits of mind that are attuned to it—are the product of racialized power that continues to reproduce violence. From the epistemological standpoint of Majority World communities, the tendency to produce knowledge without reference to the coloniality of everyday life obscures more than it reveals about the "basic" psychological tendencies that modern science proposes as natural standards for human experience. Instead, the situation of everyday life makes understanding colonial violence—and its relationship to mainstream or hegemonic psychological science—a matter of critical importance. (p. 214)

The contributors to the volume are psychologists, and their central concern is that we need a decolonial psychology that can foster new ways of producing alternatives to the domination of Euro-American psychological science. Theorizing about multiple axes of oppression such as racialized violence, poverty, economic injustices, and unsustainable development is an important goal of this project. Several international authors who contributed to this issue address various sites of injustices that are occurring throughout the world (Bulhan, 2015; Dudgeon & Walker, 2015; Segalo, Manoff, & Fine, 2015; Watkins, 2015). Decolonizing psychology means not just engaging with academic scholarship but also paying attention to the stories people narrate from the ground and finding meaningful ways to understand how they make sense of their lives.

A decolonizing perspective brings into focus those naturalized and normative cultural texts and readings in psychology that tend to overlook colonial history and current postcolonial conditions that are shaped by transnational power relations. It also identifies ways in which psychology becomes complicit in neocolonial and neoliberal forms of exploitation and makes invisible or exotic particular identities or histories of people. It theorizes how discrepant sociohistorical conditions shape the local and global power dynamic and how individual lives and their stories are shaped by these global–local intersections.

Thus, the effort to decolonize psychology is a constructive program and not just a critique of psychology; it aims to reimagine a psychology based on invisible and marginalized stories and theories. Neoliberal forms of globalization have altered the cultural dynamics in many postcolonial nations such as India and have reconfigured meanings related to culture and youth identity. Today, many youth around the world live in imagined worlds that allow them to subvert and contest deeply entrenched local beliefs about family, work, and marriage (Larson, 2002). The interactions between global and local flows challenge Eurocentric assumptions about development, identity, and youth cultures.

Shifting our gaze to the "Global South" compels us to study how those American cultural flows of media, commodities, and consumerist practices are being refashioned or reimagined in non-Western cultures, especially formerly colonized countries.[1] It also raises questions about how specific American psychological discourses of self and identity are now part and parcel of the workforce in globalizing economies such as India. These discourses reveal how both Euro-American psychological science and "American culture" as such continue to play a crucial role in how Indian youth are reimagining their "Indianness."

COLONIALITY IN EURO-AMERICAN PSYCHOLOGICAL SCIENCE

My colleagues and I have extensively analyzed how several forerunners of modern psychology played an important role in indirectly providing philosophical and "scientific" evidence to the European colonial empires to justify their Orientalist program in non-Western countries (Bhatia, 2002, 2014a; Macleod & Bhatia, 2008; Shields & Bhatia, 2009). Some pioneers of psychology unknowingly or knowingly cultivated Orientalist images of the non-Western "Others" as inferior, primitive individuals, and this legacy of the West defining the "Other" continues to impact us/the field today. Said (1979) defines Orientalism as a discourse, as a configuration of power, as knowledge, and as representation. He notes, "I shall be calling *Orientalism*, a way of coming to terms with the Orient that is based on the Orient's special place in European Western experience" (p. 1). Said argues that European scholars created the structures or references about the Orient—their language, history, society, and way of life—by employing highly specific discourses and systems of representations. These discourses were created and managed by European cultures to colonize and regulate the natives and their "civilization, peoples, and localities" (p. 203). An army of scholars, travelers, government workers, military expeditions, and natural historians brought the Orient to the archives of Western learning by creating an elaborate system of representations about the natives living in the Orient. These discursive representations were deeply integrated in the "European *material* civilization and culture" (p. 2). Western scholars transformed Orientalism into a field of study, an object of investigation, and a cultural apparatus that was "all aggression, activity, judgment, will-to-truth, and knowledge" (p. 204). Orientalism was based on the asymmetrical power relationships that existed between the Occident and the Orient. The power of the Occident was so formidable that Western armies, archaeologists, merchants, and anthropologists were flowing in massive numbers from Europe to the East, and approximately 60,000 books were written on the near Orient between 1800 and 1950. In comparison, very few people traveled from the East to Europe, and even when Easterners traveled to Europe, they were either there to admire the Western civilization or to work as servants and laborers.

For more than 100 years, Euro-American psychology has essentially provided the raw material from which the psychological portraits of the non-Western "Other" have been drawn. Key forerunners of psychology professionals, such as Darwin (1871/1888), Hall (1904), and Spencer (1851/1969), played an important role in implicitly providing philosophical and "scientific" evidence to demonstrate the innate mental inferiority of non-Westerners and the essential mental superiority of the Anglo-Saxon race (Bhatia, 2002). Such evidence was used by the political leaders of Europe to justify and rationalize the colonial oppression of their non-Western subjects. For example, Thomas Babington Macaulay (1972), a colonial British statesman, essayist, and policy reformer, wrote the following in the "Macaulay Minute" regarding Indian education:

> I am quite ready to take the Oriental learning at the valuation of Orientalists themselves. I have never found one among them who could deny that a single shelf of a good European library was worth the whole native literature of India and Arabia. The intrinsic superiority of Western literature is, indeed, fully admitted by those members of the Committee who support the Oriental plan of education. (p. 241)

Psychology's indirect role in providing justification for fulfilling the imperialist agenda begins with the rise of scientific racism. The beginnings of psychology are linked to a time when many European and American intellectuals had conceptualized the non-Western "Other" as an inferior and "primitive" savage (Richards, 1997). Such Orientalist depictions are consistently found in the work of important pioneers of psychology, such as Darwin (1859/1958) and Spencer (1851/1969).

The call for decolonizing psychology rests on the claim that contemporary psychological science bears some resemblance to the structure and mechanisms of colonization. What is the colonial form or the coloniality implicit in psychological science? The "decolonial turn" involves understanding how "coloniality" as a way of thinking continues to embody the current power relations *between* the Global North and the Global South, as well as the diverse relationships *within* the various geographies of the Global South and the Global North (Mohanty, 1991, 2003). The decolonial movement is different from postcolonial theory and postcolonialism in terms of its intellectual genealogy and specific colonial history. The field of postcolonial studies came into being largely through Edward Said, Homi Bhabha, and Gayatri Spivak's engagements with poststructuralist scholarship (e.g., Michel Foucault, Antonio Gramsci, Jacques Derrida, and Jacques Lacan) and their understanding of colonization and imperialism that was conceived within the contours of British colonization of Asia, especially India. In contrast, the "decolonial turn" is mostly rooted in understanding the European conquest of the Americas since 1500 and through the indigenous movements in Latin America. Mignolo (2010) explains,

> We highlight the decolonial projects that emerged in intellectual debates from
> the critical foundation established, in Latin America, by Jos. Carlos Maritegui,
> in Peru (in the 1920s), and by dependency theory and philosophy of liberation,
> in the 70's, and that spread all over Latin America. (p. 16)

In any case, despite the differences in intellectual genealogy, both postcolonial and decolonial projects have shared goals of social transformation and social justice (Richards, 2014).

In the "decolonial turn," coloniality, along with systems of capitalism and particular forms of domination, emerges out of the "discovery" and the conquest of the Americas (Mignolo, 2007). Coloniality does not merely refer to the colonization of indigenous culture in the Americas but, instead, refers to a whole system of thought—a mentality and a power structure that constructs "the hegemonic and Eurocentered matrix of knowledge" (Mignolo, 2010, p. 11). The "decolonial turn" does not reflect a single theory but, rather, incudes a family of scattered positions that share the view that coloniality poses one of the central challenges for a vast majority of the people in the world who are living in the age of unequal globalization and neoliberalization and thus decolonization is an important unfinished undertaking. One of the main features of decolonial thinking that is relevant for psychology is the emphasis on how coloniality, in its many forms, shapes the foundation of psychology as discipline but also how it impacts our everyday lives (Maldonado-Torres, 2007):

> Coloniality is different from colonialism. Colonialism denotes a political and
> economic relation in which the sovereignty of a nation or a people rests on
> the power of another nation, which makes such nation an empire. Coloniality,
> instead, refers to long-standing patterns of power that emerged as a result of
> colonialism, but that define culture, labor, intersubjective relations, and knowl-
> edge production well beyond the strict limits of colonial administrations. Thus,
> coloniality survives colonialism. It is maintained alive in books, in the criteria
> for academic performance, in cultural patterns, in common sense, in the self-
> image of peoples, in aspirations of self, and so many other aspects of our mod-
> ern experience. In a way, as modern subjects we breathe coloniality all the time
> and every day. (p. 243)

Coloniality is seen as a product of European modernity and reinforced through racial hierarchies, gender oppression, and oppressive forms of labor, and it also shapes the current processes of globalization. Postcolonial theories and the "decolonial turn" may have different intellectual and geographic roots, but both provide important interpretive tools to understand how coloniality is deeply embedded in contemporary psychological science.

Decolonization involves understanding the concrete experiences, stories, and narratives of people who confront poverty, racism, and gender discrimination in their daily lives. Decolonization, according to these scholars, has been occurring in various forms for centuries or since colonization began, but it became an increasingly self-conscious, collaborative global project in the 20th century. What is now known as the decolonial project is also inspired by the decolonizing struggles of leaders such as Waman Puma de Ayala, Ottabah Cugoano, Gandhi, Cesaire, Fanon, W. E. B. Dubois, and Anzaldua (Maldonado-Torres, 2007; Mignolo, 2010).

By engaging with European history, the colonial framework, and its vast repository of knowledge and thought, both decolonial and postcolonial theory "provincialize" and "localize" the universal principles that have embodied much of European knowledge. The postcolonial project does not necessarily discard or reject European thought, but instead it proposes that "European thought is at once both indispensable and inadequate" in helping us understand the diverse forms of living, thinking, and being in non-Western, postcolonial nations (Chakrabarty, 2000, p. 16). Situating key American psychological concepts within a decolonial framework allows us to trace their lineage and examine their usage in the present day.

I have mentioned the decolonizing impulses originating from postcolonial theory and decolonial frameworks, but there is a third decolonizing framework that is deployed in indigenous studies that shares some of the goals with other frameworks mentioned previously, but in many respects its efforts are for different ends. Decolonization within the broader field of indigenous studies is anchored in the the framework of settler colonialism and is primarily concerned with issues of land, sovereignty, and territory (Coulthard, 2014; Grande, 2015). The experience of settler colonialism with the United States is much different from other forms of colonialism. The settlers came with the intention of "homemaking" and "settler sovereignty," and when the settlers colonized indigenous land and converted that land for making new homes and for generating economic capital, it marked a profound act of violence (Tuck & Yang, 2012). Settler colonialism occupation resulted in epistemic, ontological, and cosmological violence (Tuck & Yang, 2012), and it continues until the present; this is why Patrick Wolfe (1999) argues that settler colonialism is a structure and not an event. Tuck and Yang (2012) explain,

Many indigenous people have been forcibly removed from their homelands onto reservations, indentured, and abducted into state custody, signaling the form of colonization as simultaneously internal (via boarding schools and bio-political modes of control) and external (via uranium mining on Indigenous lands in the US Southwest and oil extraction on Indigenous land in Alaska) with a frontier (the US military still nicknames all enemy territory "Indian Country"). (p. 5)

Similarly, Coulthard (2014) notes that the the principles of "politics of recognition," grounded in liberal multiculturalism and accommodation, have been an ineffective means of negotiating decolonization around land claims, Aboriginal law, and sovereignty between the nation state and indigenous communities in North America. He further argues that over four decades, Indigenous people's attempts to participate in the legal and political process in Canada have failed to secure their rights but instead have served to subtly "reproduce the forms of racist, sexist, economic, and political configurations of power" that were being challenged (p. 179). Thus, Coulthard reminds us that indigenous communities must continu-ally find new ways to unsettle the settler state. He states that the struggle to decolonize must adopt

> a resurgent politics of recognition that seeks to practice decolonial, gender emancipatory, and economically nonexploitative alternative structures of law and sovereign authority grounded on a critical refashioning of the best of Indigenous legal and political traditions. (p. 179)

Grande's (2015) book, *Red Pedagogy*, provides a concrete example of how decolonizing moves in the area of education and schooling require translat-ing and working across contested and different research paradigms. Her book provides a vigorous and intellectual channel between the field of American Indian education and critical pedagogy. The archive of knowledge in critical pedagogy has focused on issues of equity and social justice, but it has over-looked the struggles of American Indian history and context of schooling and education. Grande argues that American Indian scholars of education have largely neglected to engage with critical discourses of education and instead have been preoccupied with issues of identity and authenticity, historiogra-phy, tribal education, and site-based research. Her scholarship is an attempt to reimagine democratic education in the United States without demanding that Indigenous scholars adopt or completely embrace the critical pedagogy discourse.

The three decolonizing frameworks discussed previously—postcolonial theory, decolonial theory, and indigenous studies—can provide us with important conceptual tools to reimagine, renew, and build a new psychology that forges a common intellectual ground between diverse intellectual tradi-tions and geographies.

THE MODERN AMERICAN SUBJECT: ADOLESCENCE
AND YOUTH DEVELOPMENT

One of the most influential psychologists in the field of psychology is G. Stanley Hall. He played an important role in the founding of American psychology and also coined the term "adolescence." Hall was one of the first psychologists to suggest that adolescence is a separate developmental stage. Hall (1904) argued that the study of adolescence must be understood against the backdrop of colonialism, in which one-third of the human race occupies two-fifths of the world and controls 136 colonies. The process of colonization, Hall explained, had been swift and rapid since the "great competitive scramble" (p. 649) for land began in 1897. One paragraph later, he wrote that "most savages in most respects are children, or, because of sexual maturity, more properly, adolescents of adult size" (p. 649).

What is significant is Hall's emphasis that both "soldiers and thinkers" in Europe were preoccupied by the idea of exterminating other races and expanding the dominion of the West. Of course, it will be of no surprise to many readers that the political powers of imperialism had recruited armies of soldiers to "domesticate" or wipe out the resistant indigenous populations in Asia and Africa. In summary, Orientalist ideas about non-Westerners have consistently echoed in the writings of the pioneers of developmental psychology such as Darwin, Galton, Hall, and Spencer (Richards, 1997). Psychology may have moved away from representing the non-Western "Other" in stark Orientalist language, but the legacy of "coloniality" and cultural imperialism in Euro-American psychology in still alive (Adams et al., 2015).

Catherine Driscoll (2002) argues that Hall's concept of adolescence personifies the qualities of a modern subject, where individuality, agency, and biology come together to create a unified and coherent identity. Driscoll also goes on to state that "the role of adolescence as psychological crescendo, as a psychosocial crucible for becoming a Subject, is specific to late modernity" (p. 50). The linking of the stage of adolescence to becoming autonomous, self-contained, mature, rational, and unique lays out a Eurocentric cultural trajectory of psychological identity that becomes central in shaping both historical and contemporary research in adolescence and identity formation in youth in developmental psychology in the United States.

Similarly, Lesko (2012) aims to shine light on the cultural and political notions of development that have given rise to particular conceptions of youth identity or youth development in the Euro-American context. She locates the conception of adolescence as a cultural construct that was created in the late 1900s as American society was becoming modern, urbanized, and socially regulated. Youth identity then came to be defined historically and politically as a public problem, through three sets of interrelated anxieties and worries: "1) worries over racial progress; 2) worries over male dominance; 3) worries over the building of a nation with unity and power" (p. 5). Lesko argues that the concept of adolescence as a cultural construct made sense at the turn of the 20th century because it was built on the assumption that the teen years were the formative years during which White boys could be instilled with particular ideas about national and international order—which was viewed as the responsibility of the young American citizens to uphold. Thus, the concept of youth and adolescence in the United States answers a particular need at a particular time when there were deeply prevalent discourses about the *civilizing process* of youth development, sexual constraints, and the large anxieties about social disorder (Lesko, 2012; Maira & Soep, 2005).

Contemporary views of youth identity in psychology, especially as theorized in Euro-American psychology, are deeply connected to and shaped by the American historical context (Lesko, 2012). Adolescence enacts modernity as a central principle of "developing" or "becoming" as youth are always located in the discourses of "growing up" according to the proper order of development. Lesko writes,

> Adolescence re-enacts the supremacy of the West over primitive others in its psychologized (internalized) progress from (primitive) concrete operational stages to (advanced) abstract ones. Adolescence continuously enacts Western progress carried in the oppositional positions of past and present and ever points towards even greater futures. (p. 137)

The idea of adolescence that Lesko defines played an important role in shaping Erikson's Eurocentric stage- and age-based theories of youth identity in American psychology. Erikson (1963) was particularly concerned with how modernization in the West brings about a culture of mass-produced norms and a mechanized society in which standardization and centralization "threatens the identities which man has inherited from primitive, agrarian, feudal, and patrician cultures. What inner equilibrium these cultures had to offer is now endangered on a gigantic scale" (p. 413). Thus, he argued, that identity formation during adolescence becomes all the more critical because the premodern notions of community have dissolved and individuals have to seek and fashion an identity for themselves. Identity formation during adolescence turns into a *developmental task* in which all the previous identifications that have occurred during childhood have to be brought forward or assimilated in new configurations of identity.

Undoubtedly, Erikson's conceptual framework for understanding identity formation was important because it highlighted the complex interactions between the individual and society. By situating adolescent and youth identity development within a life span approach, Erikson also brought attention to social practices and rituals associated with coming of age and recognition from the community. Erikson (1968) stated that identity formation involves a process in which the society (often through subsocieties) and the individual develop a reciprocal and mutually shared relationship. However, several questions arise about identity in contexts in which there is "mutual dissonance" between the adolescent and the larger community—especially in which immigrant youth, youth of color, and queer youth often face social exclusion and discrimination (Maira & Soep, 2004, p. 249). Erikson did propose an alternative identity formation in adolescence through the concept of subsocieties that was further reworked into the theory of ethnic identity development and assimilation (Phinney, 1989). However, Erikson's influential psychosocial model of identity development is largely based on Eurocentric concepts of development, and it does not adequately speak to the realities of youth who are growing up with hybrid and conflicting cultural discourses that are made of fragments of the global, modern, traditional, national, local, and postcolonial.

The concept of hybrid narratives not only challenges linear, stage-based theories of developmental psychology but also locates young Indian lives in transnational networks that connect the cultures of the "West" and "East," and "here" and "there," in various forms of intersecting flows. Theories of identity that are based on an Eriksonian approach follow culturally specific notions of development that are constructed through a linear stage theory and are always following a teleological process. The phenomenon of globalization through neoliberalization has drawn attention to the new and creative ways in which youth imagine and reimagine the narrative of self, others, nation, and family.

Neoliberal globalization is indeed altering the landscapes of youth identity, and it challenges Euro-American conceptions of adolescence, youth studies, values, attitudes, tastes, and lifestyles (Arnett, 2002; Nilan & Feixa, 2006; Saraswathi & Larson, 2002).

One of the effects of globalization is that it produces hybrid identities (Arnett, 2002). The global–local dynamic, however, is always specific to the culture, and this is why Jensen (2003) argues that cultural identity formation in the context of globalization takes specific developmental pathways and is largely dependent on the various intersections of the global flows and local culture norms. Bame Nsamenang (2002) observes that "adolescent psychology is a Eurocentric enterprise" (p. 61), and its ethnocentrism is deeply overwhelming. He states that the majority of key scholars in the field of adolescent, youth psychology and laypeople are "unaware that the field would have been different had adolescence been 'discovered' within the cultural conditions and life circumstances different than those of Europe and North America, say, in Africa" (p. 61).

The story of African and other non-Western youth has largely been reproduced from the images, scripts, and stories of Euro-American notions of adolescence and youth identity. Most of the developmental studies on youth identity in Euro-American psychology continue to be based on theories of identity formation as linear and age- and stage-based—these theories are largely devoid of the historical and political context or are disconnected from contexts of power and social inequalities (Burman, 1994; Hammack, 2008). Furthermore, there is scant research on how neoliberalization as the guiding principle of globalization shapes youth identities in non-Western countries. Thus, examining how neoliberal forms of globalization shape youth identity in postcolonial nations or non-Western societies is an important decolonizing move that allows us to confront long-held Orientalistic or ethnocentric images that have defined Euro-American psychological science. Thinking about culture and identity through the framework of globalization also highlights how urban Indian youth are engaging with new psychological discourses and vocabularies of self and identity in their everyday lives.

CULTURE, NARRATIVE, AND IDENTITY: A SYNTHESIS IN PSYCHOLOGY

Given that culture is dynamic, contested, and relational and is not rooted or fixed in physical location, nations, or geographic regions, then culture in psychology should not be considered in terms of essences or something that we possess or own. Instead, we must theorize culture as a process and practice that is also shaped by material and discursive realities of power, history, and social practices. Following Hammack, I argue that we should study culture to understand how individuals make sense of their participation in cultural practices. Hammack (2011) argues that "culture, thus, is not something we *have*; it is something we *do*. And it is something we *talk about* doing—both to ourselves and to others—thereby reproducing the material and discursive conditions of a society" (p. 22, emphasis in original). What follows from these observations is that we must not only study culture through its rituals and social practices but also go further and examine how individuals make sense of their life in the realm of culture. Furthermore, there is no single universal idiom, symbol, or set of practices that constitutes the makings of a fixed "global" or "local" culture. Rather, individuals who are embedded in their specific cultural and postcolonial locations mediate with global–local flows and give them new meanings. Transnational connections and relations are specific to postcolonial societies given their unique colonial histories. Thus, call center work shifted to India, as Patel (2010) argues, due to access to cheap labor, differential time zones, and having millions of educated youth who were fluent in English. The call center worker is now part of a transnational service economy due to its colonial history and because of the neoliberal forms of policies that were enacted by the Indian government in the 1990s. The stories of urban Indian youth, or narrations about their asymmetrical engagements with neoliberal forms of globalization, shed light on how their identities are being refashioned in places that Cindy Katz (2004) has called the new "topographies of global capitalism" (p. xv).

Identity and Power

My concept of identity emerges out of the interdisciplinary frames of cultural and narrative psychology, postcolonial and diaspora theory, and globalization studies (Bhatia, 2007, 2008a, 2008b, 2010a, 2011, 2013; Bhatia & Ram, 2001, 2004, 2009). By locating identity within a field of fluid, asymmetrical, and intersecting histories, Stuart Hall (1996) encourages us to focus not so much on identity but, rather, on the processes of identification. He describes "identification" as an interaction or an encounter between different practices that ascribe to us an identity or "interpellates" us into becoming subjects. As Hall further argues,

> The notion that the effective suturing of the subject to a subject-position requires not only that the subject is "hailed," but that the subject invests in this position, means that suturing has to be thought of as an *articulation*, rather than a one-sided process, and that in turn places *identification*, if not identities, firmly on the theoretical agenda. (p. 6, emphasis in original)

Subjectivity and identity are both crucial to the process of identification. In Hall's viewpoint, it is not enough to examine how identities are represented in discourses but, rather, we have to go further and analyze how the subject is called upon and hailed by specific cultural discourses and why identities take up or attach themselves to certain subject positions and not others. The idea that individual subjects are invested in and are constantly interacting with their subject positions then opens up the space for examining the dynamic and multiple tensions and relationships between the psychological world (which already is constitutive of the social) and the social worlds. An individual's subjectivity or the "I" then emerges in this encounter between how identities are assigned to her and how in turn she articulates, identifies, or repositions this assignation.

Hall's (1996) notion of "articulation" is useful because it conceives of identity as an incomplete, fluid, contradictory, and dynamic site of production that emerges out of asymmetrical cultural encounters. The intersections of global–local cultural encounters have created hybrid identities across racial, ethnic, and linguistic lines. Hybridity is one of the most widely circulated and debated ideas to have emerged from the discourse of globalization (Bhatia, 2013; Kraidy, 2005; Pieterse, 2004). This term has given rise to the new configurations of multilayered identities that are described as "hyphenated," "creole," "mestizaje," "diasporic," and "syncretic." The term hybrid has evolved from being used to describe agricultural seeds, then later a doctrine that proscribed the biological mixing of races, to its contemporary usage in which hybrid now refer to gas–electric cars, architecture, music, food, clothing, and cultural mixing (Kraidy, 2005). The term hybridity captures the swirling zones of fusion and contact, difference and conflict, compatibility and rupture, location and dislocation across geographical, national, and linguistic boundaries (Cancilini, 1995).

Hybridity challenges essentialist conceptions of culture. The notion of culture as embedded within a certain, confined space becomes problematic when we consider the people who dwell on the border. How does one define the culture of the borderland or of migrant workers who live in both Mexico and the United States? Why do borderlands force us to reconceptualize received notions of culture? Anzaldua (1987) explains:

> Borders are set up to define the places that are safe and unsafe, to distinguish us from them. A border is a dividing line, a narrow strip along a steep edge. A borderland is a vague undetermined place created by the emotional residue of an unnatural boundary. It is in a constant state of transition. *Los atravesados* live here: the squint eyed, the perverse, the queer, the troublesome, the mongrel, the mulatto, the half dead; in short, those who cross over, pass over, or go through the confines of the "normal." (p. 25)

Beside the culture of borderlands, there are cases of migrants, refugees, and expatriates who move from one settlement to another, putting down their roots and carrying their "culture" with them to new places of belonging. This group represents a rupture or a clear physical break between culture and nation because these people take their culture to the new homeland and reinvent and reimagine it in their new diaspora (Bhatia, 2007).

Postcolonial scholars such as Stuart Hall (1996) and Homi Bhabha (1994) developed the early theories of hybridity. These theories sought to demonstrate the structure and patterns of domination and resistance in imperial colonies and in the postcolonial nations that came into being after colonization. These theories have explained how agency and power are enacted in practices of living hybridity in contexts in which cultures are reinscribed, blurred, and become sites of clashes and struggle (Bhatia, 2014b). Bhabha, for example, writes that mimicry was adopted by the "natives" as a form of resistance and a way of subverting the dominance of the colonial culture. Mimicry, in his view, "emerges as the representation of a difference that is itself a process of disavowal" (p. 86). Mimicry thus involves appropriating the other "as it visualizes power" (p. 86). Within the context of globalization, individuals mimic and appropriate Western cultural flows and then reframe them to create a "third space" or a "third identity" that is simultaneously/at once ambivalent, liberatory, and hybrid.

The cultural hybridity manifested in colonial times or in globalization reveals a movement between sameness and difference, ambivalence and appropriation, and continuity and discontinuity. Bhabha (1994) writes that "the social articulation of difference, from the minority perspective, is a complex, ongoing negotiation that seeks to authorize cultural hybridities that emerge in moments of historical transformation" (p. 2). Terms such as "interpellation," "third space," and "hybridity" point to complex processes of negotiation that individuals undertake as they come to terms with cultural change in their localities and as cultures, goods, and people move from "here to there." Such identity negotiations then interrogate and pose challenges to stable notions of originality, essences, or purity of cultures (Bhatia, 2010b; Bhatia & Ram, 2001). Hybridity as a destabilizing category, within contexts of globalization, raises questions about what it means to be an Indian as the global–local cultures are being reworked and reimagined by Indian youth.

The Argentinean–Mexican scholar, Nestor Garcia Cancilini (1995), defines hybridization as a "sociocultural process in which discrete structures or practices, previously existing in separate form, are combined to generate new structures, objects and practices" (p. xxv). For Cancilini, these discrete structures are not pure "points of origin" but, rather, force us to look at how hybridization comes into being as they are being recombined to form cultural heterogeneity. Analyzing the process of hybridity and identification in post-colonial societies becomes central in times of globalization as new identities are formed in the previously colonized nations. Furthermore, the study of these new hybrid identities gives us insights into how traces of power and hegemony are being reproduced within these hybridities. Hybridity therefore raises the "question of the *terms* of mixture, the conditions of mixing. At the same time, it's important to note the ways in which hegemony is not merely reproduced but *refigured* in the process of hybridization (Pieterse, 2004, p. 74, emphasis in original). The people in these previously colonized regions are making and refiguring their own cultural or alternative modernities (Gaonkar, 2001). The Western modernity of their colonial masters, in some form, has landed in the old colonized localities, and traces of newly inscribed and refig-ured hybrid identities are part of the Indian urban landscape.

The term identity is elusive and slippery, and it has many different mean-ings in various subfields in psychology as well as across different disciplines in the social sciences. The notion of identity that I employ in this book is socioculturally constituted, and I further define it by drawing on Suzanne Kirschner's (2015) formulation of identity. She argues that identity refers to the descriptions or attributions that are assigned to individuals who belong to a particular group or who are members of a society. Identities are thus "rela-tional" as an individual is "always implicitly defined in terms of what one is not" (p. 218). Identities are "historical" because we identify people by locating them in their specific historical and sociocultural practices. They are "multiple" as people define themselves through multiple categories, such as race, gender, and nationality; social roles; and through dominant master narratives. Finally, identities are "dynamic" as people agentively respond and interact to the labels and attributions given to them in varied ways, and in doing so they change the meaning of these culturally grounded labels and categories (p. 218). The definition of identity offered by Kirschner retains the significance of viewing culture in terms of history and multiplicity that postcolonial scholars have pointed to. However, I add that labels or ascriptions given to individual are not just labels, but they can be considered as discourses that carry with them, as Hall (1991b) reminds us, a whole set of histories, of interpellations, that are saturated and reflective of power. The stories that I analyze in this book give us insight into how Indian urban youth make sense of their identities in contexts of transnational mobility, global work conditions, and poverty. I examine their narratives to understand how young people in urban India refashion and subvert cultural norms and discourses and imaginatively reconstruct their identities and subject positions.

Narrative and Social Imagination

My view of culture and identity that I have discussed previously comes to life through the concept of language or, more precisely, narrative. If culture is not something we essentially possess or have and it refers to something we talk about as we reinterpret the material and discursive conditions of society, then cultural meanings about identity become articulated through language. It is here, as Hammack (2011) notes, that culture becomes a *"linguistic production—a* production that, in turn, *mediates* our experience" (p. 21, emphasis in original). The concept of narrative becomes relevant for us because "culture—including its material elements—is produced through the construction of stories about groups, their relationships, and their values and aspirations" (p. 21).

Thus, if identities are multiple, relational, and dynamic and are socioculturally constituted (although not wholly reducible to culture), then it is through the activity of narration that we understand how individuals reproduce, reclaim, or reinterpret the discursive and material meanings of culture. Therefore, it is through the *"practice* of narration that we become cultural beings and, in the process, reproduce the discursive foundations of a culture" (Hammack, 2011, p. 49, emphasis in original). Given the increasing discursive and material emergence of the worldwide phenomenon of globalization, we can no longer insist on thinking about "cultures" as contained by national boundaries or as reified entities. Scholars studying issues related to globalization make us confront questions about how culture undergoes enormous rupture and change. Contemporary global movements and globalization impulses (variously motivated) force us to abandon such seamless conceptions of similarities and differences between national cultures in favor of hybridized, "diaspor-ized," and heterogeneous notions of culture (Hall, 1993, p. 356). In other words, the relationship between culture and nation should be viewed neither as completely disjointed nor as coterminous. To posit static, immovable, immutable constructions of culture is a convenient fiction that allows us, as Hall (1991a) acerbically remarks, "to get a good night's sleep." For it allows us to believe that despite the fact that history is "constantly breaking in unpredictable ways . . . we somehow go on being the same" (p. 43). What this book delineates is the material and social conditions in which stories of hybridity are narrated, and it teases apart the various asymmetrical and contradictory components that make up the tales and trails of hybridity (Kraidy, 2005) within the urban Indian youth narratives. Thus, cultural globalization, while it may produce heterogeneity and hybridity, is articulated through the equipment of narrative and process of narration.

I integrate the primary concepts of culture, identity, and narrative to understand how urban Indian youth are both shaped by and in turn are shaping the dynamics of neoliberal globalization in India. What is it that they are narrating when they tell cultural stories about globalization at work? How do conceptions of self, fulfillment, work, and happiness, derived as they are from Euro-American cross-cultural psychology and personality theories, circulate in Indian corporations? How is Euro-American psychological science with its accompanying discourses of self and identity being reproduced in the lives of urban Indian youth? How do Indian youth's narratives about globalization reconfigure cultural meanings about family, romance, marriage, work, and money? What do these stories tell us about how these youth are refashioning their identities?

Thus, my approach to narrative is similar to my approach to culture. I prefer to describe narrative as a verb in which the focus is on "'narrating,' 'to narrate,' 'to tell,' 'to show,' and to 'make present'" (Schiff, 2013, p. 259). Narration and storytelling take us to the realm of action, imagination, and meaning-making and give us insights into why people, who are shaped by their social locations, tell particular stories to themselves, to others, or to specific audiences. I adopt a sociocultural and interpretive approach to narrative that I delineate in much more detail in Chapter 3.

By drawing on Leiblich and Josselson's (2012) scholarship, I use the term narrative to refer to a "specific genre of discourse, centered around the narrator and his or her life. . . . The kind of story or narrative which may be utilized for the study of personhood concerns accounts of events or experiences in the narrator's life" (p. 203). The focus here is on understanding narration as a form of action that reveals "why persons express themselves in a certain fashion" (Schiff, 2013, p. 259).

Questions about how young urban Indians imagine their social and cultural worlds through the equipment of narrative take center stage in this study. Although the focus in narrative psychology continues to be on the self, we know that a person's identity or self is deeply shaped by and connected to the other. One can argue that self narrative primarily derives its meaning from relationship with others (Freeman, 2014).

If we take self and other to be mutually constituted, then the narrative perspective allows me to theorize about the various spheres of otherness, which in the context of this book moves between the individual, local, national, postcolonial, and the global (not necessarily in this order). The sources of deriving meaning and purpose from something that is beyond the self can come from many domains: nature, God, meditation, family, and friends. The discourses of globalization within urban India have given rise to a distinct cultural vocabulary of self and other, and many spheres of otherness have emerged in this context; thus, my aim is to use narrative psychology to capture this fashioning and refashioning of self–other relationships in these diverse and varied cultural settings. An important feature of the stories that young urban Indians tell about globalization is shaped by their social imagination.

Social imagination, according to Greene (1995), is "the capacity to invent visions of what should be and what might be in our deficient society" (p. 5), and thus the notion of social imagination is a key concept in understanding how globalization produces culture-specific, alternative psychological discourses of self and identity. Just as colonization produced new hybrid psychologies of being traditional, nationalistic, and modern in the cultures of the colonies, contemporary forms of globalization are producing new narratives of "Indianness" in urban India. Imagination continues to be a key component in producing these new identities.

Thus, the world that is imagined and experienced in London and New York by its youth is not the same as it is imagined and experienced by the youth in Pune and Bangalore. We need to study how "Indianness" is being reimagined and refashioned through their stories of globalization and how they are reconfiguring collective meanings of self, family, romance, relationships, and work. Social imagination is about how people imagine their collective norms of their existence and "how they fit together with others, how things go on between them and their fellows, the expectations that are normally met, and the deeper normative notions and images that underlie these expectations" (Taylor, 2004, p. 23). The story of globalization, then, is always a local story that is told from a particular place, using specific cultural idioms and specific narrative imaginations. Globalization thus does not create universal or homogenized modernities or replicable modern identities but, rather, the phenomenon creates culturally constituted, place-specific identities.

NOTE

1. The Global South is usually intended to refer to countries in Africa, Central and Latin America, and many developing countries in Asia, including countries from the Middle East. The Global North refers to the countries in North America, Europe, and a few select countries in Asia. The North–South divide is represented by asymmetrical conditions of economic, political, and financial power. The Global North also refers to the "First World," and countries represented by the "First World" or the G7 (the United States, United Kingdom, France, Germany, Italy, Japan, and Canada) control much of financial assets and capital in the world, own the majority of the manufacturing operations in the world, and are able to shape financial and economic policies through the World Bank and the International Monetary Fund. The umbrella of the rich and wealthy countries that represent the Global North now includes Russia (G8).

CHAPTER 2

The Cultural Psychology
of Globalization

Constructing Desirable Identities and Spaces

The globalization of the world has created, as Inda and Rosaldo (2002) argue, a set of complex interdependencies in which immigrants and people are on the move; capital moves feverishly across borders; financial exchanges are interlinked across the globe; and cultures have acquired a mobility that brings about new struggles and negotiations about self, identity, family, and nation. Let me first make explicit what I mean by globalization[1]—a concept that is central to our vocabulary but often defies easy explanations.

Contemporary scholars have defined globalization as an empirical condition of the modern world that is characterized by complex connectivity (Tomlinson, 1999), disjunctured cultural flows (Appadurai, 1996), cultural diffusion and hybridization (Pieterse, 2004), as well as neoliberalization (Harvey, 2005). We live in a network of interconnections and interdependencies that characterize modern social life. These interconnections have been described through concepts such as networks, modalities, or flows. Not only does connectivity bring us in close proximity to places and spaces that in the past seemed very far apart but also our representational experience of distances undergoes a qualitative change. John Urry coined the terms "mobile sociology" (2010) and "mobile subjectivity" (Sheller & Urry, 2006) to study how discourses and practices emerging from migration, citizenship, transnationalism, and exile create new forms of flows, scapes, movement, and stasis and new intersections of local and global identities.

The notion of time–space compression conjures up images of a world that is shrinking (Harvey, 1990). Globalization is quite an old phenomenon, but what is different about its current form is that the scale, speed, and import have changed significantly (Hermans & Hermans-Konopka, 2010). The scale, speed, and import of globalization primarily occur through the frequent amplification and acceleration of time–space compression in economic and sociocultural dimensions of life (Harvey, 1990). Similarly, sociologist Roland Robertson (1992) notes that "globalization refers to both the compression of the world and the intensification of the consciousness of the world as a whole" (p. 8). The altering and intensification of the time–space dimension reshapes the concepts of culture and identity. Arjun Appadurai (1996), a leading scholar of globalization, writes that the "central problem in today's global interactions is the tension between cultural homogenization and cultural heterogenization" (p. 32). The acknowledgment of the interaction between global and local also prompts us to pay attention to both sides of the equation: If the global is constructed through the local, then the local is also reworked through the global (Mazzarella, 2003).

The concept of globalization is a contested term with multiple meanings, references, and the definitions vary across the different disciplines of political science, geography, cultural studies, economics, and sociology. There is a general consensus among several social theorists, however, that the economic aspects of globalization profoundly shape society, culture, and subjectivity across different areas of the world (Appadurai, 1996; Castells, 1996; Giddens, 1991; Robertson, 1992). Specifically, Pieterse (2004) argues that the emerging consensus among scholars is that globalization is being influenced by economic and technological changes, that it entails the reorganization of states, that it produces regionalization or localization, and that it is deeply uneven. It is beyond the scope of this book to undertake a comprehensive interdisciplinary survey of the economic concept of globalization, but it is important to at least briefly map out the economic theory of neoliberalization that also drives many of the current cultural processes of globalization.

The changing landscape of urban India as symbolized in the rapid development of malls, shopping centers, business processing offices, call centers, information technology (IT) parks, and gated communities was largely spurred by the opening up of the Indian market and the embrace of neoliberal economic reforms in the 1990s (Das, 2002). By most accounts, the moment of India's remarkable transformation from a "license raj" to an economic powerhouse is traced to what Das (2002) describes as the "the Golden Summer of 1991" (p. 213). A passionate supporter of global capitalism and pro-market reforms, Das writes that after 1991, India became part of a world economy and "our second independence had arrived: We were going to be free from a rapacious and domineering state" (p. xi). When radical liberalization reforms were unleashed in 1991 by the former late prime minster P. V. Narasimha Rao, the Indian economy became unshackled. Das writes that "it opened the economy to foreign investment and trade; it dismantled import control, lowered custom duties, and devalued the currency; it virtually abolished licensing controls on private investment, dropped tax rates, and broke public sector monopolies" (p. x). Contemporary forms of globalization occur through the transplantation of a neoliberal ideology in both the developing and the developed world (Kinnvall, 2004). The term *neoliberalism* has been deployed, as Flew (2014) notes, so widely that it is often used to describe the "way things are" in our society. It has also been used as a "rhetorical trope" where its meanings are assumed to be understood by a given audience. David Harvey (2005) defines neoliberalism as a "theory of political economic practices that proposes that human well-being can best be advanced by liberating individual entrepreneurial freedom and skills within an institutional framework characterized by strong property rights, free markets, and free trade" (p. 5). Harvey further adds that the neoliberal turn signifies the decline of the Keynesian principles of "national capitalism" (Flew, 2014, p. 56) and the gradual supplanting of the welfare state with free market and capitalist solutions for finding answers to enduring economic inequality.

There are distinctive sets of instruments and agencies that move the processes of neoliberalization. For instance, the International Monetary Fund (IMF), World Bank, and the "Washington Consensus" required many debtor nations in Africa and Asia in the early 1980s to pull back from their support for the public sector and state-based employment programs in exchange for participating in structural adjustment programs (SAPs). United States government-backed SAPs had severe consequences for rural farmers in Asia and Africa who owned small pieces of land (Davis, 2007; Tabb, 2002). Harvey (2000, 2005) uses the concept of *accumulation by dispossession* to explain the asymmetrical economic and sociocultural formations of globalization.

Globalization accumulates capital in an earlier stage of its history only to dismantle, destroy it, and move it away at another stage to build new geographical landscapes that provide new types of accumulation of wealth. Harvey (2000) argues that the following underlying structures undergird both old and new forms of global capitalism:

1. Space and technology: Capitalism thrives because of the constant decreases in the cost and time of moving goods and people across large distances through transportation and technological advances. Railways, automobile, jet-airways, canals, and turnpikes have enabled a faster flow of people and goods across distances, and this has happened alongside other innovations in technology, such as the postal system, radio, telecommunications, and the Internet.
2. Landed capital: Landed capital is the empowering of local fixed, physical structures that enable the circulation of capital across various circuits to support the activities of manufacturing, exchange, distribution, and consumption. Special spaces in nations have become "landed capital" and

assume importance by being marked as export hubs, economic zones, and high-tech IT parks. The effort is to make the various geographical landscapes sclerotic while creating other landscapes that are mobile and untethered.

3. Regulation of law and capital: The third element of globalization is the building of the state apparatus and territorial organizations to "regulate money, law, and politics and to monopolize the means of coercion and violence according to a sovereign territorial (and sometimes extra territorial will)" (Harvey, 2000, p. 60).

4. Global governance: The United States plays one of the most important roles in the financial deregulation and opening up of the markets by using the weight of the IMF and World Bank to move global capitalism on terms set by a few dominant economies of the world.

5. Efficiency of technology transfer: The unique characteristic of this present moment of globalization in the early 21st century is the "pace and rate of technology transfer and imitation across and through different zones of the world economy" (Harvey, 2000, p. 61).

6. Information society: The information revolution is creating an information society in which space and time compression alter social relations and thus create new types of cultural forms and communication between people.

The neoliberal agenda pushes governments to stabilize and balance their economic budgets, reduce their social spending on public goods, and coerce developing economies to open their markets to foreign investment and locate factories where cost of production and wages are low and where social policies related to taxation and human welfare are tilted toward the interests of corporations. One of the permanent features of the contemporary neoliberal order is that poorer nations cannot demand high wages or workers' rights because it has a vast reserve of cheap labor—a so-called demographic dividend that cannot move easily (Banerjee-Guha, 2010). In contrast, global corporations have technologies that are nimble and efficient and can be easily transported, so they set the terms and condition of wages, production rates, and profit margins.

In *Globalization and Its Discontents*, Stiglitz, (2002) writes about the darker side of neoliberalization in stark terms and states that globalization has neither reduced poverty nor brought political stability to much of the developing world. Instead, he writes that the unfair trade liberalization practices and agenda have been set by the countries from the North through the IMF, and the governance of globalization has occurred primarily through the *ideology* of the world financial community.

Vijay Prashad (2012) adds another important perspective to this story of neoliberalism by arguing that neoliberalism had a vigorous revival in the 1970s because of the collapse of the Third World Project. He writes that the anticolonial leaders of Asia, Africa, and Latin America established the Third World Project at Bandung Conference in Indonesia in 1955 and articulated their specific goals through the Non-Aligned Movement in 1961. The three goals of the Third World Project were "for peace, for bread, and for justice" (Prashad, 2012, p. 3), and a call for a renewed international economic order was made where economic, political, and financial power was to be shared equally across the world.

There are many reasons why the Third World Project collapsed, but one of the main factors that Prashad (2012) identifies is that the Atlantic Project mounted a forceful resistance to the Third World Project. The Atlantic Project, which was mainly made up of countries from the seven leading industrial nations of the world (the United States, United Kingdom, Germany, France, Italy, Japan, and Canada), enforced debt reductions through "austerity regimes" of structural adjustment, balanced budgets, and fiscal responsibility (p. 8). Neoliberalism also found a strong footing in the new "locomotives of the South" (Brazil, India, South Africa, and China) because the ruling classes and the elites wanted to eradicate the social–democratic welfare state of the public sector and decrease the appeal of cultural nationalism, and they eagerly embraced the discourse of individualism, productivity, profit, enterprise, and modernization. There were minority elites in these postcolonial nations who resisted the legacy of the anticolonial heritage.

IMAGINING A GLOBAL INDIA: SURPLUS LABOR AND MONUMENTS TO CAPITALISM

India is experiencing a "demographic dividend" with the youth population estimated to be approximately 350 million (United Nations Population Fund, 2014) and expected to continue to expand/increase until 2050 (Nilekani, 2008). India's demographic advantages will become "India's destiny" when the developed markets will have to rely on the vast pools of young, highly skillful, and cheap labor in India. By 2020, the average age of an Indian is predicted to be approximately 29 years in comparison to the average age of 37 years in China and the United States, and 45 years in Western Europe and Japan (Nilekani, 2008). By many estimates, these demographic trends project India to have one of the youngest populations of workers in the world. The overall increase in the current and future population of young people in India represents more than merely population statistics. Undoubtedly, the young cohort in India is at the center of cultural shifts generated by the forces of globalization. These youth are experiencing a transformation in their identities while they are simultaneously involved in transforming the cultural practices that surround them. There is a growing middle class in India that is significantly larger than the population of the United States and is expected to reach more than 500 million within the next two decades. This surplus pool of cheap and educated labor is now being exploited by global corporations and thus has consequences for ushering in profound sociocultural changes in the Indian society.

The lives of Indian youth comprise an important story of our time—a story that remains largely invisible and neglected in psychology and other social science disciplines. In much of the literature on the psychology of globalization, there has been no systematic accounting of the ways in which the social imagination of India's youth is being shaped by transnational cultural flows. There are huge swathes of Indian urban youth who are experiencing conflicting meanings about their gender roles, marriage, sexual practices, filial obligations, household responsibilities, and child care duties. Indian urban youth are at the center of globalization, and it is imperative that we examine their stories as they come to terms with new sets of discourses about subjectivity, self, social relations, and changing definitions of Indianness.

One of the most important representations of neoliberal policies in urban India is reflected in the large number of IT industries, malls, call centers, and business processing offices and the presence of multinational corporations. During the past decade, my participant observation at "home" (in India) involved jotting down elaborate notes about advertisements displayed on the streets and college campuses and in malls, neighborhoods, cafés, pubs, *bastis*, and IT parks where multinational corporations and call centers had been established. These new spaces offer insights into how transformations in spatial identity are connected to the social life of the various classes. It is through these spaces that the new middle- and upper-class consumers are "imagined as differentiated consuming units, located between multiple binaries such as 'global' and 'local' and 'modern' and 'traditional'" (Srivastava, 2015, p. 217).

In the following sections, I map out two urban spaces in Pune that have been created as part of the vision of a modern, global city and that reflect new desires of the consumerist lifestyles of the upper middle class. The construction of "global India" is an important project of the urban spatial transformation in Pune, where new forms of sociality are being cultivated to fashion a new identity that is based on redesigned urban spaces, modern forms of capital, transnational cultural symbols, and local Indian traditions and values.

Global *Desi*: Constructing "Ethnicity" in the Phoenix Mall

During my most recent visit to Pune in July 2015, my belief that globalization was a steady urban phenomenon leaving its imprint across the city was confirmed.[2] This time the city felt on fire as though undergoing an internal implosion. Within a matter of a few years, the city had stretched out exponentially, and the psychological and physical cartography of the city were being continuously and irrevocably transformed. Many distant villages on all sides of the city had now become part of a growing new Pune. New malls, IT parks, and gourmet restaurants, combined with more cars, motorcycles, and traffic gridlock, were part of the new sociocultural reality of Pune and much of urban India. The Phoenix Mall near Kalyani Nagar had been described to me by many of my participants as a "genuine mall" that topped all the other malls in Pune. In this section, I reflect on my observations of this particular mall space and how it presented an example of what Marc Auge (2008) has referred to as "non-places." He states that "super modernity" (p. 65) produces non-places, and they are the symbols of our era of globalization. In contrast, "places" have anthropological identities that are built through social relationships and activities, community, histories, and memory and are embedded in a network of other places. Auge explains:

> Place and non-places are like opposed polarities: The first is never completely erased, the second never totally completed; they are like palimpsest on which the scrambled game of identity and relations is ceaselessly written. But non-places are the real measures of our time; one that could be quantified—with the aid of a few conversions between area, volume and distance—by totaling all the air, rail and motorway routes, the mobile cabins called "means of transport" (aircraft, trains and road vehicles), the airport and railway stations, hotel chains, leisure parks, large retail outlets. (p. 64)

There are no "non-places" in absolute terms but, rather, there are differently conceived spaces that are produced by globalization and urbanization. One of the unique markers of the identity of such non-places as malls, theme parks, or airports entails the texts, visuals, and symbols they use to communicate with their customers or passengers. Navigating these spaces require one to use a map or a tourist handbook. Decontextualized instructions for customers or passengers are frequently posted on signboards to help navigate these spaces, such as "Take the right hand lane," "Proceed to security checkpoint," "Food court on third floor," "You are entering the wine region," and "Thank you for shopping with us." Non-places are homogeneous spaces that are streamlined and prefabricated so they can be frequently replicated and reproduced with similar architecture, symbols, style, and function. Non-places, too, have an identity, history, and rituals, of course, but they can easily be "manufactured" and transported across regions, borders, and throughout the world. The mall is indeed a space where people congregate and engage in social activity, but its introduction in an Indian urban city, as a result of globalization, stood out to me for its familiar "non-place" feeling and its strange juxtaposition amid the old structures of Pune.

The Phoenix Mall greets its visitors with a towering, curved, canopied entrance. My visit started with the security guard asking me to put my knapsack on a table and waving me to walk through the metal detector. The detector beeped. The young guard moved his handheld metal detector over my body and gave me the green signal to walk through. I arrived at the entrance where five young boys were relaxing on sofas and leather chairs, gazing into the screens of their mobile phones. I looked to the right of the mall and saw the Guess store and Gloria Jean's Coffee. There seemed something quite odd at that moment. It brought back memories of going to the Greendale Mall, a small mall by most standards, in Worcester, Massachusetts, in the mid-1990s. With sparkling, dirt-free porcelain tiles and high ceilings, this mall was the size of an average-size mall that one finds in America, but in Pune it looked colossal, with three floors of shopping and dining space. The Phoenix Mall was a slightly bigger, glitzier version of the Providence Place Mall—the one local to my family home in Rhode Island, which I had just visited before leaving the United States. The inside space felt simultaneously intimately familiar and strangely disorienting. For a moment, I felt as though I was back in the United States or walking through an airport terminal in Frankfurt, Geneva, or Zurich. The mall was built in the area called Ramwadi, which was once a small farm on the outskirts of Pune. Ramwadi had been recast and remade into a "non-place" or an "out of place" mall through its homage to global modernity and capitalism. The mall space evoked the culture of "sameness" because it copied the Western-style monuments of consumerism, and at the same time this space was "different" because its gleaming shine and spotless paint stood out against the grime and filth of the Indian streets.

The brand names and the consumer excesses of the West had traveled and found themselves new homes in a place that until less than a decade ago was little more than vast stretches of dry, semicultivated farmland detached from the city. I found the excesses and artificial cleanliness of the Phoenix Mall in Pune oddly disorienting and deeply alienating. The space where the mall had seemingly sprouted overnight used to be on the outskirts of Pune, with dirt roads lined by fields, local tin-roofed shops, and dwelling structures populated by a motley crew of farm workers and their families. Now, the glittering spectacle of globalization and neoliberal consumption had erased a whole slice of that organic locality and reincarnated it as a supermodern non-place, where brand names and universally recognized symbols of clothing, shoes, and other luxury items were on display. It is difficult not to feel nostalgic, knowing that the Pune that I called home was being eroded and usurped continuously and exponentially through these familiar structures and signposts of globalization.

The Phoenix Mall represented a global uniformity replete with all the standard signs found in many malls, airports, and theme parks across the world. A parade of twinkling global brands, including Apple, Nautica, Aldo, Esbeda,

Boggi Milano, French Connection, Sony, Glass Hut, Diesel, Hush Puppies, Swatch, Celio, and Gossip, lined the long spiral hallways. This global universality was punctuated with local Indian brands such as Mochi, Guru, Indigo, The Bombay Store, Crossword, Landmark, Chemistry, Star Indian Bazaar, Soch, Provogue, Pantaloons, Reliance Trends, Promod, Westend, Mogra, Ethnicity, and Global Desi. However, both global and local brands were framed with similar mall aesthetics of brightly lit, larger-than-life displays and idealized, glamorized mannequins staged to optimize and showcase brand ideologies.

In *Open* magazine, whose readership mainly consists of upper-class, educated Indians, Michael Edison Hayden (2013), an American expatriate, wrote that he goes to malls in India to overcome his nostalgia for America. When he had just moved to Delhi from America, he would frequent the MGF mall in Gurgaon to get over his bouts of homesickness that he felt during Thanksgiving or Christmas. He noted that although he only occasionally went to the mall in America, the mall space in India became an essential part of his new "expatriate" identity.

For Hayden (2013), the Indian mall invoked both nostalgia for the United States and an excitement about witnessing the future of India unfolding in real time. This mall, he observed, is a "simultaneously beautiful and a horrible mirage—a purified moment to capitalist escapism" (p. 61). The malls in Pune could be described as avenues to indulge in capitalist escapism, but they are also spaces in which the upper-class Indians could "leave India" without departing. These spaces provide urban Indians the modern materials to reimagine themselves as having "world-class" identities—where Indian spaces become contiguous and conterminously linked to First World spaces.

I walked up to the second floor of the mall and saw the entrance to the glitzy shop Ethnicity. The lettering, Ethnicity, was written in dark purple and on the right side of the entrance is a glass display window, which had approximately six or seven mannequins. These mannequins had Caucasian features, black hair, and white complexions, and they were wearing Indian *sarees, sherwanis* (traditional formal suits worn by males), and *kurtas* (loose flowing tunics).

The inside space of Ethnicity was organized and designed to create the feel of an Indian bazaar. This ersatz marketplace had erased the usual organic features of the original. The typical noisiness and messiness that emerged from the hustle and bustle of vendors and customers bargaining amid hawkers and gawkers jostling to get attention were replaced by large exoticized photo displays of the Indian marketplace.

The store was divided into named sections. On the left side was Raja Market (King's Market) for male shoppers, where *sherwanis, kurtas, mojris, Kolhapuri, chappals*, and *Jodhpuri* sandals were sold. Rani Market (Queen's Market) was located on the right side of the entrance and sold women's wares such as designer *sarees, salwar khameez*; other hybrids of Indian and Western clothes; and traditional embroidered bags from Kutch, Maharashtra, and other states. Other sections similarly used Hindi to signify the merchandise being sold, such as Chota India (For Children), Sona Chandi (Gold and Silver), Ghar Angan (Home), and Thoda Aur (Accessories).

Ethnicity's website described the store as a journey that was based on the colorful street market of India's holiest pilgrimage site, Banaras (http://delhi-ncr.mallsmarket.com/brands/ethnicity). Banaras was described as being colorful and vibrant, "inviting and seducing, native yet innovative" that created an auditory and aromatic experience for the customer. The web copy claimed that Ethnicity "revives and rejuvenates anything and everything that is Indian." The complexities and layers of Indian ethnicity defined by the fraught divisions of castes, tribes, regions, cultures, linguistic practices, histories of marginalization, and exploitation were reduced to a bricolage of commodities.

In the 1970s, foreign tourists, particularly those who identified as "hippies," would frequent Indian markets to acquire "native" handicrafts and art. For these tourists, the very local nature of these commodities made them desirable. Now in a globalized Indian economy, these local, native goods are being repackaged as chic "ethnic" merchandise to middle- and upper-class urban Indians. This rebranding of selective local goods as cool commodities to be consumed was part of the larger narrative of globalized cultural packaging at the mall.

A few hundred yards from Ethnicity, The Global Desi store was much more explicit about its mission of branding its products to appeal to a well-traveled, transnational, upmarket clientele. The website defined its product as a brand born out of a romantic affair between global fashion and Indian Rajasthani colors and designs. The website also described one of its 2014 collections as follows:

> Injecting an electrifying dose of bohemian-chic fashion, Global Desi introduces "London Calling"—a collection which resonates with the inherent travelling spirit of the "Global Desi girl." A collection which is innately urbane, yet, intrinsically Indian in essence! A mix of fashion forward ensembles, bursting with a kaleidoscope of the season's hottest hues, this latest offing from Global Desi, gives wings to your sartorial senses, and allows you to forgo the beaten track, and carve your own global fashion road. It offers a colorful glimpse of the "Global Desi girl," having a catwalk moment on the cobblestoned streets of London, as she absorbs the wondrous delights of the city, and prances around from Tate to Portobello to Hyde Park, flaunting some of the most coveted styles of the season. (http://theblahqueen.com/global-desis-calling-london-collection)

The Global Desi girl was constructed as the Indian transnational traveler who was rooted in the local with her "Indian essence" but could effortlessly transform into a global figure by incorporating what the brand defines as a "bohemian-chic" style. However, the photos accompanying this text did not display any particular, local Indian markers or characteristics. Rather, the Global Desi who is purportedly a locally produced yet globally recognized figure was nothing more than a generic version of a Euro-American model digitally inserted in stock photos such as an orchard, a stack of vintage luggage, and landscaped gardens.

Similar to its Western counterparts, the Indian mall functions as a new social space for urban, middle-class teenagers and families to hang out, socialize, and re-create their consumer identities. Malls operate to trade in cultural capital, as a place to shop and to be seen with friends. However, the Indian malls also act as portals for the urban middle and upper classes to temporarily leave the dust, heat, and grime of the Indian city streets and be transported to a "First World" space with clean restrooms, strobes of mood lighting, spotless floors, plush interiors, and boiled water in *panipuri*. The shoppers pass through the mall gateways both literally and psychologically to briefly escape the Indian-style pandemonium of the outside world.

Although the inside–outside dichotomy operates to construct the mall as a special space of escape, Indian mall designers have also been careful not to eschew a sense of Indianness. The global aesthetic of American malls with their particular standards of cleanliness and style is maintained alongside a carefully curated catalog of objects and design elements meant to invoke the regional cultural diversity of India, the feel of *kirana* shops (family-owned small grocery shops), as well as the style of local, urban, street fashion. The success of an Indian mall, Srivastava (2015) argues, requires the "seamless cohabitation between commerce, sociality, and culture" (p. 228), where India culture becomes commodified and refashioned as a consumer culture.

Although malls in urban India may be designed to be physically separated from the chaos and the dirt of the Indian street, Srivastava (2015) states that the magic of the Indian mall reflects the complexities of an Indian modernity. He writes,

> The aura of mall lies in its alignment with the gathering—and greatly admired—discourses of privatization of public spaces (through, say, slum clearance), requirements of new consumerist affects, perceptions of an easy fit between "Indian traditions" and global culture, and the superior developmental capacities of private enterprise over the state. (p. 239)

The mall spaces are reflections of an Indian modernity that is an amalgamation of class desire, consumerist aspiration, identity and lifestyle markers, and a synthesis of imagined global spatial experiences, consumer fetishization of branded goods, air-conditioned and clean environments, private enterprise, as well as local sensibilities and traditions. The urban poor or the working class are also now part of the mall culture that is symbolic of the larger sociocultural changes in India. The working-class youth now enter these spaces to shop, stroll around, or work in retail sales positions, at the food court, or as janitors, cleaners, and security guards. Their exposure to these spaces also transforms their aspirations and imaginations about consumption and allows them a glimpse of an elite or middle-class life.

Global Indo-German Urban *Mela* in a Neoliberal Context

In January 2013, when I was in Pune conducting fieldwork and interviews for this project, I visited the Max Mueller Bhavan, a branch of the German Goethe Institut. I was curious about the posters throughout the city advertising an Indo-German Urban *Mela*. I was well acquainted with the Goethe Institut, which promotes the study of German and German culture. In the 1980s, as an undergraduate student in Pune, I often borrowed books on German philosophy and literature from the Max Mueller Bhavan. I was not only able to regularly borrow books by paying a nominal fee but also able to walk around the beautifully manicured gardens. There was a small kiosk at the back of the library where I could order chai and samosas and read under an outdoor, wooden canopy. The lush greenery of the garden was accompanied by the sounds of birds, and the traffic noises that habitually drenched the city could barely be heard.

In those days, the Institut was mostly frequented by convent-educated (i.e., in schools established by British Christian missionaries), middle- and upper-class Indians, who were getting elementary and advanced diplomas in German language. Today, the Goethe Institut has a greater presence in Pune because it has become a place where IT employees, software engineers, and business management students learn the German language and culture so they can be absorbed into one of the 300 German-based companies that have been launched in Pune since 2000. Michael Flutch, Director of the Max Mueller Bhavan, commented to a business newspaper (Joshi, 2011) that there was a dramatic surge in the number of Indians who were learning German; in any given year, approximately 2000 students were enrolled in the local German language institute.

In 2012–2013, India and Germany celebrated 60 years of diplomatic ties. Germany sponsored a traveling exhibition of Indo-German culture, art, and technology through five major Indian cities, with Pune among them. A famous German artist, Markus Heinsdorff, designed several traveling, modern, multipurpose pavilions. The theme of the *Mela*, "Stadt Räume," or City Spaces, was intended to bring to light the deteriorating quality of urban life in the cities of India.[3] The *Mela* website described its vision as follows:

> Imposing malls, glittering billboards and honking cars vie for attention relegating parks, cultural and creative spaces to the background. As India gallops

towards higher economic growth and its cities and peoples struggle to keep up, it is perhaps only right that it engages with one of its strategic partners—Germany—for solutions to better prepare for this tumultuous urbanization it is witnessing. (http://www.germany-and-india.com/en/page/222/cityspaces)

My numerous walks through the main roads and small lanes of Pune had given me enough evidence that Pune, like most Indian cities, was facing immense problems of urban expansion and congestion. The city was attracting new migrant labor from rural areas. Professional skilled workers were seeking employment in cities such as Pune, where many new business enterprises and investments from foreign, multinational companies were searching for educated, cheap labor for the IT industry, call centers, and data processing companies. There were new flyovers, bridges, residential building, malls, and IT parks. This urban industrial sprawl was being built within the footprint of the old city without consideration of the needs of the existing inhabitants. Forgoing any kind of thoughtful and systematic urban planning, the local municipal government had abdicated its responsibilities to provide basic services to the urban poor in Pune. Transnational corporations were free to sweep in and take over whatever was needed to achieve their goals.

The proclamation by the *Mela* organizers that German corporations and multinational companies were going to be strategic partners in solving Pune's unbridled urban problems was supremely ironic. The promotional narrative proclaimed that German corporations were in India to provide "solutions to better prepare for this tumultuous urbanization [*sic*] it is witnessing." However, the solutions were being driven by the very corporate entities whose explosive growth in Pune had created much of the urban blight in the first place. Consider the following news statement from the German Missions in India's website reporting on the success of the *Mela*:

> From Bosch's safety systems that help avoid road accidents to a kids' lab by BASF showcasing experiments to purify water at home using natural ingredients, the pavilions are catering to the interest of all age groups. At the Deutsche Bank pavilion one can see the prototype of a solar plane, which weighs more than a medium-sized car and is equipped with about 12,000 solar cells. Also the visitors can try Siemens' digital planning game; it's a race against the clock to see how long you can keep your city going or put your driving skills to test with the Bajaj Allianz's cars stimulator. (http://www.india.diplo.de/Vertretung/indien/en/__pr/Culture__News/IGUM__Pune__Preview.html)

What was being displayed in the Indo-German Urban *Mela* was an unabashed obeisance to the rising corporate powers in India and Germany. The new avatars of global capitalism had assumed a dominant "savior" position in rescuing the Third World local practices and inhabitants. German companies such as BASF, Deutsche Bank, and Siemens had rhetorically made the local government agencies and municipalities irrelevant. The text, the story, and the cultural representations of the Indo-German *Mela* were not intended to serve the majority of working-class and urban poor youth for whom daily life involved a struggle to get access to basic necessities such as sanitation, education, employment, and health facilities.

Rather, the framing of the Indo-German *Mela* held on the Deccan College campus was that Pune and other metropolitan cities were aspiring global spaces, where European and American corporations and pop-cultural icons from Berlin, New York, and Frankfurt would arrive to lend legitimacy and validation to the localities. The Indo-German *Mela* was constructing a story of "progress" and "modernity" in which German scientific prowess and engineering capabilities were going to be used to solve local urban problems in Indian cities. Cities and urban areas are currently home to an estimated 30% of the Indian population and contribute approximately 60% to India's total gross domestic product (GDP). In the next 20 years, these percentages will increase rapidly. The Indo-German *Mela* website estimated that 40% of the Indian population will be living in cities by 2030, producing as much as 70% of India's total GDP. This means that in the next 20 years, a projected additional 250 million people will be living in Indian cities compared to today. The program went further and laid out a scenario in which life in urban India will be a nightmare—a hellish existence where city dwellers will be confronted with inefficient transportation, lack of water supplies, and a system that will be unable to properly process human waste, garbage, electronic waste, and so on.

The problems confronting "Stadt Räume," or the city spaces in India, would purportedly be solved by bringing German expertise to four areas: politics, culture, business, and academia and research institutions. The German component of the "Indo-German *Mela*" identity supplied the infrastructure, the theme, and the philosophical overview of the problems confronting urban areas in Indian cities. *Global Germany* was represented through its glittering, portable pavilions and the various science and technology exhibitions. The slogan on the website captures the motivation behind the Indo-German *Mela*. India was a place of "infinite opportunities" and Germany was going to lend its acumen in engineering, energy, transportation, resources, and waste management to Indian cities and rescue them from an impending, dystopic future.

One of the program events at the *Mela* was titled "A Goal Wall: A Shootout Challenge". The activity was described as follows: "Bend it like Beckham in this shootout match! All you have to do is shoot the football into one of the openings on the goal wall. And don't forget to yell 'Tor!' after a goal!" Adults, children, and teenagers were expected to be familiar with references to movies such as *Bend It Like Beckham* and were encouraged to "bend" the soccer ball into the nets. There were other language-related events where Indians could learn some German words and vocabulary. One such activity was titled

Schnupper Stunden, which allowed Indians to sample the German culture by learning a few German words. The participants were asked to use simple German vocabulary to introduce themselves and describe their hobbies and occupation. The local four-star hotel, Taj Vivanta, sponsored a beer garden, where the visitors—especially in the evenings—could sit under huge, white outdoor tents decked with light bulbs. Many local visitors could be seen sitting on colored benches and narrow wooden picnic tables, sampling German beer and food.

The Indo-German *Mela* provided a new cultural space in urban India—a global, elite, transnational space that was being marketed to mostly English- and German-speaking upper-class and middle-class Indian families. Every day at the *Mela*, a German clown named Shiven gave a performance. Shiven's real name was Guntur Bennung, and he performed at the cultural pavilion. His profile in the program stated that he made his first trip to India in the 1970s, and since then he has been "fascinated and influenced" by India. The program further stated, "Shiven means the one who loves the good," and it was in India that he decided to follow his inner calling to entertain children as a clown. Shiven described himself as "a clown with a philosopher's soul" who wanted to promote peace and joy through making people laugh.

Every evening, the *Mela* ended with a musical performance. The performance by Ma Faiza, a British Indian who was born in Africa and was raised in the United Kingdom, was one such example. She came to Goa to discover her "Indian" identity and started mixing underground electronic music in Goa. Ma Faiza got her big break when she was invited to play in Berlin to huge crowds. She now lives in Pune and plays in upscale hotels, bars, and music festivals throughout the world. Ma Faiza was recently voted as "India's favorite electronica D.J." At the Indo-German Urban *Mela*, D.J. Jane Ipek and D.J. Ma Faiza engaged in an "epic" battle of eclectic music. According to the program, D.J. Ipek's music would take "the audience on an 'aural journey' by stringing together music from the cultures of Turkey, North-Africa, Israel, Persia, the Balkans, Greece and Bollywood."

On January 15, 2013, cultural activities at various pavilions ended with a performance by musician Raghu Dixit. He is described as a "true representation of India." His music is ethnic and anchored in the roots of Indian poetry and folk songs, and it was described as quintessentially Indian but "global in its outlook." Therefore, the program states that it is not surprising that "Raghu has been referred to as India's biggest cultural export of recent times. . . . In April 2012, he performed for Queen Elizabeth II of England at her Diamond Jubilee pageant."

The Indo-German Urban *Mela* was indeed a cultural spectacle, where the global and local were being reproduced, repackaged, and performed in a new modern and transnational aesthetic that was made of a hybrid cultural mix concocted by German and Indian corporations, global *desis*, local performers, artists, and engineers. The style and format of the *Mela* evoked both an urban youth "pub" culture and globalized, cosmopolitan upper- and middle-class fantasies of "going global." This hybrid mix with all these elements was culturally portable, streamlined, and highly mobile. The Indo-German *Mela* had been reproduced and re-enacted in Chennai, Mumbai, Bangalore, and Delhi.

Through participant observation and writing about such scenes from the field, I was able to capture the reorganization of urban space in Pune and the way "global Indianness" was being represented and visually enacted. The mall space and the urban *Mela* became an ethnographic text through which we can decipher and decode the varieties of ways in which the global was being constructed, framed, and experienced in India by urban Indian youth and families. These spaces were reflective of the larger neoliberal cultural and social transformation that was occurring in much of urban India. They were symbols of Indian modernity that were giving rise to new narratives of mimicry, cultural icons, hybridity, elite mobility, and upper- and middle-class anxiety about being recognized as "global citizens."

For instance, at the Indo-German *Mela*, the "local Indians" on stage were strategically represented as "global Indian performers" who had repackaged their local music so it could travel effortlessly through spaces that can be described as Western, urban, modern, and yet retained an ingredient of Indian culture. The urban *Mela* expressed and created new *cultural narratives of self* that originated in a global corporatized Western society but had acquired new global–local Indian arrangements, systems, practices, usages, customs, rituals, and procedures through social constructions of class and space.

The class-based stories that I analyze in this book emerge from specific *cultural sites* that are made of rituals, practices, and habitus (Bourdieu, 1994). An examination of the stories that emerge from these distinct yet interconnected sites makes visible the contradictory practices of individual sites; their relationships to the bordering groups or sites; and how they are linked institutionally and ideologically to values of capital, consumerism, transnational connections, travel, and labor. These spaces and sites reveal an emerging montage of social class identities that make up the spectrum of urban Indian youth and show how they are synchronously positioned to each other and to the historically shifting social, political, and economic relationships within India and globally.

NOTES

1. The literature on globalization is vast and deep; different fields, such as political science, economics, sociology, and anthropology, have their own internal debates about the meaning of globalization. A search of the word "globalization" using Google results in more than 34 million hits. A quick scan of an interdisciplinary

book series on globalization by the publisher Rowman and Littlefield shows the varied approaches to understanding the phenomenon of globalization. Some of the book titles are *Globalization and Sovereignty*, *Globalization and War*, *Globalization and American Popular Culture*, *Globalization and Social Movements*, *Globalization and Terrorism*, *Globalization and Law*, *Globalization and Feminist Activism*, and *Globalization and Postcolonialism*.

2. *Desi* is a term that is derived from "desh," which means country, and it is used to describe people from South Asian countries such as India, Bangladesh, Pakistan, Nepal, and Sri Lanka.

3. *Mela* is a Sanskrit word used to describe a carnival, a meeting place, or a gathering for the purpose of cultural, religious, or political celebrations in South Asia.

CHAPTER 3

Psychology and the Neoliberal Self

Global Culture and the "New Colonial" Subjects

Neoliberal globalization is not just an economic concept or an economic condition; rather, it brings with it shifts in the *spheres of culture* (Pieterse, 2004; Tomlinson, 1999), *psychology*, and *identity* (Arnett, 2002; Bhatia, 2008a, 2013; De Vos, 2012; Hermans & Dimaggio, 2007; Sugarman, 2015). Neoliberalism's reach in psychology is quite extensive, and it is "reformulating personhood, psychological life, moral and ethical responsibility, and what it means to have selfhood and identity" (Sugarman, 2015, p. 104). Thus, several scholars of globalization who are working from their disciplinary viewpoints differ on the meaning of the term globalization, but there is a general consensus among them that neoliberal globalization is reconfiguring discourses of self and identity (Pieterse, 2004).

The growth of offshore business processing offices, call centers, and software companies that fall under the category of information technology (IT) enabled industry and information technology enabled services (ITES) in India is part of the logic of late capitalism in which the drive for maximum profit and lower production costs, highly skilled knowledge workers, and low-skilled cheap labor becomes highly valued. Thus, as capital moves across geographic spaces, it seeks "new sites of investment and new markets, it invokes, plays upon, appropriates, and transforms pre-existing cultural tropes and images, creating and re-creating new forms of cultural difference and social identities" (Upadhya, 2008, p. 102). Obviously, this phenomenon is not new because in the earlier stage of capitalism, we witnessed the large-scale creation of female "sweatshop" labor in Southeast Asia in the 1970s that made cheap shoes, clothes, and textiles for North American corporations. During the peak of colonization and industrialization, European and North American economies mercilessly used slaves and indentured laborers in Asian, African, and Caribbean colonies as disposable bodies to work in plantations, mines, agriculture, and manufacturing.

In today's transnational economies, labor has become mobile and niche oriented. Wen Liu (2015) examines how neoliberal structures have created a demand for cheap women's labor and services as maids, nannies, nurses, farm workers, and migrant labor in the developed economies of the world. There are approximately 8.2 million Filipino women workers, accounting for about 10% of the Filipino population, engaged in the "care" industry across different areas of the world (Ehrenreich & Hochschild, 2002).

The specialized transnational economy is an exemplary moment in the history of neoliberalization. The workforce around the world is now segmented by transnational knowledge workers, customer service workers, labor workers, and tourism workers who are shaped by national histories, specific economic conditions on the ground, education, and geographic convenience, and by a large cadre of mobile professionals, managers, engineers, and global workers. The story of the rise of India as one of the most globally desirable locations for offshore offices is part of this narrative of global capitalism.

During the past decade, the story of globalization in India has been linked with the implementation of neoliberal policies set forth by the government in 1990, and the "rise of India" has garnered considerable attention in American media. In 2006, both *Newsweek* and *TIME* featured cover stories on India. *Newsweek's* cover photo featured a front shot of the television celebrity Padma Lakshmi in a "namaste pose" along with the following title on the cover: "The New India" ("The New India," 2006). This title was placed above the colorful fluttering drapes of Padma Lakshmi's tight-fitting *saree*. Similarly, the *TIME* cover showcased the headshot of a young Indian woman wearing a communications headset. This young woman was obviously depicted as working in a call center, but she was wearing a *maang tikka* (gold bridal jewelry) along with two beaded strings that covered the sides of her forehead and thick floral earrings and a hanging nose ring. Beneath her face, on the bottom of the cover, the captions read "India Inc." and "Why the world's biggest democracy is the next great economic super power—and what it means for America."

The combined sector of IT and ITES in India provides employment to about 2.5 million people who work in call centers, business processing data offices, software companies, medical tourism, transcription, and so on (Mirchandani, 2012). The integration of a "virtual" global economy has created the conditions of greater contact and interaction between Western and Indian employees, managers, and customers; thus, the understanding and regulation of *cultural difference* and *identity* has become one of the main areas of concern in global corporations (Sathaye, 2008).

THE COLONIALITY OF PSYCHOLOGICAL SCIENCE
AND THE CONSTRUCTION OF A GLOBAL CULTURE

The software projects that are outsourced to Indian companies are carried out mostly by groups of Indian software development engineers who often virtually interact with other customers, colleagues, and supervisors usually at the client site or at the company site located in the United States or Western Europe. There are other times when Indian software engineers from Mumbai or Bangalore have to physically travel to meet their clients (on-site) or their teams in the United States or Europe or in other geographic regions of the world. The lack of effective cross-cultural communication between Indian software engineers, their work teams, and their foreign clients is considered to be one of the key problems in the Indian software industry. Indian software engineers and managers are fluent in English, but it is their communication style when they are interacting with Western clients and colleagues that is often viewed as deficient and problematic (Nadeem, 2011; Upadhya, 2008). Almost all Indian software engineers who work with Western colleagues or clients are expected to go through a "soft skills" training program that emphasizes intercultural communication, social skills, team building, time management, and leadership skills. These programs are essentially aimed at teaching software engineers and consultants new behaviors, dispositions, social skills, and communication styles that facilitate a smoother cultural interaction with their mostly European and Western colleagues and clients. Multinational corporations and Indian companies rely mostly on cross-cultural psychology research that has been primarily developed in the field of psychology in the United States and Europe to rectify what are viewed as deficiencies of Indian work culture (Mirchandani, 2012; Upadhya, 2008; Vasavi, 2008). The application of Euro-American psychological theories was expected to bring the "Indian techie" into the fold of what are considered as normative "global best practices."

The "Bible" of Cross-Cultural Psychology

The cross-cultural framework developed primarily by Western psychologists provided the most important tools, concepts, and vocabularies to understand "culture" in cultural sensitivity workshops and extended training seminars held for offshore companies, such as those in India. These workshops promoted highly reified ideas about culture in which Indian work culture was viewed as inefficient, hierarchical, feudal, and indirect, whereas European culture was framed as egalitarian, professional, assertive, and non-hierarchical. Thus, companies often invoked specific discourses about "culture" to explain and account for differences in work and management styles, misunderstandings, and other breakdown in communication that occurred between Indian workers and their Western colleagues. The remedy for all these intercultural problems was sought by addressing the flaws in "Indian culture" and pushing the Indian employees to adopt new principles and practices (Upadhya, 2011).

The "best global practices" in these seminars and programs were usually invented and created in the United States and then applied to the rest of the world. One of the most widely used sources for understanding the cultural differences in Indian IT companies and in other management circles is Geert Hofstede's (1980) book, *Culture's Consequence: International Differences in Work-Related Values* (Sathaye, 2008; Upadhya, 2008). Hofstede's book is referred to as the "bible" of international management studies (Upadhya, 2008, p. 104), and the term "culture" in his book is consistently conflated with "nation." According to Hofstede, the four basic dimensions of culture are individualism/collectivism, power distance, uncertainty avoidance, and masculinity/femininity. Hofstede defines individualism as "a loosely knit social framework in which people are supposed to take care of themselves and their immediate family only," whereas collectivism is characterized by "a tight social framework in which people . . . expect their in-group to look after them, and in exchange for that they feel they owe absolute loyalty to it" (Hofstede, 1980, p. 45).

The concept of "national cultures" is defined through employing various "pattern variable" schemes that are primarily based on Parsons' sociological theory of modernization and Ruth Benedict's concept of national culture (Upadhya, 2008). Hofstede (1997), whose work is much cited in the cross-cultural psychology literature, also cautions the reader to be careful when discussing cultural difference solely at the national level and offers a series of categories that include gender, generation, ethnicity, and so on. However, such categories are then put aside in favor of "collecting data" at the level of nations because he argues it makes "practical sense to focus on cultural factors separating or uniting nations" (pp. 12–13). Similarly, Gudykunst and Kim (1997), both of whom have been very influential in developing cross-cultural research on cultural differences, state that usually boundaries between cultures coincide with boundaries between countries. Other prominent scholars, such as Segall, Lonner, and Berry (1998), refer to the preponderance of interest by cross-cultural psychologists in examining the notion of individualism/collectivism as a cultural characteristic across "national samples" (Bhatia & Ram, 2001). While the application of Hofstede's framework and other psychological instruments was intended to promote better intercultural relations and communication, the purpose of these instruments in Indian companies was to essentially teach young Indian workers to fit into the dominant Western cultural meaning systems and practices of communication.

"WASP Culture" as "Global Best Practices"

Most software engineers and call center workers are expected to participate in several seminars, courses, and workshops on intercultural training. It is important to specify here that psychological discourses about managing cultural differences, identities, empowerment, teamwork, flexibility, and self-actualization were not just confined to training programs or seminars. Instead, this knowledge permeated every level of organization practices, and it shaped their mission and larger business practices. These discourses circulated as scientific knowledge throughout corporations and were frequently used to control rather than empower employees. Corporate management training thus required trainees to acknowledge their deficits, and they were encouraged to remedy their personalities "by transforming themselves into management-approved personality-type" (Upadhya, 2008, p. 116). The goal of these programs was to create "action plans" for every individual so the knowledge gained could be applied throughout the organization. What was specifically taught in these workshops or training seminars? An Irish trainer, who was conducting a training program for one of the software companies in Bangalore, opened the workshop by defining culture as "shared values" and "ways of behaving," and then she asked the participants to articulate the different descriptions associated with cultures such as "American" and "Indian.". The trainer then presented a typology of cultures by drawing on Hofstede's (1997) definitions of national cultures. Upadhya (2008) outlines this taxonomy:

1. Pluralistic—the "WASP" (White Anglo-Saxon Protestant) cultures (Australian, Canadian, and American), characterized by individualism, personal achievement, orientation to career, materialism, change as progress, and lifestyle diversity
2. Extended family cultures (Latin American, African, Middle Eastern, and Indian), characterized by social structure built around family, importance of where one is from, authoritarian power structure, family as a source of social identity, business carried out within a network, minimal social change, sharp gender differences, tradition-bound, and religious (p. 111)

The trainer argued that the cultures around the world are integrating and merging around a "global corporate culture," which is based on the pluralistic, WASP-type culture. The WASP culture was described as contrasting and colliding with the Indian culture that is based on the extended family, so the trainer then suggested to the participants that they should adapt or fit into this global culture without giving up their identities or losing their core values. The trainer, Upadhya (2008) notes, asked the participants to "accept the notion that 'I can behave differently during my eight hours in order to help my career, without changing myself fundamentally'" (p. 112).

The trainer subsequently outlined how the participants could learn new ways of thinking, behaviors, and habits, such as being assertive and direct at work—especially when they are interacting with their American colleagues or clients. The "American" personality types were directly seen as shaped by the WASP pluralistic and individualistic cultural orientation, and the Indian mindset and actions were conceived of as embedded in a family-oriented, collectivistic orientation. From this specific orientation, Americans are defined as "linear active," and Indians are defined as "multi-active" (Upadhya, 2008):

> (1) "Linear active": plans ahead methodically, likes privacy, punctual, dominated by timetables, sticks to plans, completes action chains, separates social and professional life; (2) "multi-active": inquisitive, multi-tasking, works any hours, timetable unpredictable, completes human transactions, changes plans and juggles facts, people oriented, pulls strings, interweaves the social and professional. (p. 112)

One can notice the very unacknowledged "deficit" discourse in this formulation of cultural difference, especially when the trainer emphasized that the "linear active" is the dominant way of thinking in global corporate practices and that the young Indian participants would eventually have to change their "psychology" as part of their adaptation process. During discussion time, a young woman challenged these cultural assumptions and argued with the trainer that her "multi-active style" still provided the desired result so why should she change. The trainer responded as follows (Upadhya, 2008):

> PARTICIPANT: Why don't others adopt the "multi-active style" (i.e., why should we adopt their style)?
> TRAINER: We have to be realistic—who dominates in the corporate world? It's the US, and the American system is what has come to characterize the corporate world all over, so we have no choice but to follow that style. (p. 113)

Western and Indian trainers who provide cross-cultural training are aware of the ethnocentric biases underlying these frameworks, but yet they continue to reproduce these Orientalistic images of Indians as "bad communicators," "corrupt," "feudal," and "not direct," as opposed to Americans being "easygoing," "social," forthright," and "good communicators" (Upadhya, 2008). There are two types of cultural processes at work in these cross-cultural workshops. On the one hand, the trainers encouraged their audience to embrace organizational theories that validate cultural difference and multicultural identities by emphasizing the point that cultures are "not intrinsically good or bad." On the other hand, Indian IT workers, including call center workers, are told that "they must learn to adapt to the now-'dominant global corporate culture' (which is based on the Anglo-Saxon pluralistic culture) because, implicitly, their own culture is not suitable to that context" (p. 115).

American Personality Tests and the "Scientific Imperative to Be Positive"

A battery of psychological tests and theories primarily developed in Europe and the United States were part of the evolving neoliberal management practices that were creating a particular kind of flexible and enterprising neoliberal worker in corporations. These workers were expected to follow the ideology of Western corporate culture through individual transformation; embracing a self-Orientalizing framework; and acquiring new behaviors of increased emotional intelligence, assertiveness, flexibility, productivity, and self-regulation.

Indian corporations were now heavily reliant on American "personality tests" based on career/vocational theories, and these instruments were used for recruitment, screening, promotion, and to motivate employees to become happy and positive workers (Vasavi, 2008). The IT and call center industry mostly used American personality assessment instruments to profile Indian workers and to determine whether they fit the American definitions of being "assertive," "positive," "extroverted," and "self-confident." A major appeal of these instruments lies in the assumption that they are grounded in sophisticated scientific method and that they can be taught to employees through packaged "10-point" workshop sessions.

The Myers–Briggs Type Indicator (MBTI) and Transactional Analysis (TA) inventories were two of the most pervasively used instruments for training purposes in Indian corporations (Vasavi, 2008). The MBTI purports to be grounded in Jungian archetypes and is formulated on four essential grids with binary universal personality styles: extrovert/introvert (E or I), sensing/intuitive (S or N), thinking/feeling (T or F), and judging/perceiving (J or P). Transactional Analysis is not based on universal personality traits, but it is used to teach participants the difference between "ego states" and "life states."

The MBIT is primarily used by human resource departments and consultants, and Indian IT corporations and call centers use these specific tests because they supposedly give the trainers a method for quantifying personal growth and actionable goals. These psychometric tests allow participants to "plot their responses to situation so as to 'discover' their true states-of-being or personality types" (Sathaye, 2008, p. 144). Participants were often given an "action plan" after each workshop so they could monitor their inner states and responses at home and at work. Indian IT workers and other employees were often told that they needed this psychological training because "they have lost touch with their feelings, their relationships, their values—a fact exacerbated by the technology boom and longer working hours" (p. 148). These imported instruments were justified because they were viewed as altering the social, professional, and spiritual dimensions of the employees' lives while also serving as a tool to maximize employee efficiency and productivity at work. A director of an Indian-owned multinational corporation gave several justifications for giving Western psychological training: "See, these professionals are technically very sound but their accents, mannerisms . . . are very bad, you can call them robots, actually [or perhaps simply "introverts"?]. . . . Also, it helps us because, on-site, they present a better image [of the company]" (p. 148).

Being "on-site" in the previous excerpt refers to when Indian workers were interacting with their Western colleagues, so these psychological exercises were primarily designed to make the employees fit Western cultural routines and scripts of interaction. The application of American psychological instruments such as the MBTI and TA was similarly justified in the Indian context because they were viewed as resources for psychological experiences of self-actualization, self-exploration, and self-knowledge, and it was excepted that such psychological transformation would inculcate "new dispositions" in their personality (Vasavi, 2008, p. 220).

In contemporary neoliberalized India, the new psychological discourses about work and family were based on a flat work structure; flexible time schedule; the Silicon Valley motto that "work is fun," "joyous," and "fulfilling"; and the conviction that work should bring out the full potential of a worker. Call centers and business processing offices typically operate 24 hours a day for 365 days a year (Ramesh, 2008). The work undertaken by call center agents is considered to be repetitive, monotonous, as well as emotionally and physical demanding. New systems of surveillance are put in place to monitor, evaluate, and quantify a worker's output in terms of the norms that are set up by the corporation. The call work center workplace utilizes "electronic panopticons" (Basi, 2009) by deploying advanced computer technology and hidden cameras to survey and monitor the workers. Companies use "sophisticated psychological and organizational behavior practices" to regulate, discipline, and integrate young workers in the larger organization (Vasavi, 2008, p. 222).

To minimize work-related stress in call centers and inculcate desirable personality traits, human resource departments in many corporations have developed new "rewards and recognition" practices that are based on American corporation and cultural rituals and their consumption-based practices. Vasavi (2008) explains:

> "Halloween nights" with the "Grim Reaper" visiting them on the floor; celebrations with gifts at New Year's and Christmas; outings to bowling alleys and go-karting tracks; dinner treats at expensive restaurants; and prizes of coveted electronic goods such as DVD players, stereos, televisions, and mobile phones, all compound the varied ways in which employment is masked as

entertainment and the workers are integrated into circuits of consumerism, which subsequently feeds into the formation of a new identity. (p. 223)

A whole industry of human resources workers, consultants, trainers, managers, and professors, who were using Euro-American cross-cultural psychology, personality tests, diversity training, and counseling, emerged to not just change the work culture in India but also to fundamentally alter Indian culture and society (Sathaye, 2008). First, the conception of a self that is promoted and understood as dominant in Indian IT centers is a particular conception of a specific historically contextualized American conception of self (Sathaye, 2008):

> The ideal American self lies outside social and personal realities—realities which are seen as distinctly separate from and only an interference in, the truly effective functioning of such a self. Thus the new "knowledge self," fashioned by the "knowledge economy," speaks in "I" sentences, responds to the directives of its own will, is a team player, and yet is entirely self-reliant. (p. 153)

Second, trainers, management professionals, and professors were able to seamlessly impose mainly European and American psychological conceptions of self, culture, and identity in an Indian cultural context through the power of science. The importing of these psychological techniques and systems was anchored in the belief that what is being presented to the Indian audience is a universal truth that is forged out of vigorous scientific empirical methods, American standardized psychometric tests, statistical generalizations, and the application of specialized language and vocabulary.

Data were presented via graphs, numbers, and psychometric tests, and key findings of research were often conveyed to the audiences by framing psychological training and materials as absolutely objective, universal, and scientific. Trainers often stated that the personality tests reveal the "true" nature of an individual's underlying emotional state.

Companies promoted celebrations of cross-cultural differences and touted their achievements in creating a diverse workforce, but when it came to pedagogical exercise in training (Sathaye, 2008),

> the content of a self frequently invoked—as in "self-confident," self-actualized— is treated as (self) evident. This is so despite the close relation that such a conception bears with a specific, historically produced American concern with autonomous self. . . . Trainers are able to confidently assert the universal attainability of being a "winner"—and thereby place the onus of success on the individual—because they present success as the inevitable outcome of a series of pre-charted and standardized "skills." The confidence stems from an underlying belief in the universal truth of the remedies proffered. . . . And this precisely

is the canopy under which trainers and management professionals and academics attempt to find a shelter for their work. Presented as the result of rigorous empirical observations and experimentation and standardized in the "best practices" mode, training becomes a space where a science of human behavior is brought into action. (pp. 153–154)

Sathaye is pointing to the convergence of three dominant cultures that come together to create desired identities and social practices in Indian IT industries. The first practice is the positioning of the American self in Indian companies as ideal and desired. Second, the onus of crafting a specific desired self that is approved by the management is entirely the result of an individual's enterprise and effort. Third, psychological results are presented through the power of science as hard, objectives truths that predict, measure, and judge human actions and behaviors. These three features made up an important pedagogical practice in Indian corporations.

One might be tempted to ask: What kind of resistance did the Indian software engineers and managers offer in these workshops? What counternarratives did they produce? Most of the software engineers had internalized the dominant ideology of corporate cross-cultural psychology by attempting to overcome their "cultural deficiencies" and by following the company rules and adapting to Western work norms. However, there were other employees who were critical of the cross-cultural psychology workshops and found them to be irrelevant, ineffective, and offensive.

In some instances, especially during coffee breaks, Indian workers inverted the cultural hierarchy and described their Western colleagues as "dumb (stupid *goras* [*white*])" and insensitive to the Indian cultural context (Upadhya, 2008, p. 127). One Indian manager maintained that Western workers needed to learn to adapt to Indian contexts. He stated that he had taught European workers how to improve their communication with Indians through more dialogue-based techniques (Upadhya, 2008):

These people with their white skin think they are on top of the world, but I have learnt to change their attitude. . . . Divide and rule is what they did years ago and they still practice it here. Earlier I would get bogged down by whites, but now I have fairly good relations with them. (p. 127)

One may even ask why Indian cultural psychology was not incorporated in an Indian workshop. One of the key reasons is that Indian psychology is typically viewed as inferior and less scientific in relation to British and American psychology. Furthermore, North American and European corporations had the power to decide what counted as legitimate psychology and "best global practices," and from that perspective Indian culture and psychology were implicitly seen as inadequate and inferior.

Even when training workshops drew on Indian cultural psychology concepts, they often became assimilated within the larger Orientalist narrative of Western superiority. During one workshop for call center workers, one trainer encouraged the participants to draw on the "Indian ideals of *athithi devo*—the Indian cultural norm of treating the guest as god" (Vasavi, 2008, p. 221). The trainer instructed the call center agents to treat customers as God and view their interactions with customers through devotion and service. The trainers often touched on Indian philosophical and indigenous psychological concepts, but they were ultimately just added on to serve the purpose of giving meaning to an imported Euro-American psychological science.

There are several definitions of what constitutes indigenous (or cultural) psychologies. Owusu-Bempah and Howitt (2000) suggest that in some instances, scholars equate indigenous psychologies with the psychological understanding that is embedded within traditional, and more commonly religious, conceptions and world views of self and society. In other situations, researchers are much more interested in the development of a psychology that will help with the implementation of national government objectives. For others, the eventual integration of indigenous psychologies using comparative methods is part of the search for the grail (Owusu-Bempah & Howitt, 2000, p. 29). Thus, an indigenous Hindu psychology of personhood, for example, would emphasize the following: nonlinear growth and continuity in life, behavior as transaction, the temporal and atemporal existence of human beings, spatiotemporally contextualized action, the search for eternity in life, the desirability of self-discipline, the transitory nature of human experience, control that is distributed rather than personalized, and a belief in multiple worlds (material and spiritual). (Gergen, Gulerce, Lock, & Misra, 1996, p. 498). One of the dilemmas of critiquing the importation of Western psychology is the question of what constitutes an authentic or legitimate local or non-Western psychology. The Indian Hindu indigenous psychology often borrows from Vedic scriptures or Upanishads that promote a Brahmanical view of the world and excludes the world views of Shudras and Dalits. Decolonization is a reflexive process that means being aware of the various intersections of Western and Eastern and global and local psychology and the ways in which power plays a critical role in creating hegemonic and colonizing psychological frameworks.

The Indian IT employees offered some resistance and reinterpreted the cultural norms that were imposed on them, but ultimately they had no real power to mobilize change or voice their dissent against the hegemonic corporate discourses that assumed the superiority of Euro-American psychological conceptions of self and the power of psychological science. They enacted their agency by incorporating elements of these new discourses of cultural identity to fit with their conceptions and imaginations of what it means to be an Indian in the age of globalization. While still being dominant, the "global"

American-style management practices and the circulation of new discourses about self and identity in IT companies were not transforming Indian employees into American or European cultural clones. Instead, IT employees and call center youth, depending on their class, caste, and gender locations, were deploying these psychological discourses to create hybrid discourses of "global Indianness." This is a point that I develop in greater detail in Chapters 4 and 5. The reframing or reinterpretation of Euro-American psychological discourses within Indian contexts, however, does not diminish its hegemonic force and its powerful ability to represent itself as global, normal, and natural. These dominant discourses about globalization have also created strict rules about how one should act, feel, speak, and behave in the world of interconnected digital and cyber global economies.

English Language and the New Colonial Subjects

Indian call center workers were subjected to hours of training in accent reduction, communication style, voice modulation, personality development, and so on. The Indian customer service agents were expected to do "authenticity work" on two levels. First, Indian workers were expected to come across to their Western customers as workers who are "legitimate colonial subjects," who are in awe of the West and are not threatening Western jobs. Second, the Indian agents were expected to come across as cultural clones of the West so they could establish an easy familiarity and connection with their Western clients (Mirchandani, 2012, p. 8). Customer service call center work requires establishing a connection with clients and being deferential to them even in contexts where the customers are being racist. These workers are told to respond to racist invectives with empathy and not with argument or anger. Call center agents who respond to racism with anger are often considered deviant and not fit to work for call centers. All kinds of psychological testing and training sessions are deployed to identify individuals who will deviate from the company norm. Mirchandani explains: "By virtue of their ethnicity as well as the corrupting influence of local languages, all Indians are deemed to require remedial training to be understood by Westerners" (p. 8). Indian customer service workers carry the burden of being far away from their Western clients while simultaneously being intimate in their conversations; they have to come across to their clients as workers who are capable of understanding and empathizing from a distance. The success of millions of intercultural conversations that occur over the phone between Indian call center agents and their Western client hinges on clear communication.

The responsibility of communicating clearly with the right accent, tone, choice of words, and emotion falls directly on the individual call center worker in India. Training in language and communication in call centers is imparted on the assumption that Indian English is inferior and deficient and needs to be "cleaned up," recalibrated, and adjusted to meet the demands of the foreign customers. How is that done?

Thousands of call center agents who join these companies are given training so their mother tongue influence (MTI) can be erased or neutralized. Most Indian speakers of English are multilingual, and it is often their primary or native/regional language that is seen as interfering with their ability to acquire neutral, British- or American-sounding accents. The MTI refers to the way in which the native or primary language interferes or influences how English is spoken. Many Indians are quite comfortable speaking *Hinglish*, which is a combination of Hindi and English, but the most desired accent in call centers is the neutral convent form of English. Indian elite and middle-class students who had studied in convent English schools that were started by the British missionaries often had the right accent for this job.

The training manuals valorized two kinds of accents in the call centers: the convent school-acquired neutral accent and the British or American accent. Overall, Indian English was considered deficient, and even elite and upper-class youth had to undergo formal training to correct their "Indianisms" so Western clients could understand their speech. Thus, accent neutralization, removal of MTI, speaking with the "correct rate of speech," and expressing emotions of calm, happiness, and warmth in the conversation were considered to be the goals of call center training (Mirchandani, 2012; Nadeem, 2011; Ramesh, 2008; Shome, 2006).

The Western Global Speech and the Deficient Indian Worker

The English language training industry was now an important feature of India's urban landscape, and it provided diplomas, certificates, and training that lasted from a few weeks to 6 months. The call center training, however, lasted only 2–6 weeks, depending on the speaking abilities of the individual worker. The curriculum consisted of books, textbooks, or simply thick binders and files that contained lessons on grammar and communication. The lessons were created under bold headings such as "Essentials of Grammar," "Consonant Sounds," "Diphthongs," "Intonation," "Fluency, "Pacing and Word Groups," "Speaking to Be Understood," and "Comprehending Diverse Accents," and there was one topic assigned under the heading "Indianisms and Common Errors in Speech" (Mirchandani, 2012, p. 43). In addition to these materials, other assessment sheets were used by trainers to determine and quantify the progress of agents. These sheets had scores and marks with qualitative comments on the side, such as "should not have a regional accent," "should have a neutral accent," "should have appropriate rate of speech," and "should enunciate properly" (Mirchandani, 2012, p. 43). These materials strictly high-lighted that if the Indian call center agents were to progress, they would have to overcome three types of "Indianisms."

First, English–Indian phrases, expressions, and translations of English from their regional language had to be avoided. Second, it was assumed Indians had the habit of being "unnecessarily verbose" and "speaking at twice the universally accepted rate of speech" and "having a formal, written style of verbal communication, and frequently using politically incorrect or gender-insensitive terms. The agents have to overcome these specific deficiencies" (Mirchandani, 2012, p. 42). Third, Indians had to learn to correctly pronounce certain phonetic sounds that were not part of their speech repertoire, such as the "TH" sound. These students were expected to practice their phonetic speech by following a diagram that showed the correct placement of the teeth, lips, tongue, and the roof of the mouth.

There was one chapter in the curriculum that contained instructions on how to phonetically pronounce certain American, British, and Australian accents. Mirchandani (2012) writes that there was a passage in this chapter on Indian–English that the participants had to correct:

> I am happy being due to the fact that my marriage is fixed with nice, foreign-returned boy also from Thakurpur. My brother is always pulling my legs because of that! I am also being excited because my all friends will be joining me in this happy occasion. (p. 45)

The focus on this passage was also on content and meaning so the Indian agents could discuss the varied cultural perspectives on romance and mar-riage. In this sense, there was an attempt to teach language through cultural context or usage. In contrast to this passage, the agents had to read another passage in an Australian slang (along with other British and American slang), with stated goals of learning and understanding slang terms. The passage is as follows:

> A mate told me a bloke could make big bickies in Sydney. So I made for the big smokes flat chat to have a go at trying my bizzo there. Turns out I was such a galah. I reckon I should have had a chinwag with someone who could give me good guts before I left.

It was clear that the exercise on "Indianisms" was meant to correct defi-ciencies in Indian English so the agents could speak in a neutral accent to fit the demands of global communication style. In contrast, the sections on Western slang, including Australian, British, and American, were placed under subheadings such as "Appreciating Western Culture" (Mirchandani, 2012, p. 46).

The psychological training given to Indian software engineers and call center agents points to new forms of cultural and psychological imperialism that have gained currency through neoliberal flows of outsourcing and expansion of global corporations. The particular construction of culture, identity, and cultural difference through cross-cultural psychology is not about intercultural misunderstandings or specific miscommunications between different socially situated actors. Rather, it shows how both Western-owned and Indian corporations employ narratives of cultural differences to regulate, shape, mold, and have control over their workers' real and virtual identities so as to maximize these companies' efficiency and profit.

Here, we see the confluence of global capitalism and neoliberal discourses come together to produce narratives of cultural differences that are removed from structures of power and domination (Shome, 2006). When corporate cross-cultural psychological science meets the neoliberal language of enterprise and well-being, the social reality of unequal global structures, racism, Orientalism, and ethnocentrism become disguised as simple problems of cultural misunderstandings that can be solved through individual effort and diversity training. The search for universalism in cross-cultural psychology can be considered as a modern project with its origin in a paternalistic colonialist paradigm (Burman, 2007). This type of cross-cultural research, she argues, plays a significant role in confirming "psychological 'truths,' albeit through the sleight of hand 'comparison.'" (Burman, 2007, p. 180). The cross-cultural comparisons are formulated within the Anglo-U.S. context while quantitative and experimental methodological frameworks that are purported to be free of cultural biases are utilized to examine the impact of cultural variables on the development of universal psychological processes.

The Euro-American assumptions about culture, the hegemony of psychological science, and the neoliberal cultural flow of free market, capital, labor, and control all come together to produce specific identities in young Indian employees. The way in which psychological knowledge circulates in Indian contexts opens a window on how both global corporations and Indian-owned companies are complicit in promoting specific racialized and Orientalizing language about Indian culture that then becomes accepted as a norm.

Thus, Indian culture, communication, and ways of working, thinking, and speaking become conceptualized through the language of deficits and hierarchies because they are viewed as being inferior to the "global practices" that have their origins in Western culture. The Indian-owned corporations have embraced a decontextualized, global, corporate cross-cultural psychology partly because they are trying to position themselves as global players that can compete with the multinational global corporations. Indian corporations have embraced neoliberalism as a principle that emphasizes individualization, standardization, and maximizing efficiency, flexibility, productivity, and enterprise, so these imported psychological discourses have also found a hospitable environment, which in turn mutually reinforces their existence.

In neoliberalism, Sugarman (2015) notes, not only does the notion of economic enterprise take precedence over other forms of institutional structures but also personal characteristics such as self-reliance, self-mastery, and self-enterprise are considered key attributes in the "culture" of the organization. Cultural differences are viewed as communication problems that individuals can come together to resolve through psychological training that promotes self-reflection and self-awareness. It is not just cross-cultural psychology but also Euro-American psychological science in general that has become a colonial power structure that is assumed to represent much of humanity (Adams, Dobles, Gómez, Kurtis, & Molina, 2015; Bulhan, 2015; Watkins, 2015). Its conceptions of self and identity have been historically produced and are now being circulated as universal "techniques of psychology" (Rose, 1996) through global flows of media, commodities, capital, and various other social practices of music, art, politics, lifestyles, and so on.

Modern psychology and its perspectives on self and identity have historically emerged in the discipline-at-large because it was responding to the demands of the modern Western society. Following Foucault (1988), Rose (1996) argues that psychology and psychiatry, through specific "techniques of psy" and vocabularies, have "invented" new regimes of self, identity, and personhood (p. 2). He argues that "the regime of the self that is so prevalent in contemporary Western Europe and North America is unusual both historically and geographically—that its very existence needs to be treated as a problem to be explained" (p. 2). The very particular "psy techniques," knowledge, and explanations about personhood were produced in response to late 19th-century North American and European discourses about the state, government, public services, and welfare. The "psy disciplines" emerged, specifically, to professionally shape and regulate discourses about the family, factory, childhood, industrial relations, schooling, the military, and so on (Rose, 1996).

Psychological science can be viewed as a global "psy discipline," and its concomitant vocabulary of culture, identity, training, personality testing, positive psychology, happiness, and mindfulness have spread across its borders. As corporations have become global and international, Euro-American cross-cultural psychology has particularly emerged on a worldwide scale to give meaning to complex problems of history, culture, power, identity, and conflict through uncomplicated vocabularies of collectivism versus individualism and interdependent versus independent selves. Such knowledge can be easily digested and applied where multicultural teams composed of international employees are frequently interacting and working with each other.

What is new and different about the imperial spread of Euro-American psychology broadly is that it has now become franchised, localized, universalized, and legitimized across borders through the power of science, globalization, benign meanings of multicultural diversity, transnational connections, and neoliberal corporate power. The presence of most American cultural symbols and practices, the establishment of IT industry and call centers, and the insertion of cross-cultural psychology, psychotherapy, testing, and personality psychology through science have not just impacted the work life of young Indian workers but also reconstituted the very meaning of "Indianness."

My purpose in describing how products of psychological science are used in the Indian context was to highlight the concrete ways in which specific psychological knowledge, discourses, and practices are traveling to distant areas of the world and becoming reframed within new locales. The particular Euro-American ideas about self and identity and the stories in which these selves find meaning are historically constituted, but they now represent an idealized "global self" or "best global practices." Young Indian urban IT and call center workers' exposure to the new vocabulary of self is one example that highlights how individuals negotiate the global–local intersections in their postcolonial worlds. Indian youth, whether they worked in the IT industry or were college students, were also negotiating with other powerful global flows of media, American popular culture, music, fashion, and new consumerist practice.

CHAPTER 4

Stories and Theories

Globalization, Narrative, and Meaning-Making

On February 19, 2011, *The New York Times* published an article titled "Jilted in the U.S., a Site Finds Love in India." The writer of this article, Hannah Seligson (2011), notes that three "twenty-something . . . American guys" started a website called Ignighter.com that allowed mainly young Americans to set up group dates. She explains, "One member, serving as a point person, could arrange a date—a movie, say, or a picnic in Central Park—with a group of other people and thereby take some of the awkward edge off the typical dates." In June 2009, the owners of the website noticed a heavy increase in registered users from the main metropolitan cities of India. In 2011, the website had almost 2 million users from India, and the founders claim that approximately 7,000 young Indians are registering daily on the website.

The article also notes that in January 2010, the company made the decision to exclusively market Ignighter as an Indian dating website. Adam Sachs, age 28 years and one of the founders of the website, says, "Here we are, a few Jewish guys sitting in Union Square, and we might have accidentally revolutionized the dating scene in India" (Seligson, 2011). How did this happen? The article emphasizes that contemporary young upper- and middle-class Indians who are raised on social media such as Facebook and grew up watching MTV are not using Ignighter to find a wife or to get married but, rather, to combine social networking and offline "friending" without the pressures of committing to an arranged marriage.

The website Ignighter has been renamed Step Out, and it is billed as India's number one place for dating, broadening one's social circle, and forming real relationships.[1] Many upper- and middle-class urban Indian youth who do not want to register on traditional matrimonial websites are finding their future partners on sites such as Step Out. Anita Dharamshi, the founder of another social networking and "marriage portal" site, TwoMangoes, explains her motivation for getting into the cupid business: "The whole idea of marriage and relationships was going through a revolution, and Indians, like their counterparts in the Western world, were looking to date a potential partner before making a decision" (Rajan, 2012). The introduction of the website TwoMangoes illustrates the liquid power of culture. As individuals in urban India engage with these dating sites, they are also refashioning new ideas about romance, privacy, and marriage.

The websites mentioned before bring attention to the fact that many urban Indian youth of the current generation are renegotiating the meaning of romance and friendship in the privacy of the digital world—away from the collective supervision and surveillance of the family. While the specter of arranged marriages still hangs formidably in the collective mindset of young Indians, many are ready to reinvent traditions by combining global and local practices. StepOut and TwoMangoes not only represent new online digital sites in the Indian dating landscape but also present us with new *cultural sites* where cosmopolitan urban youth are engaged in fashioning real and imagined narratives of their selves and identities (Bhatia, 2006).

These alternative stories are being developed against the shifting panorama of cultural change that is being ushered in by call centers, foreign brands, social media, increased disposable income, information technology parks, and the dominance of American media and the larger contexts of globalization. If our meanings about self and other are drawn from a diverse array of cultural landscapes and sources, then I make a case for why narrative inquiry is particularly suited to capture how individuals make meaning of their identities as they engage with these mutually shifting global–local cultural landscapes. In this chapter, I demonstrate why a narrative approach provides us with the theoretical framework to examine and understand how globalization is creating hybrid identities in India.

CONTESTED CULTURAL PRACTICES: TWO COMPETING NARRATIVES OF IDENTITY

One evening, I sat with Raj Sharma, a 47-year-old male who worked as a senior sales executive for a shipping company, at Mocha Lounge near Symbiosis College. This coffee shop was frequented by youth from nearby colleges, both women and men, several of whom were taking drags on their *hookahs* or sipping lattes and eating burgers, panini sandwiches, and crêpes. The Mocha Lounge chain has sprouted up throughout many Indian urban cities, and its décor and the theme were inspired by the *Quahveh Khannehs*[2] of Morocco and Turkey. Mocha Lounge has advertised itself as a place intended to spur conversations about politics, family, or just the weather—where people can "meet and suspend reality for a few moments" (http://www.mocha.co.in/concept.html).

Raj's Story: "We Indians Got a Complex . . . An Identity Crisis"

Raj had dropped out of college and had many short-lived careers before finally becoming a successful senior sales executive at a multinational shipping company, UniLand. Raj opened his narrative of change by stating that India is having an "identity crisis." The urban youth, Raj scanned the room as if to indict the hookah-smoking crowd at Mocha Lounge, "are having an acceptance dilemma . . . especially the young culture thinks that if they don't follow these Western trends, maybe they will be alienated, or they may be left alone." He emphasized that contemporary youth have "ready money" by working at business process outsourcing companies and call centers where they are paid Rs. 15,000 for a starting salary, which was unimaginable when Raj was younger. Raj noted that if one speaks good English and has great communication skills, one will get a job here. Raj reiterated the theme of "identity crisis" while describing the current generation. I probed further:

S: So what is it doing to their identity? What's happening?
R: They want more acceptance, and basically we Indians have got a complex . . . a very strange complex . . . that is an identity crisis.
S: What's the complex?
R: The complex is the inferiority complex. We can't accept our old traditional culture anymore. We feel shy to eat with our own hands.
S: What's our traditional culture?
R: Our traditional culture is what we had gone through earlier. The ladies . . . what do you say . . . bending down and respecting their elders, touching their feet. But nowadays . . . it's a shake hand or a hi/hello.
S: So is it superficially changing, or really changing? Are they really changing their identity?
R: Basically, as Indians, we have got that Indianness in us. But there is a superficial change also. That is just to show how Westernized, how modern you are basically.

Raj asserted that the youth were ambivalent about old forms of Indianness, and they were embracing Western and modern ways of living. He further commented that he and his teenage daughter were attending the well-known classical Indian musical festival Sawai Gandharva[3] that is held annually in Pune. This festival brings together some of the best Indian classical musicians, and the event begins late in the evening and goes until dawn. Raj observed that most of the guests who were attending this event were in their 50s or older, and he recalled his daughter's remarks: "My daughter said, 'Dad, what is this 'aaaaa'?' What's this bloody shit *raga* [Indian musical note] and all that? It's so boring."

Raj did not want to come across as a stodgy conservative in his dismissal of the youth culture, so he quickly added to his commentary by suggesting that there is a generation gap between the youth and the older generation that was present even when he was young. However, he then paused and declared that there was a difference:

> R: But we had a particular direction to go in. We had our (liberties), but within that periphery. But over here, it is all astray . . . you can go anywhere you want to.
> S: So what is this leading to?
> R: Identity crisis.
> S: Are they becoming more individualistic?
> R: Could you just imagine an 18-year-old girl smoking in our time? Now it's common over here. Classic Milds is made for these young girls, and they openly. . . . Your next visit, you'll find that a girl and a guy will be smooching on the road, or a boy walking with a beer can on the road. So what is this? This was never in our culture earlier. It is changing. Women have become. . . . But it is changing for good in one way. . . . Earlier it was that Indian women . . . she was treated like a servant of a man. It was a male dominated society. Now both are at par. And Indian woman has got a freedom to express at least. But due to this freedom, the chances of taking undue advantage of this freedom is also growing. So that's why the divorce rates are also going up. Multiple affairs are also going up.

Raj was equating English-speaking, young urban Indian women's experiments with smoking and drinking and their liberal attitudes toward sexuality as a sign of decline in Indian cultures. This was not a new perspective. Women have always been considered as bearers of culture and tradition and have been held up as symbols of family purity and as representing the nation (Chatterje, 1993). The changing of women's role—their ability to access education, their participation in the economic sector, their financial independence, and their capacity to have input or "choice" in romance and marriage—was considered to be a threat to patriarchy, morality, and orthodox traditional Indian values.

Raj acknowledged that the discourse of patriarchy had suppressed women in India and now these women were breaking free. He, however, attributed the ongoing decay of "Indian culture" to globalization and women's liberal attitudes. The young, urban Indian women I had interviewed for this project had also equated globalization with breaking of boundaries and becoming more empowered. But their narrative told a different story.

Sunaina's Story

In contrast to Raj's perspective, consider the perspective of Sunaina, a 20-year-old studying at a liberal arts college in Pune. She grew up in the exclusive area of south Bombay, where her father made machinery for textile mills and her mother bought and sold paintings in the domestic and international art market. Sunaina belonged to the elite class and had traveled with her parents to the United States, Spain, England, and Switzerland, as well as Indonesia, Malaysia, and Thailand. She told me that her parents valued the education that comes with travel. Sunaina observed, "One cannot become aware of the world by just being in one city."

Sunaina had participated in a focus group interview that I had conducted with eight other students, and she wanted to continue a private conversation with me. She sought me out at the cafeteria and talked to me about how globalization is transforming and changing her identity. She began by telling me that globalization had made her "broad-minded." I prodded her to elaborate what "broad-minded" meant to her. The reply came quickly:

> The stereotypical mindset of an individual in India would be girls should be quiet, girls should get married early, girls shouldn't smoke or drink, girls shouldn't have premarital sex, everything that we spoke about yesterday. After getting their undergrad they should stop studying, and all of that. But now I'm extremely open to stuff like guys, or drinking. Like, we get hammered quite a bit in my batch.

Sunaina compared cultural transformations of Indian urban youth to the Euro-American countercultural youth rebellions and hippie movements of the 1970s. She singled out America and the United Kingdom as the primary cultural sources from which college-going urban Indians received ideas about an ideal lifestyle. She highlighted that these two countries, after all, gave the world "pop culture, hippie culture, the peace movement, the drugs, the sex, the rock and roll, and everything." Sunaina grew up on American media, watching shows such as *Desperate Housewives*, *The Simpsons*, *Family Guy*, and *South Park*. These shows allowed upper- and middle-class young girls such as Sunaina to imagine living a life outside of India. Sunaina asserted that shows such as *Friends* and *Sex and the City* have common themes because they project the possibility of an independent and glamorous life in New York. These shows gave young, upper-class women the material for creating a hybrid self where the movement between Pune and Mumbai and New York and London appeared culturally seamless so that, as Sunaina stated, "You feel like that's where you want to be. You want to have your own apartment, and live with your friends, and have fun, and go out, get drunk, meet new guys, stuff like that." Although exposure to American television serials had shaped Sunaina's identity narrative, it would be misleading to characterize her story of self as being singularly shaped by American culture. There was another competing voice lurking in the discursive space of her overall narrative.

Sunaina stated that "American culture" was too permissive, where young girls, out of cultural expectations of dating, tend to have limited taboos about sex and drugs. Her narrative underscored the importance of incorporating Indian values in a globalized identity. She went on to state that the young girls at her college were open to having relationships with boys, but most of the girls were still virgins and proud to have experimented with sexuality where the final physical act had not been completed.

I pressed Sunaina to define "American culture." She observed that American culture is "very loose and extremely lonely." She made it clear that she would not live in America because it would be difficult to raise children in a culture that has no family values and is morally depraved. Sunaina believed that American culture lacked a moral foundation because drugs and alcohol were easily available to youth. The high rates of teenage pregnancy were reflective of a culture that promotes a "loose" lifestyle. American culture, Sunaina continued, is based on "a very lonely lifestyle. Everyone's independent. You know like, you don't meet your grandparents, or your uncle and aunt for like . . . you'll meet them once a year for Christmas or something like that. Not all the time."

In the initial part of the interview, Sunaina mentioned that American culture as a global culture had given her an opportunity to experiment with alcohol and drugs and also had given her ideas about individual freedom. She believed that the tradition of the joint family system in urban India needed to be unshackled because modern couples should have the freedom to live their own lives—without experiencing interference from their parents. I asked Sunaina, "Since you described America as depraved, morally inferior, and a place that did not value family relationships, why would you want to import American-style family values?" Sunaina replied that she did not perceive any contradictions in her views because experimenting with drugs made her independent but not a "drug addict"—an affliction that many young Americans experience. She described those contradictions as quirks:

So it's kind of like those few Indian quirks about us are still there. We have our limitations about stuff. Like girls over there lose their virginity at the age of

14/15 and stuff. But over here most of the girls in our batch are still virgins, and we're proud that way. *Like, we're proud to be virgins.* It's not that we're like, "Oh my God, I'm a virgin, and she got laid, and she's so much more superior than me." It's not like that. And we're 18.

In her narrative of globalization, Sunaina associates American culture with drugs, sex, divorce, and loneliness. She explicitly describes it as a morally corrupt society while still believing that American culture as *symbolic of Western modernity* can strategically be used in the Indian context as a counterpoint to Raj's narrative of locating India's declining cultural values in young women's embrace of Western culture.

Raj's and Sunaina's narratives are both *imagining* and *constructing* particular images of American and Indian cultures by drawing on their understanding of globalization. Their narratives of globalization and "Indianness" are produced from two generational viewpoints. Raj's views are more accurately representative of the experiences of Indians who grew up in a pre-liberalized India. Sunaina's narrative is shaped by her experiences of growing up in an urban upper-class India that was undergoing tremendous change as a result of neoliberalization, the introduction of satellite TV, and the spread of the Internet and various forms of social media. Their narratives give us a glimpse into their negotiations with identity, but they also shine a light on how Raj and Sunaina are being shaped by the contradictory and conflicting cultural flows of globalization and localization.

At this historical juncture in urban India, as individuals face the winds of uncertainty and anxiety, the construction of a coherent and intelligible narrative account of self is all the more urgent and unequivocal. Even more pressing for psychologists is to begin to understand how these cultural materials are being strategically deployed by young Indians to create multilayered meanings of tradition, modernity, and "global–local Indianness."

These narratives about globalization force us to examine how key concepts in American psychology, such as "self," "identity," and "identity crisis," take on new cultural and psychological meanings. In the remainder of this chapter, I make a case for why narrative psychology is particularly suited to capture how individuals such as Sunaina and Raj make meaning and reimagine their self–other relationship as they engage with new contexts of globalization. I briefly sketch the story of "identity" in American psychology. The story of identity that I sketch is not exhaustive because such a task is beyond the scope of this book. Instead, I provide a selective offering of theories or historical moments that are crucial to understanding the trajectory of the concepts of self and identity in American psychology. It is against this larger historical framing of identity in American psychology that the story of "narrative psychology" or the significance of a narrative perspective is articulated.

The concept of self and identity has been dissected, analyzed, and explored by scholars and theorists from a wide range of disciplines, such as history, philosophy, literature, anthropology, theology, and psychology. The term *identity* has been the subject of discussion for over millennia, and we continue to preoccupy ourselves with this "God term" (Burke, 1969, p. 105).[4] The notion of self and its vicissitudes has been endowed with innumerable meanings. Each discipline formulates its own distinct representations and interpretations of the concept of identity. For example, psychology embodies the view of the Western self as firmly bounded, highly individualized, and atomistic (Cushman, 1990; Sampson 1993). From the mid-20th century onward, the field of psychology has witnessed an outpouring of theories on personhood, self, and identity and has given popular culture a language of interiority. We have a long history of a robust and ever-expanding "Psy complex" (Rose, 1996) that has mostly produced a static and reified vocabulary of self-construal, self-esteem, self-exploration, self-judgment, self-regulation, self-efficacy, self-states, and selfish motives. We have also witnessed, in one form or another, a renewed interest in producing relational and socially constituted identities in psychoanalysis, social constructionism, cultural psychology, cross-cultural psychology, critical psychology, discursive psychology, and narrative psychology (Ashmore & Jussim, 1997).

The identity projects of American psychology or American social science can be traced to late modernity or the late modern age, where the trajectory of self-identity, as stated in Chapter 1, is bound up with the questions of identity: Who am I? Where do I belong? How shall I live my life? The project of selfhood, especially within the context of the post-traditional societies, becomes a *reflexive project* (Giddens, 1991, p. 32). Modernity also breaks the intimacy of the small communities and makes our relationships with others impersonal and detached. The project of self-fashioning and creating self-narratives—with its attendant language of feeling, memory, and experience—becomes an important pursuit in modern times. Giddens (1991) writes,

> A person's identity is not to be found in behavior, nor—important though this is—in the reaction of others, but in the capacity to *keep a particular narrative going*. The individual's biography, if she is to maintain regular interaction with others in the day-to-day world, cannot be wholly fictive. It must continually integrate events which occur in the external world, and sort them into the ongoing "story" about the self. (p. 54, emphasis in original)

How is the narrative of self reconfigured within conditions of globalization or the new discourses of globalization? What constraints and possibilities do powerful local forms of modernity that position themselves as "global" offer for the reconstruction of self in non-Western localities?

Taylor (1989) argues that the question of identity or the search for an identity is usually presented in the form of the question, "Who am I?" One can answer this question by giving a name or referring to one's ancestry and genealogy, but that reference does not tell us what gives meaning to our lives or what is significant about our identity. To know who I am, then, entails knowing where I stand. My identity, as Taylor asserts, is

> defined by the commitments and identifications which provide the frame or horizon within which I can try to determine from case to case what is good, or valuable, or what ought to be done, or what I endorse or oppose. In other words, it is the horizon within which I am capable of taking a stand. (p. 27)

What translates from Taylor's view is that an identity crisis is an extreme form of disorientation that is expressed not just in the condition of not knowing who one is but also in being gripped by moments of radical uncertainty characterized by not knowing *where one stands*.

To know oneself or one's identity is to be positioned in a moral space in which questions about what is good and meaningful are examined. These moral spaces are defined by our histories, cultural practices, and other selves, "One is a self only among other selves. A self can never be described without reference to those who surround it"; Taylor, 1989, p. 35). In particular, Taylor (1985, 1989) views modern identity and its relation to culture and society as primarily informed by the moral frameworks of the 18th-century Romantic and the Enlightenment images of human nature. In essence, modern Western psychology draws on these philosophical frameworks to articulate definitions of identity that connect the individual and society and the social and psychological realm. The psychosocial framework, in which the notion of identity passing through successive stages becomes articulated, is an important foundation for the field of American psychology.

ERIK ERIKSON AND THE NARRATIVE OF IDENTITY CRISES

Erikson's concept of identity is based on eight psychosocial stages in which each individual, from birth to death, is confronted with specific developmental conflicts or psychosocial challenges that are brought about by the specific stages. As the individual passes through each successive stage in the eight-stage model, "the social context of development broadens somewhat, and the developing person moves forward to address issues whose resolutions depend in part on how the preceding issues and stages have been resolved" (McAdams, 2006, p. 51). Erikson (1968) defines identity as a process that is located in the "core" of the individual and "yet also in the core of his communal culture" (p. 22). Erikson has also defined identity as "ego synthesis" and as the interaction between an individual's body and thought and the sense of continuity and sameness that the "I" experiences across the life span. His book, *Identity: Youth and Crisis* (Erikson, 1968), explains the process of identity formation that becomes critical during the stage of adolescence and youth. He locates the period of Western youth's identity crisis in a particular historical moment that was brought about by the Industrial Revolution, urbanization, as well as the birth of worldwide connectedness and communication. Erikson provides a clear description of the process of identity formation:

> Identity formation, finally, begins where the usefulness of identification ends. It arises from the selective repudiation and mutual assimilation of childhood identifications and their absorption in a new configuration, which, in turn, is dependent on the process by which a society (often through subsocieties) identifies the young individual, recognizing him as somebody who had to become the way he is and who, being the way he is, is taken for granted. (p. 159)

His view implies that identity formation is a stage of development in which new patterns of thought and structures materialize, and through these configurations an adolescent is able to negotiate the previous and new identifications that arise.

The so-called adolescent stage, the adolescent mind, is essentially a "mind of a moratorium" (Erikson, 1968, p. 262) where individuals are exploring new identity commitments through their peers, religion, or cultural icons. These identity crises or disruptions, then, are critical turning points where the "ego of the individual" has to "integrate the time table of the organism with the structure of the institutions" (p. 246). Although Erikson argues that the ideology of social institutions and history shapes our identities, his stage-based model is primarily a universal model that aims to explain continuity and discontinuity in human development across all cultures.

Occasionally, when Erikson ventures into understanding the identity formation of "Black Identity," for example, he resorts to stereotypes and the racist language that was prevalent in 1950s America. When he describes the loss of identity in Black children, Erikson (1963) writes that

> Negro babies often receive sensual satisfaction which provides them with enough oral and sensory surplus for a lifetime, as clearly betrayed in the way they move, laugh, talk, sing. Their forced symbiosis with the feudal south capitalized on this oral sensory treasure and helped to build a slave's identity: mild, submissive, dependent, somewhat querulous, but always ready to serve, with occasional empathy and childlike wisdom. (p. 241)

Erickson further notes that the American "Negro" parents' corporeal and bodily socialization practices prime the child to develop a set of primitive sensory behaviors that are reflected in the child's language and interpersonal interactions. He argues that Black children's physicality or their sensuality makes them malleable to acquiring a slave identity. Thus, Black identity mainly develops out of their sensorimotor experiences within slave culture, and Black children are viewed as devoid of having advanced intellectual or cognitive capacities that White children may possess. Erikson argues that this underdeveloped Black identity is passive, dependent, submissive, and enabled African Americans to assimilate into the Southern plantation culture. The split in Black identity occurs when the "Negro" begins to identify with the master race of White people and the master race in turn protects and asserts its own dominant identity (Erikson, 1963).

The "Negroes" who leave the poor "havens" of their local, southern home to find work and employment opportunities in the North have developed only one "historically useful identity (that of the slave)" and thus they are unable to integrate any other form of identity (Erikson, 1963, p. 242). Thus, Black families who arrive in the North usually encounter violent disruptions to their previously developed identities. As a result, Erikson argues that Black children generally develop three types of identities: "(1) mammy's oral sensual 'honey child'—tender, expressive, rhythmical; (2) the vivid identity of the dirty, anal-sadistic, phallic-rapist "nigger"; and (3) the clean, anal-compulsive, restrained, friendly, but always sad "White man's Negro" (p. 242).

Erikson's observation about minorities and "colored" children is based on the racist foundations of knowledge and prejudices that were in circulation in American society in the 1950s. He was clear that there was an Anglo-American model of development that constituted an ideal form of identity development and that minorities in America would struggle to integrate this ideal. Erikson (1963) writes,

> I have mentioned the fact that mixed-blood Indians in areas where they hardly ever see Negroes refer to their full blood brothers as "niggers," thus indicating the power of dominant national imagery which serves to counterpoint the ideal and the evil images in the inventory of available prototypes. No individual can escape this opposition of images, which is all-pervasive in the men and in the women, in the majorities and in the minorities, and in all classes of a given national or cultural unit. (p. 243)

It is important to contextualize and situate Erikson's psychosocial stage model because it was primarily based on the experiences of the White male American adolescent, the assumed superiority of White Anglo-Saxon culture and practices, and the concept of frontier life and American individualism. His racialized model of identity formation and identity crisis provides the foundational language in American psychology and continues to influence present-day scholarship on adolescence, youth, and identity formation.

In response to self-contained and depoliticized conceptions of self, we have witnessed several movements in psychology, mostly emanating from the margins, that have sought to critique as well as reconstruct psychology's approach to understanding the role of culture and history in the construction of selves and identities (Bhatia & Stam, 2005). Contemporary psychologists who work on the mutual constitution of self and culture have emphasized the inseparability of the psychological and cultural realms and are described by Kirschner and Martin (2010) as being part of the "sociocultural turn" in psychology. Kirschner and Martin note that sociocultural perspectives have become increasingly visible and important in psychology. Such perspectives "envision psychological processes, such as the mind and the self, as phenomenon that are socioculturally constituted—that is, actually made up within, as opposed to merely facilitated by, culture and society" (p. 1). Similarly, Valsiner and Rosa (2007) note that the conceptual map of sociocultural psychology, while being theoretically heterogeneous, emerges out of "historical dialogues with psychology, sociology and anthropology" (p. 3). In Chapter 1, I provided a deeper analysis of how the concept and phenomena of "culture" and "identity" are being reframed within the context of globalization and migration and its implications for narrative psychology. Here, however, I describe some of the key moments of the "narrative turn" in psychology that in many ways were spurred by the sociocultural and interpretive turns in psychology. I begin by telling a story about my own encounter with narrative theory as a graduate student and the possible worlds it opened up, allowing me to pursue an alternative psychology.

CULTURE, NARRATIVE, AND MEANING-MAKING: A PERSONAL STORY

My entire graduate education in psychology in India was negotiated within the terrain of American psychology, where theories of self and identity were studied through the lenses of behaviorism and cognitive science. When I was doing my graduate work in psychology at the University of Pune in the 1980s, my professors repeatedly emphasized that "psychology is a science of human behavior" and what was of utmost importance to them was that we study behavior, in all its varied manifestations, that was "publicly observable." All our textbooks and the psychologists we studied were American or British. While the dominance of B. F. Skinner's behaviorism had been usurped by the cognitive science revolution in the United States, we were assiduously toiling away, studying and "memorizing" facts about learning theories formulated by the pantheon of well-known American psychologists: Skinner, Tolman,

Thurstone, and Hull. We were also repeatedly told that pursuing questions of identity through the frame of culture was a meaningless pursuit unless "culture" was reduced to a variable in an experiment (Bhatia, 2011).

In the outside, so-called real world, we believed that we were surrounded or bathed in cultural meanings. Culture was everywhere—on our streets, in our homes, and in all the rituals, rites, ceremonies, superstitions, and class-based hierarchies that were enacted around us. Our meaning-making activities about culture or identity happened outside the realm of psychology in spaces that were usually reserved for banter over chai and samosas, on cricket grounds, or while discussing the "dialogue delivery" of heroes in Hindi movies, sharing jokes, and telling stories to each other. We were a bunch of young graduate students, full of questions about the world around us, carrying copious loads of stories about our evolving identities, yet we could not bring any of our subjective alienation and angst to the psychology classroom.

Much of my psychology education in India occurred within a pedagogical context in which larger questions about the relationship between culture and self were not examined and we were largely dissuaded from pursuing questions about identity.[5] Our stories as young Indians were not part of the psychology textbooks we were reading. There was a complete erasure of our stories in the *theories of identities* that we were studying. Questions of "culture" and "subjectivity" were often dismissed as being too philosophical or anthropological, or they were deemed to be messy variables that contaminated the experimental process. Therefore, we could never bring our earnest critical interrogations of the discipline to the classroom, our exams, or our conversations with our professors because the mainstream (i.e., dominant form) of scientific British/American psychology disallowed it.

It was only when I came to study as a doctoral student in psychology at Clark University that I first discovered that stories of identity could be studied through narrative and the frame of culture. There, I discovered the power of "culture" and "narrative." After reading Jerome Bruner's (1990) *Acts of Meaning*, I recall being in a trance about realizing that my pursuit of the study of psychology was not a futile endeavor. In Bruner's work, I had found not only an entirely new way of doing psychology but also a blissful escape from the grip of the dominant psychological frameworks of that time: behavioral, cognitive, and biological psychology.

As someone who had lived in India, I had assumed that I was innately predisposed to know the *psychology of culture*. Growing up in India, my generation's history books, teachers, parents, and relatives had pounded into our minds the story that India may be poor, but Indians have the gift of "culture." We were constantly reminded that India hails from a 5,000-year-old ancient spiritual heritage. "Indianness" was juxtaposed against the other narrative that the West may have material possessions and economic prosperity, but it lacked the splendor of "culture" and the inner tranquility of a spiritual civilization. We were comforted by the knowledge that in the long life span of a civilization, America was a new kid on the block—a "cultural adolescent"—whereas we Indians were wise sages who had the perennial wisdom of a deeply spiritual culture.

I did not have to read Bruner to know that the story about the glorious "Indian culture" was a single story, told from a particular point of view. What Bruner's work had opened up for me was the simple but powerful idea that individuals and groups use narratives to make sense of their lives, and their sense-making activity is deeply shaped by their cultural settings (Bhatia, 2011).

WAYS OF KNOWING THE WORLD

More than two decades ago, Bruner (1990, p. 19) outlined a vision for cultural psychology in stating that psychology must move away from being preoccupied with "behavior" and shift its focus to how we make meaning of our "actions" as intentional agents located in cultural practices and socially situated settings. In short, Bruner was concerned with how people use canonical and ordinary understandings of events to interpret and give "narrative meaning" to breaches, deviations, and other extraordinary mitigating conditions in everyday, cultural life.

The use of narrative as a way of knowing the world, according to Bruner (1990), is "one of the crowning achievements of human development in the ontogenetic, cultural, phylogenetic sense of that expression" (p. 67). He was arguing against the cognitive revolution—specifically against the Piagetian rationalist framework, which had mainly conceived of the *telos* of child development in terms of producing "little scientists" and "little logicians." In elevating narrative knowledge as equal to paradigmatic knowledge, Bruner wrote that the "central concern is not how narrative as a text is constructed, but rather how it operates as an instrument of mind on the construction of reality" (Bruner, 1991, p. 6).

Bruner (1986) laid out his vision for a narrative psychology by boldly stating that there are two modes of "cognitive functioning, two modes of thought, each providing distinctive ways of ordering experience, of constructing reality. The two (though complementary) are irreducible to one another" (p. 11). The possibilities for knowing that are afforded by the narrative genre are different from those afforded by the paradigmatic framework. The paradigmatic imagination is concerned with hypothesis creation, issues of cause and effect, empirical verification, logical deduction, abstract variables, and statistical correlations. Imagination, in the paradigmatic domain, as Bruner (1986) argues,

> leads to good theory, tight analysis, logical proof, sound argument, and empirical discovery guided by reasoned hypothesis. . . . Paradigmatic "imagination" (or

intuition) is not the same as the imagination of the novelist or poet. Rather it is the ability to see possible formal connections before one is able to prove them in any formal way. (p. 13)

The narrative and the paradigmatic worlds afford different imaginative possibilities, and the language that is used to embody these possibilities is different as well.

Thus, it is the *meaning-making* capacity of narrative, with its ability to shed light on how people create meanings about their experiences through narrative, that became attractive to psychologists in the 1980s. Along with Bruner, there were other key scholars who played an important role in galvanizing the movement for creating a narrative psychology (McAdams, 1993; Freeman, 1993; Polkinghorne, 1988; Sarbin, 1986). Bruner and other psychologists were building on the overlapping postmodern, linguistic, and narrative turns that had already spread through the intellectual scene of the humanities in the early 1980s. The focus on narrative had spawned an immense interest in theorizing about narrative in disciplines such as history, literary criticism, psychoanalysis, law, philosophy, ethnography, and cinema studies. This "virtual explosion" of interest in narrative led Martin Kreiswirth (1992, p. 630), a literary historian, to ask a series of questions: "Why narrative? And why narrative now? Why have we decided to trust the tale? And what does this say about how we define, talk about, and organize knowledge?" I believe Kreiswirth's questions still hold considerable currency even in the present day as we ask larger questions about how we approach self and identity in psychology from a narrative perspective.

FOUR TURNS IN NARRATIVE PSYCHOLOGY

At the outset, I want to make clear that terms such as narrative, narrative theory, and identity have different meanings across different fields. My intention is not to provide a wide-ranging and inclusive account of narrative theory or its subject but, instead, to map some key historical moments in narrative theory in psychology. I thus highlight the relationship between narrative and identity in psychology so as to support the arguments that I make in this book about globalization and identity.

Theories of narrative have been proposed in diverse forms across the disciplines of history, psychology, literature, and psycholinguistics. The widespread use of narrative as a theory and concept across different disciplines has made it a "hot topic," but narrative "is an elusive concept, and narrative psychology is equally elusive" (Schiff, 2012, p. 33). In recent years, all of these fields combined have produced a plethora of literature on the structure, form, function, meaning, ideology, and discursive aspects of narrative.

One cannot point to a singular narrative turn that marks the rise of the narrative framework, but instead we can point to at least four narrative turns that came into being at distinct periods to answer different sets of questions about identity and self (Hyvärinen, 2012; Schiff, 2013). The first narrative turn in North America came about with the publication of *On Narrative* by W. J. T Mitchell in the early 1980s, when doing theory had high currency in literature, anthropology, and linguistics (Schiff, 2013). In France, however, the first narrative turn came about much earlier in the 1960s, when structuralist theories of narrative were on the ascent.

The second turn, very briefly, is located in historiography with the publication of Hayden White's (1978) *Metahistory*, in which he argues that interpretation is a key element in historical narrative and we make certain epistemic choices about what to include and what to leave out in historical narratives. Narrative as a mode of representation in history is essentially a political act. The hermeneutic orientation of narrative, as articulated by White, becomes adopted by social scientists, and the third narrative turn occurs when narrative theory travels to psychology, sociology, education, social work, medicine and anthropology, business and management, as well as applied, or therapeutic, contexts. Social scientists, especially psychologists, find narrative theory, with its emphasis on human meaning-making and collective and personal identity, a useful methodological and theoretical counterpoint to the dominant frameworks of positivism, scientific rhetoric, and experimental methodologies.

Several key works were published in the 1980s and 1990s that provided the theoretical and methodological foundations for building a narrative psychology (Bruner, 1986, 1990; Cohler, 1982; Freeman, 1993; Josselson & Leiblich, 1993; McAdams, 1997; Mishler, 1986; Polkinghorne, 1988; Sarbin, 1986). This third narrative turn was particularly influential in psychology because it opened up an alternative space for thinking about psychology. Sarbin (1986) introduced the term "narrative psychology" to the field of social psychology and argued for adopting the narrative framework as a *root metaphor* for understanding the development of self and identity. Gergen and Gergen (1984) suggested that a narrative account needs to establish a telos or an endpoint. Such a goal or endpoint can be established by the "value of a protagonist's well-being, the destruction of an evil condition, the victory of a favored group, the discovery of something precious, or the like" (p. 175). The description of the goal state allows the narrator to "*select and arrange preceding events in such a way that the goal state is rendered more or less probable*" (p. 175, emphasis in original). McAdams (2001) wrote that there was a time in psychology—across developmental, social, and personality psychology—in which the "psychological lexicon became filled with terms such as life scripts, self-narratives, story schemas, story grammars, personal myths, personal event memories, self defining memories, nuclear scenes, gendered narratives, narrative coherence, narrative complexity, and the like" (p. 101). By focusing on the "singularity" and "particularity" of stories, as opposed to searching for generalizability and predication, psychologists were able to make interpretive claims about identity by examining single or multiple narratives that were connected to larger cultural practices (Brockmeier, 2012). The third narrative turn in psychology has been enormously helped by the creation of the journals *Narrative Inquiry* and *Narrative Works* and the publication of 11 volumes on narrative that were edited by Ruthellen Josselson and Amie Lieblich and later joined by Dan McAdams. The publication of the *Handbook of Narrative Inquiry* (Clandinin, 2007), along with many other books on theory and methods (Bamberg, 2006; Daiute, 2014; Mishler, 1986; Riessman, 2008), has also contributed to the makings of a narrative psychology.

The fourth narrative turn arrives, according to Hyvärinen (2012), when narrative practices are used in media, advertisements, and health and illness discourses to reach audiences that are beyond the academic boundaries of the social science disciplines. For example, news becomes packaged as "breaking," "inspirational," or "top" stories and is presented differently for various demographic audiences. With the advent of 24/7 news, cable news channels such as FOX and MSNBC are compelled to turn out stories that become laced with ideological content and are put forward to mirror the belief systems of their audiences. The growing attention given to narrative studies does not stem entirely from narrative theory or any one turn; rather, all these turns combine together to contribute to the making of narrative psychology.

The four narrative turns in literary studies, history, social science, and culture, as both Hyvärinen (2012) and Schiff (2013) remind us, should not be framed as part of a sequential and continuous plotline. Rather, the different disciplines have reinterpreted the theory or concept of narrative according to their disciplinary and research interests. In any case, J. Hillis Miller (1990) recalls that in the last decades of the 20th century, the social sciences and humanities witnessed such a tremendous expansion in theories of narratives that it made his "mind ache to think of them all" (p. 64). He goes on recount all the theories that examine narrative and collectively contribute to the making of each narrative turn, such as the "Russian formalist theories of narrative, Bakhtinian, or dialogical theories; new critical theories; . . . hermeneutic and phenomenological theories; structuralist, semiotic, . . . Marxist and sociological theories; reader response theories; and poststructuralist and deconstructions theories" (p. 67). It would suffice to say that each of these theories provided the momentum and the material to make the various narrative turns. These theories also supplied the theoretical foundations for creating a mild paradigm shift in psychology and other social sciences and humanities. The reframing of psychology from a narrative perspective then must begin from how narrative provides us with an important tool for understanding self and identity.

A basic principle that is integral to the project of narrative psychology essentially begins with the idea that we must focus on the experiential and contextual dimensions of human experience because individuals live in contexts and not outside them (Freeman, 1997, 2010). By moving our focus outside the contrived conditions of the lab, our data may be disordered and messy, but it makes human psychology avowedly *cultural* (Freeman, 1997). A second important aspect of narrative psychology emphasizes that there are infinite narratives and stories circulating in the world through a variety of narrative genres that are constituted in and expressed through language. In a famous quotation, Barthes (1975) mentions that

> among the vehicles of narrative are articulated language, whether oral or written, pictures, whether still or moving, gestures and an ordered mixtures of all those substances; narrative is present in myth, legend, fables, tales, short stories, epics, history, tragedy, drama, [suspense drama], comedy, pantomime, . . . stained-glass windows, movies, local news, conversation. (p. 237)

Beyond the presence of narrative in various forms and genres in society, one of the functions of narrative is *communicative*—narrative facilitates and gives meaning to socially shared understanding about everyday activities in conversation and interpersonal talk and in cultural practices of marriage, romance, and organization of religious rituals. Narrative enables the reproduction and re-creation of reality via the means of language. The second function of narrative is *empathetic*: A benefit of using a narrative psychology approach is that we can create "empathetic" knowledge by focusing on the subjective stories and experiences of both the researcher and the participant (Brockmeier, 2012).

There are several approaches to studying narrative based on different and often incompatible theoretical and methodological assumptions. One common agreement among scholars whose work is influenced by the narrative turn is that "identities and selves are shaped by the larger sociocultural matrix of our being-in-the-world" (Smith & Sparkes, 2008, p. 6). Schiff (2013) provides a helpful taxonomy—one that has some overlap with Smith and Sparkes' analysis of narrative but is distinct because it provides a way of locating the varied perspectives in contemporary narrative psychology. The *cognitive approaches*, as envisioned by Bruner (1986), conceive of narrative as a cognitive instrument of the mind that can be used to interpret and structure the experiences of oneself and others. A cognitive approach would, for example, examine how an individual's storytelling structure reveals some fundamental aspects of his or her thought processes or cognition. Cognitive psychologists are interested in exploring reasoning processes: how children construct stories about their mental states and how the narrative form aids individuals in understanding their self and comprehending other people's minds (Fivush & Nelson, 2004).

The second way to study narrative is to use *personality approaches*, which are most widely associated with the work of McAdams (2006). In these approaches, the life story is a "unit of personality that sits above traits and cognitive strategies" (Schiff, 2013, p. 251). Based on Erikson's (1963) theory of psychosocial development and Henry Murray's thematic analysis, these approaches advance the view that one's life story is shaped by childhood experiences, and then the questions of identity are examined in late adolescence when individuals attempt to provide a unified and coherent account of self. Smith and Sparkes (2008) describe this perspective as a psychosocial approach in which identities are characterized as an

> internalized life story that develops over time through self reflection. Thus, an individual's ability to develop and maintain a coherent, unified, and positive life story is said to require the cognitive capacity and inclination to draw meaningful connections across one's past, present, and anticipated future. (p. 9)

Researchers have studied how personality traits are shaped by life stories and how the developmental trajectory of narrative sense-making is reflected in adolescence (McLean & Pasupathi, 2013).

The third way to study narrative is to use *cognitive and personality approaches* that draw on script theory, autobiographical memory research, psychosocial theory, personality theory, and life-story perspectives (Singer, 2004). These psychosocial elements of the narrative approach are integrated with the cognitive and personality approaches. The group of psychologists who employ this approach to narrative are interested in understanding the "processes or strategies that underlie stories" (Schiff, 2013, p. 252). Those who embrace a psychosocial perspective tend to conceive of having a "thick individual" focus with emphasis on the internalized processes and a "thin social" role in the formation of identity.

Schiff (2013) categorizes the fourth perspective as *"interpretive" approaches*. While acknowledging that this label is broad and imperfect, he states that researchers using an interpretive perspective view "narrative as process in which persons construct a version of themselves, the world and others. . . . The focus in on how persons interpret their life experience and make these interpretations explicit" (p. 252). The interpretive approach also focuses on uncovering the hidden meanings of the texts and is generally embraced as an approach to critique the mainstream psychology's overemphasis on experimentation, "science," and statistical methods. The emphasis in the interpretive approach is on providing performative, evocative, compelling, and rich analysis of narrative texts to show how people interpret the meaning of their life and why they tell stories and to whom

(Brockmeier, 2009, 2012; Bruner, 1990). These theorists emphasize the role of narrative and culture in co-constructing a relational understanding of self and identities. Interpretive researchers, according to Schiff (2013), focus on problems that give us insights into how significant others shape one's personal identity, how agency is enacted, how meaning is constructed through reflections on time (hindsight) and through relationships with others (Freeman, 2010, 2014), and how narratives play a role in moral development (Day & Tappan, 1996). In contrast to the personality approaches to narrative, researchers who use an interpretive perspective are not necessarily focused on understanding how individuals achieve narrative coherence or narrative unity in their stories. Furthermore, they also question whether life story is an internalized form that develops over time through engaging in self-reflection.

Schiff (2013) categorizes the fifth perspective as the *sociocultural approach* to narrative. There are significant commonalities between the interpretive and sociocultural perspectives. Sociocultural approaches are concerned with how narratives are shaped through cultural contexts—how modes of telling, sharing, and positioning shape the production of narratives. From this perspective, there are narrative theorists who, to varying degrees, acknowledge the interiority of self, locate the self in the ongoing intersubjective process of self and other, or advocate the self as constructed through a "thick relational perspective" (Smith & Sparkes, 2008, p. 24).

Researchers who employ a thick relational perspective approach do not focus not on cognitive scripts or understanding the inner realms of an individual (Gergen, 1999). Rather, they conceive of narratives (Sparkes & Smith, 2008) as a

> *vehicle* through which our world, lives, and selves are articulated and the way in which such narratives function within social relationships. . . . There is a shift in emphasis from an individuated, psychologized image of the person to a perspective that stresses narrative as form of social action and a relational, sociocultural phenomenon. (p. 299, emphasis in original)

The sociocultural approach focuses on uncovering patterns of meaning in single or multiple stories that are shaped by political, cultural, and social contexts. Scholars who adopt a sociocultural approach often anchor their research in the following questions: How are identities performed within social relationships and cultural practices (Gergen, 1999), and how are they fluidly positioned within language, conversations, and relational patterns (Bamberg, 2007; Georgakopoulou, 2007; Harré & Gillet, 1994)? How do larger cultural discourses about power and ideology shape the understanding of self and others (Benham, 2007; Bhatia, 2007, 2013; Clandinin & Rosiek, 2007; Hammack, 2011; Squire, Andrews, & Tamboukou, 2008)? Many of these theorists are interested in understanding what narrative accomplishes and how it is told and retold in differing cultural circumstances over time. Those who examine narrative through the "small story" approach are interested in exploring how stories emerge out of daily practices of conversation and what people "do" with narratives (Georgakopoulou, 2007).

Despite the varied and often conflicting approaches to narrative, many psychologists are drawn to narrative to explain the simple but powerful idea that individuals and groups use narrative to make sense of their subjective lives and their social worlds. The approach to narrative that I have adopted shares many concerns articulated in cognitive and personality approaches, but my definition of narrative is hybrid, much like the subjects of my study. As explained in Chapter 1, I adopt an interpretive and sociocultural approach to understanding narrative.

TOWARD A NARRATIVE PSYCHOLOGY: IDENTITY IN CULTURAL PRACTICES

When psychologists use the term *narration*, they refer to instances of oral or written storytelling. These stories may be a part of an everyday conversation about people, places, or events. Narration can also involve the act of reconstructing and sharing stories about one's self through autobiographies, life histories, memoirs, or personal accounts and everyday conversations. Psychologists often use the terms *narrative* and *story* synonymously and use narrative to refer to verbal utterance, texts, conversation, novels, or full-fledged autobiographical accounts. As mentioned in Chapter 2, the narratives that I analyze in the Indian urban context were elicited through formal and informal interviews. There are some interviews where the participants present a "big" story of their unfolding life in urban India, and the narrators take a distanced and highly reflective stand and provide a polished and planned account that has a neat beginning, middle, and end. In contrast, there are other interviews where participants share fragmented "small stories" about their life and the cultural practices in which they are immersed. These stories do not necessarily have neat beginnings or endings, and they often take the form of explanations, reflections, and commentary.

Narrative provides meaning a *telos* or the endpoint to the chronological dimension of life. Arguing against theorists who put too much emphasis on the chronological order of the narrative, Ricouer (1981) suggests,

Any narrative combines in varying proportions, two dimensions: a chronological dimension and a non-chronological dimension. . . . The activity of narrative does not consist simply in adding simply episodes to one another; it also constructs meaningful totalities out of scattered events. (pp. 278–279)

The chronological dimension refers to the sequential episodes, such as "the king died, and then the queen died" or "if x, then y." The second dimension of narrative is the configurational dimension that holds or grasps together the actions or the scattered events of a story into a meaningful set of relationships through the process of emplotment. Both the chronological and the configurational mode make the story "tellable" and "followable" and are an important part of the overall narrative function. Questions about narrative are concerned with not only the sequential timeline of life events and the logical connections between events but also how we give our experiences meaning, and it is this question that preoccupies poets and storytellers and those who are concerned with building a narrative psychology (Bruner, 1991).

Is there some kind of hermeneutic imperative that pushes us to continuously engage in making sense of our lives or impose order and coherence (Freeman, 2010)? Our propensity to actively construct a coherent meaning of our selves is a "need imposed on us whether we seek it or not" (Carr, 1986, p. 97). Coherence, however, is not a given, and our life's work is aimed at retelling and re-storying events to create an account that has intelligibility and integrity (Bochner, 1997). We may live our lives forward but understand them retrospectively, which is why the act of narration is not only intended to make meaning of our lives but also serves the purpose of making meaning *with others* and *for others* as we navigate our social worlds (Bochner, 2014). This is why Bochner (1997) argues that we are social beings and we live storied lives through the tales that are transmitted to us and the stories we claim as our own. Storytelling thus has two functions: It is way of a knowing and a vehicle for narrating about our lives.

At the simplest level, there are three fundamental presuppositions that make up narrative psychology and are integral to fashioning a broader psychology that is based on narrative or interpretive understanding of the human condition. First, there is the story that is made up of a point of view or a meaning that the narrator constructs. Second, there is the positioning of the story—with its potential for fluidity and amorphousness—that is used for a particular audience in a given social interaction. Third, there is a cultural and social world with all its contradictions and contestations in which the narrator, the audience, and the narration are interactively located (Brockmeier, 2012).

Whether the narrative world-making occurs by drawing on stories of personal experience or the common stock of stories that are drawn from our old and new mythologies, the most compelling dimension of narrative resides in its potential to claim *human agency*. Narrative has an empowering function for individuals because it gives them the opportunity to shape the texture of their identity by strategically selecting what story is told, how it is told, and to whom it is told in interactions and through self-reflection and hindsight (Freeman, 2010).

It is this agentive dimension of narrative that I previously discussed in Chapter 1 that makes it particularly important for understanding how the "individual as a subject" is able to reassert him- or herself in his or her cultural context. The identity of the "subject" or "person" is not autonomous and prior to society, but it emerges through its placement in the sociocultural surroundings.

Individuals do not necessarily just passively absorb their ascribed identities through a totalizing discourse but, rather, use narrative (among others forms) to revise and resist these external discourses or assignations as they occupy their multiple cultural sites or locations. Individual can use narrative and stories as language-based equipment to express their subject positions and give meaning to the uniqueness and singularity of their experiences. Being interpellated by power structures or created through systems of cultural power does not mean there is no room for individual story-making or agency. The urban Indian youth make and remake their identities as they narrate stories of their life through the lens of their social class location; their rootedness in history of colonization and postcolonial culture; their exposure to discourses of globalization; and their particular embeddedness in social practices of education, employment, and traditions. These urban Indian youth use narratives to voice their agency, but they are not "free to thwart or fabricate narratives at will" (Sparkes & Smith, 2008, p. 301). When people narrate stories, they draw on a range of narrative resources that are not equally distributed in our society. People live in conditions of structural constraints and oppression, and they cannot make up any story line that suits them. Thus, the stories that people tell are inevitably shaped by what anthropologist Michael Jackson (2002) calls "the politics of storytelling."

IDENTITY CONFLICTS AND WEBS OF MEANING: THE NARRATIVE OF VALENTINE'S DAY IN INDIA

In the past few years, Valentine's Day in India has been used to provoke debates about the purity of Indian culture and the so-called contaminating influences of Western cultures. The believers of the Hinduvata movement, who espouse a right-wing, violent, and exclusionary form of Hinduism, have regularly mounted attacks on urban youth as they celebrate Valentine's Day.[6]

In 2009, Matt Wade, a reporter for the *Sydney Morning Herald*, reported that six men belonging to the right-wing Hindu organization Shiv Sena were arrested in Agra, where the Taj Mahal is located. The Hindu nationalist men were arrested because they forcibly cut the hair of couples who were displaying public affection in a park. Similarly, in Pune, Shiv Sena members stopped two couples and forced them to enter a marriage at the scene, then and there, by garlanding each other. In Ujjain, Hindu fundamentalists physically assaulted a brother and a sister whom they assumed to be a couple demonstrating public affection. In the smaller Indian cities of Aurangabad and Bijnaur, several Hindu fanatics blackened the faces of couples who were perceived as not behaving in accordance with Hindu traditions (Wade, 2009).

Wade (2009) also reported that Molla Ram, a policeman from the northern state of Haryana, attacked a female college student by grabbing her hair and spinning her around several times. Hindu nationalists from the newly developed city of Gurgaon, outside Delhi, took their protest to malls, where they urged young Indians to boycott Valentine's Day. Satish Mann, who represented the Hindu nationalist agenda and was the main organizer of these protests, said, "We have been and will keep protesting against these Western concepts. Our culture is the greatest and we can't allow youngsters to ape the West and indulge in indecent acts, like dating" (Wade, 2009).

In February 2014, the newspaper *Indian Express* reported that more than 100 couples had gathered at the Sabarmati River in Ahmedabad to celebrate Valentine's Day. Hindu mobs belonging to nationalist parties Bajrang Dal and Vishwa Hindu Parishad threw rotten tomatoes at the couples because they were seen as indulging in immoral and indecent celebrations. Bajrang Dal president Jwalit Mehta justified their actions by stating that Valentine's Day is a Western tradition and an "obscene celebration" that must be discouraged in Indian youth.

The Valentine's Day protest in 2009 came on the heels of another much publicized event when an angry mob of protesters attacked a young Indian woman who was drinking alcohol in a pub in Mangalore. As a response to these attacks, Renuka Chowdhary, then the Minister for Women and Children, accused the Mangalore attackers of wanting the "Talibanization" of India. In response to these escalating attacks on urban women, a young woman named Nisha Susan started a Facebook group called the Consortium of Pub-going, Loose and Forward Women. This group, which has men and women supporters, urged women to visit their local pubs to buy a drink as a mark of resistance. In protesting against these attacks that were justified in the name of the "culture wars," this group also urged its supporters throughout the country to send pink *chaddis* (local vernacular for underpants) to various collection points across the country and to the main headquarters of the Sri Ram Sena. The actions of the Consortium garnered 32,000 supporters on the web, and several newspapers around the world picked up its story.

If we view narrative practices as embedded in cultural practices, then the telling and retelling of individual stories happens through the medium of language and the social discourses of families, communities, and the culture that surrounds us. The Valentine's Day story in India points to the crucial role of culture and how one "global event" produces two contested and divergent cultural narratives about what constitutes Indian identity. The struggle concerning Valentine's Day also points to the deep connection between culture and narrative. Thus, in studying individual narratives, we are essentially studying cultures. This point is made succinctly by Freeman (1997):

> Insofar as lives are lived in culture—in language, in social relations, in communities, in the web of quite specific rules, conventions, beliefs, discourses, and so on—then in studying lives, we are, as a matter of course and necessity studying culture as well. (p. 172)

The study of "life-in-culture" points to a paradox at work because at the very moment we focus on individual narratives and take the individual life as the primary unit of our analysis, we are required to transcend the individual and move into the cultural realm in which individual life takes meaning. Thus, the narrative study of lives is essentially a hermeneutic enterprise because it places narrative understanding squarely in the domain of meaning. What makes the study of narrative a hermeneutic enterprise? What hermeneutic meanings do the cultural clashes about Valentine's Day in Indian reveal?

An interpretive study of human beings and their cultural realities is based on local knowledge or emic concepts. Emic concepts are also called experience-near concepts and describe why individuals find their experiences meaningful. In contrast, etic concepts or experience-far concepts are used by scholars to make generalizations about how their participants understand their own cultural worlds (Brockmeier, 2012). Emic concepts are seen as providing an insider view and the etic perspective is considered as delivering an external or an outsider's perspective on the life of others.

When individuals are engaged in telling their stories, they are not necessarily thinking about their stories through the lens of etic analytical frames, discourse analysis, plot structures, "story lines," or semantic and discursive registers. By paying attention to the experience-near, emic concepts, we become aware that "people engage in very different stories about themselves (which is to say that there is no single "narrative identity')—irrespective of the fact that these narratives can be subject to the same categorical distinctions of "story," "discourse," "plot," and so forth" (Brockmeier, 2012, p. 440).

This does not mean that these theoretical frames or the categorical plots and discourses do not give us knowledge about the situation; rather, they give us only one side of the story—a story that is mediated by our vocabulary and deflects attention from the language used by insiders to convey their reasons for telling and sharing their story. Emic concepts or views of the world are based on how individuals see their world from within. These subjects tell stories about their lives that they consider meaningful, and there are no a priori, predetermined universal characteristics of storytelling. What is considered a story and the various sets of events and episodes that make up the story are co-constructed by the narrator and the audience.

A "culturally thick" notion of narrative supports Bruner's (1990) claim that a culturally sensitive psychology must pay attention to not only what people do but also what their story is about, why they did what they did, and how others perceive their doing and acting (Brockmeier, 2012). With the emphasis on saying, doing, and telling, we are in the world of narrating—our narratives emerge from everyday interaction with practices and significant others. Narrative psychology becomes emic when "it is based on experience-near stories of what people, at a certain point in time, consider to be meaningful in their lives" (Brockmeier, 2012, p. 446).

From an emic point of view, we are not always concerned with meaning-making that happens in a tightly organized, neat plot-oriented narrative that has thematic continuity and a coherent development of events, actions, and dramatic resolutions. Rather, we pay attention to personal narratives and stories that people share in everyday conversations that have interruptions and seem incomplete and where meaning is co-constructed with input from conversational partners and audiences.

What we see in the story on Valentine's Day are two or three emic narratives being told. First, the Hindu nationalists are anxious about the loss of tradition and how Valentine's Day has come to represent immoral Western values. Second, the young Indian women who started the Pink Chaddi campaign are creating a story about gender rights, oppressive religious discourses, and moral policing, and they are redefining what love and romance mean within Indian culture. In addition, by starting the Consortium of Pub-going, Loose and Forward Women, they are challenging deeply entrenched patriarchal discourses of the Hindu nationalist and conservative notions of "Indianness" that are being unfairly projected onto young urban women.

The celebration of Valentine's Day is not just a story that is circulating in urban India. Through corporate backing and advertising, it has created a set of cultural practices that includes couples giving roses to each other, sharing cards, and perhaps going out for special dinner dates. Every year, people who support the conservative, right-wing narrative violently resist Valentine's Day celebrations by upholding some essentialist ideas of "Indian culture" so they can drum up votes and publicity for their political party. Their narrative describes Valentine's Day as immoral and selectively overlooks how their own conservative and deeply patriarchal narratives of Indian cultural *values* promote the structural and institutional oppression of women.

The young Indian women who have been targets of these attacks have mounted a hybrid counternarrative against the Hindu nationalists by yoking together the theme of gender rights, the Gandhian philosophy of peaceful protest, and the affirmation of their right to celebrate Valentine's Day with their significant others. The young women who decided to send pink chaddis to the army of Hindu nationalists strategically described their movement as nonviolent and Gandhian. The Consortium of Pub-Going, Loose and

Forward Women thus represents the cultural struggles over tradition and modernity while it also reveals how being "global" or "Western" and being "Indian" are imagined differently by different groups of people within the same culture. The young women who are resisting the Hindu nationalists are also showing that their identity is derived from many horizons of meaning or spheres of otherness: postcolonial, Gandhian, global, traditional, urban, and religious. The women are engaged in creating hybrid cultural narratives of their identities that simultaneously connect them to an imagined transnational community that celebrates some version of Valentine's Day while allowing them to thwart and resist the cultural policing mounted by the Hindu fundamentalists.

By sending pink chaddis to the Hindu nationalists, the women were sending a strong cultural message about autonomy and women's rights, and they had simultaneously creatively adapted to cultures that had traveled from elsewhere and had taken root in their social spaces. The idea of creative adaptation is a hallmark of alternative modernities, as Gaonkar (2001) asserts, but it does not mean that one can freely choose and reinvent one's identity from the cultural offerings of globalization and modernity. Rather, it refers to the "manifold ways in which people question the present. It is a site where people 'make' themselves modern, as opposed to being 'made' modern by alien and impersonal forces, and where they give themselves an identity and destiny" (p. 18).

The young women's hybrid narratives suggested acts of "making," expressing their subject position, acting, responding, and reacting, rather than being "made." They further indicate that the youth were not simply resigning themselves to passively embracing Western ideas of romance but, rather, were renegotiating these global–local cultural tensions and contradictions. Globalization and conditions of modernity in various forms act as both lure and threat, so the elite and everyman rise up to these forces to fashion a new amalgam of narratives in their own imagination.

Even prior to the onset of contemporary neoliberal forms of globalization, people living in non-Western societies had to negotiate with various expressions of colonial and postcolonial modernity. If you revisit the culture of Calcutta in the 1940s, the preoccupation with modernity was everywhere. Drawing on Chakrabarty's (2000) work, Gaonkar (2001) explains:

> Everything in sight is named modern: "modern coffee house," "modern talkies," "modern bi-cycle shop," "modern tailor," "modern beauty salon," "modern bakery," a newspaper called *Modern Age*, a magazine for the "modern woman," a call for "modern education," an agitation for "modern hygiene," and so on. Those who submit to the rage of modernity are not naïve; they are not unaware of its Western origins, its colonial designs, its capitalist logic, and its global reach. (p. 21)

By naming objects and businesses as "modern," the urban dwellers of non-Western societies were experimenting with hybrid identities and meanings. Today, the vocabulary of "modern" is still in circulation, but to some extent it has become attached to the vocabulary of "global" images, events, media, festivals, and celebrations that are shared by youth from across many cultures. The discourse of globalization and the accompanying language of modernity are no longer Western-centric, and they are being used to question the present, interrogate traditions, reinvent heritage, and reshape youth culture and identity. The dominant story of Western modernity is anchored in the ideas that it flows outside the confines of the West and it is seen as naturally linked to progress and development. Contemporary postcolonial scholars of globalization have also reminded us of another perspective of modernity (Shome, 2012). They are interested in denaturalizing the association between Eurocentric modernity and progress. In the contemporary era of globalization, intersecting scapes of finances, media, commodities, and capital shape these alternative modernities or cultural-specific subjectivities (Appadurai, 1996). The Valentine's Day example gives us multiple insider perspectives within a given culture, and it also makes us aware of the cultural stories about gender, modernity, and traditions that urban Indians tell themselves. This is essentially a culturally contested story about globalization that insiders use to construct identities for themselves—it is a story that varied groups of urban Indians tell themselves every year to reaffirm their perspective on what constitutes Indianness.

Geertz (1973) has noted in his classic study of Balinese cockfights that those scholars who treat the cockfight only as a text or a rite or a pastime or as reinforcing status distinctions in Indonesian society are overlooking the Balinese interpretation of this ritual. The function of the Balinese cockfight is essentially interpretive:

> It is a Balinese reading of Balinese experience, a story they tell themselves about themselves. . . . Drawing on almost every level of Balinese experience, it brings together themes—animal savagery, male narcissism, opponent gambling, status rivalry, mass excitement, blood sacrifice—whose main connection is their involvement with rage and fear of rage, and, binding them into a set of rules which at once contains them and allows them play, builds a symbolic structure in which, over and over again, the reality of their inner affiliation can be intelligibly felt. (pp. 448–450)

Participating in cockfights in some ways is no different from participating in other sports such as soccer and cricket because it a form of a ritual in which the individual's subjectivity or psychological world opens up along with and to those of others. Such public rituals are collective, yet inherently personal—where one roots for a side and feels, thinks, erupts with joy, and is largely consumed by the unfolding excitement of play.

Thus, from an interpretive point of view, "culture" does not stand *outside* the event or the phenomenon or the story as an isolated, powerful independent variable. In order to understand the meaning of a Balinese cockfight or the struggles about celebrating Valentine's Day in India, we have to understand how the culture provides the webs of significance to individual sensemaking. What the rituals of Valentine's Day and Balinese cockfights suggest is that the individual actors are placed in and shaped by the "cultural webs of significance" that they have spun through language and particularly through the *mediation of narrative*. Therefore, in order to spin tales and weave webs of signification—whether etic or emic—for others and ourselves, we need the equipment of narrative. Without narrative and language, the cultural meanings we have spun remain closed, which is why culture and narrative shape each other and are bound in and by a hermeneutic circle—a point that is cogently explained by Brockmeier (2012):

> On the one hand, I argue that without narrative, these cultural webs of meaning cannot be spun, which is to say without the use of narrative, human beings cannot communicate, interpret their experience, and guide their actions, except in a restricted way. At the same time, I propose that without narrative, we cannot investigate these webs and the way they are spun—that is, without the use and analysis of narrative we cannot scientifically and scholarly interpret people's cultural self- and world-interpretations. This hermeneutic circle inherent to this approach has often been explicated as an unavoidable part and parcel of every effort to understand human action and mind. (p. 442)

Scholars working within the narrative tradition have made the case that if psychology has to capture the meaning-making aspect of human activity, then it must recognize that notions about the self and world cannot be conceptualized as brute data that are "out there" in the world. Rather, human beings as actors in the world postulate the meanings of culture, and these meanings in turn act as frames that make our experiences meaningful, valid, and comprehensible (Bruner, 1990; Denzin, 1997). It is in the realm of meaning that competing narratives about Valentine's Day in India assume their significance—they provide the link to culture and also show us that narratives are multivoiced, as well as dialogically and relationally constituted (Hermans & Hermans-Konopka, 2010).

NOTES

1. Although *Step Out* and *TwoMangoes* are considered popular sites for dating and finding partners in urban India, the most successful website for matrimonial and arranged marriages is Shaadi.com. This web-based portal is advertised as the

world's largest matrimonial service, and it states that it has redefined how "Indian brides and grooms meet for marriage," claiming its services have "touched" more than 35 million people (http://www.shaadi.com).

2. The website states that Mocha Lounge is inspired by the *Quahveh Khannehs* of Morocco and Turkey. These "warm and homely coffee shops are the perfect place for people to come over, order a coffee and talk about their day. About politics, family or just the weather if they so please. It's a place to meet and suspend reality for a few moments. That's what Mocha was designed to be" (http://www.mocha.co.in/concept.html)

3. The website states that the "Sawai Gandharva Bhimsen Mahotsav, the biggest festival of classical music in India, organized every year by the Arya Sangeet Prasarak Mandal which was founded by Bharat Ratna Pt. Bhimsen Joshi, shall take place between December 11th and 16th this year. Like the previous years this festival of music shall be organized at the New English School Raman Baug grounds" (http://sawaigandharvabhimsenmahotsav.com/about-festival).

4. Burke's (1969) notion of "God terms" is also derived from the concept of terministic screens, which he defines as follows: "Even if any given terminology is a reflection of reality, by its very nature as a terminology it must be a selection of reality; and to this extent is must also function as a deflection of reality" (p. 45).

5. At that time, there were no indigenous psychology frameworks on identity and culture that were in the psychology curriculum, and unless questions of identity could be converted to a testable "hypothesis," students were usually discouraged from asking larger questions related to society or culture.

6. In 2015, there were several protests against Valentine's Day celebration and *India Today*—a leading English magazine—reported that there were several cities in which right-wing Hindu fundamentalists carried out their attacks on youth (http://indiatoday.intoday.in/story/valentines-day-bajrang-dal-protest-vhp-hindutva-hyderabad-police-shiva-ramulu-hyderabad-cyberabad/1/418954.html).

CHAPTER 5

Traveling Transnational Identities

Imagining Stories of "Ultimate" Indianness

The June 2008 cover of the monthly city magazine *Simply Mumbai*, sold along with the nationally known magazine *India Today*, shows two tall, thin, young women with charcoal-colored shoulder-length hair. They are standing on a golf course with golf clubs in their hands. One of them is pictured in a full frontal shot wearing emerald green shorts, a floral top, and dull gold sandals. The other is captured in a full-body side shot and is wearing a purple top, beige shorts, brown gladiator sandals, and a yellow crochet necklace as a bracelet. The headline on the cover, printed in white and pink colors, reads "GET SHORTY: Stay Stylish and Cool in Your Choice of Shorts from Mumbai's Stores" (Mothiar, 2008). The two Indian women are portrayed as urban, wearing short shorts and playing golf—a sport that only the very affluent in India can afford. These women supposedly are shown as having arrived on the global stage—without the traditional trappings of a *saree* or a *salwar khameez*. These young urban, upper-class women are presented as having two identities: They are *Indian* and *global*. The models were posing as confident, urban, fashionable Indian women who have a transcendent, metropolitan location—the picture could have been taken in a New York suburb or in the Parisian countryside. In short, the image conveyed to the reader is that one could be a young *global Indian* in Mumbai by playing golf and wearing colorful and revealing shorts, shirts, and sandals.

The symbolism is quite powerful because it affirms the point that it is no longer a social taboo for women to wear shorts. In the Western world, women wearing shorts, even rather abbreviated versions, in summer while playing sports is unremarkable.[1] In India, shorts-wearing women were more the exception than the rule. Hence, the idea that shorts are the preferred *mode couture* for a Mumbai summer is quite remarkable. The phrase "new gusto" provides the verbal frame in which new visions about India were being articulated. This new India is shown as young, confident, vibrant, cosmopolitan, and shedding its older, staid, stoic, and traditional shell.

I had picked up the *Simply Mumbai* magazine in a Mumbai hotel in August 2008 as I was getting ready for my return to the United States, having just collected interview data with upper- and middle-class urban youth and families in Pune. My conversations with urban upper-class and affluent youth about India were mostly peppered with phrases such as "India is happening" and "India is on the rise." Television and media had also played an important role in presenting India's rise as a global power. Over hot chai lattes at new coffee houses, such as Café Coffee Day and Barista, these urban Indians provided sophisticated critiques of the rise of globalization. Many participants pointed to an interesting paradox: They were against American-style globalization but were quick to suggest that globalization in India has given them a new interior self—a self that is cosmopolitan, confident, and equal to the American/ Western self. In other words, their narratives reveal "an explicit object of contestation and negotiation" with their engagements and interactions with practices of globalization (Lukose, 2009, p. 205).

In this chapter, I show how the elite, transnational "children of liberalization" construct their identities as they engage with global cultural images of media, fashion, and romance. The transnational youth I describe in this chapter are indeed "children of liberalization" because they have spent their entire childhood and youth in a post-liberalized India of new wealth, exposure to media, and access to branded material goods, and they have participated in acquiring new forms of social and transnational mobility. These upper-class, elite participants have an optimistic and liberatory view of globalization; they generally believe that India's moment has arrived on the world stage. The question that is central to this chapter is the following: How do the urban upper-class and elite youth in Pune think *about* and *with* terms such as global, globalization, and Indianness? How do they participate in the discourses of globalization?

CONTEXTUALIZING ELITE INDIAN YOUTH: THE GLOBAL MOMENT OF LIBERAL ARTS EDUCATION

I conducted interviews with 20 students from Meridian College[2] individually and in two focus groups. I also conducted additional interviews with two faculty members and one staff member of Meridian college. In addition, I briefly spoke to the president and several senior leaders in upper-level management at Meridian College so I could get their perspective on urban youth culture in India and their philosophy of liberal arts education. The private, undergraduate Meridian College (henceforth, Meridian) was established in 2004 and was one of the first colleges in India that combined an American liberal arts education with an indigenous educational perspective. I place Meridian in its current cultural context so readers can grasp what is new and different about the curricular philosophy of this college and how it might also indicate how these youth are being shaped by their upbringing in a liberalized India.[3] The college catalog describes Meridian as "the first institution in India with liberal education" that aims to "blend traditional values with liberal education and revive the *Guru–Shishya* ethos" (teacher–disciple) by having an active mentorship program.

When I was growing up in India in the 1980s, most young middle-class Indians who attended college had only three degrees that they could pursue: arts, science, or commerce. Besides engineering and medicine, which were reserved for a select few, these were the only three educational options or tracks that shaped the career and life of college-aged Indian youth. Thus, if a student was enrolled in an arts degree program, he or she could not take courses from the science or commerce/business programs and vice versa. Meridian, where my fieldwork was located, did not adopt the fossilized arts curriculum of my time but instead had taken the curriculum that one finds in American liberal arts colleges and mixed it with indigenous philosophical concepts of nonviolence and humility. The mission of Meridian was to foster its students' imagination so they could be transformed into critical thinkers and moral citizens.

A Meridian catalog stated that the college goes beyond the traditional education of arts, science, and commerce and allows students to take courses across disciplines of physical and natural science, humanities, social sciences, and fine and performing arts. Meridian advertised that it "empowers students to think for themselves and become responsible, active, global citizens." The message throughout the catalog was about learning and self-discovery: Meridian College was going to provide a college education that mimicked a *yatra* (journey), and the importance was not on report cards and grades but, rather, on the journey of discovery and growth. The marketing materials were slick, with picturesque aerial photographs of the college highlighting its surrounding hills, green farmland, and beautiful architecture.

Discovery of Self: The Liberal Arts in Indian Context

Meridian provided a liberal arts education that encouraged independent inquiry and taught students to break free from conventional thinking. Students could take courses in global studies, logic, rhetoric, writing, and public speaking, and they were required to engage in a "Discover India" project and internship program. Connecticut College, where I teach, states that its liberal arts mission is to educate "students to put the liberal arts into action as citizens in a global society." The mission and vision statement in the Meridian catalog was filled with statements on learning that fostered creative and analytical thinking and skills of interpretation and communication. This was an important moment in the history of the Indian education system as American-style education with a focus on liberal arts was being blended with business management training, communications, sciences, and Gandhian principles of moral living, humility, and respect for human dignity. When I first visited the campus in 2008, the long, winding road through the hills was not yet paved. The monsoon rains had made the approach road quite slushy, and I had to use the college's van to get to the campus because no auto-rickshaws could make the trek. I wondered how a 75-acre campus, about 7 miles from the University of Pune, was carved out from what was once a remote village. The infrastructure on the campus was still being developed, and new residential houses and large classrooms were being built. I first spotted the campus when the van in which I was riding navigated through a set of small hills and then suddenly the road opened out onto a valley. As the van made its downward descent, I saw a lush green golf course, tiny dots of concrete structures in the distance, and the Shayadri mountain range in the background.

From a distance, I could see a small temple, a river brook, and tropical trees swaying in the foothills. Once I reached campus, I was given a tour by a faculty member, and the architecture and the natural beauty of the campus impressed me. The high-tech classrooms were spacious, arranged executive style, with high ceilings, flexible seating, and beautiful wooden benches and desks. When I revisited Meridian in 2013, the campus buildings looked fully developed, with additions of new structures such as a picturesque plaza, a reflecting pool, and a garden pool that sprayed mist around the lawns. The architects of the campus state that the campus was designed as a "bazaar of education" to reflect the theme of an Indian bazaar that is marked by constant change and chaotic social interactions. Buildings were named after Indian poets and philosophers, such as the Kalidasa Performing Arts Center, the Tagore Lecture Theatre, and the Vivekananda Library. The concrete buildings were connected by a public walkway and opened out onto a common plaza, just like many open-design schools in California.

Founded on private land by wealthy businessmen, with millions of dollars in investment, the liberal arts Meridian College was becoming a valued commodity in the Indian education system. In 2008, I was invited by one of the professors at Meridian, who taught social psychology, to give a few lectures on "cultural psychology" and to give a public lecture on my book, *American Karma* (Bhatia, 2007). I spent several weeks with students, talking to them about their education; how they viewed the sociocultural changes in urban India; their understanding of globalization; and how they were reimagining Indianness in the context of new media, brands, increasing materialism, and greater exposure to Western cultures. A large number of students who studied at Meridian were youth from upper-class and wealthy families, who had lived in cities such as Mumbai, Ahmedabad, Bangalore, Pune, and Delhi. A few had come from the United States. Meridian was gradually being recognized as a college that provided expensive American-style business management education to wealthy students, and it was also acquiring a reputation for being a a place where the privileged youth came to discover their selves and identities.

"EXPOSED" INDIANS: IMAGINING POSSIBLE SELVES AND IDENTITIES

The youth at Meridian equated globalization with openness and having a chance to connect with other youth through social networking sites. Globalization was also associated with new high-paying jobs in information technology (IT) and call centers, freedom, independence from parents, the loosening of sexual attitudes, and the lifting of traditional constraints on young women. Akshay, a 19-year-old student, noted that the "mindset" of the youth in India is different from that of the previous generation, and they are now connected to multiple cultures and worlds beyond their towns and cities. Unlike the previous generation, the contemporary urban youth believed that they were more aware of, exposed to, and knowledgeable about the world. Akshay said that globalization has meant "entry of new brands" to India and "exposure to new ideas." Shalini, a 20-year-old student, summarized what several young participants had expressed to me in their interviews; she said that globalization has allowed her to "imagine, that yes, a lot of things are possible. A lot of things are possible. . . . A lot of things that you might have otherwise just thought or dreamed about, are easily accessible because of globalization." Another student, Reena, noted that globalization meant that the entrenched culture of patriarchy is weakening and women can take on new roles: "Everyone wants to have an identity for themselves. . . . Globalization has given me freedom in terms of a person. In terms of being a girl." She further observed that freedom also meant that the Indian youth's values were being Americanized or Westernized, and many more young women were smoking, drinking, and having sex before marriage.

Reena further noted that adopting Western ways was "ruining the culture . . . and [the pull to] dance, drink, [and] smoke" were becoming an integral part of the youth culture. The discourse about acquiring cultural capital through a globalized form of Americanized identity, therefore, was also laced with a cautionary note. Reena stated that although they have freedom today, the youth are becoming corrupt and Indians are blindly adopting the values of the West. The "rising India" discourse was also marked by expressions of anxiety about the loss of traditional Indian values and the creation of a Western culture that leads youth to pursue money and materialism while disregarding parental authority.

Shilpa, a 19-year-old student at Meridian, told me that Indian culture was always very stable and conservative. She argued that the roles and jobs associated with women and men were clearly demarcated. In present times, however, she remarked,

> Because of globalization and Westernization, it is no more the same. Like, earlier we had joint families, staying together, people looking after each other. But now you have nuclear families. They have broken up. And people are just concerned about just their lives. Not the family.

Globalization was not an abstract concept for the youth—their social practices and everyday life spaces were being deeply impacted by transformations occurring in urban India.

During one of my interviews, I asked Nina Jain, a 19-year-old undergraduate student at Meridian, to define how globalization was impacting Indian culture. She answered,

> Honestly speaking, I don't think I am the right person to define Indian culture, because the culture which I have grown up in is not an Indian culture, it's a metropolitan culture. I could be in Bombay [Mumbai] or I could be in New York, it would be the same. It is . . . about the things I do.

Nina's comments on the similarities between New York and Mumbai may be far-reaching, but her comments reveal a widespread belief among the transnational urban Indian youth that metropolitan Indian cities such as Bangalore and Mumbai are the new centers of global Indian cosmopolitan culture.

The cultural spaces in these cities create cross-cultural bridges between youth who live in New York, London, and Mumbai. Undoubtedly, Nina's experience with globalization is unique and particularly marked with her ability to access cultural scapes that connect London to Mumbai through her privileged social class status. This attempt to view global youth culture as shared across cultural spaces in Paris, London, and Mumbai reflected the yearnings of the global elite. These "children of globalization" were not just appropriating Western culture but also making it their own by blending "global cosmopolitanism" with "regional identity and local cultures" (Lukose, 2009, p. 25).

Many of the participants, whom I describe as belonging to the transnational class, repeatedly used the word "exposure" in their conversations with me. These youth considered themselves as "exposed Indians"—who from an early age were exposed to American/Western education, knowledge, and culture. The concept of the "West" is described as a generic, all-encompassing category that is used by the participants to refer to mainly America and the United Kingdom and some other Western European cultures and countries.[4]

The experience of global modernity through forms of neoliberalization had moved from being a foreign allure to an object that was being negotiated and contested in their everyday relationships with their friends, family, and the nation state. These transnational Indian youth did not have to go to America to bring back their credentials of modernity and be recognized as "global youth." Instead, their exposure to the world outside their locality and the opening up of the culture were allowing them to reimagine new narratives of global Indianness. The stories of globalization articulated by the Meridian youth were not about Western or American imperialism; instead, they were framing the external cultural flows as giving them opportunities to re-create meaning about Indianness at home and abroad.

AMERICA'S GLOBAL "MANIFEST DESTINY" IN INDIA: INDEPENDENCE, LIFESTYLES, AND EXPLORATIONS OF SELF

Throughout my research, Indian urban youth described globalization as a social phenomenon that was "changing" Indian society such that Indian culture was "coming out of the old." A phrase I heard often from them in Hindi was *"badal raha hai yaar"* ("things are changing here"). When I asked the participants in a focus group at Meridian to define what this sociocultural change meant to them, they unanimously responded by using phrases such as "breaking way from the family" and "becoming independent" in their thinking. I pushed the participants from the focus group to tell me how their exposure to globalization has brought about more independence in their thinking. Nalini explained:

> Till 60 years ago, girls were staying with their parents till they got married off and sent off. Not all our grandparents are educated for that reason at the moment. But now it's not that lifestyle anymore. Now we have broken away from that sort of society. Now we're expected by our parents who are more global, to be out in the open, to go explore on our own. In America, kids leave the house when they're 18 and go live on their own.

The theme of "breaking away," "becoming independent," "exploring," and "living on one one's own" appeared consistently throughout the youth narratives at Meridian. This theme of "independence" was rooted in their real and imagined ideas about American youth culture. The references to America and American youth culture played an important role in the narratives of Meridian youth. During one of the focus group discussions, Akshay, a 19-year old young man, raised his hand and remarked, "I guess when we talk about the 'West,' its America. It is just that we know more about that place, and its more economically powerful than the rest of the world. So you compare yourself always to that." American culture, including their imagined ideas about America, played an important role in shaping their narratives. During my time at Meridian, the students wanted to know more about the youth at Connecticut College—where I had taught for more than a decade—and what American youth generally studied in their colleges. They asked questions about the liberal arts curriculum, how American college students spent their weekends, and how widespread was the "hookup" culture and "binge drinking" on American campuses.

I was asked to translate and decode the mind of an undergraduate American student with the hope that in my answers I would place both the Meridian youth and their American counterparts as equal in terms of intelligence, creativity, and "coolness." Exposure to American culture via travel or through media constituted an important aspect of the Meridian youth's perceptions about being *global citizens*. The phrase "global citizenship" had become an empty slogan that some of these students used to characterize their distance from their parochial locality and their affinities with "youth culture" around the world. The elite young generation aspired for the American-type independence, but they were also critical of the excessive freedom that was given to college-going youth in America.

Akshay was eager to give me insights into the culture of Meridian, and he had remained after the interview to talk about my book project. I began by asking Akshay, "Why are Meridian youth interested in knowing about American culture?" He explained that the youth watched American media and were avid consumers of Hollywood movies and "a lot of our influences are dictated a lot by America. . . . And our standard has always been the American standard." This "American standard," he said, is used whenever anyone in urban India sees a foreigner or someone who is "white"—that is, has fair skin. He commented that the urban upper class youth's tendency is to equate white with being American and being superior. I asked Akshay the same question that I had asked many youth during my interviews at Meridian: "Why were the youth embracing styles, ideas, and popular culture from America and not other countries?" Akshay replied that urban Indian youth could trace their preoccupation with American culture to colonial times when Indians believed that the British culture was superior to Indian culture. After the independence, during the postcolonial phase, Indians looked "down upon" the British because they had colonized India for more than 200 years. Then he stated that the next superpower was America, and Indians had to look to another culture to reconstruct their identity:

I mean you need somebody . . . you need a country . . . you need somebody to look up to—a "father figure"—in that way. And it happened a little bit with Russia, when Russia lost. . . . But again, the influence exerted by Americans is very, very high.

Akshay further argued that globalization had accorded American culture a hypervisibility, a super power status, and a standard that urban Indian youth and youth from across the globe admired. His friends at Meridian grew up watching American television shows such as *Scrubs, Grey's Anatomy, Boston Legal*, and *Friends* and listening to music by Bruce Springsteen, Brittany Spears, and a host of other American musicians and pop singers.

The "Americaness" of America was not just an alluring imaginative space for Akshay and his friends. The point was not to embrace American culture as it was shown on American TV but, rather, to appropriately reimagine it in India as part of their transnational identity. Akshay told me that there are *Americanized Indians* in India who do not want to go to America, but they want an American identity in India:

A: But they want America in India. 1 in a 100 would actually go and stay in America. They want to replicate the entire model here.

s: Because they have certain privileges here they don't want to give up?

A: Exactly. You have somebody who does your laundry, who washes your dishes, washes your car.

Akshay and his cohort of friends were aware that the American culture that was being appropriated by them and other Indian youth was a "television culture" and often devoid of complexity. He acknowledged, "We really don't know what American culture is." He elaborated that in India they tend to associate jeans, Coke, and Hollywood movies with American culture and that Indians have stereotypes about Americans as being rich and having fancy houses and many cars.

The Meridian youth imbibed the plot, the cultural references, and the themes that were presented in television shows such as *Seinfeld, The OC, Boston Legal, Big Bang Theory, Scrubs*, and *Friends*. These imported media texts had become shared cultural texts that were used by the students to create their self-narratives and to understand the psychology of their college-going peers. There were some youth at Meridian who were into meditation or Yoga, but they shied away from talking publicly about their spiritual pursuits. Akshay explained, "Realizing that contentment and such things are not passé. If that was passé, you wouldn't have your Baba Ramdev doing pranayama and having a massive following people doing it." I asked Akshay why the youth do not perceive yoga and meditation as having social status. He responded, "Its uncool. C'mon, you do Pranayam? Seriously, man?"

Taking an extended pause in our conversation, Akshay questioned his generation's fascination with American culture, brands, drinking, shopping, cars, and crass materialism. Akshay gave me a long explanation about how Indian society is changing and that American media was the new *cultural text* that gave youth and many middle-class families novel stories to define their lives. He had embraced many of the values that he was associating with American culture, but he was worried that these new ideas were "shaking the foundation of the Indian society as such." The Meridian students were searching for alternatives in a society that was dominated by corruption, casteism, and other gender inequities.

Akshay specifically singled out the IT boom and the import of serials such as *Nash* and *Baywatch* as creating cultural shifts in Indian society in the 1990s. He asserted that divorce was not a stigma anymore, and embracing materialism and becoming money-minded were not frowned upon by society. Once again, I pushed Akshay to be more specific about why he believed that American culture could be having such a strong influence on the youth at Meridian:

s: So is this American influence? That you are getting exposure of the West here?

A: I'm coming back to America because, you know, a lot of what we see, read, eat, and drink comes from America. . . . Because, if you really look at it, the biggest brands . . . you know, you have your Coke, Pepsi, McDonald's, fashion labels—Tommy Hilfiger, and Gap, and all of that. American movies infuse a lot of their culture in them. A lot of it! I mean, the cars you drive—you have your Cadillacs and all of that. And you have your big SUVs. And, like I said, you don't see a lot of movies from Australia, Europe, and Russia. Like I said, Indians have always considered American things as a standard. To live up to them is truly you know—becoming world citizens or global citizens. We don't have any standards of our own.

Akshay was anxious that elite, educated youth in India were becoming "homogenous" by embracing the materialism of American culture, and he was afraid that his generation was losing touch with their *Indian culture*.

Akshay told me that there will come a time when the misguided youth at Meridian will need to be reminded about their Indian roots. Akshay pondered, "I think General Motors had an advertisement, 'Made in America,' 'Be American, Buy American' thing which they had launched. That will start happening. Very, very, soon." The irony was not lost on me that Akshay cited an American car advertisement as a model to address some futuristic Indian youth for whom the essential qualities of Indianness would have become weakened.

What these narratives reveal is that media images that are enshrined and heavily coded with local cultural meanings beam out to new places to find their home in television sets across distant continents. In his article on youth culture in Bangalore, Saldhana (2002) writes, "Thus, the way global youth in Bangalore construct their sense of place within India's modernity and globalization can only be understood by interpreting *their* images of the West within India's specific geohistory" (p. 344, emphasis in original). The youth studying at Meridian in Pune were creating their story of global Indianness by interpreting their images of America within their specific local practices.

NINA'S STORY: THE "ULTIMATE" GLOBAL INDIAN

I met 19-year-old Nina, whom I mentioned previously, for several interviews at a newly built, high-tech classroom that was located in the center of the Meridian campus. Nina was wearing shorts, a sleeveless top, basketball shoes, and a nose ring. Her nonverbal behavior reminded me of the undergraduate students who I taught at my college in the United States. Nina's nonchalant pose was deliberate, and she relished her reputation of being a rebel and described herself as someone who is irreverent toward boundaries. Nina told me that the general student body perceived her as promiscuous and that there were rumors circulating on campus that she had "gone out with 37 boys."

As soon as we sat down for the interview, she said, "Don't get confused about the cross, I'm Gujarati." She was eager to impress upon me that she is a Hindu but wears a cross because key messages from the Bible had an impact on her. Nina was from an elite, wealthy, traditional Gujarati family. She lived in Dadar, a middle-class suburb of Mumbai. Nina studied at an all-girls private school, St. Mary's High School, and then after fifth grade, she transferred to Bombay Academy, an elite co-educational school. The children of Bollywood families, wealthy businessmen, upper-class professionals, and generally children of "famous people" attended this prestigious school. Nina explained that she currently lives in Dombivili, which is known as a conservative area, mostly populated by "orthodox Gujaratis." Her relatives and neighbors disapproved of her transfer to the new co-educational school. However, her transfer to this school was a transformative moment in her life; Nina noted, "The person I was, and my way of living, and behavior, in a lot of ways changed."

"Mean Girls" in Mumbai: Becoming "The Cooler People"

Bombay Academy allowed Nina to intermingle with other upwardly mobile and well-traveled, cosmopolitan friends. Nina's new cohort of friends ridiculed students who were excelling in academics; "You are not cool enough or popular enough if you are academically superior to others." It is at this juncture in her life, Nina proudly proclaimed, that she overcame the awkwardness of her preadolescent body, glasses, and "bad" physical appearance. She started wearing low-cut sash dresses, cut her hair short, and stopped applying oil to her hair so she could get the "attention of the nice and cooler people." Nina told me that her physical makeover made her attractive, preppy, and cool. I asked Nina to describe what "cool" meant to her. She responded, "The cooler people were the ones that everyone looked up to, the ones who had the first preference at the cafeteria tables, something like the [scene] from the American movie, *Mean Girls*."

In order to be popular with the girls and boys, Nina transcended her geeky image by deliberately starting to do poorly in school. Despite the assistance of expensive private tutors and intense parental supervision of her schoolwork, Nina barely managed to complete 10th grade. She finished 11th and 12th grades at another private and exclusive school, Mumbai's Matthews College. Finding herself yet again in the company of other privileged Mumbai youth, she began to push the boundaries of tradition and disciplinary rules that were enforced at home. Nina sought out friendships with a core group of wealthy students who became her peer group, and with fewer structures or direct supervision from school or parents, she began experimenting with alcohol and drugs. She remarked, "So I got into the entire party circle at that point. And because it was a new thing, it was very cool at that stage. And the people I'm meeting are my best friends from that school." Subsequently, Nina transferred out of Matthews College in Mumbai and decided to attend Meridian, where I was interviewing her.

I asked Nina how she views "Indian culture." She replied that she does not follow Indian culture but, rather, a global culture. I asked her to describe this global culture. She stated, "Next Wednesday I'm leaving after class gets done, to go back for a party in Bombay, and coming back for an 8 o'clock class in the morning." Her father, a wealthy investment banker who lives in Dadar, was going to send a chauffeur-driven car to pick up Nina at Meridian in Pune. She would then be driven to Mumbai so she could attend a graduation party hosted by her friends from Matthews College.

Nina told me that while she was on her summer vacation from college, she did not live with her parents in Dadar but instead stayed with a friend at an exclusive apartment in a South Mumbai location. Although Nina's father could afford to live in an expensive flat in South Mumbai, he chose to live with his parents in Dadar. Nina explained, "My grandparents don't want to shift out, and my dad doesn't want to break the tradition of family. So I still live there." Nina confessed that she feels slightly embarrassed telling her friends that she lives in the middle-class, conservative section of Dadar. South Mumbai is the symbol of urban cool, where signs of global fashion, brand-name stores, nightclubs, and malls are clearly visible. By staying in an apartment with her friend in cosmopolitan South Mumbai, she has access to a life that involves going to pubs, clubs, shopping, and being with friends who, according to Nina, personify global sophistication.

I asked Nina what being "global" or "Westernized" meant to her and if she felt superior in knowing English, traveling abroad, and adopting American codes. She smiled, said "Yes!" and then explained,

> There's this sort of connection. Especially when you talk about Bombay, the social circle of my level, my class, is such that even if there are around 6,000 kids my age, we know almost everyone. And we are supposed to be "the ultimate," what everyone else aims to be.

I was taken aback by Nina's honest acknowledgment of claiming to be from a superior class. I replied, "Really?" trying not to sound too sarcastic. She continued, "Because you have the confidence in you, and the way you carry yourself off, and the way you look glamorous, because you've seen it somewhere else. Like, [if] you read *Vogue* [it] is better than reading *Femina*."[5] Globalization, in Nina's view, was equated with urban youth who were acutely aware of fashion, music, and styles and had upper-class status. She remarked that her social circle has money, class, status, connections; they watch media that is "cool"; and they know where to shop for the right brands.

In other words, Nina was impressing upon me that she and her elite friends had the right kind of financial, cultural, linguistic, and social capital. Through her father's connections, she had met important business people and famous Indian actors such as Shahrukh Khan, Aamir Khan, Hritik Roshan, John Abraham, Kajol, and Naseeruddin Shah. She identifies herself as a "global woman" who goes shopping with her friends to the United Kingdom, where she will not hesitate to spend 400–500 pounds on an item of clothing or jewelry. I asked Nina to define what "class" meant to her. She replied that

> class status means that if there's a riot going on in Bombay, I will not be touched by it. . . . When you see, for example, communal riots, these people getting killed, and you read the newspaper about that blast and this thing and *blah blah*, it doesn't affect you.

I asked Nina to elaborate why she had immunity from riots and bomb blasts. Nina clarified that she lived in a gated community and she moved in cultural spaces that allowed her protection from the unpredictable chaos that middle-class and poor families encounter every day in Mumbai. In addition to being financially well-off, Nina remarked that her father had a network of powerful friends so no one would harm her.

Nina told me that India is now becoming globalized, and the youth are becoming psychologically more like teenagers from across the world—"Like, any other teenager. Like, if you go to Germany, you'll find my clone out there. Or in Europe, anywhere else in Europe." I was curious to know what were the particular shared psychological characteristics of this "global clone" that connected youth from Singapore to Sydney and from London to Chennai. Nina and her friends emphasized that all global teens have shared knowledge about global brands, movies, fashions, and educational institutions. According to Nina, travel is an essential ingredient for becoming knowledgeable about the world: "I've traveled globally. I've traveled to UK a million times, US, Singapore, China, Thailand, Africa, Mauritius, all of Europe." Nina argued that if urban youth describe themselves as "global" or "cosmopolitan," then they *ought* to have broad knowledge about imported brands, commodities, and products. She remarked that most youth "should have a certain attitude towards life, a certain amount of knowledge about things." I asked Nina to explain what kind of knowledge the urban youth need to acquire if they are to be considered part of the global youth culture. She illustrated her point with an example:

N: If Prada is having a sale at Vama (an upscale fashion store), it's important knowledge.
S: Vama is an Indian brand?
N: No, it's a shopping complex where you have only exclusive brands.
S: Oh! OK. So Vama is a special exclusive (shop).
N: Ya! So it's something you should know about. Like any person who is *anyone*, would know about it. Or if there is a new line Victoria's Secret has brought out, you would *know* about it. Or then, the season 4 finale of *Grey's*, definitely watched it. Or the new song by Infected Mushroom, totally got it. And the new movie, *Mamma Mia*, watched it. *Sex and the City*, the movie, watched it.

Nina's narrative is tied to what Mazzarella (2003) called a "consumerist ontology" (p. 13). This ontology, which is reflected in Nina's discourse, overlooks the dichotomy between true and false needs, between necessity and luxuries, and does not consider consumerism as exclusively elitist. Within the Indian sociocultural milieu, Nina's position on consumerism is overtly elitist. It idealizes media products that are Western and valorizes knowledge acquired through American media and also creates a narrative rooted in a superficial philosophy of cosmopolitanism. The demarcations of what constitutes global youth culture are clearly staked out through reference to Victoria's Secret, *Grey's Anatomy*, and *Sex and the City*. The key phrase that needs to be brought under analytical scrutiny is "watched it."

What does it mean for Nina and her transnational elite friends to define identity through consuming "Prada at Vama"? The phrase "watched it" signifies that Nina occupies a site of privilege in which consumption of foreign commodities and media texts creates an exclusive norm for referencing individuals who belong to the private club of elite youth. The phrase "watched it" signifies exclusive modalities of consumption—rising above the masses that do not have the capital, resources, and knowledge to "watch" and consume the foreign commodities. Elite consumption practice signifies for Nina both seeking pleasure and identification with commodities that travel in limited social circuits in urban India.

Nina mentions that she usually buys Abercrombie and Fitch, and most youth throughout the world recognize this brand. This identification with friends and products from abroad positions her not only as different but also as superior to her middle-class friends. Nina explains:

> No, to some level, to be completely honest, it makes me sort of feel superior to most people who are here. You are more globally (well-connected) than they are. And that again brings a divide between you and the girls. Because you feel that you are better off, you feel that you are more superior to them.

She makes it clear that her cosmopolitan knowledge about America gives her instant recognition as a global teen when she travels abroad. This knowledge was crucial to the development of her global self because she used it to forge connections with youth from America and Europe and also simultaneously used it to create distance from the ordinary middle- and working-class Indian youth.

The youth at Meridian had used their wealth to build what I call a "politics of originality" that surrounds their consumerist practices. They did not have to buy cheap imitation luxury bags, watches, clothes, and perfumes that many middle-class Indians bought from street vendors or inexpensive department stores. Going to London or taking trips to Delhi or Mumbai to buy expensive branded goods was not just about public displays of social status and conspicuous consumption. Instead, it signaled that these youth were able to engage in practices of exclusivity by going to the source of the original store or the city from which the so-called cultural commodity emanates. These youth have now become authentically global. It implied that one's self extends beyond the local to a series of branded global spaces in Dubai, Manhattan, or London that are associated with the "original modernity" or the "original forms of the West." It means that one can shop in New York at brand-name luxury stores such as Nieman Marcus and Tiffany & Co., dine in gourmet restaurants, and watch Broadway musicals while also meeting one's Indian relatives who live in diaspora communities.

Nita Mathur (2010) argues that there is an intergeneration gulf between the parents of "liberalization's children" and the youth who have grown up in a liberalized India and how they view practices of debased materialism and unchecked hedonism. She writes that there is indeed an ideological shift in the younger generation of the middle and upper classes as they move away from Gandhian idealism to ostentatious consumerism. This shift also signals a reshaping of the younger generation's self-narratives as they become more preoccupied by their personal gains and desires and are less concerned about the general welfare of the collective, public good. There are three main implications of adopting a consumerist ideology for the reorganization of social values in contemporary urban India.

First, this transnational class has the power to attach status and eminence to displays of fashion and the flamboyant buying and owning of luxury commodities. Second, Mathur (2010) writes that the possession of desirable goods has become a way of life that sets up aspirational goals for the entire society. The pursuit of brand-name goods has now emerged, she argues, as a "contemporary basis of understanding distinctions in society and as signifiers of personal identity that sets an individual apart from others" (p. 226). Third, for young urban Indians, there is a distinct shift from having virtues of austerity, modesty, and sharing to open and unencumbered exhibitions of personal wealth and commodities. The transnational urban Indians tend to embrace a cosmopolitan outlook, have global aspirations, invest time and energy in becoming professionals, take risks, and demand efficient leisure-time services, but they are also careful about not entirely dismissing Indian values of thriftiness and their moral obligations to their family. In one psychological study conducted with youth in India, Rao et al. (2013) found that Indian youth were highly self-reflective about how globalization was shaping their cultural identities. Nina's narrative thus embodies the new upper-class generation and also captures the ideological shifts in today's youth and their self-reflective talk about globalization.

American Media: Translating *Friends* and *Scrubs* in India

Nina's psychology of self and other, her understanding of how global teens should behave and interact with each other, and her understanding of the types of knowledge they should possess were mainly shaped by American television. I asked her what type of television serials she watched. Nina enumerated, "Right now I'm finishing my third season of *Scrubs*. But I finished *Prison Break, Lost, OC, One Tree Hill, Friends*, oh I love *Friends*!" Nina singled out *Friends* as one of her favorite shows because it reminded her of her friends and the "crazy stuff" they do. She insisted what is shown on *Friends* can be applied to her circle of friends on campus and in Mumbai.

Nina was quite keen about letting me know that what is shown on *Friends* is not strange—it "is not unheard of, it is the kind of stuff we do." Nina made attempts to convince one of her housemates, with whom she had several recurring conflicts, to watch *Friends* together. She recalled:

> Like, I had tried to make my roommate watch *Friends* with me once. I was trying to be nice to her, and she totally got disgusted by the way Joey acts. And I was like, that is how most of the guys in a club would act when (you are there). And she's never been to a club. So I was like, "Why wouldn't you do that?" so I don't get it.

Here, Nina was acting as a sophisticated translator of American popular culture, decoding the cultural meanings of friendship and American dating rituals for her roommate. Her espousal of a transnational perspective seemed obvious to her. Nina uses this television text to teach her friends how to act appropriately in a pub or a club. Her roommate, Nina says, is reluctant to use *Friends* as a template for guiding her romantic life. Nina cannot comprehend her roommate's dislike of *Friends* because she believes that Joey is a universally adored character.

According to Nina, most urban upper-class young men in India, when they go to clubs, act like Joey from *Friends*, and if her roommate wants to be a part of the dating scene, then she should watch *Friends*—especially the way Joey relates to women and his friends. Nina's attempt at persuading her roommate to watch *Friends* seemed somewhat caricatured, but that was not her main point. She emphasized that the *cultural knowledge* acquired by watching *Friends* or other well-known American television shows creates a shared identity for the urban elite and becomes a basis of forming an exclusive cosmopolitan community with other youth.

Nina's other favorite show is *Sex and the City*, and as an ardent fan of this show, she has watched all the episodes. *Sex and the City* is about the social and romantic lives of four white, single women in their 30s and 40s who live in New York City. How did Nina, a 19-year-old teenager who grew up in a traditional Gujarati family in Dadar, Mumbai, relate to the themes of *Sex and the City*? I asked her this question. Nina answered that this television show provides an accurate representation of lives of contemporary young women in Pune and Mumbai. She explained:

> Women talk about men, be it New York or Bombay, it's the same thing in all places. Like you can relate to it. Like, my best friends and me would sit and make Cosmos for ourselves, following the *Sex and the City* tradition. And all of us would sit and watch it at one of my friend's place. And we'd say, "Oh my God, that is so true." And get into our own little gossip about how that applies to our life.

Nina's narrative engagement with American media texts revolves around the process of importing selective themes that remind her of her social life.

She uses specific episodes of *Sex and the City* and *Friends* to understand the local cultural meanings of her romantic relationships. This type of selective cultural reading of media texts is similar to what Janice Radway (1984) called reading as an "act of discovery" in which each reader interprets the meanings of the text to suit his or her individual cultural realities. The meanings of these American texts are negotiated by Nina and her cohort within their interpretive communities. Indian youth use these American television serials to instantiate their beliefs about being in a community of global teens. Their financial resources allow them to travel to American and European cities where these texts are used as a vehicle to form connections with other transnational youth. The shared discourse about American clothing, television, and music and European fashion gives the elite urban transnational India youth a way of feeling that they are above the daily grimness of the Indian context—where the airports, roads, and schools are less than adequate, and frequent power outages and corrupt state bureaucracies are the norm.

How are the transnational youth I described previously "making present" their subjective experiences within cultural contexts to themselves and others in a society that is undergoing rapid change? Arthur Frank (2012) writes that a dialogical narrative analysis "understands stories as artful representation of lives, stories reshape the past and imaginatively project the future. Stories revise people's sense of self, and they situate people in groups" (p. 33). He further highlights that stories are always narrated within dialogues where the act of storytelling is essentially a response to others—who are actually present or merely imagined. Stories anticipate immediate and future responses, which incorporates the retelling of the story in different contexts. Two central questions that emerge from the narratives discussed previously are (1) How do the multiple voices of being global and Indian manifest themselves in the identity narratives of Meridian students? and (2) What type of hybridity is constructed as a result of the dialogical interactions between these different positions?

POLYPHONIC NARRATIVES: INDIANNESS, *JAYA PARVATI*, AND THE LURE OF GLOBALIZATION

One fruitful way to understand the multiple and competing voices in the narratives of the upper-class Indian youth is through Bakhtin's (1981) term *polyphony*. The term polyphony emphasizes "how one speaker's voice is always resonant with the voices of specific others—people whom the speaker listens to and whose response she or he anticipates" (Frank, 2012, p. 35). Hermans and Kempen (1993) argue that the polyphonic self moves in "an imaginal space," inhabiting different *I* positions simultaneously, with each position entering into dialogical relationships with one another, "agreeing or disagreeing with each other" (p. 47). In their application of Bakhtin's concept of voice, Hermans and Kempen conceive of the dialogical self in terms of a number of dynamic but relatively autonomous *I* positions that are in dialogue with real, actual, and imagined others. The *I* is not static but, rather, can move from one position to another with changes in time and circumstances.

From the perspective of the dialogical self, any given individual or *I*, depending on the sociocultural constraints, can take a stance or a position of ridicule, agreement, disagreement, understanding, opposition, and contradiction toward another *I* position. For Bakhtin (1981), utterances and words are "double-voiced" because the utterance is directed toward the speaker and anticipates the response of the real and the imagined others.

Extending on Bakhtin's theory, Raggatt (2012) writes that the most elementary positioning process that can be found in a story or a narrative is the movement between "*I* position" and "counter-position," and this dynamic movement sets up the foundation for multiplicity and decentralization of self. He further elaborates:

> When the *I* takes up a position in relation to the world, or one is positioned by others, movement is immediately implied by a range of potential counter-positions, whether these positions are internal to the self or have origins outside. In either case, some degree of dynamic, developmental or cultural tension is implied by the process of positioning and counter-positioning. . . . At the cultural level, for example, the process of globalization has created opportunities for innovation of the self across borders and cultural divides that are new. . . . At the same time, countervailing processes of localization emerge (or re-emerge), and these can lead, in their defensive forms, to race tensions and conflicts, to a closing-off of new positions, and even to a resurgence of fundamentalisms characteristic of the pre-modern era. (pp. 31–32)

The narratives of the Indian youth are polyphonic and exemplify this ambiguous and dynamic movement between positions and counter-positions as a result of their engagement with practices of globalization. Nina' story is illustrative of this movement, and one can find these global–local intersections present in the stories of a large segment of the transnational Indian youth.

In my study, several Indian youth who belong to the elite transnational class defined globalization as making them aware of world events, giving them an increasing ability to travel, having easy access to the world through social media and TV, availability of foreign brands, as well as forging connections with youth from foreign countries through social networking sites.

At a minimum, we find two competing positions in these narratives. One position is acquired or appropriated through the process of globalization. The other dominant position seeks to interpret and reframe their "Indianness" through the positions that are represented as global and largely American.

What are the qualities of these two positions and how do they interact with each other in their narratives? What does the global position represent? What does Indianness represent?

Nina's narrative definitely leans toward a construction of self that is based on a dynamic movement between positions and counter-positions of being a *global Indian* woman. She reiterates that one can be a global and a traditional urban Indian woman without having to give up one's culture. India or Indianness for the young women and men at Meridian was associated with traditions, preserving the family, respecting elders, following a moral code, and observing sexual restraint before marriage. Indian traditions were seen by the youth as a set of moral values that would sustain and nurture them as their culture increasingly became "Westernized" or "Americanized" (Mazzarella, 2003). The younger generation of Indians whose lives resembled the identity narratives of Meridian youth spoke to me about India's potential to become an "advanced" and "highly developed" country. However, they were simultaneously alarmed at the "Americanization" of their lives and the discursive positions that accompanied those *foreign ways of being* in India. Indianness was conceived and described as a cultural shield that gave them immunity from potential overindulgences in the "global" dimension of being a global Indian.

An important element about being a global Indian involved dispelling myths about India when the urban Indian youth traveled abroad. Their self-esteem in many ways was tied to India's progress through globalization, and they were keen on seeing a positive image of India portrayed, primarily in Europe and America. The descriptions of "Indianness" and "Indian nation" became blurred as these youth spoke of revamping India's image abroad.

It was clear that these youth, while traveling abroad, were confronted with stereotypical images of India as poor, underdeveloped, and traditional. Nina gave the following example:

> The first time I went to a summer school abroad, and people weren't that aware of India. They were like, "Oh, so do you have like snake charmers on the road" and "People wear *ghagara cholis*" and "Do you wear sarees" and everything.

Nina's comments in this focus group highlighted the point that the new generation of transnational youth had viewed globalization as catapulting India into the league of nations that are considered powerful and advanced. Through their international travels and contact with other young Euro-Americans, these participants were engaged in translating for others a new vision of the Indian nation—they were acting as cultural brokers and educating Americans and Europeans about the global transformations that were occurring in India.

When she was studying at Oxford University in the United Kingdom, Nina observed the ritual associated with *Jaya Parvati*. This is a fasting ritual practiced by many married women who primarily live in Western regions of India.

As part of the ritual, women are required to avoid consuming salt for 5 days. This *vrat* (fast) honors Lord Shiva and goddess *Parvati*, and it requires women to avoid wheat and vegetables as well. Young women also observe this fast with the hope that they would get "ideal husbands" in their marriages. On the fifth night, the women—who are fasting—are expected to participate in a *Jaya Parvati Jagran* (all-night vigil and prayer). While at Oxford, Nina practiced this ritual, and all her friends "who were from all over world" respected her Indian tradition.

Nina told me that her friends were from China, Switzerland, and Italy, and her "boyfriend there was from Germany"; the six of them participated in this ritual. She emphasized that her friends from all over the world respected this Indian ritual of not eating salt and food grains, and they went with her to shop for the special food that was associated with this ritual. Nina said,

> They would respect the fact that I worshipped a plant for that time being. They stayed up with me on the last night because I had to stay up. They respected my tradition, my culture. . . . The fact that we can relate to each other's traditions and culture is what makes you global. I mean, the reason I have a cross around my neck is because I have read the Bible, and I really like some things in the Bible.

Nina's version of global Indianness is based on the idea of benign multiculturalism and the concept of world citizenship. She emphasizes that globalization implies tolerance, acceptance of different views, and honoring tradition. These "ultimate global travelers" at Meridian self-select cultural traditions that continue to affirm their sense of Indianness while imagining themselves to be a part of a global world culture. This identity is based on reimagining both Indianness and American and Western culture within an upper-class, elite, urban context.

The transnational identities at Meridian were primarily constructed through a selective reading and application of American cultural symbols. The fluidity of American global culture as represented through music, food, fashion, and clothing seeps its way into the lives of transnational youth in urban cities such as Pune, Delhi, and Mumbai. These elite youth have been socialized in urban cities, and they have come of age in a post-liberalized India that valorizes identities that are deeply connected to consumption practices. Derne (2008) notes that

> by consuming Pepsi rather than local Thums Up or Domino's Pizza rather than a roadside *samosa* (at a cost—in the case of the pizza, which might be 35 times higher), one presents oneself as a cosmopolitan transnational mover who is oriented globally rather than locally. . . . The elite Indian who prefers Pepsi and Pizza Hut may see himself or herself as having more in common with

the Western consumer than with non-elite India who can only afford locally-produced goods. (p. 103)

Although Derne's observation about the elite Indians' consumption practices is somewhat applicable to the lives of Indian transnational youth, it does not fully explain how these youth strategically use their *Indianness* to be become "global Indians." How does their Indianness fit within the realm of their imagined global identities and vice versa? The orientation of the transnational youth at Meridian is indeed global/American, as reflected in Nina's narrative, but it would be premature to dismiss Nina and many Indian transnational youth as being bereft of Indian traditions or disconnected from local sensibilities. This is where we see the narratives of Meridian youth coming into dialogue with positions that strategically attempt to redefine their image of what it means to be an Indian. How is "Indianness" represented in the dialogical narratives of the urban Indian youth?

The concept of "position" not only highlights the multiplicity and plurality of cultural selves that exist within a single individual narrative but also allows us to foreground the tensions, contradictions, and asymmetrical power relationships that exist within that narrative. Recognizing and identifying the polyphonic construction of self helps us understand how, for many urban Indian youth, becoming global Indians suggests that acculturation within the context of globalization is a dynamic, plural, and infinite process that results in new cultural meanings and definitions—many of them contradictory and always resisting finitude. As we go through the interview corpus of the transnational elite Indian youth, we can ask the following questions: Who is doing the talking? What does it mean for them to be home in a world in which the global is seemingly seductive, modern, and liberating? What areas of their identity were being transformed by this polyphony of positions?

SEX AND LOVE IN ROMANCE AND ARRANGED MARRIAGES: CONTRADICTIONS IN CULTURAL VOICES

The polyphonic quality of the narratives of the transnational Indian youth that I described before was dialogical and multivoiced, but these narratives also showed tensions and contradictions with respect to their ideas of sexuality, romance, and marriage. What was clear from Nina's interview and the other interviews conducted in this sample was that globalization was associated with imagined American cultural practices. These practices were appropriated by youth in shoring up an identity position that can be defined as global, cosmopolitan, and traditional. The construction of the global Indian identity was also used as a strategy to critique certain elements of Indian traditions and social practices. *Indianness was positioned as a counterpoint to modernity and American culture.*

While the cosmopolitan, well-traveled Meridian youth had formed narratives of themselves through a global consumerist discourse, they also had anxieties about managing and maintaining their Indianness. Throughout the interview, Nina gave me the impression that it was important for her to define and frame her identity as a young Indian woman whose experience with globalization was primarily mediated through consuming American popular culture. In addition, she used *Friends* and *Sex and the City* as texts to understand her romantic entanglements with young men who she encountered at Meridian and in Mumbai. Despite having a boyfriend, Nina proudly asserted that she was a virgin and she wanted the "act" to be special: "I'm totally open about it. Considering I'm the last virgin in all my friends, and they've told me that. . . . Not yet. Came close to it, nothing against it. Would love to do it. Just not with any random guy."

One of the most radical changes I observed in many college-going youth in Pune, especially the young women, was their willingness to talk openly about sex and intimacy in their romantic relationships. When I was growing up in India, sex was a taboo topic, and it was a matter of shame and dishonor for women to express sexual desires before marriage or even to engage in conversations about sex and love outside of marriage. Even during my college days in India, only a tiny minority of select young upper-class, mostly urban men and women had experienced sexual intimacy with their romantic partners. However, by and large, the youth of my generation viewed sex and sexuality through the prism of a moral and patriarchal discourse.

Young men were allowed more latitude to engage in talk about sex, and they also sought out opportunities to have sex before marriage. However, most men and women in traditional India were going to find their partners through arranged marriages, where the wishes of their parents and community overrode their individual choice. Despite modern ideas about dating and romance, the traditional sexual practices, usually associated with women abstaining from sex and keeping their virginity until marriage, still continue to exist in various forms in much of India. Most of the youth at Meridian were open to talking about their premarital sexual relationships, having love marriages, and exploring live-in relationships, but at the same time they believed in arranged marriages and going through the ritual of finding a suitable spouse through their family networks.

The youth of Meridian were creating two contradictory views about sexuality. One view referred to their private lives: experimenting with sex, embracing the language of individual desire and going on dates, finding intimacy within romantic relationships, and marrying someone of their choice. This discourse was similar to the language used by American youth. These same youth were also expressing a discourse about the need to honor the sacredness of sexuality, finding ways to be sexual while still persevering their virginity, choosing a "traditional marriage," and respecting their parents' wishes and the rituals of the arranged marriage system. The contradictory juxtaposition of traditional and emancipatory views about sexuality was an important feature of the narratives of transnationally oriented youth.

Ira Trivedi (2014) captures the dual and contradictory conflicts that many young Indians were experiencing in her book, *India in Love: Marriage and Sexuality in the 21st Century*. She claims that economic globalization has spurred on new forms of social and cultural change in attitudes toward family, sex, and romance in the middle and upper classes of India. Upon returning to India after studying in the United States, Trivedi noticed that the sexual mores in her peer culture had become highly polarized. She observes:

> I found myself living in a bizarre mélange of traditional Indian culture where arranged marriage was expected but also where a Big Apple style dating culture was the norm amongst the *same* people. So someone could be meeting prospective partners for marriage through the arranged marriage process, while dating and mating rampantly on the side. (p. 5, emphasis in original)

The youth at Meridian were indeed part of the cultural transformations in sexual practices that were occurring in urban India. Abraham (2004), who studied low-income college-going Mumbai youth, writes that urban youth are more likely to embrace sexual liberalism in the contexts of economic liberalization and globalization. What are the new symbols of this revolution? She argues that there are new representations of sexuality in print and visual media that depict "the objectification of the male body, the unabated pursuit and pleasure of desire and multiple sexual relationships" (p. 211).

The long-established system of arranged marriages is on the decline; divorce rates are increasing; and a small segment of the urban middle- and upper-class youth are also embracing liberal views toward gay identities and lesbian relationships. Trivedi (2014) writes that 75% of urban youth between the ages of 18 and 24 years have engaged in premarital sex. In addition, she notes that a sizable number of urban teenage high school students have engaged in sex, and these urban teenagers frequently talk about dating and wanting to have sexual partners. She concludes that Indian society is not just going through a sexual and a love revolution. She explains:

> Young people are having premarital sex, same sex relations have been decriminalized and recriminalized, more people are defiantly declaring their sexual preferences, and women are demanding their sexual rights. Essentially, sex is coming out of the bedroom, and on to the streets. And the love revolution has led to the break-up of the arranged marriage as more people decide to marry for love than community or caste. (p. 378)

What had become evident to me as I spoke to both the youth and the older generation in Pune was that the rapid pace of technology has been crucial in generating a cultural shift in attitudes toward sex across the various social classes. Young urban Indians were now able to channel their sexual desires and fantasies instantly through cable television, Facebook, YouTube, Twitter, online pornography, and chat rooms. Along with technology, the pace of urbanization and industrial expansion, exposure to Western media, the decline of the joint family, the increasing number of nuclear families, and increasing divorce rates are some of the key factors that are driving the sexual revolution. Today, young Indians are also frequently exposed to sexual images through television, Bollywood movies, songs, advertisements, magazines, and fashion wear.

Trivedi (2014) writes that when she was growing up as a young child in India, she and her friends would tease each other by singing the popular grade-school jingle that was imported from America: "First comes love, then comes marriage, then comes (Smriti) in a baby carriage." Although they sang the jingle in jest, they knew all along that the order of first love and then marriage was completely out of place in the Indian context. Until even about two decades ago, first marriage and then love were the most pervasive culturally coded moral prescriptions that had to be followed by women. In contrast, in today's urban India, the sexual revolution is being spearheaded by young urban women as they are reframing the stereotypes of being a "good Indian" woman.

After interviewing and listening to hundreds of women, Trivedi (2014) came to the conclusion that on urban college campus and universities in India, having premarital sex is more a norm than a deviation. She writes that "free from the clutches of family and the mores of middle-class India, girls are keenly interested in sexual exploration. This sense of experimentation is mirrored in the bustling nightlife and social scene—in night clubs, bars, hookahs" (p. 35).

My interviews with the young men and women of Meridian confirmed some of Trivedi's (2014) conclusions about the sex revolution that was taking place on campuses in major cities in India, but I found these stories of sexuality filled with contradictions and tensions. Although American culture was embraced, these transnational youth also deployed the rhetoric of strong "Indian family" and "Indian cultural values" to critique American values of individualism and materialism. Sex was associated with shame and being a virgin, yet everyone I spoke to had a boyfriend or a girlfriend.

An imagined and, to some extent, a pure form of Indianness was an important theme in their narrative. This pure form of Indianness was constructed through traditional forms of family, ancestry, heritage, traditions, religion, diversity, and plurality. Indianness was thus framed as an enduring legacy of family values that were transmitted through the lens of an "old civilization."

For instance, Nina's close friend Rakhee, who was also an upper-class student at Meridian, described Indianness as being family oriented, "very close to families," "not discarding your body and giving it to anyone," and "having self-respect and knowing one's limitations." In the same interview, she also described "Indian views" as strict and restricting. Their invocations of Indian traditions to understand their sexuality are a legacy of what Abraham (2004) refers to as the "pativrata" culture in India. *Pativrata* frames women as "pure" and "good," and it "embodies the confinement of female sexuality through the complete devotion of a woman to her husband regardless of how he treats her" (p. 213).

The Meridian youth's juxtaposition of their global cultural view with the local Indian views brings out the conflicts and tensions within their self-identity. Their stories symbolize the modern views of liberal sexuality while still being circumscribed within the traditional discourses of family, tradition, and purity. Adopting a dialogical framework encourages us to examine the contradictions, complexities, and interminable shifts of identity construction (Bhatia, 2007; Bhatia & Ram, 2001).

MULTIVOICEDNESS OF POWER AND PRIVILEGE: HYBRIDITY IN NARRATIVES OF GLOBAL INDIANNESS

The narratives I collected are deeply multivoiced and polyphonic, and they exhibit a fundamental tension in their identity. Interpreting Bakhtin, Wertsch (1991) notes that one way in which dialogicality comes into being is when one or many utterances of the "speaking subject" come into contact with, and "interanimate," the voice of the other. The utterance is an important element of dialogicality because of its focus on "addressivity," a concept that requires at least two voices—the author and the addressee, the self and the other (p. 52).

The urban Indian youth are not just dialogically engaging with American media and Western brands but also reimagining these "other" cultural practices to "interanimate" and bring to life the stories of their multiple identities. The interviews reveal that globalization and localization are not diametrically opposite forces but, rather, mutually constituted through an evolving dialogue that creates tensions as well as new types of dialogical hybridities. When Bakhtin uses the term voice, he does not mean "auditory signals" but, rather, the "speaking personality" or the "speaking consciousness" (Wertsch, 1991, p. 12). In this regard, Wertsch notes that the real challenge of studying dialogicality is to spell out exactly how voices or self–other positions come into contact with each other and change each other's meanings. If we were to take a Bakhtinian view of identity, then we have to ask, What is the quality of hybridity that emerges in these narratives?

Hybridity not only synthesizes and combines cultural forms and categories in a given sociocultural milieu but also has the potential to disturb, unsettle, and adulterate old singular identities. The Argentinean–Mexican scholar, Nestor Garcia Cancilini (1995), defines hybridization as a "sociocultural process in which discrete structures or practices, previously existing in separate form, are combined to generate new structures, objects and practices" (p. xxv). For Cancilini, these discrete structures are not pure "points of origin" but, rather, cultural forms that allow us to look at how hybridization creates "multitemporal heterogeneity" (p. 47). Thus, forms of religious rituals, syncretism, cartoons and comics, graffiti, popular culture, and television programs all comingle to form hybrid identities that simultaneously involve fragments of the ancient, magical, local, global, and national. The varied ways in which transnational urban Indians develop *personal narratives* to make sense of their practices of globalization highlights the critical role of narrative and the understanding of both the psychology of globalization and the process of self-making.

These narrations or stories (Schiff, 2013) reveal an individual psychology and also show how these hybrid narrations are embedded in larger transnational social practices of "flexible citizenship" (Ong, 1999) that allow "global Indian" youth to travel across borders easily and become part of the community of international mobile travelers. The social imagination of the Meridian youth is shaped by the circulation of global capital, their elite liberal arts education, and the neoliberal structures that place a high value on "global citizens" who can work in a flexible economy.

The construction of hybrid identities is essentially a dialogical process that combines incompatible positions, competing values and ideologies, and connotes a struggle, a contestation, and a tension. The narratives of the Meridian youth point to a dialogically constructed hybridity that moves between various positions of Indianness and Americaness, autonomy and relatedness, as well as tradition and modernity. I argue that the transnational youth are developing a dialogicality of "global Indianness"—a hybrid identity—that is essentially fashioned through three dialogically constituted practices: transnational class, traveling Indianness, and consumer citizenship.

Transnational Class: Stories of Global Self

The symbols and language of globalization in any given place are performed and expressed through specific cultural categories. The youth at Meridian were part of the elite transnational class that comprised a tiny minority of India's population, yet they were playing an important role in defining various forms of Indianness. What does it mean to say that the youth belonged to the transnational class? There are three important dimensions that make up the transnational class. First, members of the transnational class in India live in a social space through which they have acquired economic power by having access to wealth and financial capital. Bourdieu (1994) argues that our position in a given "social space" or class is constructed by the quantities of the various kinds of "capital" we possess (p. 229). The families of youth at Meridian are what Leslie Sklair (2009) has described as individuals who belong to a transnational capitalist class.

This class is the old elite class that is transformed by its participation in new forms of a globalizing economy. This transnational class is composed of owners and controllers of transnational corporations, global bureaucrats and politicians, global knowledge workers, IT professionals, and upper-level management employees (globalizing professionals) and merchants and media consumers. There were other students from upper-class families, whose parents were upper-class professionals—doctors, engineers, lawyers, professors, and merchants—and they were in part benefitting from the globalizing economy in India because they had access to transnational capital (finances), education (at home or abroad), and social spaces such as malls, colleges, airports, and iconic vacation destinations.

The second key element of having a transnational identity involves having a sufficient amount of cultural capital. Bourdieu (1994) extends the language of economics and argues that an agent's position in a given social space is also defined relative to other forms of capital. The other forms of capital are defined as "cultural capital" (knowledge of art, literature, and technical skills) and "linguistic capital" (knowledge of educational, public, poetic, and official forms of language). The youth at Meridian have been educated at some of the best convent-run or private English-speaking schools and have acquired appropriate cultural knowledge about American or European popular music and media, and they use Internet technologies to mediate their social relations. For Bourdieu, cultural capital functions as a specific "form" of capital, "convertible with but irreducible to economic capital" (Beasley-Murray, 2000, p. 101).

Acquiring cultural capital thus involves being socialized as an agent in a particular field where specific practices or *habituses* of cultural knowledge, competence, world view, preferences for food or sports, and dispositions are highly valued (Bourdieu, 1994). The acquisition of specific types of highly regarded cultural knowledge equips the individual to have both empathy and appreciation for those social fields and practices where this knowledge is discussed, displayed, or produced as a an artifact. Johnson (1993) notes,

> The possession of this code, or cultural capital, is accumulated through a long
> process of acquisition or inculcation, which includes the pedagogical action
> of the family or group members (family education), educated members of the

social formation (diffuse education) and social institution (institutionalized education). (p. 7)

The youth stories at Meridian reflected their proficiency in English and their ability to speak with a neutralized Indian convent school accent, and they also knew when to insert their native Hindi or Bengali words in their communication with their friends or families. Many of these students had the privilege to be educated by private tutors, experts, and coaches; they had attended competitive schools to master specific forms of knowledge and literacy practices that had become highly valued in India and abroad.

Linguistic capital is often subsumed under cultural capital, and it is defined in terms of its "market value." Bourdieu (1994) makes the case that in the linguistic market, one will find some linguistic products that have more value than others, and individuals become competent speakers when they reproduce speech acts that have been assigned a high value in the marketplace. The students who belong to this class have access to spaces and institutions that themselves are a product of the neoliberal global moment: malls, educational institutions, media, and finance and private residential communities.

For example, Meridian had specifically emerged in the context of a new "global India," and one of its missions was to create a generation of Indian youth who had a psychological outlook that incorporated the global and local aspects of their culture. The faculty who taught at Meridian were mostly Indian scholars, activists, performers, and scientists, but many of them had studied or acquired professional degrees in the United States, Germany, France, the United Kingdom, and Canada. The mission of Meridian is to give students the experience that makes them "a citizen of the world" through their diverse, multicultural education. In this context, "India" and "Indianness" become a subject of study and discovery—a piece of cultural capital—that is juxtaposed against global liberal education. An important aspect of belonging to a transnational class is their ability to be mobile travelers within the nation and beyond the nation state. Most of the Meridian youth have been abroad—as tourists, for adventure trips, and for family vacations.

The third dimension that made the Meridian students unique was their engagement with discourses of self. The vocabulary and language of self-growth, human potential, and self-discovery were now part of the larger curriculum of most of the institutions that wanted to produce "global Indian" students, workers, and professionals. My conversations with the deans, students, and faculty at Meridian had reaffirmed for me that a new "language of subjectivity," largely created out of American psychological discourse, was becoming a mainstay at Meridian.

One could witness it in Meridian's catalogs and courses and in everyday conversations at the college. In catalogs, the Meridian educational experience was described as an education that aims to create a globally adept breed of managers but also produces students who will be "critical thinkers" and "emotionally mature." The students were told that they were at Meridian to pursue their inner passions: "Build your course of study by choosing courses that appeal to you. It lets you be, it lets you explore and gives you time to understand which career path best meets your goals and objectives."

Girish Khanna, a student who describes his experience of being at Meridian in the school's catalog (2013), states that he let go of his stereotypes and inhibitions and that he has learned the true meaning of the word "potential" as he has learned to "harness his creativity" and found "balance" and "clarity" (p. 37). Another student, Anupama Sethi, describes the experience of being at Meridian as follows:

> The journey at Meridian has brought along times filled with fun and frolic, laughter and cries, agreements and disagreements, likes and dislikes, adjustments and alterations. But most importantly with all these emotions it has helped me carve out my identity. (p. 37)

The youth of the transnationally oriented families believe in accumulating global experiences or using travel to acquire cultural capital about new trends, fashions, or what Bourdieu (1994) calls "taste" and "preference."

Some of the youth had traveled abroad and visited Europe and America to visit relatives in the Indian diaspora; visited tourist attractions; and gone on shopping excursions in Dubai, New York, and London. The youth from the transnational class acquires a global subjectivity by participating in ritual and practices of work, recreation, shopping, and fashion that have a "franchise culture" across different areas of the world.

Carol Upadhya's (2011) research shows that the IT industry in India has contributed to the specific discourses of globalization and what it means to belong to a socially mobile, transnational class. First, she notes that Indian professional workers are situated in multinational corporations where narratives about cultural identity and multiculturalism are in circulation. These workers interface with workers from the United States and Europe and have to participate in mandatory workshops that force them to make their Indian culture transparent. They are expected to participate in workshops that expose them to new narratives about self, growth, human potential, and cultural sensitivity and that require them to have communication skills that allow them to interact with people throughout the world. Second, the success of the software industry and the large export of contract workers who work in the knowledge economy have brought IT workers global recognition. Thus, the success of the IT industry as a source of "global pride" becomes fused with Indianness and Indian culture. The software industry takes credit for the positive media stories about India that appear in India and the United States. This new nationalism or nationalistic discourse about being Indian is now "reconstituted within the discourse of globalization, creating a kind of global nationalism" (Upadhya, 2011, p. 175). The software professionals exhibit a nationalist pride as India is viewed as an economic powerhouse and not just a "Third World" country anymore.

A third way the IT industry has brought an element of transnational culture in the upper and middle classes is by importing American organizational and human resource language such as the inner self, personal growth, and producing the image of a "global Indian" professional who works in a global workplace. The transnational professionals participate in a range of "psychological practices" that distinguish them from other Indians. They participate in training programs on time management, self-actuality, personality development, assertiveness training, emotional intelligence, and other management techniques to produce "empowered" workers. Upadhya (2011) states that

> such training, and the experience of "global knowledge work" itself, inflects IT professionals' subjectivities and alters their orientation towards work, the self and others. . . . These training programs adopt a range of Western psychological concepts and techniques or "technologies of the self," to inculcate desirable personality traits such as "assertiveness" and "self-confidence.' (p. 176)

The vocabulary and language of self-growth, human potential, and self-discovery are now part of the larger curriculum of most of the college institutions that want to produce "global Indian" students, IT workers, and professionals. My conversations with the deans, students, and faculty reaffirmed for me that the language of identity, largely created out of Euro-American psychological discourses, had become a central feature of social life at Meridian.

The Meridian youth I had spoken with wanted to study in a college or university that had an American-style curriculum that emphasized individual growth as opposed to being exam- and marks-oriented. The youth who lived in Mumbai, Delhi, and Bangalore were aware of how the youth in their cohort made trips to Europe and America, and this type of mobility was becoming commonplace. Several of them mentioned that new circuits of "cool mobility" involved experiences of hiking and parasailing in the United States, doing adventure sports in Spain, or just traveling to learn more about cultures in Africa or South America. New types of mobility involved seeking out unconventional travel experiences that combined education, self-discovery, extreme sports, and making connections with youth from other cultures.

"Cool Traditions": Traveling Indianness

Nina and her peers believed that clothing, music, and movies that were cultural products of American popular culture represented modern "ideas" and "traditions" of the West. As the world was becoming more globalized, the youth argued that the young people across India needed to be aware of these developments in the West far "more than in India." The youth I interviewed at Meridian believed that these new global cultural brands, mainly emanating from the United States, had the power to give them—especially women—a new confidence and outlook on life. It was quite evident from my conversations with Nina and her peers that these youth were largely disconnected from youth of other classes who did not have the credentials of being global and were not part of the upper-class, English-speaking strata.

The global, transnational Indianness is constructed by upper-class and elite youth by drawing on diverse cultural privileges. Radhakrishnan (2011) explains that transnational Indians' symbolic and material privileges are derived from their dominant position of being a part of the successful worldwide narrative of globalization and having the power to produce notions of a *globalized Indian* culture that are naturalized, applied, and streamlined in the public and private space. This transnational class has the power and means to create "influential, resonant notions of a new and improved Indian identity—an appropriate difference with cosmopolitan sensibilities" (pp. 34–35). The narratives of Meridian youth that I analyzed yoke together appropriate notions of Indianness with cosmopolitan feelings and outlook.

What are the appropriate notions of Indianness? Indian cultural psychologist Nandita Chaudhary (2004) argues that "familism," in contrast to individualism, is one of the most significant sociocultural realities that influence the formation of personhood in India (p. 109). Separating or breaking away from the family ruptures the inner world of the child and enables the creation of insecurities. Kakar (1996) observes,

> Whatever the necessity or reason for such a step, not only brings a sense of insecurity in a worldly, social sense, it also means the loss of "significant others" who guarantee a sense of sameness and affirm their inner continuity of self. (p. 121)

Traditional conceptions of personhood in India (Misra, 2003) are based primarily on social, interdependent familial relationships, where family harmony is viewed as essential to the stable and secure self.

Cultural practices such as touching the feet of elders for their blessings, sacrificing oneself for the good of the family collective, or being responsible for the financial and psychological well-being of others are considered to be moral values. We have to take into account other nonpsychological factors to explain the Indian tendency of constructing the self in family terms. Locating the self within the context of a family for "indulgent socialization" (Chadha, 2011) for reputation, name recognition, and other economic factors also needs to be considered. Identification with the family provides the primary psychological locus of anchoring one's self, but the family also serves as the bedrock of economic security in times of economic crisis.

In India, the majority of the population cannot depend on the government for social security, medical care, and unemployment wages. In the event that one's father falls ill, lack of monsoon rains destroys crops, or a young child becomes disabled, there are no governmental support systems that can be accessed. This is why Indian psychologist Kakar (1996) writes that an individual's identity—a person's self-worth, individual decisions, initiatives, and actions in the world—is always being interpreted within the context of the family.

Chaudhary (2012) writes that there is a "collective 'mulitvoicedness' that characterizes Indian cultural reality" (p. 171). She further writes that "social positioning" plays a more profound role than "personal positioning" in how Indians construct their sense of selves and others. Within the context of the dialogical self, Chaudhary argues, "Thus if we accept that personal and social positioning are two dimensions of self-configuration, there is clear evidence of a prevailing focus on the latter in Indian culture" (p. 172). It is important to highlight here that almost all the narratives of Indian youth in the Meridian study were incorporating some elements of the "Indianness" that have been discussed by several Indian psychologists (Chaudhary, 2012; Kakar, 1996).

The transnational Meridian youth in particular were reconciling their image of themselves as global and cosmopolitan while continuing to retain an image of being an Indian who respects traditions, customs, and values associated with strong family bonds. This was not an easy task because, if you recall, the Meridian youth describe globalization as breaking the shackles of tradition, giving them exposure and making them different from their parents. In their narratives, they viewed the concept of "Indianness" different from their parents' generation—the pre-globalization generation or the midnight's generation—as being highly rigid, oppressive, rule-bound, and constructed through the binary of East and West.

These youth did not want to discard *familial Indianness*, which was seen as the moral bedrock of their selfhood, but it had to be revised and given new perspectives from their position as being transnational youth with access to global cultural capital. How was this strategic voice of Indianness created within the polyphony of other voices?

During my interviews with the Meridian youth—both with individuals and with focus group participants—globalization was equated with producing what Radhakrishnan (2011) has described as *appropriate difference* or *appropriately conceived* global Indianness. Being a global Indian meant displaying a kind of transnational *cultural difference* that had the right currency and credibility and that could be transported to other countries, where it would be accepted as legitimate, valid, and as having a world-class standing. My interviews with Nina, Rakhee, Akshay, Shilpa, Malini, and the focus group participants made it clear that a "culturally streamlined" notion of India was being invoked (Radhakrishnan, 2011). Selected parts of Indian culture, as represented through ritual marriage or codes of interaction with elders, could be adopted in Oxford or New York in their travels and study-abroad stints. Nina could easily observe the *Jaya Parvati* ritual in Oxford because the fasting rituals associated with this Indian tradition were viewed as a transferable set of norms that even her friends from Germany and Italy found easy to appropriate.

The youth from Meridian tended to view culture and cultural practices as multicultural *mobile components* that could be made compatible with the culture of modernity, liberation, and individualism. This mobile and modular notion of global Indianness was largely apolitical and divorced from the social inequalities that were rife in the system. The narratives of the members of this transnational class were highly individualistic but family oriented. They believed in an optimistic notion of Indianness and "the progress of an unfettered individual taking off on the global scene, and that Indianness is upheld in family relationships, in respectable women, in practicing a certain kind of decontextualized version of Hinduism" (Radhakrishnan, 2011, p. 200).

The youth at Meridian used their financial power, cultural capital, and transnational privilege to engage in practices that gave rise to a traveling notion of Indianness that was able to cross boundaries, places, and institutions. These youth wanted an Indianness that becomes world class, and by becoming world-class Indians, their identities gain legitimacy in the eyes of the rest of the world. In other words, it is important that the youth are not only perceived for their "Indianness" abroad but also recognized as having a global Indianness that is compatible with a cosmopolitan and Western sensibility at home and abroad. These upper-class participants are involved in the production and consumption of this "transnational" Indian culture, which is largely created through their access to a networked society where new Internet- and social media-based technologies amplify and refashion old social hierarchies and networks.

The type of "global Indianness" that the Meridian youth were constructing is effectively captured in one of India's top-grossing, super-hit Hindi movies of 2011, *Zindagi Na Milegi Doobara*. Anjali Ram (2014) undertakes a textual analysis of this film in her book, *Consuming Bollywood*, to show how the protagonists of the film are producing a global Indian identity. I utilize Ram's analysis to shed light on the narratives of Meridian youth and the *appropriate Indianness* that is being constructed in their narratives. The basic plot of the movie *Zindagi* revolves around the lives of three young urban Indian men—Imran, Kabir, and Arjun. The three men have been best friends since childhood, and they meet in Spain to celebrate Kabir's bachelor party. This party involves a road trip through the scenic areas of Spain that is interspersed with adventurous extreme sports, such as parasailing and scuba diving.

Imran works as a copywriter in an advertising firm in Delhi, and Kabir is an affluent young man who runs a multinational business that he has inherited from his family. Arjun is a highly successful financial analyst who works in London. The female characters are similarly given an aura of being both Indian and global. Laila, who is played by the well-known British–Indian actress Katrina Kaif, is shown as having a generic "global identity." When Imran meets her for the first time, he mistakenly thinks she is Brazilian. Laila tells Imran that she has a hyphenated identity and that she is part Indian and part American and she lives in London.

Kabir's fiancée, Natasha, is an interior designer who is Indian but travels around the world with ease. Ram (2014) writes that Natasha frequently uses the word "Babe" in her conversation and wears clothing that symbolizes fashions of Indian elite youth and bears a resemblance to fashions advertised in foreign magazines such as *Vogue*. The third female character of the movie is Nuria, who is Spanish and is Laila's friend and somehow becomes included in the plot, thus highlighting the ease with which Indian identities can travel with other cultural identities without carrying the baggage of standing out or feeling foreign in Spain.

Ram (2014) writes that the central narrative plot of *Zindagi* occurs entirely in Europe, and this is not a new development because foreign locations in the West have frequently served as adding a glamorous background to Hindi movies. However, what is unique about *Zindagi* is that Spain as a cultural location becomes the *transnational space* in which three young Indians discover their "Indianness" abroad. They discover their "self" by facing their fears and by participating in adventurous sports such as scuba diving, parachute jumping, and participating in the "running of the bulls" ritual. These men find themselves confronting their fears and inhibitions and also reinterpreting the meaning of Indian traditions and parental and social expectations as they make their road trip across Spain. They realize that familial expectations, as well as their roles and responsibilities to be a "good Indian," can be hypocritical and restricting.

Unlike in Hindi movies of the past, Ram (2014) reminds us that in *Zindagi*, the West is not viewed as being immoral, materialistic, and highly sexualized but, rather, it is associated with values that foster individual decision-making and freedom that is unfettered by the force of traditions. Ram (2014) writes,

> The identity exploration in *Zindagi* is not a rehashing of the eternal, imperishable, Hindu/Indianness that is highlighted through difference with the West representing amoral modernity. . . . Rather Spain becomes the sphere within which the three male buddies "find themselves." . . . Their embrace of new, challenging, dare-devil experiences, their seemingly unlimited access to wealth, and effortless transnational travel signal a new, globalized, affluent, consumer-defined India. (pp. 184–185)

Although the three young urban Indian men in *Zindagi* reconstruct their identity in Spain, I argue that spaces such as Meridian in a neoliberal India provide a similar function. The participants of Meridian considered themselves as world-class Indian citizens because they, to some extent, believed that they were on par with youth from the United States and Western Europe. The main difference between the characters in *Zindagi* and the youth from Meridian is that the youth's college space had become an educational playground for them to experiment with alternative global modernities.

Consumer Citizenship: The Search for "World-Class" Indianness

The construction of global Indianness that was produced at Meridian did not grapple in any serious way with the failures of economic liberalization and the widening inequities it has created. The global Indianness that I saw being constructed at Meridian, and other similar spaces across several urban Indian cities, reverberated with an Indianness that was largely apolitical and devoid of a social justice orientation. Undoubtedly, there were several students I met at Meridian who were deeply committed to social causes, volunteering at several local non-governmental organizations, and taking courses that focused on social inequality and caste divisions. However, the majority of the students, while concerned about the growing poverty and injustices in India, seemed mostly interested in cultivating a neoliberal "global" identity that would benefit their lives and careers. It was a type of Indianness that Radhakrishnan (2011) had observed in the identities of young Indian IT professionals and knowledge workers. This type of global Indianness, she argues,

> collapses the dizzying diversity of religious and community practices within India into a singular kind of difference, just one more in a world panoply of global cultures. In an unexpected throwback to the discursive effects of Orientalism, Indian cultural production becomes oriented towards something singular and nationally agreed upon, even when only a few voices have agreed, or even been consulted. Indianness becomes again a cultural commodity to be produced and reproduced, not only for a Western gaze, but also for the consumption and display of Indian cosmopolitans the world over who care to partake. (p. 201)

A central part of the narrative of this commodified/Orientalized global Indianness is created by participating in acts of consumption of media, brands, fashions, and luxury goods that are considered "world class." Globalization, according to the transnational youth, had strengthened India's standing in the world, and now they view themselves as "no less" than their counterparts in the West—their identities and desires have become "world class."

These English-speaking upper-class and elite youth had created cultural reference points for self-making that were based on the transnational codes of fashion; brands; and media habits such as watching *Sex and the City*, *Friends*, and *Seinfeld*. What does the consumption of world-class commodities and being in world-class spaces mean for these young Indians? A hybrid world-class Indian identity consisted of having selves that could travel easily across borders—Indian youth would inhabit the same space as youth from other Western countries. Another part of having this world-class identity was structured around their desire to see India's infrastructure, such as roads, airports, educational institutions, theaters, housing, and sports stadiums, as equivalent to "First World spaces."

First, it is important to be clear that when Meridian youth use the concept of "world class," they are actually *not* referring to the world. They are invoking the practices, institutions, facilities, infrastructure, and the *culture* of America and Western Europe. Second, the idea of "world class" is being constructed in opposition to their perception that India had for a long time belonged to a "Third World" space or a country in which the living conditions were subpar and in most instances considered "third class." Third, the term "world class" at Meridian did not refer just to Euro-American standards of excellence but also to a new class of privileged Indian youth who had the financial capacity to travel to America and Europe and interact with youth from these "First World" countries. In essence, globalization had given the English-speaking, upper-class and elite families both the social capital and the structural legitimacy to cultivate "world-class" identities.

The youth at Meridian used their symbolic power and their transnational privileges to engage in practices that allowed them to create world-class narratives of themselves. In other words, their performance of "Indianness" needs to be recognized as "credible Indianness" that is compatible with a cosmopolitan and Western sensibility at home and abroad. In short, the narratives of these transnationally youth in India are deeply multivoiced and polyphonic.[6]

In summary, what the narrative analysis reveals is that the Meridian youth believed that although they were culturally different, globalization both as worldwide phenomenon and as discourse had created a certain "sameness" with other European and North American youth. During my focus group interviews, I asked a group of six students the following question: "Can I ask, are you closer in some ways socially and culturally to some of these people outside India?" All of the participants responded with a unanimous "Yes!" Akshay reflected the collective thinking of the group. He observed that exposure means that

we're different only in the way we think. . . . Sometimes if you try to associate with something which you would define as more Indian, you'd probably look at that as something alien, saying that you cannot associate yourself with being that Indian, because you're not.

Similarly, Malini, a 19-year-old participant from the group, further elaborated: "Wherever . . . if I meet my relatives, or my mum, elders or whatever, sometimes I feel a certain dissociation from their side saying that 'She has changed'."

This move to establish their equivalence with youth from the "First World" countries was seen as progressive and emancipatory: It would empower elite younger generations of Indians to interrogate the oppressive elements of tradition so as to reimagine their Indianness in a way that puts them on an even playing field with First World counterparts. This type of hybridity gave them the agency to re-create their dialogical stories where Indianness and Americaness, tradition and modernity, were constituted through each other and strategically employed. This exposure and constant negotiation with "globalization" gave them the freedom, for instance, to participate in the sexual and marriage revolution and emboldened them to give new meaning to the private sphere of romance, marriage, and sexuality.

Nadeem (2011) has noted that globalization works like a fugue or a derived counterpoint in a musical composition. The first line of the composition reveals the major theme of the music, and this is followed by a response or an answer that is similar to the main theme but nevertheless is presented in a distinctive key or a different note. This response or answer does not form a one-to-one correspondence with the major key but, rather, engages in a simulation or a counterpoint that has different characteristics. What we learn from these interviews is that shrinking of time and space has spurred on a complex connectivity between cultures and given rise to new forms of psychologies, lifestyles, and identities.

A small minority of upper-middle-class and elite youth were producing new and powerful narratives of their "ultimate global Indianness" that also circulated as "master narratives" (Hammack, 2011) in the popular imagination and across other classes. We know that narrative practices play a central role in shaping human development. They play a "pivotal role in binding the individual into a cultural world and binding the meaning of this world into the individual's mind" (Brockmeier, 2012, p. 439). As culture and its accompanying psychological constructions of self get dislocated or disembedded from specific territories and place, they also simultaneously get inserted in new places, localities, and territories through individual narratives and stories. The analyses of the narratives of transnational youth show that the disembedding and embedding or the de-territorialization and re-territorialization of cultures do not happen in a vacuum. Instead, their cultural meanings are uprooted from one locale to another, and they resurface in individual stories that highlight their narrative engagements with identity.

NOTES

1. While it has become somewhat the norm for urban middle- and upper-class women to wear shorts, there are still strong taboos and social codes about *lajja* (shame and purity) that prohibit women from exposing their body, so shorts tend to be longer than those found in Western fashion. However, reading *Simply Mumbai*, one may get the impression that it is quite common for urban Indian women to be seen in shorts. Journalist Jhilmil Mothiar (2008), author of the story for this fashion segment, states, "The pair of shorts that we've loved and sometimes outgrown never really went off the racks. This season, it's hitting wardrobes with renewed gusto—and in all lengths. From short shorts in all the spring colors, knee length ones in linen and corduroy, to the hottest and newest kid on the block, the jumpsuit, it's all here for you to bag. Pair them with flip-flops, gladiator sandals or pumps. As toted by celebrities internationally, the seeming innocent pair of shorts is a red carpet hit too. Dress up your black satin shorts with a party shirt and sink in your favorite five inches."

2. Meridian is not the actual name of the college and is being used to preserve anonymity.

3. Vishakha Desai, in an op-ed for India's English newspaper *The Hindu*, makes a very persuasive case for why the Indian education system needs to be grounded in a liberal arts curriculum. Her point is that the vocational training institutes and the top-notch Indian institutes since Independence have both always privileged the teaching of math, science, and technical education over a liberal arts curriculum that is rooted in humanities and the social science. There is a growing recognition that a liberal arts curriculum should be integrated within all curricula, including vocational schools (http://www.thehindu.com/opinion/op-ed/liberal-arts-education-in-india/article7190808.ece).

4. The students very often conflated Americanization and Westernization because American culture and Western culture were frequently synonymously associated with each other. The presence of "American" popular culture in its various forms was quite a ubiquitous feature of the Indian media landscape.

5. *Femina* is a popular Indian magazine that focuses on women's issues such as health, family, beauty, and fashion.

6. Hermans (1996, p. 44) reminds us that dynamic movement between different *I* positions in a story opens up possibilities for the dialogical self to show "individual differences." Therefore, he emphasizes that within any dialogical self, some positions may be temporary and others can occupy a more permanent place. There are some positions that are supported and others that are condemned by institutions, traditions, and various collective groups. Many positions take on an imaginary character and frequently enter our imagined and "real" selves even when we have no direct face-to-face contact with them. Finally, some positions fluctuate between positive and negative dimensions. Some are enjoyable, affirming, and validating, whereas others are irritating, intimidating, and threatening. The idea of self with its emphasis on multiplicity and dynamically shifting meanings captures the different kinds of dialogical negotiations one has to undertake in the wake of departure, dislocation, and movement from being on a familiar territory to being a stranger and a foreigner in a distant location.

CHAPTER 6

Outsourcing the Self

Work, Love, and Money in the Call Center Culture

Meera, a 25-year-old woman from Guwahati, Assam, had moved from Delhi to Pune after working briefly at the Dell Computer call center near New Delhi. I interviewed her in Pune, where she was sharing a room with her friend Ruth, another call center worker, in a small apartment near Quarter Gate. Meera told me that while growing up in Guwahati, she had learned "voice modulations" and "correct pronunciations" by "watching these ladies on BBC." In preparation for getting a call center job, Meera told me that when she was in college, she would imitate the BBC news anchors on television. When she practiced the British accent, she said that her "lips trembled with a lot of expression" and then the "accent stuck" with her.[1] Meera explained that for her, globalization meant that she got a job in a call center and broke away from the "cocoon" of her family, relatives, and friends. Working in a call center had forced her to face the outside world.

The interview began with Meera telling me about her initial interactions with customers from America. It was a life-altering moment as she felt a rush of excitement when the first calls came in from America. She described her initial interactions in the Dell call center as being a "whoa!" moment as she experienced speaking over the phone to people from a *foreign* country. However, as Meera got deeper into the call center work, her supervisor told her that her conversations with American customers were not up to standards and she needed to improve her communication style. Her supervisor said that her calls had a dimension of "no confidence at all." Meera found the American customers quite demanding, and their questions and comments rattled her. During her low moments at work, Meera's colleagues reminded her that in her daily conversations with others, she came across as a confident speaker, but somehow when the call beeped into her headphone from the United States, she became scared. Meera explained:

> So that's when I started realizing where things lacked, so I started realizing that they're just human beings—I don't need to get scared just because they're Americans. Because, they're very demanding. Americans, as people, are extremely demanding, and they expect the best. Not like Indians who would settle for the second best, or maybe the third in line . . . and it used to be very intimidating earlier.

Meera's supervisors were impressed with her affable personality and her strong work ethic, so they put her through an intensive training in voice modulation, accent reduction, and intercultural training in "American culture." The trainers also told her that she needed to "be herself" during the conversations and that she should express her individuality with "a smile on her face."

At the time of the interview, Meera was feeling confident of pulling off the scripted conversations that were demanded of her when she was on the floor. When I asked her how her life had changed as a result of being in a call center, Meera told me that she had become confident and independent. However, the most profound change occurred when she realized that Americans were not how they were depicted in movies, "and what you see in movies does not happen in real life. So we had this very glossy picture of the people there. But I did not really know them as human beings." This was a significant revelation to her, and she commented that people in America are very ordinary—"that the person is someone just like me, very real-life." Her perception that Americans were not how she had imagined them to be was a learning moment that made her feel both culturally similar and distant from her American customers.

Meera wanted confirmation from me that the knowledge she had gained about Americans and "American culture" was accurate. She asked me questions about how Americans lived their lives in suburbs, why their marriages failed, and how they had acquired a sense of superiority—which she saw as a desirable trait. Meera also had to undergo various training workshops in which she was taught how to rework her emotions when she had to deal with demanding clients. Many call center agents who work in the transnational service sector have to undergo training in mimicking accents and related soft skills training that supposedly increases their communication effectiveness. These call center "culture" workshops give rise to new subjectivities as young Indians internalize the psychological discourses of time management, self-actualization, creativity, and generally becoming professionally driven, autonomous individuals. Meera told me that moving to Pune and living by herself had created new experiences for her. She could wear "Western dresses," go to bars, interact with men, and embody what Vasavi (2008), who has extensively studied the call center work culture in India, has called a "strongly Westernized and individualized orientation" (p. 223).

Meera is part of a growing brigade of transnational, cheap labor who work in the call center industry, and her story, to some extent, upends the norms of the traditional, urban Indian family structure. Her narrative emerges out of the intersections of local, colonial, postcolonial, and global historic moments. Growing up in a working-class family and making the journey from Guwahati to Delhi and now Pune, Meera's identity has been shaped by colonial and postcolonial legacies of studying English, mimicking BBC anchors, and now working in a global call center. Two powerful cultural forces shape her hybrid narrative. On the one hand, as a call center worker for Dell, she makes $200 a month, making her part of a global economy that is dependent on cheap labor, low wages, and exploitative work conditions. On the other hand, the call center job has given Meera the identity of being an independent woman who "has made it on her own." She has a measure of control over her life, and she gives financial support to her family in Guwahati.

Meera struggled with the accent training and voice modulations that were required at work, and she found American customers to be extremely demanding. At one point in her fledgling call center career, she had lost confidence in her ability to take calls from abroad, but the excitement of getting that "first call" from an American customer spurred her to improve her accent. As Meera negotiates between the expectations of family and work, she experiences what Basi (2009) refers to as "virtual migration" and a widening of "the discursive practice of identity construction" (pp. 159–160). This emergent dialogical self among urban middle-class youth is embedded in the practices of globalization. These global–local identities, according to Basi, reflect "a biography and a trajectory from the past to the anticipated future. But it is in the physical world, grounded in the local, that identities take on stronger meaning" (p. 160).

In this chapter, I investigate the process of identity construction or biographic narration in the stories of call center workers whom I interviewed. In particular, this chapter is concerned with the following questions: What are the contested notions of Indianness that emerge in the narratives produced by call center workers? How do young women who work at the call centers navigate between new freedoms of mobility, independence, and traditional expectations of gender roles? How are neoliberal, American psychological discourses of self incorporated to create an identity that is individualized yet rooted in a familial notion of Indianness? The narratives that I examine in this chapter are created out of an asymmetrical context of power as young Indians work as "subjects" of a global economy who primarily serve "First World" customers. The interviews reflect how tradition and modernity, mimicry and authenticity, collude with each other to dialogically create new middle-class subjectivities. I conducted interviews with more than 15 young call center workers in

Pune, ranging in age from 21 to 28 years, and in some cases I also interviewed participants who were older than age 30 years. Several of them had grown up in Delhi, Calcutta, Nagpur, and Guwahati and had migrated to Pune to work in the growing call center sector. In addition, I interviewed a chief executive officer (CEO) of a well-known accounting firm and a business processing office (BPO) and also interviewed an English language trainer, a journalist, three parents of call center workers, and several other young information technology (IT) workers to get a well-rounded sense of the call center "culture" in Pune. I use stories gleaned from 20 interviews to analyze how young workers at the call centers navigate between new freedoms of mobility, independence, workplace expectations and traditional cultural expectations.

YOUTH AS CYBER LABOR: INDIA'S DEMOGRAPHIC DIVIDEND

There are approximately 2 million—mostly young urban—Indians working in call centers and BPOs in India (Mirchandani, 2012). The call centers and back offices, according to Tharoor (2007), are not just providing coolie labor for computer-related troubleshooting, airline reservations, and automatic billing. Rather, Tharoor proudly proclaims that urban Indian youth are analyzing actuarial work for British companies, interpreting magnetic resonance imaging charts for American hospitals, managing consulting companies for global firms in the United States and Europe, and writing software for the airline industry. This remarkable economic acceleration and the concurrent outsourcing of both low- and high-skilled jobs from American companies to India compelled Thomas Friedman (2004), an ardent advocate for free-market globalization, to write in one of his *New York Times* columns, "When I was growing up, my parents told me, 'Finish your dinner. People in China and India are starving.' I want to tell my daughter, 'Finish your homework. People in India and China are starving for your job.'" Friedman presents an overly positive account of the call center work culture in India and overlooks the ways in which the Indian youth are being exploited as cheap labor.

The phenomenon of globalization, as such, also presents an historic moment for psychology to study how youth cultural practices are being reconfigured in non-Western and non-European spaces. Indian call center workers on average earn between 10,000 and 20,000 rupees per month, which is the equivalent of about $2 per hour, or $5,000 per year. Because India's per capita income is approximately $1,000, a call center salary of $5,000 per year places these youth in the middle class category. The Indian call center industry has succeeded because of cultural factors such as a large youth population, fluency with the English language, low-cost wages, and the time differences between India and both the United Kingdom and the United States. Most call center workers in India earn about one-sixth or less of the salary earned by workers in the United States and the United Kingdom, and the average salaries in Indian call centers range from $150 to $400 per month (see Marantz, 2011).

Reena Patel (2010), an anthropologist, writes that the creation of transnational call centers in India primarily came about because India could provide low-cost, English-speaking, educated labor. These operations came into existence as transnational corporations decided to employ 24-hour workers across various time zones. Drawing on Barbara Adam's work, Patel notes that corporations have now begun a process in which they have the power to colonize time by setting the Western clock as a standard commodity. As Patel notes, "*Temporal imperialism* and *temporal entrapment* have also been used to define the shifting relationship between the timescapes of the Global North and the Global South" (p. 28, emphasis in original). The restructuring of the US immigration policy led to the reduction of H-1B visas along with a sharp economic downturn that was experienced by the IT sector in the United States in 2000. This was one of the main reasons that US-based firms outsourced highly skilled engineering jobs and low-skilled call center jobs to India. Patel concludes that the call centers were created in India "essentially, because the Indian worker could not migrate to the United States, the work migrated to India" (p. 29). The Indian government also enabled the presence of call centers in India by removing import licensing requirements and moving from a "permit Raj" to a liberal economy with fewer bureaucratic constraints being imposed on multinational corporations.

The deregulation of the telecommunication industry, the policies of corporate downsizing in the West, new technological advancements, trade reforms, the privatization of the IT industry, and the creation of a new consumer-oriented middle class led to the creation of call centers in India. A call center is typically defined as "a dedicated operation in which computer-utilizing employees receive inbound- or make outbound-telephone calls with those call processes and are controlled either by and Automatic Call Distributions (ACD) system or predictive dialing system" (Taylor & Bain, 1999, p. 102). There are two types of call centers throughout India: One sector is called the "voice processes," and the other sector is called the "non-voice processes" or, as it is commonly referred to, the BPO. Thus, the common acronym that describes both these processes is ITES-BPO, which stands for "information technology enabled services–business process outsourcing" (Basi, 2009). The standard night-shift hours in a transnational call centers in India can range from 10:00 p.m. to 6:00 a.m. or from 8:00 p.m. to 4:00 p.m. The non-voice or business processing work such as data entry can be conducted during normal work hours in India. This service sector is expanding in India because the work hours are usually 9:00 a.m. to 5:00 p.m. and the workday is well suited to the local Indian work conditions. The government website "Business Portal of India" (http://www.archive.india.gov.in/business) estimates that in 2008 the

Indian call center and BPO sector was worth $52 billon, and the average age of employees in the ITES industry was between 25 and 30 years. There are seven main locations of call centers in India: Bangalore, Mumbai, NCR (National Capital Region, which consists of New Delhi, Noida, Gurgaon, Faridabad, Haryana, Uttar Pradesh, and Rajasthan), Hyderabad, Pune, Chennai, and Kolkata. In 2004, NCR had 53 call centers; Mumbai had 45 call centers; and each of the major cities, such as Bangalore and Chennai, had about 35 small and large call centers (Basi, 2009). Pune is one of the cities that experienced an urban churn starting in early 2000, and it has about 12–15 major call centers, including WIPRO, Infosys, WNS Global Services, IBM Daksh, Convergys, Mphasis, Capital India, Vodafone, Accenture Services Ltd., GAIA ITES Pvt. Ltd., and several other small ones.

The city of Pune is known as an educational center, and it attracts students from all over India, who come to Pune to study engineering, management, medicine, and communication studies. The call center and IT industry boomed in India in the mid-1990s and continued to rise at a feverish pace until 2008. Pune became very attractive to multinational corporations because it had a strong middle class; a large number of educated, English-speaking Indians; and provided easy access through transportation. In the past two decades, the city has also witnessed a growth in engineering colleges, technology industries, and other educational institutions that provide training in language-based services and soft skills, such as English language learning, accent reduction, and voice modulation. The attrition and "burnout" rates in the call center industry are between 40% and 60%, so there is a constant demand for additional English-speaking, college-educated workers (Ramesh, 2004).

VIJAY'S STORY: BRANDED CLOTHES, BRITISH ACCENT, AND "INDIAN AT HEART"

Vijay's story of becoming a call center worker in many ways reflects the lives of many other young, English-speaking, middle-class, urban call center workers. He grew up in a joint family that used to own a profitable shop selling bicycles in the heart of Pune city. Vijay's grandfather had started the bicycle business in the 1950s, when the bicycle was one of the most common modes of transportation in India. As a child, he had lived with his grandfather, grandmother, uncle and aunt, and cousins in a midsized apartment in a "colony" where many Punjabi businessmen had arrived after the partition of India in 1947. Over the years, Vijay's grandfather, grandmother, and uncle died. After his aunt moved out of his house, Vijay's father, Ashok, became the sole inheritor of the house and the shop. The old building that housed the bike shop, like many structures built during the colonial era, collapsed during an unusually intense monsoon season.

Vijay's family sued the owner of that building for compensation in the mid-1990s, but the case moved slowly through the bureaucracy of the High Court, and it took almost a decade for the family to recuperate some of its investments. Vijay, who was 25 years old at the time of the interview, had two sisters; this nuclear family had experienced the brunt of the financial upheavals due to the loss of the bicycle business. However, Vijay's family had inherited the family's apartment, and they regarded themselves as having "good karma" that at least they did not have to shell out money for rent or a monthly mortgage.

Vijay's father, Ashok, did not have the financial means to buy or rent a shop to open a new bike business, so instead he and his wife started a catering business from their home. This modest business brought them a relatively small income, but it was enough for them to meet their monthly expenses. Vijay had competed his undergraduate education in the "commerce stream" at a night college and had been unable to secure a steady job for several years. He was unemployed for long stretches of time and was always searching for a job that paid him a decent salary.

The call center and BPO companies were expanding in Pune and were recruiting a large number of the educated unemployed youth. Vijay's good social skills and his basic fluency in English secured him an entry-level job at the call center, and at the time of my interview with him, he had completed 4 years as a call center worker. He was very eager to share his story with me. We decided to meet at a coffee shop in one of the new office complexes that represented the ongoing urban expansion of Pune.

"Tight Tops" and the Decline of Indian Culture

I arrived at the Café Coffee Day that was located in a small office complex on Boat Club Road, which is one of the most expensive residential areas in Pune. The first floor of the main building housed newly built upscale restaurants, such as Mainland china, La Dolce Vita, Moti Mahal, and Sigri. Café Coffee Day was tucked inside the foyer of the entrance to the building and had a scattering of chairs and tables and an efficient wait staff. We ordered our lattes, and I began our conversation by asking Vijay, "How do you define Indianness?" He responded, "I can smoke, right?" Then he lit up his cigarette and, without the slightest hesitation, he launched into a rather bombastic critique of the call center workers and the youth of his generation. He bemoaned the lack of patriotism in his generation and the call center owners who expect Indians to work during major Indian holidays and cultural festivals, such as Republic Day, Holi, and Diwali. In his view, although the corporations were located in India, their business practices were created to satisfy customers who were residing in Europe and America. He told me that Indians should not forget their culture. I asked him, "What is their culture?" Vijay pointed out that he could see the cultural deterioration in urban areas by observing how college-aged women behaved in public. He said young women have started smoking, and both young men and women prefer live-in relationships rather than staying with their parents. He offered his reasons for the current "decay" in Indian culture:

> The way the females behave nowadays, wearing tight tops, and wearing clothes which are not decent enough . . . see, even if you wear Western clothes, there's no problem. But there are kinds of dresses. For example, wearing a tube kind of a bra, and showing people their breasts. 40% of their breasts are—specially going into pubs and all. Smooching with guys, kissing with guys in the pubs. I don't think that belongs to the Indian culture.

Vijay frequently visited the nightclubs in Pune and commented on the decline of "Indian culture" as a result of youth participating in the social events that were happening as part of the city nightlife. He had seen the call center and BPO industry evolve within a short span of time, so he spoke with the confidence of being an insider and someone who was an eyewitness to the cultural shifts that were occurring in his generation.

Marriages in India, he continued, are coming apart because husbands and wives are traveling to different cities for BPO jobs and they do not see each other so they are having extramarital affairs: "Some females sleep under high-posted guys for promotions. Some females do that." Vijay believed that new money and women experimenting with drugs, sex, and alcohol were the large-scale cultural changes that were corrupting Indian youth. He advised me to see the Bollywood movie *Corporate*, which he believed captured the decline of Indian culture and values. The call center jobs in Pune had provided new opportunities to make good money, but those jobs were largely considered low skilled and highly stressful. Vijay began his workday at 10:00 p.m. and returned home at 7:00 a.m., and the only time he had to communicate with his friends and parents was during the weekend. When at work, Vijay wore a headset, receiving up to 50 calls a day from customers from the United Kingdom. Vijay viewed globalization and the mushrooming of call centers and IT technology companies as a miracle that had altered his standard of living. When Vijay's father lost his bicycle business, Vijay did not have a professional education that might have allowed him to acquire a job as a computer engineer, doctor, lawyer, accountant, or entry-level IT professional, so the call center work beckoned him. His relatives reminded him often of his failures and his directionless future, "At one time, nobody used to ask [about the well-being] of our family. . . . I just bought a car for myself, and everybody started upgrading my family."

John Miller, Mercedes, and the Removal of Mother Tongue Influence

Vijay raised his hand and spoke in a disconcerted voice when he shared several stories about how his relatives and friends had told him that his life was not worth much and he "was not worth doing this and worth wearing that." In contrast, today he was independent, and he believed that he had proved his detractors wrong. He started out with a salary of Rs. 7000 ($100) per month and was now making Rs. 30,000 ($350) per month. Vijay proudly announced to me that today he had an identity and status in the world. He made a gesture toward himself with an expression of contentment on his face, "For example, I don't wear anything unbranded . . . Yesterday I just purchased two pants of John Miller. I wear Provogue, Lee." The call center salary was not just about securing a job or having a new source of money to fulfill his needs. Instead, his narrative demonstrated that he had become part of a global network of young workers and had attained *psychological freedom* from his family and relatives. His work, branded clothes, and a secondhand car gave him the feeling that he now belonged to the middle class.

Vijay insisted that now when he is sitting with "high-profile people," his branded clothes give him confidence, composure, and standing. He told me that in the corporate world, everyone is reading everyone through their clothes, cars, and how they speak. Vijay asserted, "When you speak in front of managers, when you're sitting with high-profile people, you come to know what you are." He insisted that the residential areas in which you live, the house you own, and the car you drive are the personal identity markers in a new India. Vijay wanted to impress upon me that globalization may have weakened Indian cultural values, but India has new material symbols of foreign cars, credit cards, and easy money. We are now sitting near Boat Club Road, he notes, which is a prestigious location.

He then reminded me that if I walk around Boat Club Road for a couple of hours, I will find "at least 10 Mercedes-Benz S Class, Limousine, Pagero, Ferrari, name the car, you have in India today. We drive the best cars of the world today." I asked Vijay why branded cars are important in India. Vijay said that cars represent India's new wealth and status in the world. Once again, he made his point by telling me a story about his "Sardar"[2] childhood friend, Vicky, whose father was a well-known financier in Dubai. Vicky, he declared in a long monologue that seemed reminiscent of a hero in a Bollywood movie, beats all odds and goes from hero to zero. Instead, Vijay presented an anticlimactic ending by telling me that Vicky used to ride a simple scooter at one time, but his father had gifted him a Mercedes S class and he currently has assets worth a million dollars in India. Globalization, Vijay avowed, is about having status and money, "because at the end of the day, the power of money matters a lot." Vijay's dreams were about experiencing the neoliberal power of money, finding a working wife, a new flat, moving out of his class location, and becoming an operations manager responsible for the entire floor of call center agents.

Vijay got his first job at the call center after doing four rounds of interviews. The first round, called a "jumbled HR interview," is very critical in getting a call center job. The human resources personnel ask candidates questions that force them to talk about themselves. The success of call center workers depends on their conversational skills, their ability to placate a distressed customer, and especially their ability to speak English that does not have *mother tongue influence* (MTI). Within the call center context, MTI is basically described as the varied ways in which the speech patterns and vocal intonations of one's native language, such as the Punjabi or Gujarati or any Indian language, influence the individual's English accent and vocal inflections.

I probed further and asked Vijay to explain what happens when a candidate has MTI. He answers, "The mother tongue influence is not acceptable at all. For example, if 'e-f-f-e-c-t-i-v-e' is 'effective,' and a Maharashtrian, right now we are seated in the State called Maharashtra, he will pronounce it as 'effect-tew.' Most people from the United States, United Kingdom, Australia, or any country, Vijay emphasizes, will sometimes not understand Indians because of their strong MTIs.

"Bloody Indians" and the Racism of Call Centers

Vijay explains that companies want agents who can speak with an American, a British, or a neutral accent. If they can pull off the mimicry or imitation, then there are many benefits, but what these call centers want is agents "who can speak neutral English." In India, there are more than 22 languages and more than 2,000 dialects; thus, Vijay argues, the influence of MTI is widespread, and most candidates do not make it through the first round of interviews. For candidates interested in seeking jobs at call centers, several major educational institutes across India provide training to candidates so they can master the call center speech and the requisite MTIs can be erased. The second round of interviews is called a "voice and accent round," in which the candidates are judged on their sentence construction, command of grammar and syntax, and interpersonal skills. Thereafter, they take some basic math, English, and logical reasoning tests.

Undoubtedly, the selection process is competitive, but Vijay made it sound far more challenging and ruthless—"Because all these are elimination rounds. You do not clear one round, you're out." The fourth round, he told me, is a final interview with the assistant vice president, and then the candidate is selected. One challenge that every call center worker must be prepared for is to be subjected to racial abuses and taunts that customers from abroad may hurl at them. Vijay noted that most customers are demanding but not racist, but if the clients are not satisfied with the interaction, they will sometimes resort to making racist remarks: "'You bloody Indians,' yes, they do speak that way!" I asked him specifically how many such irate calls he handles on a daily basis. He said that he has his share of angry, racist interactions on a weekly basis, but most customers do not use racist language. He interrupted his train of thought to remark that just the previous day an older women from the United Kingdom told him she did not want to speak to him because he was an Indian. I asked him to recall the details of the incident. The customer asked him where was he speaking from, and Vijay clarified:

> I said, "Where am I speaking from? You are speaking to . . . I'm in India." She said, "Don't mind, no offense. I don't want to speak to an Indian. Please transfer/divert my call to. . . ." So what I did, even I said, "No problem. I did not take any offense. That's your call. You provide me your call back number. I'll email them and I'll request them to call you back."

Vijay considered handling such difficult calls an achievement, and his supervisors praised him for his efforts. He said if an agent does not handle these calls properly, then the first step is that they take him or her aside and do "counseling," and then the agent will have to "Y-Jack" with someone else.

A "Y-Jack" step essentially involves undertaking a series of remedial training lessons with a call center agent, where the supervisor puts on headphones so he or she can simultaneously listen to the conversation the agent is having with the customer. Vijay told me that the remedial counseling sessions also involve doing psychology-based, self-help courses on building confidence and discovering one's inner potential. If, after 3 months, the worker is unable to improve his or her interaction with the customer, he or she is fired.

Vijay said that a successful call center agent is someone who can form a connection with the customer and is able to answer customer questions clearly. The agent should be able to maintain his or her composure and speak clearly in the language that any foreign customer can understand. I asked Vijay if he or anyone in his company had retaliated against a customer. Vijay said that retaliation or speaking back even when the customer is abusing the call center agent is strictly forbidden; however, he recalled one incident in which an American customer called and ranted about the primitive and underdeveloped conditions in India: "I have heard there are still bullock carts in India." Vijay was extremely proud when his colleague defended India with the following response: "Excuse me, sorry to interrupt, but today we drive the best cars of the world. We drive Pagero, we drive Mercedes-Benz S Class, we drive Honda City, we drive Corolla . . . name the car, and we have it in India." The influx of new imported cars was a point to which Vijay returned quite often in the interview, and he equated the significant rise in the number of cars on the road with India's arrival on the global stage. In his view, the availability of cars symbolized India's emergence from primitiveness to advanced development, and that was Vijay's colleague's main rebuttal to the caller's description of India as being "primitive." Several of the youth to whom I had spoken also often reminded me that one of the differences between "old" and "new" India was the very visible presence of both foreign-made and Indian cars on the roads throughout most urban cities and smaller towns.

Vijay admitted that although the pay from call centers is competitive, the work is extremely demanding, involving fielding 50 or up to 75 calls in some instances during a shift. The night shift is often characterized as the graveyard shift, to accommodate the American or European schedule, and workers often do not see daylight for weeks because they sleep during the day and even on weekends. This work is intense, and over time it takes a toll on their bodies and their relationships because their work schedules do not match those of their family and friends. Vijay considered working in a call center as a temporary assignment so he could gain enough experience to move into management.

Being a team leader was the next step for Vijay, but he ultimately wanted to have a career like that of Mr. Jitendra, who started as a door-to-door collection agent, became a team leader, assistant manager, operations manager, and then a regional manager, and is now CEO of a multinational BPO and call center operations in India and Nepal. As our conversation was concluding, Vijay regretted that he might have been too negative in his evaluations of the call center culture. He wanted me to relay some positive messages back to American citizens and "my" government back in the United States. He straightened himself, put his head toward the recorder, and then he made a brief speech:

> I would like to really thank the United States of America for giving Indians a chance to make their bread and butter, and I would request them not to stop the BPOs in India, because if the BPOs are stopped, the economy of India will . . . people will not even be able to have their two meals. Secondly, the economy would totally be—I can't get the word—wiped out.

Vijay' story is polyphonic, exhibiting a range of positions that are shaped by contexts of disparities and asymmetrical power relationships between "First World" and "Third World" economies. He is aware that his job is dependent on the American and British corporations and to some extent his newly acquired class status is also connected to a global economy that is being controlled by forces outside India.

MADHURI AND NAMRATA'S STORIES: GENDER, AGENCY, AND "GOOD MONEY"

In 2005, I met Madhuri, a 25-year-old woman who had been recently divorced, had moved to Pune from Delhi, and was working as a human resources manager for a local software development company that had grown from 300 to 1,800 employees within a short period of time. Madhuri and her parents had experienced long stretches of conflict between them because her parents had a difficult time accepting her divorce from her husband—an officer in the Navy. Her parents lived in a small town in Kerala, India, where the stigma of divorce typically brought shame and dishonor to the family.

Marriage and the Stigma of Divorce

Madhuri had moved to Pune to further her career and live as a single woman, where her status of being divorced did not carry such a heavy social stigma. She told me that her life story did not map onto the wishes of her parents, and they blamed her Westernized and "Anglicized" friends for causing her divorce:

> So they, in some ways, my parents blame me for the marriage not working out. They think that I got my priorities mixed up and I let my career manage my life. My mother has a problem that most of my friends are Christians. So she thinks I've become very Anglicized and that I've lost my roots completely. So my parents think I'm close to being an, you know, atheist.

Madhuri viewed most marriages in India as being stifling for women—where their identity was primarily determined by their roles as wives and mothers and everyday life had to be negotiated within a patriarchal cultural space. She was clear that she did not want her aspirations and desires to become secondary to those of her husband. Madhuri told me that she did not want a relationship in which her husband had power and authority over her decisions and individual desires; "And, secondly, for me . . . how do I put it? I didn't see marriage as the end of my own identity. My identity was equally important."

The search for her identity, outside the confines of marriage, has meant living separately from both her parents and her former husband and moving from a conservative small town in Kerala to Delhi and now Pune, where she held an executive position in the human resource management division. Madhuri's primary responsibility at her company was to facilitate meetings with upper-level management so there was open communication and transparency between different departments, team leaders, and technical personnel. In addition, Madhuri also worked as an English language trainer to help employees who could not communicate effectively in English and needed help learning "correct pronunciations." At the time of the interview, Madhuri was working with a large number of software engineers and management personnel who were mainly from small towns of India and needed English language lessons.

During the interview, Madhuri told me that most of the employees she had trained were males from conservative families, and they had very little experience working with women colleagues. She described these men as being "socially awkward in front of women" because they had lived their lives "straitjacketed" by tradition and small town customs. For many new high-skilled migrants from India's small towns, living in a metropolitan city such as Pune or Mumbai was similar to experiencing a culture shock. She said,

> I was the only woman there so it sort of made them feel odd. And certain things they find it odd that it comes from me. I mean, like, let's say if you talk about (beer), for instance, you know, the (non-English speaking youth pronounce the) word "b-e-a-r"? Most (English-speaking) people pronounce it as "bee-uh." So the way I choose to correct it as, "Beer is what you drink." So that they remember.

The coworkers that she was training were shocked to know that she drank beer and were taken aback by her public declaration of her liking for beer.

Madhuri believed that cultural change in India was redefining what it meant to be a middle-class Indian woman. She believed that financial independence was not the only reason why women were feeling more empowered in urban India, but that they had more choices in terms of seeking employment in call centers, airlines, and IT companies so that gender roles both outside and inside the home were undergoing change. Her stint as an instructor teaching English language skills to youth who were seeking to gain employment in call centers in Delhi had profoundly altered her perceptions of how the youth of her generation were different from previous generations. She remarked that her generation of women are open to experimenting with different kinds of relationships—live-in and short term—and when couples face hurdles or conflicts, they are likely to go their separate ways. Madhuri commented that when she worked in Delhi, "I discovered that this concept of live-in relationships was a direct fallout of call centers." She referred to New Delhi as a melting pot of cultures where young men and women from all areas of India were coming to Noida and Gurgaon,[3] which was a growing hub for IT companies, call centers, BPOs, and other IT-related industries in India. As an instructor, she spent months training the large number of aspiring call center workers who came from families that had very limited financial means and, relatedly, limited English-language skills.

During the training course, Madhuri became friendly with these young students, and she witnessed remarkable positive changes in their self-identities— how they dressed, spoke, and interacted with others. She claimed that these youth were being transformed by their search for call center and BPO jobs in Delhi and by the experience of living in a city, sharing a room with other students, working odd jobs, traveling by bus, and finding romance and sexual intimacy in the city. Madhuri emphasized that the call center workers who came from modest means had achieved a certain measure of independence from their families. She also mentioned that young women who worked in call centers had developed a reputation of being promiscuous and "loose girls."

Compared to previous generations of women, Madhuri stated that young women in call centers were out more often in public spaces with their colleagues in buses, office spaces, bars, clubs, and so on. These young Indians from middle-class families, Madhuri emphasized, "all came with big dreams of making it big in a call center." During her interactions with these young men and women, she also noticed the dark side of the call center culture—where youth were misusing their new freedom in her view: They were living their lives on their own terms, without having to be accountable to their parents or other family members.

Namrata's Story: From Housewife to Call Center Worker

Namrata, a 38-year-old middle-class Hindu woman, worked for a call center that sold cell phone service to customers in the United Kingdom. Having been a housewife for almost 15 years, she had entered the workforce after her husband had become unemployed. Namrata was from a traditional Hindu family where the idea of *bahu* (daughter-in-law) and *beti* (daughter) working outside the realm of the home was considered a sign that the *pati* (husband) and other *aadmi* and *khandaan* (men and family) were not capable of taking care of the family. However, during the past 4 years, call centers in Pune, such as Cybage, Convergys, Mphasis, and Msource, had become the new avatars of capitalism that had hired thousands of women such as Namrata. She worked in Pune in a sprawling high-tech park near an urban residential township called Kalyani Nagar.

Namrata has been one of the beneficiaries of the outsourcing industry in India. She was educated in a convent school called St. Anne's in Pune and was employed at her current call center after she gave four successful interviews. Namrata opened her conversation with the following thoughts:

> I had many ups and downs in my life and there was a need for me to go out and look for a job. Times have changed . . . because of this globalization. I have work—a part-time job and money. . . . The people who are at my call center are mostly housewives. My father is the one who came for the interviews.

Namrata's father was supportive of her decision to work at a call center because he acknowledged that Indian society was changing and so were his *purane khayalat* (old-fashioned ideas). The men and women employed by these call centers were usually young and worked 10–12 hours during the night shift. Namrata elaborated on the few customers from Britain who used racist, profane, and abusive language to express their frustration at job losses in local counties in England as a result of the outsourcing of jobs to India. Namrata said,

> Last week, I had a customer who told me that Indians are criminals. Your standards of living are low. He was using four-letter words in every sentence. He was abusive and he used foul language that I can't say to you. We do get some irate customers from time to time.

Namrata's story is an interesting study within the context of the Hindu family. She is the sole wage earner in a traditional Punjabi household, and the power dynamics within her family had shifted considerably since she joined the call center. Namrata's self is entwined in a number of complex sociocultural relationships. She resists the patriarchal structure of her traditional family by working outside the house to support her two children and husband.

At work, Namrata becomes Lisa—a pseudonym given by her company in order to have effective communication with her British customers. On the one hand, she feels emancipated by gaining financial independence, whereas on the other hand, she bemoans the invasion of "Western culture" in Pune as "live-in relationships" and "high divorce rates" are becoming common. While occasionally she may be subjected to racist abuse from irate customers residing in England, she accepts it as part of her workload. Namrata feels independent by defining herself as a working woman in a multinational company. However, she is also going through a period of reconstruction and reflection in her life. She regrets discontinuing her education immediately after her marriage, and her new financial and psychological independence has altered the traditional hierarchy in her family.

Madhu, a 28-year-old single woman whom I interviewed, echoed several of the themes mentioned by Namrata. She is on the marriage market, and Madhu's mother is looking out for marriage proposals for her daughter. However, Madhu believes that working at the call center in Kalyani Nagar has decreased her chances of getting good marriage proposals because women who work at the call centers are viewed as liberal and sexually permissive. Madhu told me that this new generation of men and their families want a working spouse, but they do not want someone who works the night shift. She further elaborated how these families want all the "good money" that is brought through these jobs at the multinational companies by *bhaus* (daughter-in-laws). Yet, they expect the women to play the role of dutiful wife and mother during the evening.

CALL CENTERS AND NARRATIVES OF
INDIVIDUALIZED INDIANNESS

Despite the stigma associated with call center work, Madhu continued to work in the call center because it gave her a professional "identity." She moved up rapidly through the corporate ladder of the call center to become a quality control manager, where her job was to inspect the quality of the interactions between the agents and the call center workers on the floor. The cultural forces of globalization were, bit by bit, altering the social identities and the family dynamics in urban India. Like Namrata and Madhu, there were huge swathes of the middle-class, urban Indian population who were experiencing conflicting meanings about their gender roles, marriage, filial obligations, household responsibilities, and child care. In this vein, Nadeem (2011) writes,

> What is threatening about globalization is its emphasis on individualism, the sense that personal skills and achievement, not family, caste, or class, are what make a person. . . . Economic independence can therefore mean freedom from family. . . . Gainful employment is not synonymous with "empowerment," but in a social setting where women are often considered repositories of family honor, being able to work at night with men is no small matter. (pp. 64–65)

R. C. Tripathi (2011), an Indian psychologist, argues that in contemporary societies, we have much quicker mutations and connections between cultures than was the case in the past. New cultural seeds can transplant themselves rather surreptitiously and become integrated within established social and cultural meaning systems. However, Tripathi also warns us that this does not mean that traditional cultures are going to be diluted or that there will be one single, homogeneous global culture. He argues that the "central values of cultures may become weak but their memes will survive and their understanding should help in understanding of the individual as well as collective consciousness" (p. 372). Therefore, he notes that psychologists will need to find new

> paradigms, models and methods that are based on concatenation of cultures or new cultures that have evolved and will be evolving. The challenge which psychologists face today, therefore, is in developing theoretical frameworks or paradigms based on cultures as they have evolved and are evolving and not based on culture as they once were. (p. 172)

If we take Tripathi's lead, we have to ask what identities are being constructed in Vijay, Madhu, Madhuri, and Namrata's stories about their work at the call centers. How does working at a call center reflect narratives of mobility and independence?

Vijay, Madhuri, and Namrata's stories show that they are engaged with breaking boundaries and creating new meaning of their identities. The call center workers inhabit a space where ideas about the local are produced through the global and vice versa. The stories that I discussed previously move between narrative negotiations of online and offline identities. The production of identities in call center workers involves "transnational mobility, through virtual migration," and it brings into sharper focus new "modes of identity construction" (Basi, 2009, p. 23). The intercultural work of the call center workers can be characterized as "diasporic journeys" taken through the digital world, and the stories of call center workers, Basi notes, "are lived, re-lived, produced, and reproduced through individual and collective memory, thus differently imagined" (p. 23). If we use the analytical frame of hybridity to describe the experiences of call center workers, then what are the dialogic overtones and contested ideas about the self–other relationship that emerge in these narratives?

These narratives, like the stories of the transnationally oriented youth discussed in Chapter 5, are dialogical and plural. They demonstrate how agency and individual choice are articulated within the constraints of their gender and class positions. The hybridity of the call center workers is situated in the logic of capitalism, where they earn good money to support a middle-class lifestyle and become independent, but at the same time, these young Indians work in stressful conditions and with demanding and sometimes abusive customers. Thus, there are three themes that seem pivotal to the construction of what I describe as narratives of *individualized Indianness*: becoming independent, resisting surveillance and countering stories of mobility, and dialogicality of mimicry and authenticity.

Becoming Independent: Indian Family Values and "Becoming Somebody"

Madhuri, Vijay, Namrata, and Madhu's narratives navigate between continuity and change, stability and instability, sameness and difference. These narratives do, indeed, demonstrate to us the process of identity disruption and re-creation that is so central to narrative psychology. Amia Leiblich and Ruthellen Josselson (2012) write that identity provides an answer to the question, Who am I? They note: "'In what sense am I the same person yesterday, today, and tomorrow?' 'What makes me unique, namely different from others?' 'What do I stand for in the world?' and 'To what do I devote my life?'" (p. 205). These are crucial questions that individuals ask about their selves as "I" or "Me" as they try to make meaning about who they are and how they should be in the world. However, the interviews analyzed before also show there are other questions that become far more contested and challenged when identity questions are framed not only as questions about self but also from the point of view of *others*: What do my traditions demand of me? What ought I be in the eyes of my religion, family, community, and others? How do I fulfill my duties as a mother, wife, and sister?

One dimension of Vijay, Madhuri, Namrata, and Madhu's narratives essentially attempts to re-create well-assembled cultural plot lines that are being challenged by new contextual details, uncertain actions, ambiguous and conflicting cultural knowledge, and extraneous happenings (Ochs & Capps, 2001). Globalization is framed as signifying freedom and emancipation while simultaneously diluting notions of Indianness: family, honor, a stable marriage, and high regard for tradition. Namrata and Madhu's narratives, for example, highlight how notions of "Indian family" are changing within the context of contemporary middle-class, urban India. In particular, Namrata's story illustrates how globalization through neoliberal interventions is changing a woman's role in the family and the meaning of family itself. Although Namrata is still working within the contours of the Indian familial self, the transformation in her gender role allows her to re-interpret her social positioning and her psychological world. Namrata stated that her "husband does not like that I work, but we have no choice. My sons are growing up and I need to support them. I have to assert my voice."

Through her call center work, Namrata has acquired financial independence, and she is able to assert her power in the family. Going against her husband's wishes, Namrata got a job at the call center. She finds the job extremely demanding, but it gives her a new social position within the family hierarchy. Namrata conveyed to me that each day after she finishes her job as a call center worker, she has to return home and be a wife, which entails ensuring that meals are cooked, the house is taken care of, and her children have done their studies. Initially, when she worked on an evening schedule, her life was not synchronized with her family's schedule, and very often when Namrata returned home at night, her two sons had already gone to sleep so she rarely saw them. Call center employment had given Namrata and Madhuri social status, new career opportunities, and financial independence, and they were able to assert their agency within the contexts of family hierarchy. This agency did not connote unlimited freedom where they could reinvent themselves, but working at a call center meant that they could experience psychological freedom through small acts. These interviews show how urban, middle-class women are creating new "counternarratives" of self, where their identity formation is no longer dictated by feminine labor at home but, rather, they can be "seen" and "heard" in the public space.

When I interviewed Satish Kapoor, the CEO of Global India Technology—one of the fastest growing, mid-tier IT companies in India—he began by telling me that today's Indian youth are much more expressive and less constrained by group norms. He had inherited his father's small but well-recognized accounting firm, which he expanded in 1990 just as India was becoming liberalized. I asked him what particular changes he had seen in Indian youth in the past 20 years. His said that young employees refer to him by his first name, they are not afraid to question company policies, and he referred to the younger generation as being both individualistic and family-oriented. He told me that Indians, especially the youth, are "getting globalized" and have a better understanding of the world. He explained:

> Yes, yes. There is also another thing that is happening, which is that: We Indians are changing because of our current place under the sun. See, because, there is a tremendous degree of self-confidence within Indians that didn't exist a few years ago. Today you travel anywhere in the world and even (at) a small airport in the US you will find some Indian kid with a backpack, and completely at peace with himself . . . not feeling out of the world, not feeling in any way kind of suppressed.

Satish emphasized that the older Indian generation had to temper their aspirations and desires, and in the olden days if a young Indian man saw someone driving a Mercedes, he would believe that "I will never have a Mercedes. Somebody else will have a Mercedes." In contrast, the youth of today, Satish noted quite energetically, are very different: "You talk to a young kid, and he will say, 'I am going to buy a Mercedes.'" The most important difference in middle-class Indian youth is a transformation in attitude and that "they feel they have a chance." I shared with Satish that many working-class youth I had interviewed had not experienced any real benefits of globalization, and it seemed to me that attitude alone was not enough to achieve equity in Indian society. I then asked him to comment on how many parents from the middle and upper class had shared their anxieties with him regarding youth becoming much more materialistic, Western, or narcissistic. He refused to engage any further with those questions, saying, "Maybe it is so, but I haven't come across that. Maybe I am probably outside that whatever." Satish's point that there is an essential Indianness despite the changes wrought by globalization was echoed repeatedly in many interviews and focus groups. While many of my participants were quick to point out the radical differences between generations, they would follow up with the notion that the youth are still "Indian" in their values. The reconstitution of "Indianness" in the context of dynamic cultural change was an important theme that surfaced across the narratives.

Globalization and the Reconstruction of Agency and Personhood

Globalization, outsourcing, and neoliberalization are not abstract terms and concepts in the lives of Vijay, Namrata, Madhuri, and Madhu. Their personhood was getting reconfigured as they were engaging in practices of globalization, and their self-narratives were being reinvented through overlapping and contesting frames of modernity and tradition, freedom, and restraints, as well as consumption and choice that were dictated by the free market. Namrata regrets discontinuing her education immediately after her marriage, and her new financial and psychological independence has also altered the power dynamics in her family.

In the global world of call center culture, where "accent neutralization" is an accepted pedagogy and speaking good English is a ticket to connecting with the virtual West, Namrata had become one of the millions of India's "Macaulay's (cyber) children" (Nadeem, 2011). The now infamous, but then celebrated, *Macaulay Minute*, written by Lord Babbington Macaulay in 1835, stated with imperial certitude that "we (the British) must at present do our best to form . . . a class of persons, Indian in blood and color, but English in taste, in opinions, in morals and in intellect" (Macaulay, 1835/1972, p. 249). Namrata's ability to speak in a globalized British accent had saved her family and provided resources for her children. She was grateful that, finally, a moment had arrived in her life when she could put her English education to good use. The English language, she asserted, had made her a working woman and had given her a new social identity.

Madhuri's narrative also shows her struggle to redefine the concept of marriage within the Indian family. Her parents perceived Madhuri as being dismissive of religious traditions and "the culture of the place" that had shaped her parents, their relatives, and friends in the community. Madhuri reiterated that there was a wide gulf between urban, metropolitan cities and small rural towns in India regarding the cultural expectations of gender roles. From her parents' point of view, there was a cultural script that she was expected to follow: what she should wear, when she should get married, whom she should get married to, when she should have children, how she should behave with her in-laws, and so on.

Going against the orthodox views of her parents and community of Brahmins, Madhuri did not believe that "okay, once married, you're married for life." She believed that new educational opportunities had brought about cultural change in India and being a divorced woman was not a stigma anymore in her workplace or social circle. Her job as management executive had given her a new identity as an independent urban Indian woman, and this job signified both economic and psychological independence. Madhuri was not looking for just any job but, rather, employment that drew on her talents and made her day-to-day work meaningful and creative. In the initial years of her marriage, Madhuri's husband and family did not object to her working as a schoolteacher or doing other part-time jobs. However, Madhuri had been searching for a job that gave her life meaning and purpose, and that is when she decided to look for a permanent full-time job as an English language instructor in one of the language training institutes in New Delhi. When Madhuri started searching for full-time jobs, with the prospect of building a career, her ex-husband and his family objected to her plans:

> So I realized that after that, after a year or so, their attitudes have changed, so they were like, "Why do you have to do that? Why can't you just teach some kids at home, take some . . .?" And then I'm like, "I'm not going to do that. I would never do that. It doesn't interest me." I like to work not to—I mean, for me, even now money is not the big consideration. Now, yes, I'm single and I have to support myself, yes. I will definitely look for a job, but that's about it. For me the job has to be interesting. The content has to be enriching . . . a lot of the traditional men that are there, you know, they have these terrible double standards, okay? I experienced it myself. So it's like the woman has to be completely domesticated and at the same time be presentable, blah, blah, blah, and, you know, be sophisticated, as the men require. And, you know, I was just at a loss to understand what I'm supposed to do. And it's very difficult for me as an individual to keep changing according to somebody else's whims and fancies.

Madhuri' narrative was essentially a story about her asserting her agency and becoming independent. Her narrative was about resisting the demands of marriage and "domestication." Traditions and customs were important for Madhuri, but she wanted to self-select those traditions that broadened the role of an Indian woman. Her narrative centered around the theme of "autonomy"—an identity that was not based on "double standards" or "domestication" or "somebody else's whims and fancies." In Madhuri's narrative, we see a search for an identity that is not predetermined through marriage or the traditional roles of being a housewife and a mother.

In contrast, Vijay's narrative highlighted a preoccupation with the weakening of the "Indian family" bond and unity. He emphasized that young men and women are experiencing new freedoms, through their financial independence, so they smoke, take drugs, drink alcohol, and party, and they are not accountable to their families. Vijay, who grew up in a joint family and lived with his parents, believed that the core family unit and old values are changing in India. This basic foundation of the "Indian family unity," he stressed, was based on the notion of family sacrifice. He sustained his critique of Indian youth culture by pointing out, "Nowadays, nobody sacrifices for the family. Everybody is thinking about himself or herself. Indians have become selfish nowadays, very selfish. Like, they don't have any respect for parents."

Globalization, according to Vijay, had changed the family dynamics because young, college-aged boys who are barely 20 years old earn more money than their fathers, so now they do not have to listen to their fathers: "At one time the father used to be the head of the family, and he had some power in his hand but now . . . a kid becomes the head of the family." The current youth have different sets of values toward family, consumption, and marriage. Vijay said that he frequently observes in his cohort of friends that fathers will try to intervene in their sons' lives when they see excessive indulgences of drinking and staying out until late at bars and having girlfriends. Vijay stated,

> Like, for example, you are a parent today and you say to your son, "You have par-
> tied enough since the last two days," and you try to stop your son from going to
> bars, the son will say, "What's your problem? I'm earning my own. I'm spending
> on my own. You have no right to tell me."

Vijay believed that liberalization had opened up "pent-up desires" in Indian youth –especially the middle classes who were raised with old cultural values of saving their money, spending less, not going out, and sacrificing their lives for their children and families. This generation, he repeated, has realized the *power of money*. There was no other option, Vijay alleged, but to accept globalization and move with the world. Globalization had brought new jobs, money, and overseas travel, and he was of the view that the younger generation in India is benefiting from this economic development.

What I found echoed throughout the interviews is that the call center workers had internalized and embraced the larger discourses about call center work. In these larger public narratives, call center jobs were associated with an underlying concern with the urban Indian youth losing "family values" and "respect for traditions" and becoming sexually promiscuous, materialistic, and self-centered (Basi, 2009; Mirchandani, 2012). The younger generation *ventriloquized* their own personal narratives through the larger social anxieties and moral panics of the society.

Social Ventriloquation: Speaking to the Other

The process of ventriloquation allows voices "to speak through the other" (Valsiner, 2000, p. 9). Furthermore, in the ventriloquation process, one voice infuses the other voice and uses it as a medium to express its own voice or its *I* position. I use ventriloquation to imply not a single dominant voice but, rather, how various voices continuously shape others and create new voices or what Hermans and Hermans-Konopka (2010) call *third positions*. The metaphor of "refraction," or one position speaking through other positions, seems apt to describe the dialogue occurring within the narratives discussed previously. The ongoing negotiations and communication between these positions produce new third positions. Hermans and Hermans-Konopka state that "when two positions are involved in a conflict, they can under specific conditions be *reconciled* in a third position in which the conflict between the original position is lessened and mitigated" (p. 15, emphasis in original).

The process of ventriloquation in the narratives implies not just the act of imitating or copying the position and perspectives offered by others but also reconstituting them as part their narrative identity. The act of ventriloquation suggests a twofold process where positions are *spoken with* and *through* each other, thus changing the dynamics of both positions and creating a new position or identity. The "third position" that the call center workers create is the result of an ongoing negotiation between concerns about losing their Indian values and embracing work that encourages materialistic, Westernized, and consumerist values/behavior. The youth reconcile the conflicting positions by claiming a third position of being "independent" or being a professional worker or being "somebody." This status of being "somebody" was an important third position that evolved out of the ventriloquation between the voices that represented the fear and loss of Indianness and their access to a materialist and consumerist lifestyle.

Vijay's story reflects the creation of a hybrid position of becoming a "somebody" after he became a call center worker. While Vijay equated call center jobs with a generic loss of Indian values or with dilution of his imagined views about "Indian traditions," he simultaneously used his call center job to become "somebody." The voice of the cultural dilution of Indianness was constantly being refracted and read through the voice of having a car, nice clothes, and then "becoming something in life." This third position of having status, as an identity, was crucial to the development of Vijay's narrative. On many days, he reported feeling that he was a "cyber coolie" (Nadeem, 2011) who was put in a back office station where he was providing service to "First World" customers because his labor was inexpensive. He lived in an artificial world in which he had access to an air-conditioned office floor and beautifully landscaped office building, uninterrupted access to computer and electricity, and was immersed in a semi-Western "atmosphere." When he went home, he was usually tired after his 12-hour workdays, and he smoked incessantly and needed a few drinks to fall asleep.

Vijay's concern for the loss of "Indian values" is juxtaposed against becoming materialistic and living like Westerners, but the call center work had redeemed his life and allowed him to have a third identity of being an important person. Being a call center worker had given him a professional identity, and he was able to consume name brands and drive a second-hand Indian-made Maruti car. After his father's business collapsed, Vijay stepped in as the sole wage earner for his family and contributed a regular monthly income to his parents. He had secured a few promotions in the call center industry, and in 2011 he moved from voice to non-voice process—working for a bank that collected business-to-business loans. His promotion and the money he gave to support his family had made him "somebody" in the eyes of his relatives and family. His life had not yet amounted to being a *sahib*, but there were moments when he experienced "high social status" by going to expensive restaurants and imbibing imported whisky.

Bakhtin (1981) writes that ventriloquation essentially points to a process of hybridization. A hybrid construction, he states, "is an utterance that belongs, by its grammatical (syntactic) and compositional markers, to a single speaker, but that actually contains mixed within it two utterances, two speech manners, two styles, two 'languages,' two semantic and axiological belief systems" (pp. 304–305). Bakhtin further emphasizes that the process of ventriloquation with a mixture of positions and voices essentially points to tensions, cultural contradictions, and paradoxes. Madhuri's narrative, for example, reveals this paradox.

Madhuri's work as a management executive at a well-known IT company had given her freedom to move across cities and to be open about her status of being a divorced woman. She found the traditional role of an "Indian woman" to be stifling and constraining, and her position as a management executive required her to work with Indian men who were "socially awkward" and were scandalized by her drinking and her liberal views. Out of these two positions, she created a third position that involved being a single woman with an identity of a woman who did not have to live by the "whim and fancies of a man"; she could pursue an identity that was independent—a kind of *individualized Indianness* that is autonomous yet somehow deeply Indian. This was a position of an alternative Indian modernity (Gaonkar, 2001) where traditions are reinvented through specific cultural frames and practices.

This process of ventriloquation also points to the burdens of carrying a double-voiced discourse and the labor of crafting new identities by going against cultural expectations. The creation of these "third positions" is not easy because they require negotiating with the power structures of one's family, workplace, and gendered norms about what it means to be an "Indian woman." The women who worked at the call center could not assert their agency in all areas of their lives. Despite having financial freedom, many women still had to work out their agency within the patriarchal discourses set up by their male bosses, boyfriends, husbands, mothers-in-law, and parents. The call center work was difficult and demanding, and it was further complicated by larger media and public sphere debates about young Indian women "losing touch" with some essentialist "Indian culture" as they acquired Western values of dressing and independence (Basi, 2009; Patel, 2010).

A young Indian woman's successful transition at the time of marriage is determined by her ability to adjust to and negotiate new sets of relationships and hierarchies in her husband's extended family. An important part of this successful transition involves having children, "which brings both emotional satisfaction and improved status in the household" (Seymour, 2004, p. 457). With the onset of adolescence, young Indian girls are socialized to maintain strict sexual and interpersonal boundaries with men, and their sexuality becomes highly regulated because the purity of their bodies is seen as connected to family *izzat* (respect and honor) and *naam* (reputation and social standing). As many middle-class women are becoming part of urban cultural life, acquiring skills to enter the workforce, girls are beginning to assert their rights and are "not wanting to be 'door-mats,' with often one or more family members supporting the endeavor" (Chadha, 2011, p. 184). The call center women whom I interviewed for this project were breaking away from the straightforward path of socialization—their entry into adulthood was taking a different route. The call center and other globalized forms of work were thus creating new gendered positions that were threatening to the traditional patriarchal structure of the Indian family and the value system associated with those practices.

Public Surveillance and the Mobility–Morality Narrative: "What Will People Think?"

The Indian call center industry has gone through a process of "pinking." A "pink-collar" worker was a term originally used to describe women who worked in the computer industry in the Caribbean. The women were employed as data entry and "informatics workers," and their work in the professional industry was considered a departure from working in the cane fields and kitchens in which their mothers and ancestors had labored (Basi, 2009). Women are overwhelmingly represented in the call center industry because they are constructed as having an innate ability to be empathetic, patient, and calm in their conversations with clients from abroad (Mirchandani, 2012; Patel, 2010).

In 2003, women comprised approximately 40–70% of the staff at call center workplaces (Mitter, Fernandez, & Varghese, 2004; Ramesh, 2004), and most of these women came from lower-middle and middle-class families. There were structural reasons that prompted many women to join call centers. Those jobs that require sharp communication and interpersonal skills were conceived as temporary or short-term entry-level jobs that women embraced because the top managerial positions were usually offered to men. Second, the call center jobs, as described by Namrata, were flexible, and women could enter and leave the profession with ease. Women who were pregnant, for example, could leave these jobs and return when they had suitable caregiving arrangements.

Call center work has provided many middle-class young Indian women with disposable income, autonomy, and financial independence. The money earned through call center work was usually used for supporting the family; paying tuition; buying groceries; and buying personal items such as clothes, cell phones, and household items. Patel notes (2010) that the night shift provided single women, who lived independently or with families, a *great escape*. The discourse of becoming independent while still being connected to the family was one of the principal reasons given by the participants for joining the call center. Being single, away from the private surveillance of families, these women could work in a *global* and *modern* environment, take vacations, and make independent decisions about marriage and their social life. While some young women found "liberation" through call center work, they had to continue to obey patriarchal rules at home, their work was degraded, and a call center job was considered to make them less attractive in the marriage market. For some women, doing call center work was seen as becoming "autonomous" and modern and defying tradition. Thus, a woman working at a call center was viewed as someone who would not take her place in the family hierarchy and would most likely put her needs before those of the family.

Gendered Rules and Patriarchal Discourses About "Good Girls"

In 2000, one of India's leading magazine, *India Today*, depicted on its cover the face of an Indian woman wearing a headset and a microphone. The headline printed below the woman's face read, "Call Centers, Housekeeper to the world, India's fastest growing industry employing millions and earns million." This image was intended to reflect the rise of the middle-class Indian woman as a liberated, educated, and global woman who was transcending tradition and creating an identity in which she is not merely a wife, sister, and mother but also a working woman. My interviews with the participants of the study revealed a heightened anxiety about young women leading "promiscuous" lives in Pune as the result of working the night shift. The infusion of women in the call center industry was creating larger anxieties about gender roles, and the "dilution of Indian cultural values" was usually located within the context of women "stepping out" of their home and their boundaries and hanging out in public spaces such as bars and dance clubs and moving about "in the night." Women's work in call centers is viewed through a "mobility–morality" narrative that creates norms about what behaviors are acceptable for women in the public space and gendered rules about where they should or should not be seen (Patel, 2010). Apart from having fluency in the English language, the second most important requirement for getting selected for this job is being willing to work the night shift. Thus, physical mobility, going to and returning from work, and temporal mobility (going to work when one is expected to be at home) for middle-class Indian women invite strict regimes of surveillance and patriarchal regulation. Patel explains, "Because leaving home at night is generally considered inappropriate for and off-limits to Indian women, companies offer transportation as part of their recruitment strategy" (p. 2).

Meera, whose story was discussed earlier in this chapter, told me that the women call center workers were judged by a different standard than the men. During weekends, she and her roommate, Ruth, went to bars together to "release their tensions" and to "socialize with other people." Meera told me that "we go to bars to just have a good time, but people think it is not okay." Meera was worried that her neighbors, landlady, and friends were judging her escapades in the nightclub life. This mobility–morality narrative is activated by the question, "What will people think?"—how women's reputations are sullied as they are deemed "bad girls" by others who see them moving about in the night. Patel (2010) observes,

> Going to a mall with friends in the early evening is okay; unwinding at a bar after a long night of work is not okay. This narrative also requires women to look proper. Before stepping out of the house, a woman must scrutinize how she is dressed in relation to the time of the day and where she is going. Unlike her male counterparts, her choice of attire comes from remaining aware of how patriarchal regimes of surveillance perceive her bodily existence—whore versus homemaker—and reflects how far some men believe they have a *right* to go—from unwanted gazes to rape—when they consume a woman's body. (p. 61, emphasis in original)

Women's work in call centers and in the labor force in urban India is an example of how narratives of gender, culture, and identity are being remade through both local and global practices. While call center work provides many women a sense of becoming "individualized Indians" who have a decision-making capacity in the family and have the freedom to organize their social life, they are also burdened by practices of surveillance, consumerist identity, and exploitation of labor. Patel (2010) thus gives us the following insight:

> Conceptualizing globalization as a force that liberates women from local traditions is tricky because it can inadvertently be used to disguise and rationalize the exploitation on which this "liberation" is based. This is not to suggest, conversely, that globalization always increases exploitation. (p. 53)

My interviews with call center women confirmed Patel's analysis that the women were being culturally positioned through a patriarchal and conservative binary discourse of "public" and "private," "homely" and "bold," "bad character" and "decent woman," "liberated" and "traditional."

In my interviews with Namrata and Meera, they talked about how call centers in Pune attracted a large number of middle-class young women. The appeal of call center work, despite its tedium, was its lucrative pay and the call center culture that gave young women an opportunity to "be themselves." As young women became more independent, they were also willing to seek out romantic relationships with men in call centers because they could pursue their relationships outside the public and family gaze. In response to patriarchal surveillance and public scrutiny of women's behavior, call center workers became strategic about their relationships with their boyfriends—meeting secretly at certain cafés, bars, and during office times—so their relationships would not invite attention. Call centers had also come to symbolize spaces where "going out" with a male was a norm rather than an exception.

Working in call centers required young women to adopt a "strategic" view about their individual identities—they used the call center environment to assert their identities by not being bound by their traditional roles in the family. They wore "Western clothes" to work, had boyfriends, moved around in public spaces, visited bars and disco clubs at night, and embraced a consumer ethos. The struggle to break away from their family and gender roles also invited scrutiny from the family and the public. Basi's (2009) research confirms, "Women did not necessarily enter the call centers specifically to find marriage partners; however, the sexually liberated, charged atmosphere produced conditions in which it was almost a requirement to have a partner" (p. 113). This independence gained by the women through their movement outside the home was a cause for familial anxiety and censure. Their individuality and possibility of being sexually expressive and active positioned them as unfit to take an appropriate gendered place in the family hierarchy and acquiesce to collective needs.

Women's work in the call centers demonstrates that globalization is generating new cultural concepts of gender roles and gendered identity that are contradictory, contested, and overlapping. The Indian nation, as a postcolonial society, was reconstructing itself within modern discourses of neoliberal globalization, and the opening up of the night shift in the call center industry had created new gendered positions (Hegde, 2011). As more women became the face of the call center industry, they were constructed as young, free, consumer-oriented, influenced by the West, and having inferior sexual mores and values. In this vein, Hegde writes that "the consumer identity ascribed to call-center employees accentuates the stereotype of the Westernized, sexually available woman. Call center workers, particularly women, are routinely associated with being 'call girls' or are considered sexually permissive and 'Westernized'" (p. 186). The call center women were simultaneously marked as emerging consumers of a global economy and as sexualized objects that could be commodified and "consumed" in the larger media and public discourses.

The call center work for many women represents a space of empowerment with higher levels of income and access to financial and social independence. However, it also simultaneously represents an exploitative space because of differential time zones, low wages relative to those of American workers, and an extremely stressful work environment. Furthermore, the very independence that women experience and express through their newfound economic roles positions them for social disapproval and potential for bringing dishonor to their families.

BECOMING GLOBAL: MIMICRY AND IDENTITY IN
THE CALL CENTER WORLD

One way to understand the hybrid narratives of young Indians within the call center context is to examine how identities are constructed by what Nadeem (2011) has called "modern mimicry." He argues that contemporary forms of mimesis are not only directly linked to colonialism but also intertwined with corporate globalization. British and European colonialists contrasted their superior Western civilization against what they considered as the backward culture of the primitives. Contemporary forms of globalization continue these hierarchies between the "First World" and "Third World" and the developed and the developing worlds. According to Nadeem,

> Both produce a strong compulsion to imitate, particularly on part of the privi-
> leged strata in the so-called developing world. Today, with the waning appeal of
> postcolonial nationalism, consumer oriented mimicry has emerged as an inte-
> gral component of class and personal identity. (p. 46)

What these consumer and transnational corporate-oriented practices denote is not a modernist attempt to create an "authentic" Western identity, a "child-like tendency to copy," where the "West" becomes a "cathetic object that is invested with emotional energy" (Nadeem, 2011, p. 47). Rather, the mimicking of Western lifestyle and consumption commodities, goods, images, and symbols gives call center workers a sense of autonomy, but it also requires them to invest their "emotional energy" at work in creating professional identities that are based on American discourses of "self-fulfillment," "being happy," and exploring their "creative self."

To some extent, the youth and many middle-class, urban Indians were deriving pleasure and were "choosing" to identify with a consumerist life-style that they associated with most American practices. However, the practice of mimesis in the stories of call center workers was largely created by the harsh structural inequalities of the global economy, cheap labor, and corporate-driven globalization. The Indian call center work culture and its practices of acquiring British and American accents are created out of a "complex interplay of colonial histories, class relations, and national interests" (Mirchandani, 2012, p. 3).

Workshop Identities: Accent and Cultural Training

Vijay, Madhu, Meera, Namrata, and several others whom I interviewed had to undergo training in voice, accent, and understanding British and American culture. Vijay told me that once the candidates are selected to become call center agents, they are trained by specialists to imitate British, American, and neutral accents. Vijay was trained to use both American and British accents, and I asked him to give me an example of his voice training:

s: So, can you give me examples of a UK accent?
v: Okay. I'll give you some basic example. A UK "c-a-n," C for Charlie, A for alpha, N for November. (he imitates both accents).
s: Hmm. So you have to do this at work?
v: Yes, I have to do this.
s: So, you have to be conscious of your accent when you're speaking?
v: Yes, you have to be.

Vijay's imitation of the British and American accents for stock phrases such as "Can I get your account number?" or "Is that okay with you?" was quite on the mark, but he told me that he could not pull off a conversation in foreign accents if he had to go off script.

Vijay told me that there are usually two types of training that call center agents are expected to go through: accent training and cultural training. In the initial stages of outsourcing, Indian call centers would train their young agents to acquire British and American accents. The demand for globalized speech has led to the creation of dozens of specialized institutes in urban and small Indian cities. These institutes are geared solely toward the erasure of what is now very widely known in call center circles, and as mentioned previously, as mother tongue influence in speech. MTI training neutralizes and erases the hard "r" and "s" of the Indian accent. In addition, call center agents can be fired if they are caught speaking in their native Indian language on the premises. Having a speech that is shorn of its local MTI is viewed as an asset—these workers can work in any market.

A key aspect of cultural training is to teach middle-class, urban Indian call center youth how to connect with mostly American and British customers. The call center workers I met during my fieldwork had never traveled abroad, so the training was created to bring the *foreign culture* home—to train youth to have familiarity with mostly American and British ways of speaking and making small talk. The call center socialization into American culture is organized around role-playing routines of acquiring foreign identities, namely Western-sounding names, at work; requiring workers to be familiar with American football and basketball scores; and knowledge of American conversational rituals of "small talk." These call center workers were taught the codes of "American culture" by exposing them to American television serials such as *Friends* and *Seinfeld* and movies such as *American Pie, Independence Day*, and *J.F.K.* Shome (2006) notes how youth working at the many call centers throughout urban India facilitate their hybrid identity as they are compelled to take on roles as "Indian by day" and "American at night." Their traditional Indian names would be replaced, and so "Suman may become Susan, Nishara may become Naomi, or Amit may become Alex or Alan" (p. 112).

The globalized identities of call center workers were being constructed in contradictory and problematic ways. For example, Meera, Vijay, Namrata, Madhu, and several others who worked in call centers were expected to go through a process of "accent neutralization," "de-Indianization," or "voice neutralization" (Shome, 2006). Boussebaa, Sinha, and Gabriel (2014) describe offshore call centers as the result of a worldwide phenomenon of "corporate Englishization." They argue that the call center does not improve transnational or intercultural communication but, instead, these interactions reproduce colonial-style hierarchies, mimicry, and power relationships between the Western, Anglosphere countries and those that are subordinate to them in the Global South. This form of mimicry is rooted in a consumerist culture that promotes a false utopian ideal of a global village and global citizenship. Mimicry in this sense is not a subversion of the language and modes of dressing and customs of the dominant majority as Bhabha (1994) has argued but, rather, is seen as essential to the survival of the global workers. This imitation has earned call center agents appellations such as "phone clones" or "cyber coolies." In the larger public discourses and debates about outsourcing, initial studies done on UK-owned call centers in India labeled them as "dark satanic mills" and "cyber sweatshops" (Basi, 2009). The narrative meaning-making that occurs in call center culture is shaped by the unequal context of a transnational service economy, corporate guidelines, and the demands of the Western customers. The subjectivities that emerge out of the call center narratives are linked to institutional and historical forces of colonialism and reproduced within the "West versus Rest" framework in neoliberal times. There are clearly marked contexts of power that shape the dialogical relationship between an Indian call center agent and the Western customer.

Mirchandani (2012) reminds us that one aspect of this interaction is defined by the perception in the West that these are "distant workers" who speak in strange or not-quite-right accents and pose a threat to their domestic jobs at home. Second, the workers have to appear authentically "just like" their customers in the West by becoming familiar with their cultures and codes of speaking. The successful conversation requires that the call center agent create a connection with the Western customer through proper emulation of cultural styles. The concept of authenticity or *authentic mimesis* provides an important context in which to situate the narratives of these transnational workers. On the one hand, call center workers are located in different historical and cultural contexts from their customers. On the other hand, from their cultural positions as Indian workers, they have to continuously create (apparently) "authentic" or "culturally seamless" interactions with Western customers (Mirchandani, 2012). This paradoxical and contradictory dialogicality between sameness and difference becomes an integral part of the stories of the lives of the call center agents. These narratives are hybrid and plural, but their hybridity is also created by asymmetrical cultural and economic contexts and practices. The role of social and institutional power in shaping their individual narratives and the voices within them is central to understanding identity formation. As opposed to physical labor, service work in transnational call centers involves "emotional labor" wherein the workers are expected to display particular emotions (and hide others) with their customers (Hochschild, 1983).

American Psychological Practices and "Happy Selves" at the Workplace

The neoliberal and global management practices are used to shape the work culture of call centers and IT industries (Upadhya, 2008). During training sessions, call center employees are repeatedly told that their customers can sense their mood through their voice, so they need to smile, ensuring their positive mood comes through. The workers are told to maintain their calmness when customers become angry and hurl racist abuses at them.

Emotional labor refers to more than just managing one's emotional expressions while reading the screen and being attentive to the customer. It also refers to being culturally sensitive in their interactions with Westerners, where agents are prohibited from displaying their natural emotions while sharing superficial feelings that they do not genuinely experience. Even after intensive cultural training, Ramesh (2008) writes, "quite often the awareness of the agents about the cultural, socioeconomic and geographical background of the customers is too weak to deliver quality service" (p. 250). The burden of understanding the culture of American and British customers and "getting the conversation right" with Western customers is considered to be one of the most stressful aspects of the call center job.

The daily drudgery of interacting with customers from abroad and ensuring that their interactions are marked by a dialogicality of authenticity and sincerity is also one the main reasons why the call center industry has such high attrition rates (Ramesh, 2008). The constant monitoring that occurs in a hierarchically oriented work culture also adds to the psychological alienation that is experienced by the workers. In order to stem the high attrition rates and stress levels in call centers and other IT industries, human resources departments often resort to using Western psychological practices of counseling employees and creating an "illusionary sense of empowerment" (p. 252).

The global corporations that own these call centers and many other IT companies have adopted a global management discourse that involves applying psychological intervention and giving psychological counseling to these workers. As mentioned in Chapter 1, the Silicon Valley organizational culture of "work as fun" or "workplace as campus" is imported to give call center agents a sense that their work is creative and stress-free and that they are part of a global knowledge economy. Human resource departments promote a culture of "freedom" and "flexibility" in the call centers while simultaneously subjecting employees to constant electronic surveillance and monitoring of their quality of interactions with customers.

Modern call centers actively promote the idea that working in a call center is entering into modernity, where they can be middle class, have access to air-conditioned spaces, commute in luxury buses, and work in high-tech facilities that are beautifully landscaped. In summary, self-worth and self-confidence are constructed through corporate forms of globalization. The call center workers to whom I spoke expressed to me that they had to undergo several workshops and training modules in which a highly "individualized" self was constructed. The call center and many entry-level IT workers across the industry were told they should not appear scripted in their conversation but, instead, should appear "happy," "spontaneous," and "authentic." They were told to partake in workshops to build their self-esteem and to self-actualize through finding "peak experiences," "flow," and "happiness" at work. The self-help courses and psychological tests that were aimed at assessing the personality traits and the motivation levels of call center workers were mainly imported from management techniques that had been used widely in Europe and America (Vasavi, 2008).

In this vein, Sonali Sathaye (2008) notes that the imparting of "soft skills" through "self-help" courses to Indian workers in the software industry, BPOs, and call centers essentially occurs through an erasure of "Indian values:" She writes,

> Indian values are conspicuous by their absence in this version of self-help courses. Indeed when Indian meanings, concepts or feelings do crop up in the course of sessions, employees are taught to relearn those in favor of more "universal"—typically American—understandings. The can-do interpretations of intangible phenomena taught in soft skills training run smoothly alongside management techniques, which place a high premium on individuality. (p. 138)

The North American and European global corporations and the Indian-owned local corporations draw on what Nikolas Rose (1996) has called the "Psy expertise" or psy disciplines, which refer to the creation of psychological techniques and discourses that produce conceptions of self that are aligned with neoliberal concepts of personhood as autonomous, free, and highly self-regulated. One of the implications of the importation of the global corporate culture in Indian call centers, BPOs, and software companies is that "Indian culture" and Indian values often become subject to a language of otherness and difference. They reflect practices of new types of *corporate Orientalism* where Indian culture and identity itself become scrutinized and internalized through a language of "self" that is taught in customer orientation workshops and cross-cultural training seminars.

Psychology has played an important role in creating the language of the unregulated, enterprising self in the neoliberal turn (Sugarman, 2015). Rose (1996) argues that psychology has given us the apparatus and the technologies and techniques to tell us what it means to be human: how we can discover our self, be our self, love ourselves, and be loved for the self we really are. Psychology as an enterprise has profoundly shaped the management of personhood, identity, and subjectivity in schools, prisons, factories, hospitals, armies, and the church. Multinational corporations that now manage the Indian call centers have imported the "Psy enterprise" from the West to train, regulate, and manage the identities of the Indian youth. Babu Ramesh (2008), who has conducted extensive studies on call centers and BPOs, states,

> The philosophy of work organization in BPOs is based in individualisation. Agents are moulded to act as individuals who report to and are monitored by another individual. Even in project-based teamwork, this is the core principle that structures work relationships. This norm is widely internalised by call center agents. . . . Promoting individualised situations leads to greater isolation and lower likelihood of establishing networks of information and support. (p. 256)

What is important to remember, as we unpack these complex forms of intersecting identities that involve the global, modern, and the local, is that call center culture does not produce exact replicas of the American professional worker. Call center workers are actually imagining a type of corporate Americaness, a particular concept of an "individual" that does not even exist in America. The copying of Western lifestyle and consumption commodities, goods, images, and symbols gives call center workers a sense of autonomy, but it also requires them to invest their "emotional energy" at work in creating professional identities that are based on American discourses of "self-fulfillment," "being happy," and exploring their "creative self."

The identity narratives of call center workers emerge out of many intersecting and overlapping forces that Shome (2006) characterizes as "gazes." From a narrative standpoint, these gazes give rise to a multitude of voices, and the call center worker's identity is shaped by interactions among different positions. First, there is the gaze of the instructor who trains the call center recruits to speak in a "de-Indianized" global accent. Second, there is the gaze of the computer screen that the agents monitor and that often shows weather descriptions and the general cultural conditions of the city from which the customer is calling. Third, there is the gaze of the customer, who cannot visualize the worker but imagines the Indian workers through his or her British or American cultural frame. Fourth, there is the gaze that the call center agent fixes on herself or himself as she or he tries to perform the identity of being an American or British worker or feels the pressure to speak without an accent. Fifth, women call center agents who work the night shift and step out into the night space are under the "cultural gaze" of police, family, friends, and acquaintances; as such, they have to make sure they act like "good girls." Sixth, all call center workers are expected to internalize the "psychological gaze" that scrutinizes their level of self-actualization, self-esteem, work as fun and creative, and so on so that they can create "authentic" and "right" culturally seamless connections with their foreign customers.

It is imperative that we place the existence of these call centers in a postcolonial, transnational economy where the offshore companies are often unregulated by their own governments and the Western transnational corporations create a work culture and new psychological practices that are driven by the principles of maximizing profits and shareholder value. These transnational "asymmetrical relationships" between different entities and regions can be seen as "reproductions of institutionally established provisions and constraints on communicative activities" (Hermans, 1996, p. 45). Wertsch (1991, p. 124) suggests that these asymmetrical relations and constraints force us to "privilege" one voice over another. Valsiner (2000), in turn, refers to the privileging of one voice over another as "domination." In some cases, he notes, such domination can quickly transform into the complete "expropriation," extinction, and erasure of all voices. On such occasions, Valsiner argues, the dialogical self becomes completely "monologized" and one-dimensional (p. 9).

What is important to recognize here is that the voice-to-voice or phone interactions are not just created out of isolated, decontextualized positions but, rather, individual identities are shaped by the power of corporations, institutions, and imported psychological discourses of self, work, community, and fulfillment. In summary, one of the most important visible markers of the new India is the ever-growing participation by, and the presence of, youth in the cultural practices of globalization. In this chapter, I drew on stories of middle-class, urban Indian youth to show how they are negotiating their identities in the face of sweeping cultural and economic transformations. The stories are intended to orient the reader to the tensions and contradictions that urban Indian youth are experiencing as they straddle a neoliberal economy of global corporate culture, engage in expressions of individualism while reinventing tradition, search for autonomy and relatedness, and play with new forms of authenticity and mimicry in rapidly changing cultural contexts.

NOTES

1. The British way of speaking English, with its intonation and inflections, was considered by many middle- and upper-class families as "standard" English. One of

the significant colonial legacies in India was the social prestige accorded to "British English" or the English spoke by the news anchors from BBC. Hundreds of new institutes had opened up in Pune that taught basic, intermediate, and advanced English and "accent reduction" through "personality development" courses.

2. Sikh men are also referred to as *Sardars*.

3. Gurgaon is one of India's most modern cities and was built to accommodate the growing demand for offshore call centers, BPOs, malls, and high-end residential and gated communities. There are more than 200 multinational corporations in Gurgaon that are featured in the Forbes *Fortune 500* list.

CHAPTER 7

Identities Left Behind

Globalization, Social Inequality, and

the Search for Dignity

*P*anchsheel *basti* (slum settlement) in Pune is located on the outskirts of two neighborhoods that had experienced a sudden, then continual, influx of brand-name stores, upscale restaurants, European tourists, and multinational information technology (IT) parks. However, everyday life in Panchsheel *basti* is disconnected from these new swirls of global flows and symbols of affluence. I draw on the interviews I conducted with young women and men who lived in this *basti*. In 2013, there were about 10 functioning stalls of public toilets for more than 1,500 people in Panchsheel *basti*. In other words, this *basti* was emblematic of the other India—an India in which, according to United Nations (UN) estimates, more than 600 million individuals have no access to toilets or basic sanitation.[1] The cultural flows that enveloped the adjacent "high society" areas had bypassed this locality. The young participants from the Panchsheel *basti*, one after another, furiously gestured at me, "What globalization? What progress? Our lives have remained the same!" The stories of the young men and women in Panchsheel *basti* exemplify lives that are lived in the "circuits of dispossession" (Fine & Ruglis, 2009). Their interviews demonstrate how urban youth living in slums have ambitions for a better life, but they are unable to find an exit out of the *basti* life. The youth I spoke to wanted a middle-class lifestyle—access to educational opportunities; a clean, livable space away from the *basti*; a motorcycle; a small one-bedroom apartment; and, above all, a private toilet. Globalization, in their corner of the world, represented a meaningless phenomenon that did not deliver much. These youth were aware that the phenomenon of globalization, referred to in the local Marathi language as *jagtikikarana*, was full of promise and hope for others—people who lived a mere few hundred feet outside the perimeter of their *basti*. The stories that I heard from the *basti* youth reflect their engagements with *jagtikikarana*[2] and are shaped by their imagined and real construction of youth that they refer to as *hi-fi* classes or upper and elite classes. I use Arjun Appadurai's (2013) concept of "capacity to aspire" to argue that the *basti* youth's capacity to aspire and have ambition is not just an individual psychological trait. Rather, their aspirations are shaped by their caste identities, structural conditions of poverty, their schooling in the vernacular language, collective social practices, and the prestige accorded to speakers of English in urban India. However, this aspirational discourse is interlaced with moral discourses as the youth assert their agency and difference from the affluent youth who live in close proximity to their neighborhoods.

TOPOGRAPHIES OF DISPOSSESSION

The best way to understand a locale is to describe what it consists of and what it is surrounded by in order to examine how the various geographies are connected or separate. Cindy Katz (2004) employs the notion of "countertopographies of globalization" in her book, *Growing up Global*, to call attention to how "particular people in disparate settings are pressed and 'excessed' by globalization's effects" (p. 179). A countertopography, as Katz argues, is a "productive and spatialized means for understanding how global neoliberal reforms produce uneven developments of 'space and scale' and social relations and practices" (p. xiv). Her book draws out the structural similarities between the daily routines of children growing up in Howsa, Sudan, and New York City. By drawing on specific connections between the different network of spaces, Katz argues, we can reveal the particular "global" effects of the material and social practices associated with capitalism in very different locales. In this section, I explore how this idea of "countertopographies" emerges in the context of Panchsheel *basti*.

When I was growing up in Pune, Boat Club Road and Koregaon Park were known as "high-class" neighborhoods or "posh localities" where the elite, professional upper-class, wealthy families lived. Hotel Blue Diamond, the Osho Rajneesh Ashram,[3] and the lavish bungalows and palatial houses that were tucked away in the various lanes spoke of a different India—where the affluent and the foreign tourists were both cordoned off from the rest of Pune. Their lives were inaccessible to us, but we could bike through their tree-lined lanes to get a glimpse of affluence from the outside. We often saw imported cars parked in front of the houses, high fences guarding the owners' privacy, and white marble facades that adorned the heavily guarded entrance gates to cloistered communities. Riding on bicycles with friends from Pudumjee

Compound, where I lived, to Koregaon Park was akin to being a tourist at home—the wide footpaths, the green and clean spaces, the meticulously landscaped gardens, and the relative scarce population in this area gave us a feeling of gazing at an exotic locale.[4]

Panchsheel *basti* is situated close to Koregaon Park and Kalyani Nagar, where the new centers of IT offices were being built along with expensive and exclusive residential apartment houses. Before I headed to the *basti*, I wanted to immerse myself in the surroundings to get a sense of the spatial and visual symbols that surrounded the *basti*. I asked myself the following questions: What do the youth and families see around them as they go back and forth from their settlement? What is the material and visual topography of the space around the *basti*?

Locating Symbols of Affluence: Topographies of Possession

During my visit to Pune in early January 2013, I headed to the *basti* by starting my walk from Boat Club Road toward North Main Street in Koregaon Park. During the past few years, I had made this walk to the *basti* more than a dozen times, but this time I was greeted by huge posters advertising various New Year's Eve parties at hotels, open grounds, and special celebrations to accommodate thousands of youth in Pune. Growing up in Pune, I had visited Koregaon Park innumerable times, mostly on my bicycle and later on my Luna moped, and I was always struck by its affluence and distinct geography. During this visit, I wanted to pay close attention to the transformation in the various surrounding neighborhoods of the *basti*, so I took down detailed notes about my observations.

Uber Luxurious Apartments: "Development with a Conscience"

As I was walking on North Main Street, I saw one poster with three White women standing sideways on their toes with their hands stretching horizontally as though they were flying. I continued my walk across the open stores where Kashmiri merchants were selling Buddha statues, bronze and brass Indian handicrafts, marble jewelry boxes, gemstone necklaces, and other ornaments. The handicrafts included heavily sculptured brass figurines, silver hookahs, along with floral utility bowls and walnut woodcarvings of lotus flowers and bedside tables; these were exhibited outside. I wondered how much labor and time it took to bring out these heavy items every day and then put them back inside the store at closing time. I continued my walk across the bus stop and passed by a coffee shop and a tattoo studio, and across the road I saw the branches of a lone enormous tree nudging a narrow, vertical advertising board. The billboard had printed pictures of three high-rise towers that were built on five acres of prime land. One tower consisted of 21 apartments, and the other tower contained 59 apartments. The slogan on the outdoor advertisement read, "Somethings you don't look at. You only look up to." Below the image was the following phrase: "A private community of uber-luxurious, ultra exclusive apartments." The perimeter wall of the space where the buildings were being constructed had a series of printed posters that contained sketches of European street scenes circa the 1920s.

One such scene depicted a generic main street with cast iron lamp posts, antique horse-drawn sleigh carriages, and a chauffeur driving a vintage automobile. The scene included a silhouette of a modern, European-looking woman dressed in a red hat and skirt, walking a dog and marveling at the Windermere sign, which was the name of the compound that housed these exclusive residential buildings. Another scene depicted a male silhouette standing on a carved wide bench. He, too, was taking a picture of the sign titled "A Modern Classic." On the left side of the perimeter wall was the logo of the real estate building company. The logo was presented on a card that looked like a combination of a finely etched scroll and a formal American wedding invitation. The slogan read, "Vascon: Development with a Conscience."

I found it quite ironic that the real estate company was developing exclusive, luxurious apartments with a conscience for one of the wealthiest segments of the Indian society. One is likely to hear an assertion linking development and conscience at a local nongovernmental organization (NGO) or at development conferences held by UN-type international organizations. The real estate developers who were selling these ultra-luxurious residences had somehow found a way to market their buildings by merging capitalism with the notion of conscience. Past the Windermere sign was a huge art studio followed by a narrow lane banked by rows of small shops that sold mostly designer clothes, with names such as Naksha, Olive, and Boutiques. I stopped at the Miracle Uni-Sex Salon, Slimming and Spa advertising board outside a store that was promoting a sale of spa and beauty treatment for Rs. 2999 ($50). The five services in this package could include deep tissue body massage, head massage, a basic haircut, wash and blow dry, pedicure, full arm waxing, or eyebrow shaving.

The promotion displayed a headshot of a young White woman with an oval face, full lips, and green eyes. Her auburn-colored hair was cut in the style of a choppy bob and had bronze highlights. A few yards away, a store called Olive sold upmarket fashion clothing and had three mannequins placed outside the shop. The white mannequin was wearing a black, open-back, summer dress with a wig of straight black hair. One of two Black mannequins had a V-neck T-shirt over a miniskirt, and the other one wore a tight floral dress. These two mannequins were wearing neon pink and orange punk rock-style wigs sporting blonde highlights.

In front of these shops, there was a modern, multistory, glass office building with a large, rectangular sign on the front that read Kaya Skin Clinic. There was a picture of a young male model with shoulders exposed and two close-up face shots of young women. All three models had light skin and could pass for White Euro-Americans.[5] As I walked farther, I noticed a sign on a wall of Rajput Restaurant on the other side of the road; the sign was painted blue and red and stated, "It feels Beautiful Today." There was a stray dog sitting in front of the sign, impervious to the pedestrian traffic and the cars whizzing by on the road.

Europe in India: Villas, Townhouses, and Cobbled Streets

I ambled across the Koregaon Park Bridge to Kalyani Nagar and encountered a cluster of oversized advertising billboards. These were some of the largest outdoor advertisements I had seen in the city. They were placed at the intersection of the bridge that connected Koregaon Park with Kalyani Nagar—both areas where English-speaking, urban elite residents lived and coexisted with the prosperous IT businesses in similarly manicured office parks. One of the publicity boards proclaimed, "New Year Bash at the Pune Marriott: Twist, Feast, Celebrate," and the one next to it read, "New Year Bash: Studio 53: The uber chic new year destination for Pune!" As I walked across the bridge, I spotted another huge advertising board for "Limited Edition homes from 2000 to 6000 square feet." This board showed a background of golden hue and a series of flats rising up and touching the blue sky. The board read, "PARKING FOR YOUR LIMO, RIVER AS WATER BODY, 24K [Gold] AS HOME." I could see the actual cluster of congested "24K" apartment buildings in the distance, which barely resembled the "golden hued apartments" pictured on the board. The Mula–Mutha River flowing through the apartment complex was parched dry save for a thin sluggish rivulet. Kids played cricket on the open, dried riverbed. Despite this desultory, dried landscape, advertisements showcasing luxury homes amid verdant greenery were everywhere—main highways, roads, theaters, glossy magazines, hotel lobbies, and alleys and lanes. Modern, Western-sounding names, reminiscent of the colonial era, were deployed to evoke an aura of European affluence and luxury: Oxford Riverside, Princetown Apartments, The Glassy Junction, The Royal Mirage, A City of Joy—Luxury Apartments, Serene Homes—Paint Your Imagination, Landmark of Happiness, Green Luxury, Eco Life, Bella Vista, Swiss County, Costa Rica, Capriccio, and Silver Mist were some of the advertisements that I spotted in and around Pune.

One luxury real estate developer, Marvel, has specifically made delivering "sophisticated" and "unparalleled" luxury to customers its mission. The Marvel Aurum project was located just a few miles from the Panchsheel *basti*.

The advertising blurb on the Marvel website for this project proclaimed it as "most-top-of-the-line project (ever)," located in Koregaon Park. Koregaon Park, Pune's exclusive residential area situated in northeastern Pune, was described as a green jewel surrounded by huge "rustling trees that canopy the quaint lanes." The website further elaborated how this elite space is dotted with sprawling bungalows, elegant towers, boutique stores, luxury spas, and world-class restaurants. The Koregaon Park space was presented as a backdrop for luxurious living that gratifies the senses. The advertising content further informed its readers that the moment one enters the lobby of the Aurum building, a concierge will greet its residents and the experience will simulate living in one of the most luxurious hotels in the world. The four-bedroom apartments, each 3,400 square feet, were asserted to be "beautifully planned," and Marvel Aurum's "crowning glory is a swimming pool in the privacy of each large, landscaped terrace. The one-touch automation just adds to the incredible luxury." In addition, the building would be protected by a distinctive *jaali*—a facade that works like an "elegant filigree sun-screen reducing the heat and glare inside." Above all, the advertisement for Marvel Aurum guaranteed that the residents will have so much power over nature that "even the seasons will dance to your tune." The idea was to remove oneself from the dirt, filth, and chaos of Indians streets and leave India to be in a global, mall-like space. Marvel makes it clear that these apartments are for those "seeking a world of their own" (see http://www.marvelrealtors.com/mail/aurum.html).

In their insightful study on advertisements of gated communities and high-end residential buildings in Bangalore, Chacko and Varghese (2009) argue that these exclusive residential buildings construct an image of a community or a home that is primarily based on class rather than on caste, kinship, or religion. These advertisements were mostly targeted to wealthy "global" Indians and Indian immigrants who were returning from the United States to work in Bangalore, Delhi, and Pune. The transnational and international culture that was promoted in advertisements near the *basti* implied a clean, structured, and organized living, away from the turmoil and grime of urban cities. The advertisements for gated enclaves, for example, incorporated an idealized form of European architecture and American space and landscaping with emphasis on cobbled patios and walkways and European-style villages. These rhetorical messages used signs and symbols to connote a lifestyle that was refined, "high class," and communicated meanings related to what it means to be "Indian," "global," and "cosmopolitan." Chacko and Varghese note,

> The near-absence of vernacular architecture in the built environment of the gated enclaves and the widespread adoption of the terminology of "villas," "townhouse" and "condominiums" that is standard in gated communities the world over, speak of the supplanting of local built forms by those with a global identity. . . . Such names and spaces identified as "servants" quarters, "foyers,"

"parlors," or "powder rooms" may also evidence a desire to replicate the settings of the privileged lives of former colonial masters. (p. 62)

As I continued my walk through Kalyani Nagar, I came across the store Bread Story: All Time Best Seller and Ad Labs Theatre, where the Hollywood movie *Life of Pi* was playing along with the Bollywood movie *Dabbang 2*. Crowds of college-aged youth were hanging around outside the theater and moving in and out of both the local Kalyani restaurant and the nearby McDonald's. Taking a left turn from the theater onto Kalyani Nagar Road, I was amazed to see a large number of beauty/fitness and health clinics that operated within the small residential area.

LOCATING PANCHSHEEL *BASTI*

To make my way to Panchsheel *basti*, I walked from Kalyani Nagar back to Koregaon Park, turning left onto Lane No. 5. My walk on this lane ended rather abruptly when I came upon an entrance to a railway track. As I walked across the railway track, I saw half a dozen young men playing cards. The busy railway track was the back entrance to the *basti*; this small slum settlement was tucked behind the wealthy, exclusive topographies. I walked through the back entrance that was used by several of the families in the slum and took the mud road that led to the interior of the *basti*.

The community of Panchsheel *basti* was established in 1965 near the railway line. It was a "declared slum" built illegally on the railway land owned by the Central Government. Joshi, Sen, and Hobson (2002) carried out the first comprehensive surveys and "poverty mapping" of slum settlements in Pune. They estimated that 45% of Pune's population lives in slum settlements. The residents of Panchsheel *basti* were a small part of the growing population of residents who lived in slum settlements. A designation of a "declared slum" by the local municipal government meant that the slum was entitled to basic amenities such as electricity and running water. Joshi et al. explain:

> The definition of "slum" is further complicated by the process of "declaration," which applies to settlements on privately owned land. When a settlement is recognized by the local municipality as being one where living conditions are below a specified standard, it is "declared" under the Maharashtra Slum Improvement Act (1971). Once declared, a slum is eligible for basic improvements including water supplies, common toilets, paving, electricity and drainage. In practice, many slums with poor living conditions have not been declared. Slums located on land owned by the public sector can be provided with basic amenities without being declared, although in practice this seldom happens: Many lack basic infrastructure and are similar to the undeclared slums (pp. 226–227).

The local municipal government has largely been indifferent to the needs of the slum dwellers and has portrayed them as illegal citizens, filthy, undeserving of assistance, and as people who steal land. It is important to understand that the *basti* youth throughout Pune have been battling both the crippling indifference of the government and the apathy of the public at large.

The Panchsheel *basti* had 501 households, with 1,724 people residing in these dwellings: 74% of families were Hindu, 15% were Muslims, and 11% were Christians. The majority (87%) of the families resided in semi-*pucca* (semi-permanent) houses, which were made with a combination of mud, bricks, and tin. Sometimes slum dwellers built the walls with bricks and the roof with corrugated tin sheets. Eleven percent resided in *kutcha* houses (temporary or makeshift mud-based dwellings) in which the roof, walls, and doors were typically composed of unfortified materials such as cardboard, tin, or asbestos sheets with either mud or cement flooring. Only 2% of the population had *pucca* houses, which are solid or permanent and made of bricks and cement. Most of the residents worked in the informal sector as construction laborers, security guards, rickshaw drivers, plumbers, maid servants, and night nurses. Many did odd jobs, serving as cleaners, janitors, and custodial workers for the new apartments and IT offices nearby.

Slums, Wages of Living, and Illegality in City Lights

In his book *Planet of the Slums*, Mike Davis (2007) argues that the world's urban labor force has doubled since 1980. He notes that the current population of cities is 3.2 billion, a number larger than the total population of the world when John F. Kennedy was the US president. He predicts that by 2050, almost all of future population growth—which is expected to reach 10 billion—is going to occur in cities and small, peri-urban areas and towns that reside next to the megacities. The sum of all the urban populations of China, India, and Brazil is almost equal to the entire population of Europe and North America.

The rapid expansion of urban areas across the world has created more than 24 megacities with populations that exceed 8 million people. There are now several "hypercities" with populations of more than 20 million. Davis (2007) forecasts that by 2025, Asia will be home to 10 hypercities that include Jakarta (24.9 million), Dhaka (25 million), Karachi (26.5 million), Shanghai (27 million), and Mumbai (33 million). These overgrown cities with their uneven geographies will consist of societies characterized by deep chasms of social inequality within cities and between cities.

Davis (2007) also argues that along with the rise of the megacities, there will be an exponential growth of second-tier cities and urban areas where rural families will not have to migrate to cities, but the cities will migrate to their living spaces. For example, there are now 35 medium-sized Indian cities that have reached beyond the 1 million mark. These future human settlements will be a mix of urban and rural settlements where "there will be polycentric webs with neither traditional cores nor recognizable peripheries" (p. 9). Much of this urbanization in the current climate of neoliberal globalization is largely disconnected from factors of growth, production, and sustainable forms of employment. Urbanization without growth is a common phenomenon in Latin America, the Middle East, and most of South Asia, and according to Davis, it is more the legacy of

> global political conjuncture—the worldwide debt crisis of the late 1970s and the subsequent IMF-led restructuring of Third World economies in the 1980s—than any iron law of advancing technology. . . . Policies of agricultural de-regulation and financial discipline enforced by the IMF and World Bank continued to generate an exodus of surplus labor to urban slums even as cities ceased to be job machines. (pp. 14–15)

The important question that economists have asked is why did urbanization in much of the developing world continue at such a rapid pace despite high urban unemployment, low wages, a shortage of housing, and high inflation? For example, Davis (2007) notes that in the 1980s, much of the African continent experienced stagnant unemployment and low agricultural productivity but experienced an annual urbanization rate of 3.5% or 4.0%. Cities across Asia and Africa have experienced negative growth and also simultaneously experienced meager investments in infrastructure, education, public housing, and education.

The rural-to-urban migration has ruptured the classical stereotypes of labor-intensive countryside and capital-intensive cities, and instead there are many reverse examples of capital-intensive countryside and labor-intensive cities. The phenomenon of "overurbanization," according to Davis (2007), is driven by "the reproduction of poverty, not by supply of jobs. . . . As a result, rapid urban growth in the context of structural adjustment, currency devaluation, and state retrenchment has been an inevitable recipe for the mass production of slums" (p. 16).

The phenomenon of globalization that has spread through the instrument of neoliberal capitalism has intensified the creation of more than 200,000 slums throughout the world, and it is now estimated that more than 1 billion people live in slums and experience absolute poverty. The city of Mumbai, for example, has an annual shortage of 450,000 formal housing units, which leads to an analogous increase in the creation of more than 500,000 informal slum dwellings. Out of a total of 500,000 people who come to Delhi annually, 400,000 of them become integrated within the existing infrastructure of slum communities (Appadurai, 2013). South Asia is home to one of the greatest concentrations of slums spread out in the cities of Delhi, Mumbai, Kolkata, Karachi, and Dhaka.

In India alone, there are three mega-slums, and more than 150 million people reside in slums (Davis, 2007). Mumbai has approximately 10–12 million squatters, and it is now considered the global capital of slum dwellers. According to the UN, a slum is officially defined by dense settlements; overcrowding; degraded, poor, or informal housing; inadequate access to safe water and sanitation; and insecurity of tenure (Davis, 2007). Panchsheel *basti* was indeed one of the small slum settlements that was built on railway land owned by the government, and thus the residents were technically considered to be *illegal*.[6] Neoliberalism has produced what Harvey (2005) calls uneven geographical development. He makes a distinction between capital accumulation and accumulation by dispossession. The former occurs through the growth of capital, and the latter is a phenomenon that occurs when public goods are privatized, such as the privatization of access to public services of water or education.

In most of the developing economies, the idea of a state that is strongly committed to public housing, social welfare, job development, education, and sanitation has been withering away. For a very long time in these nations, the governments have largely abandoned their responsibility to the urban poor, and they have been rather complicit in creating social conditions in which the philosophy of "accumulation by dispossession" takes root. Fine and Ruglis (2009) argue that neoliberalism produces state-sanctioned policies in which the discourse of personal responsibility and corporate profit replaces the basic duties and the obligations of the state and creates specific "circuits and consequences of dispossession" (p. 20). The youth all over the world are one of the casualties of this radical dispossession because neoliberal policies foster socially unequal societies and redistribute young people's "dreams and aspirational capacities" (p. 20).

Gender, Dignity, and the Search for Private Toilets

Everyday life in Panchsheel *basti* is disconnected and dispossessed from the swirls of global wealth that surround its neighborhood. Reportedly, 94% of the 500 families, or 1,700 individuals, use the five community toilet blocks in the settlement, with only a minority (6%) of families having access to individual toilets. This is a representation of the other India—an India in which, according to UN estimates, more than 600 million individuals have no access to a toilet or basic sanitation. The struggle for survival in the *basti* was evident as the urban poor in this slum eked out a meager living and experienced the daily indignities of public defecation and high unemployment. Most of the youth were not aware of the term globalization because they spoke Hindi or Marathi and very little English. In Hindi, globalization was defined as "bhumandal-ikarana," "sarvabhaumikata," and "pragati," and in Marathi it was referred to as "jagatikikarana," but these were esoteric words that were used in academic or journalistic writing and had not entered the colloquial usage. These words implied awakening, worldwide activity, or progress, but for the families living in the slums, globalization was usually perceived as a social phenomenon that had only improved the lives of upper-class and affluent families.

Zainab, a 19-year-old female who studied at Dr. Ambedkar College and lived in the *basti*, identified "water logging"[7] and lack of toilet facilities as add-ing to the daily stress of living in the slums:

s: But have the conditions in the *basti* improved?

z: No.

s: What is the major problem here?

z: Water logging in homes especially during rains.

s: Where does the water come from, apart from rains?

z: Due to the leakage in drainage lines.

s: And what about toilets?

z: We have common toilets built by government. It is another problem.

s: What is the problem with the toilets?

z: During rains, water accumulates on roads. So the roads actually become invisible. We face difficulties in going to the toilet.

s: So you have 10 toilets for about 1,500 persons?

z: Yes.

s: So you face problems in using toilets?

z: Yes. And there is no hygiene. The woman appointed for cleaning bath-rooms is not doing her work properly. Nobody shows any interest in cleaning the toilets.

s: So there's a lot of filth around there?

z: Yes. We can also see overflowing garbage bins.

s: The garbage is also close to bathroom?

z: Yes. And in rains it adds to the problems. The garbage spills out of the bin and it stinks.

Zainab believed that having degraded public toilet facilities was one of the greatest challenges for the women in the slums, and it was a problem that had deteriorated throughout the decades as the population of the *basti* swelled. While the toilet situation was singled out as an overarching problem that overwhelms the families in the *basti*, Zainab also talked about other chal-lenges, such as not having access to education, secure employment, and per-manent housing, that shaped the life of the people in the *basti*.

Zeenat, who worked as a social worker for the local nonprofit organiza-tion, Shelter Associates, lived in Panchsheel *basti* and had introduced me to several youth who had spent their childhood and most of their adult life in this slum. She said, "You should talk to a young man, Aman. He is shy but if you can engage him, he might speak." Zeenat gave me some background about Aman's family. Aman had four siblings, and two of his sisters were married. His father was an alcoholic and particularly abusive to his wife and his children.

Aman had suffered from polio as a child, and his legs were paralyzed. Zeenat said that when Aman's father "comes home from work, sees Aman sitting on the bed, doing nothing . . . he hits him. Then he gets physical with his wife." Aman was enrolled in a basic computer program in school, but he could not afford to pay hostel fees so he was forced to drop out. When I entered his 200-square-foot house that was made of mud, cement, and a tin roof, I found Aman sitting on a black metal bed. He told me that he is free these days because he is unemployed. He said, "I feel bad due to polio. I could not walk properly. I was affected with it when I was one and a half years old." Then I asked him what are the basic necessities that he cannot afford to buy:

s: What are the essentials that you want but are unable to purchase?
A: There are many such products.
s: Can you name them?
A: Computer, products required for luxurious lifestyle, car, good house in a good society.
s: What do you mean by luxurious lifestyle?
A: It means a prosperous life, where nothing is lacking.

Aman said the he notices the youth from other societies showing off their luxuries, such as cars, jeans, and other brands, and then he spoke about how the lack of private toilet facilities is a torturous indignity that he has to experience every day. He wakes up at 4:00 a.m. to go to the public toilets so he can avoid the long lines. Aman uses his hands to move his body forward, and the road to the toilet is dark and often filled with muddy water. Often when he is inside the public toilet, people bang on his door, urging him to finish his morning rituals. He told me that he really wants "a private toilet" in his house so he does not have to wake up at 4:00 a.m. to use the filthy toilets.

Aman's tone was stark, matter-of-fact, and he mentioned to me that he is looking for just one break and one opportunity in his life. He had visited Hinjewadi, a newly built IT park, for an interview at a domestic, Marathi-speaking call center. Aman did not get the job. He explained, "There was a problem. It was on fifth floor. It was not possible for me to walk to the fifth floor daily. There was a vacancy at a hotel too. But they wanted to hire a person who could walk properly." After my conversation with Aman, I went to Zeenat's house to have tea. I invited Aman, but he was not interested in continuing our conversation with others around us. Zeenat told me that *aapaij log* (disabled people) and young women sometime have to defecate outside because the public toilets are busy or not working.

The 2012 United Nations' "Millennium Development Goals Report" (United Nations Development Programme, 2012) states that 626 million people in India do not have access to a toilet and practice what is called "open defecation." Every day, millions of women and girls in India experience teasing, sexual harassment, stalking, violent assault, and rape when they go out to defecate in the open in bushes, fields, and gutters on the road. Dasra, a philanthropic organization in Pune, published an extensive study in 2012 titled "Squatting Rights: Access to Toilets in Urban India." This study reported that 30% of women from the underprivileged sections of Indian society experience violent sexual assaults every year because lack of sanitation facilities forces them to travel long distances to find secluded spots or public facilities to meet their bodily needs. This report specifically highlights that 70% of girls living in Delhi slums experience teasing and verbal assaults when they are searching for places to defecate. Sanitation is a matter of both public health and gender equality. Every day, 1,600 Indian children younger than age 5 years die due to lack of proper sanitation. They die from diarrhea, cholera, typhoid, and parasitic or worm infections.

For many women in urban and rural India, lack of sanitation is linked to issues of health, safety, dignity, and education.[8] Toilet access increases school attendance for girls because parents are more likely to send their daughters to school if they know they can dispose of their sanitary products in safe toilet facilities when menstruating. Recently, families in some villages in the state of Maharashtra, India, have refused to marry their daughters into families that do not have proper toilets. The 2008 UN fact sheet on sanitation mentions that these families have painted signs in their village that states, "Daughters from our village are not married into villages where open defecation is practiced" (UN-Water, 2008).

Every major report or study on sanitation published in the past decade notes that toilets give women dignity, access to education, security, and improved health. Almost everyone I interviewed in the *basti*—young and old, men and women—singled out lack of toilet faculties as being crucial to how they viewed themselves: urban poor who cannot afford basic amenities. Both Zainab and Aman expressed that not having a private toilet was a matter of dignity, and it impacted how they viewed their progress in life. The families living in the slums emphasized that having access to toilets was about dignity and privacy, but it also protected them from diseases and ensured environmental sustainability. Lack of access to sanitation constituted one of the major threats to the security, stability, welfare, and development of children, youth, and families living in slums.

RAVI'S STORY: CLASS INEQUALITIES
AND DANGEROUS LIVING

As I walked from Zeenat's house through the narrow lanes, I passed by exposed drains and women washing utensils and clothes using water collected in buckets. The stench from the public toilets and overflowing garbage bins punctuated the spaces. Scooters and bicycles were lined up neatly against the walls of the small homes. It was mid-afternoon, and the rare soothing and gentle chill of the December sun enveloped the *basti*. The houses were mostly semi-*pucca* and hugged each other with common partition walls. Most of the by-lanes in the slums were paved and kept reasonably clean because the lanes functioned as a social space where the neighbors congregated, cooked, bathed, and argued with each other.

I interviewed Ravi Kartik Yadav, a 22-year-old male, at his house in the *basti*. When I entered Ravi's house, his mother walked out to give us privacy for the interview; "I will work outside so you can talk," she offered helpfully. His house was a one-room space with a small "kitchen corner," and on the other side of the room was a tiny enclosed space for bathing. A small television sat perched on the Godrej stainless-steel cupboard along with a framed Bachelor's Degree in Commerce diploma certificate from the same college where I completed my undergraduate degree in psychology. We sat on a bed that served as multipurpose furniture, and we began the conversation by talking about our alma mater, Wadia College.

I remarked to him that I had recently visited the college and was surprised not to see a "cycle stand" as it was replaced by a parking space for mopeds and motorbikes. Ravi laughed, "That was another time . . . there are also many cars now." Ravi was born in this *basti*, and he had spent his childhood and youth in a 200-square-foot room. His father, he said, did "service" in Khadki and brought in a very meager income. His mother was a housewife. He had another brother and two sisters, and all of them lived in that small space.

Monsoon Rains, Miniskirts, and the Hi-Fi Class

I asked Ravi to tell me what globalization had meant to him and if the growth of IT companies and the new economic prosperity had made any difference to this slum or his life in general:

R: No. Nothing has changed in our slums.
S: You are staying here for the last 20 years. Haven't you seen any change?
R: Nothing has changed in the slums. Changes have taken place outside.
S: What kind of changes have you seen outside?

R: Towers, residential buildings and commercial complexes, big companies, huge projects like Magarpatta City, Trimbak City have come up.
City is progressing, but nothing has progressed in our slums. Though
there are some development works here like construction of roads.

S: So there is not much change in your life?

R: No change.

Ravi explained that one of the most difficult challenges faced by the slum
dwellers is not having access to clean toilets. There are just a few stalls for
more than 1,500 people, so many people end up defecating outside or they
wait in long lines in the morning. The public toilets are unclean, and for many
in the slum, having a private toilet inside one's house is considered a luxury.

The other problem, he identified, was the excessive water logging that
occurs in the low slopes and nonpaved lanes of the *basti* during the monsoon
season. He took me outside his house and showed me the space just beyond
his door where the water accumulates: "Last monsoon, all this water had come
up in to our room . . . it was unmanageable." However, not having a toilet
inside the house was a source of even more immense stress. Ravi said that
although his family could save money to build a toilet, there was no space to
install it. A toilet would replace the entire bathing space, and that would be
just as inconvenient. He further added, "Suppose guests come to the house
when females in the family are taking a bath. When the females come out of
the bathroom for changing dress, all the gents have to move out of the house.
They cannot change dress in the same room." He said maneuvering around a
small space on a daily basis and accommodating to the needs of five people is
an ongoing struggle, but everyone adjusts. Ravi said there are larger families
in the *basti* that have to make due with a one-room space, with husbands,
wives, children, and in-laws all staying together under the same roof.

In Ravi's view, the discourse of "globalization equals progress" was superficial because it had brought no meaningful change in his life, although he
had observed significant cultural and economic shifts in the affluent areas
around the neighborhood. When he was growing up, Ravi said, he saw more
young women wear sarees and dresses, and now they wear "minis and even
micro-mini dresses. Girls also enjoy cigarettes." Ravi seemed outraged at what
he perceived to be the deterioration of Indian cultural values. He argued that
in the past only the older men consumed alcohol, and now even schoolgoing
children drank alcohol and smoked. He characterized the affluent families and
youth around him as being from a "high society" or being from a *hi-fi* class—
drinking, driving fancy cars, and being indifferent about the world was a fashion statement for the hi-fi class.

Ravi argued that young people also consumed alcohol in his *basti* and that
could be justified because they were experiencing hardships, unemployment,
and a bleak future. I asked him to describe what the term *hi-fi* meant because

it was a word that I had heard used by several others who had lived in the *basti*. Just as in the West, hi-fi originally referred to the quality of music that was produced through "high-fidelity" technology—abbreviated as hi-fi. In colloquial, English-speaking urban Indian discourse, hi-fi referred to "high-level thinking" or "high-level living" or a certain style of urban living that was reflected in lives of the upper and affluent classes. Ravi said that a hi-fi lifestyle referred to living in nice apartments in an upper-class neighborhood, wearing branded clothes such as jeans, having a motorbike or a car, and going to bars and discos.

Hi-fi also symbolized a liberal and modern outlook, that gave permission to adolescent girls and boys to being romantic in public with their partners. A hi-fi young woman smoked, went to bars, and wore miniskirts. A hi-fi young man wore jeans, branded sneakers, drove a car, and displayed a "carefree" and "confident" attitude. A person labeled as hi-fi spoke fluent English with a neutral or a "convent school" accent. Ravi claimed that having a hi-fi lifestyle was associated with having money and a high standard of living. He told me that the youth from the *basti* could not become hi-fi because becoming hi-fi was connected with having material luxuries and having a specific lifestyle. Ravi remarked that a young person from a *basti* whose father works as a servant or does odd jobs cannot even dream of becoming a hi-fi person. In contrast, children born to businessmen and professionals from places such as Kalyani Nagar inherently have access to resources leading to the hi-fi lifestyle—they can go abroad, hang out at exclusive clubs, and give the impression that they are having a good time.

The youth from the Panchsheel *basti,* he noted, mostly used buses or bicycles to move around, and those were not symbols of being hi-fi. I asked Ravi to explain why he believed that the *basti* youth could never attain a hi-fi identity:

s: You talk about high life, hi-fi, high standard. What do you mean by that?

R: I used to go to my school and college on a bicycle. And my friends used to come on two-wheelers. Some of them used to come in four wheelers. Then at the canteen, I could only afford to purchase a *vada pav* (bread and potato fritter) and they were purchasing costly burgers. It was not possible for me to spend Rs. 50 a day.

s: For them, this amount (Rs. 50 a day) is small?

R: Yes. My dad used to give me Rs. 5 every morning. The money was meant for repairing my bicycle if it gets punctured. I used to save this money for purchasing my books, paying my class fees and other educational expenses.

Ravi emphasized that there are profound class differences between the hi-fi youth and the youth from the *basti*, and the divide can never be bridged because the hi-fi people consider the urban poor as "cheap log" (cheap people). The word "cheap" in the Indian urban context implies moral defects, vulgarity, and having a working-class lifestyle.

Class Struggles and the Impending Anxiety of Eviction

Ravi told me that most of the hi-fi youth who studied with him at Wadia College were not focused on their studies. The hi-fi youth, he said, could neglect their academics because they were aware that they had a strong financial and well-connected familial support system that would ensure them a decent future. He commented that "going to Inox (modern multiplex cinema hall) was a routine thing for them.[9] While, my friends were spending time in library, solving accounts problems." Hi-fi youth hung out at malls, watched movies at multiplex cinemas, and drove cars and fancy bikes; the boys hung out with girlfriends who wore miniskirts, and girls had boyfriends who were into drinking, smoking, and wearing fashionable clothes.

Ravi argued that the social and class barriers in India were not a new phenomenon because the chasm between the rich and the poor had existed throughout Indian history. Ravi said that as the neighborhoods around him were becoming more prosperous, the youth from the *basti* were also searching for ways to go beyond their limited lives. He had a close set of friends from his *basti* who shared his class background and values, and he felt emotionally connected to them. In college, however, he had developed a social network of friends and acquaintances from a range of classes—some he described as "two wheeler" class (motorbike) and others "four wheeler" class (cars). The navigation and negotiation of social class differences was extremely stressful and demeaning for Ravi. He did not disclose to his middle- and upper-class friends that he lived in a *basti* and that his family was part of the urban poor in the city with limited resources. He remarked that he felt not just different from his hi-fi friends but also inferior to some of them:

> Yes, it has happened many times. I used to feel ashamed, inferior while going to the college on my bicycle. So I was parking my cycle on the rear gate. And then I used to walk into the college from the main gate. My fashion sense was not like theirs (rich students). I got some money from parents for paying college fees, which itself was a big thing. There was a different group of poor students that I used to hang out with.

Ravi also resented the physical encroachment of the hi-fi society on the areas around the *basti*. First, the "big companies" came to his neighborhood, and then industrial high-tech parks, restaurants, clubs, residential buildings, and call centers had taken over much of the space around *basti*.

Growing up, Ravi said, Panchsheel *basti* had many green spaces for play and open grounds for taking walks. He pointed to an apartment building near him: "There was open ground with a few trees where we now see Clover building. We used to play cricket on this ground." Ravi wanted to move out of this settlement, but he was losing hope that he would ever be able to afford a small apartment anywhere near his neighborhood. He remarked that he did not have a job and not even a small-time family business, so there were few options for his future. What made his family and him most insecure, however, was not having ownership of the house in which he had grown up. He had some security knowing that he lived in a "declared slum" so his family could not be evicted easily, but the events of 1995, when the local government demolished some houses in the *basti*, gave him nightmares.

Ravi's *basti* existed on land that was owned by the government, and in "legal terms" all the houses were temporary housing built on public land. Ravi was infuriated and worried that despite living in Panchsheel *basti* all his life; his family still could not claim their house as their own:

> Yes, I wish to leave the slum. But this is the only house we have. Where will we go if this house breaks? No, this is not a permanent house. It is constructed on railway land. So if this breaks, we don't know where to go. In 1995, we have seen houses being demolished here and people actually living on the pavements. We understand the problems they suffered.

Ravi argued that it was fairly "dangerous" for youth to live in the slums because many were unable to deal with day-to-day stress of lack of sanitation, not having permanent employment and earning daily wages, and living with the fear that they could become homeless anytime. Ravi and other youth whom I had interviewed believed that the young boys in the slums had taken to drinking cheap liquor because six new liquor dens had opened in and around the *basti*:

R: Yes. It has increased. Reason is unemployment. Because they don't have work, the youths spend time gambling, playing cards and drinking liquor.

S: Does that result in quarrels, or fights?

R: Yes. Even small disputes are giving rise to major clashes. Police cases are filed against those indulging in fights. Once a police case is filed, these youth then start thinking, it will not matter even if they are booked in another case. But many youth in our slum are educated. However, they don't have good jobs.

At the end of our conversation, Ravi told me that he felt good sharing his story, but he reiterated the point that he does not believe that everyday living in the *basti* has changed in any significant way. He observed, rather philosophically, "There are many problems. In fact life itself has become a problem. And the only solution is keep living your life."

What is the narrative "tone" and "imagery" of these stories? McAdams (1997) argues that identity stories have certain identifiable structures, content, and components narrated in a setting; the stories reveal conflict and drama between the characters, significant scenes, and turning points, and they are made of resolved and unresolved endings. Life stories also display an overall emotional tone or an attitude that may be, for example, pessimistic, resentful, buoyant, or positive. The life story is also shaped by particular metaphors, similes, sounds, and the imagery that capture unique experiences of the narrator. Therefore, "an individual's favorite metaphor and symbols are reflective of what his or her identity is about" (McAdams, 1997, p. 66). Drawing on the work of MacIntyre and Taylor, McAdams argues that the creation of identity through narrative requires an individual to have a moral orientation in the world. These moral orientations are deeply ideological and reflect the political, social, and religious belief system of the narrator.

The imagery in the narratives of Panchsheel *basti* youth is largely about the lack of basic amenities in their lives and the social inequality that they witness around them. The youth with whom I spoke asserted their agency and voice through political mobilization, employment, and education to bring about change in their lives, but they had little hope that the structural conditions of the slum were going to change in the near future. The aspirations of the slum youth were in many ways similar to those of the other middle-class youth—they wanted upward social mobility, name-brand goods, and luxuries that they noticed around them and on television. However, their aspirations were essentially shaped by their inability to transform the power structures around them.

PRIYANKA'S STORY: CULTURAL PRACTICES AND MAPS OF ASPIRATION

Priyanka's story echoes the struggles expressed by Ravi and Zainab and others from the *basti* regarding the futility of individual effort in the face of asymmetrical power relationships, lack of material resources, and diminishing opportunities. Priyanka, a 21-year-old woman who had lived all her life in the *basti*, did much of her schooling in a Marathi medium school (the instruction was in the local Marathi language) and then transferred to the all-women's St. Meera's College to complete her 11th and 12th grades, where the instruction was in English (English medium) and the academics were fairly demanding. She was compelled to drop out of college because her parents could not afford her college fees:

I had to leave studies due to family problems. It was mainly due to lack of money. My parents don't earn much. My sister has completed her graduation, B.A. I also want to do some courses. We are three sisters and there is nobody else to look after the family.

Priyanka had been practicing taekwondo for the past 2 years with the hope that she would be recruited as a constable in the local police force. She had intended to resume her college studies once she was selected for training in the police force.

Mall Culture, Maid Servants, and Education

One of Priyanka's sisters was married off after she completed 10th grade because their parents did not have the financial means to take care of their daughters:

> Our parents feel bad that they do not have a son. All three are daughters. So they got her married early. But we want to do something. We want to move ahead with the world. Wherever we go, computer knowledge is required.

Priyanka had decent prospects of getting a job in a mall as a sales assistant, but her parents prevented her from applying because the job required her to work in the mall until 10:00 p.m. She said, "So my mother did not allowed me to do the job. She said the people would talk bad about me if I came late." I asked her why people would talk about her negatively if she worked late hours in the mall. Priyanka said that her parents believe that malls are for high-class or hi-fi people and not for traditional girls with "middle-class" values living in her slum. Priyanka stated that there is a fear among the parents that malls are places where young girls will meet boys and become intimate or have "affairs" with them. The families in the slum, she added, viewed young women as being wives, caregivers, and housewives, and someone working in the mall was viewed as breaking traditional roles.

According to Priyanka, the slum would never progress because young girls and women are not perceived as intelligent enough to go to school and have careers. Her neighbors and relatives constantly put pressure on her parents to get the girls married off when they had just graduated from high school. Priyanka noted that there is a deep gender bias in the slums, and she wanted to prove that girls are as intelligent and hard-working as boys. She wished to show she could be independent, but the system did not allow young women to realize their full potential:

> We don't even get any help for education. One of my friends could not pay her college fees in grade 12 due to her father's illness. None of her teachers came

forward for paying her fees. I felt sad that I could not help her. I am not rich and so I was unable to help her. Poor people don't ask for money for everything. But they should at least get some help for completing education.

Priyanka was ambitious and had planned her future carefully so she could move out of the *basti* in the future. She got admitted to an English medium college (in which the primary instruction is in English), learned the basic computer applications, and then found a job in a mall and was practicing martial art skills to prepare for a career in law enforcement.

Priyanka was self-confident, assertive, and had aspirations for her family, but the obstacles she faced were fundamentally tied to not having resources. Her catalog of frustrations regarding the short supply of basic amenities and the lack of access to resources in the *basti* by now had become a familiar theme in every interview I conducted in the slums or with the local social workers: a shortage of toilets; lack of educational opportunities; overflowing garbage; the smell of decomposing food; the unsustainable ratio of 1 toilet to 50 people resulting in many people defecating outside; indifferent and corrupt local politicians; strategic, self-interested visits by the power elite during election time; vulnerability of families who had lived in the slum for decades but feared eviction at any time; the incessant sounds of passing trains making it difficult to study in the evening; lack of job security due to working in the informal economy; crumbling and decrepit walls in their homes; leaking tin roofs that threatened to cave in every monsoon; and lack of English fluency prohibiting the youth from being competitive in the globalized local job market.

Priyanka's father was a day wage laborer who held temporary jobs in the construction industry a few times per week. During the monsoon season, he had no employment because building work slowed during that period. She was currently spending time preparing for her police training exams and was mainly working at home helping her mother with chores such as cleaning and cooking. She had witnessed first-hand how rich people lived because she had worked as a "maid servant" during vacations doing *jhadu-pocha* (sweeping and cleaning) for several well-to-do families in the area. She said, "If I missed a day's work, the wages would be subtracted from a $12 monthly salary."

Priyanka remarked the only way out of slum life was through acquiring an education that gave her reasonably good employment. She argued that upper- and middle-class youth have the advantages of education, well-connected networks, and living in surroundings that are conducive to their health, body, and mind. The upper-class youth get all the "facilities," and she further emphasized, "I wish I also get all the things they have, but I don't have them. I will work for them." However, Priyanka promptly dismissed her wishes and remarked that the youth from the slum can dream big, but they will not have a car or a nice house in a posh residential complex. Marrying a rich boy was not a realistic possibility either:

> No, no. I will get married someday, but no boy from a rich family will marry us. It only happens in films that people from rich families join relations with slum people, get married to a girl from slum. In reality, I have never seen anything like this. In my case, my parents would get me married to someone in our relation, where situation would be same. Only house will change, but the problems would remain the same.

Priyanka blamed the conservative "mentality" of the families living in slums and the indifference of the government, the politicians, and the wealthy class for contributing to a lack of economic progress in the *basti*. The local politicians, she argued, win elections because of the *basti* votes, but once in power they become disengaged. The politicians who get elected by the *basti* voters, Priyanka emphasized, need to investigate the realities on the ground in the slums. She reminded me that a "few days before we went to the local corporate for proof of residence certificate. But his men said that he was sleeping and asked us to come later. These politicians speak a lot, give many assurances, but do not do any work."

ASPIRATIONS, IDENTITY, AND STRUCTURAL PRACTICES

The stories of Priyanka, Ravi, Aman, Zainab, and other youth I met shed light on the dark side of neoliberal globalization—where large numbers of citizens are left out of the narrative of progress. These youth had ambition, hope, energy, and what Appadurai (2013, p. 189) refers to as a "map of aspirations." However, the structural conditions in the slums did not provide them with the resources, opportunities, stories, or tools to implement their hopes and desires. As Appadurai reminds us, aspirations are "never simply individual. . . . They are always formed in interaction and in the thick of social life" (p. 187). For Priyanka, her aspirations were not just connected to her individual desires but also given meaning through the cultural norms and practices of the collective social life within which she was embedded.

Aspirations about the "good life" in the *basti* were intimately connected to local ideas about marriage, gender, divinity, cosmology, work, leisure, respectability, health, and virtue. Yet, Appadurai (2013) argues that the capacity to aspire is a "navigational capacity" (p. 188). Due to their lack of opportunities, poorer members of society are unable to flex their capacity to aspire in tangible, realistic, and concrete ways. This limitation, due to their circumstances, in turn prohibits their ability to exercise their "voice." Drawing upon Hirschman's (1970) work, Appadurai notes that the poor tend to move between loyalty and exit. Here, loyalty refers to an attachment or acceptance to norms, and exit in this case could imply violent protest or total apathy. Rather, Appadurai calls for initiatives and interventions among poorer communities that can nurture the "faculty of 'voice'"—"the capacity to debate, contest, inquire, and participate critically" (p. 189). For the *basti* youth whom I interviewed, the rhetoric of globalization and its promise of progress and prosperity were a distant, unrealizable horizon. While their narratives certainly express individual agency, their aspirational capacity and their hopes for a better future are continually battered and hemmed in by the exigencies of their present.

In the past decade, psychologists and behavioral economists have drawn on the social psychology literature of willpower and self-control to analyze how poor people make everyday decisions about food, money, recreation, medicine, alcohol, and calorie and food consumption. The key finding can be summarized as follows: Exercising willpower essentially involves making rational decisions when we are faced with conflicting choices in our lives. Willpower is a limited resource, and it uses a "cool cognitive system" rather than a "hot emotional system." From this view, the exercise of willpower is related to personal goals (Bauemister & Tierney, 2011). The behavioral science research on this subject has come to the conclusion that the self-control that the poor have to exercise on an everyday basis has much more devastating consequences for the poor than for the rich. In this regard, Abhijit Banerji and Esther Duflo (2011) explain,

> Because self-control is hard to buy, self-aware decision makers take other defensive actions against the possibility of being tempted in the future. An obvious strategy is not save as much, because we know that we will just waste the money tomorrow. We might as well give in to the temptation today, if all we are going to do is give in to it tomorrow. This perverse logic of temptation operates in the same way for the poor as it does for the rich, but there are good reasons that the consequences may be much serious for the poor than for the rich. . . . The result is a vicious circle: Saving is less attractive for the poor, because for them the goal tends to be very far away, and they know that there will be lots of temptations along the way. But of course, if they do not save they remain poor. (pp. 198–199)

Thus, in addition to citing the structural problems that impede the progress of the poor, these studies have provided us with important insights about how the poor think and make decisions about their resources. However, many of these behavioral economics studies are also based on a "rational choice model" and an "ethics of probability," so they tend to define aspiration, self-control, and choice as constructs that are mainly located in the individual (Appadurai, 2013). Such an individualized conceptualization largely ignores the cultural contexts and structural constraints that frame and give meaning to the narratives of the youth living in slums.

We need to move away from thinking of aspirations as arising out of an individual cognitive system; rather, we should locate them in the practices of everyday life. Upper-class women from Mumbai and Chennai have different views of happiness compared to a working-class woman in rural Pune. What is important to note here is that in every instance, aspirations of a "good life" are closely linked to a system of ideas located, in Appadurai's words (2013), within "a larger map of local ideas and beliefs about: life and death, the nature of worldly possessions, the significance of material assets, the value of peace or warfare" (p. 187).

My central argument here is that the capacity to aspire, to regulate one's behavior, and to exercise self-control is deeply linked to the cultural practices and other stories that circulate in the lives of the urban poor. The stories that the youth in the slums narrated in my research are highly class bound and show that their *capacity to aspire* is not just an individual trait or a psychological ability. Rather, aspirations, willpower, and other so-called rational choice-making activities are shaped by larger narratives of power and cultural capacity, which are in turn unevenly distributed in our society. Thus, it is the meaning-making capacity of narrative, with its ability to shed light on how people interpret their experiences through stories, that can be used to understand the process of identity formation of the youth living in slums.

The concept of imagination, as previously mentioned, is linked to the "narrative way of knowing" that Bruner (1986) believes is essential to understanding personhood. It must be noted, however, that in the field of psychology, there are very few accounts about how non-Western populations living in urban poverty are using their narrative imagination to come to terms with their changing conceptions of personhood and identity. Following Appadurai (2013), I emphasize that I am not arguing that the poor do not have the capacity to aspire, have ambition, and voice their needs. However, part of being in the condition of poverty is having reduced opportunities and therefore lacking the power to enact and pursue their aspirations, practices, and experiences to achieve favorable outcomes. The capacity to aspire is not equally distributed in a given society, and the affluent and well-to-do classes often have an advantage in having a much more developed capacity to aspire. Appadurai (2013) elaborates:

> It means the better off you are (in terms of power, dignity, and material resources), the more likely you are to be conscious of the links between the more and less immediate objects of aspiration. Because the better off, by definition, have a more complex experience of the relation between a wide range of ends and means, because they have a bigger stock of available experiences of the relationship of aspirations and outcomes. . . . They too express their aspirations in concrete, individual wishes and wants. But they are able to produce justifications, narratives, metaphors, and pathways through which bundles of goods and services are actually tied to wider social scenes and contexts, and to still more abstracts and beliefs. (p. 188)

The stories I heard in the *basti* reflected individual aspirations. However, the propeller of power and material resources to transform these nascent aspirations into realistic and productive outcomes was missing, thereby limiting their "navigational capacity." Building on Appadurai's (2013) ideas regarding "navigational capacity," I propose the notion of *narrative capacity* as the ability of the poorer urban youth to create stories that matter in the larger society and the maps that are required to realize their aspirations. The narrative psychology perspective provides us with a theoretical framework to connect the individual concepts of "voice," "self-control," and "capacity" to larger collective and cultural practices.

If we accept the premise that culture-is-in-self and self-is-in-culture, then individual narratives about aspirations are shaped by collective norms and belief systems about aspiration, and thus individual human capacities are dialogically connected to local norms, values, and interpretations. It is through narrative that individuals make sense of cultural webs of meaning (Brockmeier, 2012). What is important to recognize here is that the aspirations of the slum youth are in many ways similar to those of the other middle- and upper-class youth: They want social mobility and the brands, goods, and luxuries they see around them and on television. The basic difference is that the upper- and middle-class youth whom I interviewed had the advantage of having structures of wealth, legacy, education, social networks, and also stories of aspiration that empowered them to imagine and navigate their way to success in their education, business, or employment. The upper- and middle-class youth also had collective storytellers—parents, teachers, peers, and supervisors—who were able to expand the horizons of their aspirational understanding. This enabling of their navigational capacity as *narrative capacity* stands in contrast to Priyanka, for example, whose parents were limited in their capacity to imagine a different and better future for her due to their own structural disadvantages.

One of the important arguments made by Appadurai (2013) is that the capacity to aspire is not so much about conceiving the past through the lens of tradition but, rather, about defining the "future as a cultural fact." Within economics and the broader UN approach to poverty, development is always about designing economic futures. In contrast, scholars in anthropology or cultural psychology work with cultural concepts that are based on "pastness." Bringing the "future" into the fold of culture allows us to design futures in which there are possibilities of fashioning new stories of self and identity. Thus, cultural patterns that give rise to specific beliefs about aspirations can be changed and modified through debate, collective mobilization, and strengthening of the collective voice of the poor.

This change requires psychologists to link debates about poverty to both individual psychology and how collective narratives about success and scarcity shape an individual's capacity to aspire. The burden of creating specific narratives and navigational capacities should not be entirely the personal responsibility of the urban poor. Rather, the combination of government intervention, creating social policies that reduce social and economic inequality, the willingness of dominant classes to redistribute capital, and the collective mobilization of the urban poor together are required to create new structures through which poor children and youth can reimagine and alter their cultural and narrative maps of aspiration.

The well-known Indian economist, Amartya Sen (1999), argues that "freedom of agency," or individual freedom, is shaped by the social, political, and economic opportunities that are available to us. Thus, Sen writes, "Development consists of the removal of various types of unfreedoms that leave people with little choice and little opportunity of exercising their reasoned agency. The removal of substantial unfreedoms, it is argued here, is *constitutive* of development" (p. xii, emphasis in original). The linking of agency and identity with development or culture, then, directly takes us into the heart of psychology—a humanistic science of sense-making.

Ultimately, concepts of voice and aspiration have to be viewed through what Taylor (1989) calls a hermeneutics of "ethical horizon" in which concrete human capabilities can be shaped, made sustainable, and given meaning and expression in local contexts through others. This means creating a new language for psychology. Mark Freeman (2014) argues that much of psychology gives priority to self and is "essentially egocentric" (p. 1). In contrast, he makes a plea for fashioning a new psychology that is other-oriented psychology or *ex-centric* and that is based on the priority of the other. An "other-oriented" narrative psychology will allow us to examine how our individual aspirations and capacities are connected to structural conditions of inequality, lack of educational opportunities, and the lives and everyday practices of the hi-fi class. In this context, part of understanding the "language of otherness" means we have to strengthen the "narrative voice" of the poor and think of them as partners in the battle against poverty.

The well-to-do youth from the adjacent neighborhoods were important *others* for the Panchsheel *basti* youth, and they played an integral role in shaping their identity narratives. The youth from the *basti* mostly described the middle class and rich as being "morally" adrift in their pursuit of money, who were mostly occupied with frivolous romances and excessive drinking and smoking. Their narratives were shaped by their encounters with structural inequality, their cultural maps of aspiration, and the affluence that surrounded them.

HI-FI IDENTITY, EDUCATION, AND ENGLISH LANGUAGE SKILLS

The narratives analyzed previously are dialogically connected to what the *basti* youth perceive as the "hi-fi" class. Hi-fi youth are described as living in posh houses and apartments, driving motorbikes and cars, wearing fashionable branded clothes, hanging out with girlfriends and boyfriends, and having a lifestyle that is seemingly free of worry or anxiety. Repeatedly in my interviews, the youth expressed such imagined constructions of upper- and middle-class youth who had heterogeneous lives that were differentially shaped by gender, education, social networks, and varied financial circumstances. However, what is important to note here is that the "hi-fi" construct played an important role in shaping their *stories of identity*. The hi-fi youth were visible in media, malls, and surrounding areas of the Panchsheel *basti*, and they were also portrayed as the new symbols of globalization: English-speaking call center agents and IT workers. Many youth from Panchsheel *basti* viewed the rich and the affluent class as being indifferent to poverty and morally corrupt, but they also expressed a yearning for having access to their symbolic and material privileges.

The youth of Panchsheel *basti* were accustomed to seeing their wealthier peers drive motorcycles and fancy cars in the evening, throw parties on weekends, and drink expensive alcohol at local bars. In contrast, most of residents in the slum held low-paying jobs as rickshaw drivers, security guards, waiters, and maids or worked in the construction industry as manual laborers. The families owned very few necessities, yet almost all the houses that I visited had a television set with a basic cable package that gave them access to more than 50 Indian and Western channels. Many family members watched mostly Hindi and Marathi television programs on a regular basis, but they also were fond of some dubbed English movies and television programs. During a focus group discussion, the young people of the *basti* told me that there was a gradual but perceptible change in cultural identities of the youth—the girls wore jeans, they were encouraged to go to school and college, and some whom they knew had recently entered love marriages rather than traditionally arranged partnerships.

The Importance of "Personality"

The major source of entertainment for these youth was watching television shows, movies, and cricket games and also copying the fashion of Bollywood stars. Sohaib Khan, a 19-year-old who was studying commerce at Poona College, told me that there is a "craze" for Star Plus serials and soap operas in the slum. He remarked, "People leave all work and see these serials. And what they see in the serials they try to do the same in real life. They wear the same kind of dress that actors in these serials wear." Sohaib lived with his three brothers and parents in a small house, typical of the *basti*. Sohaib, too, began the interview by identifying the lack of clean toilets as one of the daily stresses of his life. He said that the toilet doors were broken, there was not enough light in the toilets so it was difficult to move around after dark, and the rotting garbage that accumulated near the toilets worsened the situation. He told me that the hi-fi class had basic immunity from these problems and that was one of the reasons they were successful.

Sohaib argued that the high-class, hi-fi people were culturally different from the youth in the slums. He said that they received all the benefits of globalization, such as good clothes, jeans, branded T-shirts, cars, and fancy gadgets, and what ultimately made them different was their "personality." I asked Sohaib to elaborate. He said, "They have a different personality. They have a different thinking. They think big. They don't mix with us. They don't speak properly to us. They curse us, abuse us. They can't tolerate the sight of poor people around them." Sohaib linked having a *hi-fi personality* to having the financial and cultural capital to pursue their aspirations and fulfill their potential. His comments invoke Appadurai's (2013) notion of "navigational capacity" because he recognized the cultural capital and power of the hi-fi class. They had robust financial resources and social networks through which their aspirations could find the right pathways to become positive outcomes, and repeated failures did not signal the end of one's career or opportunities.

Sohaib's father was a street performer who did magic shows outside the Pune railway station. His work resulted in an unstable income ranging from 30 cents a day to $8 on exceptional days. Sohaib could not expect any pocket money from his father, but he wanted to live a hi-fi lifestyle by moving into a "good flat." He stressed that not having the ability to speak fluent English the way the hi-fi and middle-class people spoke English prevented him from getting jobs at the call center, malls, and in the service industry:

SOHAIB: Yes. I wish I could speak English fluently. I felt bad when I failed in an interview.
s: Why did you feel bad?
SOHAIB: My friends speak good English and hence they got job. But I failed.
s: How can they speak such good English?
SOHAIB: They are my school friends. They don't stay in slums. Here nobody is so educated. Also I could not go to private classes. I did not have the money to pay the fees.

Ravi, whom I introduced previously in this chapter, similarly told me that English was not just required for the jobs in the global economy but also gave youth who spoke it well an *identity* and a feeling of superiority. He reminded me that the *basti* youth could learn from the "hi-fi class" how to act and be successful, but they will not take the initiative to socially interact with them.

I asked Ravi if he ever spoke to or interacted with the hi-fi girls from college or the neighboring areas. He remarked that he freely interacted with the girls from the slums, but interacting or even coming near the girls from the hi-fi class was considered overstepping his boundaries. He explained, "We are afraid that they may say something hurtful and this may make us feel very bad. So we never tried to speak with them. Also they never felt the need to interact with us." Ravi explained that the *basti* youth do not have the same "confidence" in themselves as the hi-fi youth, and not being able to speak fluent English puts them at a great disadvantage in the job market as well as in social situations. In focus group discussions with the *basti* youth, the point about not being able to speak fluently in English and with the right accent was reinforced repeatedly.

The parents whom I interviewed from the *basti* also claimed that almost all of the children from the *basti* went to inexpensive schools where Marathi was the primary language used. The youth perceived fluency in the English language as essential to belonging to the hi-fi class, but many were also interested in using it as a skill to acquire jobs at a call center. The *basti* youth were aware of the economic developments that had occurred in their area, and they had witnessed the migration of middle-class urban youth from different areas of India to Pune. The youth wanted jobs that paid well and required them to make conversation in English with foreign clients. However, for many of them, passing the interviews in English was an arduous, stressful, and virtually impossible task.

The English-Speaking Class as the New Caste

Wasim Akhtar, age 23 years, from the *basti* had been interviewed for call center jobs on several occasions, but he was never offered a job. He noted that the main difference between the affluent youth who live in Kalyani Nagar and Koregaon Park and the "poor class" is that the latter do not have access to English education. Wasim argued that even call center work required fluency in English and a basic undergraduate degree, and being educated in the Hindi and Marathi vernacular school was an impediment to their progress and social mobility:

s: So you don't get a job if you don't know English?
w: Some of them manage to clear the first round, but fail in clearing the second round. It has happened with me four times. So we now think of starting some business. Some youths sell vegetables, some drive auto rickshaw as jobs are not available.

Wasim had dropped out of school after 10th grade to support his family, and he noted that *mehnghai* (inflation) was the root cause of suffering in the slums. He worked as a tailor, cleaner, and an office boy. He wanted to get a bachelor's degree in commerce so he could support his family.

Wasim said that globalization and economic development in Pune have created opportunities for the wealthy people from Pune and Mumbai and for Indians from "foreign countries." He singled out the corrupt politicians as being responsible for stagnation in the lives of the urban poor. The politicians, he stressed, "are dirty and responsible for keeping us in poverty—they give fake assurances, but do nothing." Wasim remarked that "poor people here are cursed" and the *basti* needed good teachers and political leaders so the youth can get educated, but most leaders who oversee the *basti* are themselves uneducated.

Wasim wanted to speak fluent English so he could get a job at a call center to support his family and get his sisters married. He said he needed to save Rs. 50,000 for each of his sisters' weddings. Wasim often reflected on his family's circumstances: "Many times I question myself and also God. I feel those who don't require get lot of cash and those who require it most have nothing in their hands. I wish my life was like those rich chaps." I asked Wasim what would be the first thing he would do if he got some money. He replied that he would go to college to become educated so he could speak fluent English.

Given the large available pool of middle-class youth who had good English-speaking skills, the odds of getting a job at a call center were stacked against Wasim and his peers. Vasavi (2008) states that English-speaking skills are acquired by those youth who have studied in English medium schools or private schools, and so jobs at business process outsourcing companies (BPOs) and call centers by default only become available to those who belong to the higher socioeconomic group. The stories of *basti* youth revealed that they wanted to acquire English language to "mimic" youth from the hi-fi class and also, more important, to get a well-paying job. Thus, the acquisition of English language had come to represent, in Bourdieu's (1994) terms, access to symbolic capital because English was associated with being hi-fi, modern, and having prestige and social status. Learning to speak English had also become associated with "becoming an educated" person, and it was assumed that a person who spoke English was knowledgeable, skillful, and competent.

The "English-Speaking Curse" and the Global Economy

Speaking in the English language was part of the Indian postcolonial identity, but English had become defined as the language of success and speaking it had become a requirement for being part of the global economy. The youth in the *basti* told me that most parents in their neighborhood wanted their children to go to "convent"-run English language schools, but the competitive selection process and lack of funds made it difficult for them to be a part of the "English caste system." Sohaib had experienced the anxiety of being rejected from this caste system: "I was rejected in an interview recently. So I became anxious.

They asked me to do a 3-month course in English. Only then they would give me a job."

In an article titled "The English Speaking Curse" that was published in the magazine *Outlook*, Puri (2008) wrote that English is a new source of anxiety and worry for students from poor and low-income families in India and for those youth who study in non-English medium schools. Puri noted that college students frequently commit suicide because of their inability to master the English language. However, such stories do not get profiled on the front pages of English newspapers. Her article exposes urban Indian youth's unequal access to English and how it has created new linguistic divides in Indian society. The linguistic barriers between those who speak and those who do not speak English have always existed in postcolonial India. English as cultural capital is an indelible and powerful feature of the colonial legacy that has shaped the class hierarchies in India.

What is new about the existing demand and interest in English language skills in India is that having a basic undergraduate degree and fluent English language skills alone is now sufficient to acquire jobs in call centers, BPOs, malls, hotels, and other service and retail industries. The working-class youth were acutely aware of how not having fluency in English positioned them as being "vernacular," regional, *chote log* (lower-class people), and lacking a modern and hi-fi Indianness. Puri (2008) noted,

> Another unequal world is that of the English language teaching industry, that teeming hub for seekers of "good" English. They want "good" English, not just for BPO jobs and scaling linguistic walls that prevent them from studying or working abroad, but also for better-paid jobs in malls, retail chains, airlines, hotels, restaurants, media, banking and finance. "Good" English also gets you better treatment, English-speakers tell you poignantly, in malls, fancy showrooms, from sellers of financial services.

The stories that make the front pages are the ones that reinforce India's image of an expanding English-speaking middle class and the advantages it gives them in a global economy. In addition, tales of Indian writers of English novels and nonfiction gaining recognition at home and abroad, winning international prizes, and the rise of English-language teaching institutes in India garner attention. Because English has become the aspirational language associated with the hi-fi class, large numbers of youth from places such as Panchsheel *basti* and India's small towns and cities mistakenly believe that these training institutes can give them the credentials to get jobs in call centers, malls, or the service industry.

The English language institutes perpetuate the myth that the English language has become a commodity that one can purchase to upgrade one's life. There is an expectation from students and parents that English can be learned and mastered quickly, and it can be used to get employment and a personality makeover. Puri visited one such premier institute in Delhi and found that the spoken English curriculum that was being taught was deeply flawed. She observed that (as quoted in Puri, 2008)

> a mish-mash of definitions of auxiliary verbs, hackneyed proverbs (man proposes, god disposes), American "slangs" and "jargons" (airhead, hunk, chocoholic), tongue-twisters, teaching exercises that seem to have been written for Chinese students, with references to common Chinese errors. American English is the place's forte, I am told, and a class could begin, says one teacher, by her walking in and saying, "Hi dudes and dudettes."

The rise of the call center industry and a rapidly expanding service and retail industry had resulted in the creation of many small and large English language institutes across India. During my travels in Pune, I noticed there was one institute called "The English Clinic," perhaps implying that a lack of English-speaking skills was equivalent to some form of pathology or disease. The British Council had decided to enter the Indian market to meet a growing demand to teach "good English" to teachers, corporate workers, engineers, and call center workers. The British Council was the United Kingdom's main cultural organization and representative across the world, and there were 10 British Council centers in various cities in India. One of its functions was to expand the use of English language and expose people to British culture through libraries, teaching English to youth and adults, and training the young Indian population to be "global citizens."

The Cultural Imperialism of British English and "Fake Teeth"

Former British prime minster Gordon Brown visited India and announced that teaching English to the world was going to be one of the United Kingdom's major exports and it was going to train 750,000 teachers in India to speak English. The demand for English language skills had also created new parental anxieties about their children's ability to speak "proper" English because basic fluency in English was considered an important criterion for gaining admission to some of the elite, private schools in India. There was a general recognition in urban India that government-run vernacular schools did not teach proper English in their curriculum. Most children from the basti had graduated from these municipal schools as they were inexpensive and getting admission to them was easy. Gauri, a 60-year-old grandmother from the *basti*, wanted her grandchildren to learn English in a private school, but her children could not afford the fees, and there was no one at home who could supplement their English language instruction:

No, we'll put them in Marathi medium only. See, we are not that strong in English so we'll not put them in English medium. Why lie about it? Why show your fake teeth? We'll do whatever is in our capacity. In Marathi medium, also there is English after the 5th grade, so if the kid studies well, he'll speak the language properly. Like my son speaks good English, studies well. If he studies with concentration then Marathi school is also good, but they should realize the difficulties he faces. Marathi school is also good. Our heart desires that we should be able to enroll our children in English schools but we should have that kind of money. Where will we get so much money? We don't have money. That's why Marathi schools are better for us. What can we do?!

Gauri likened not knowing English to "fake teeth," and the learning of English then gave them the opposite: real teeth. What the interviews with the youth and families in the *basti* revealed is that learning English symbolized a step toward permanent employment and also an entry into a global economy that was seen as controlled by the hi-fi class. The youth did not want to become exact replicas of the hi-fi class; rather, they wanted to become part of those global, language-based practices that made them competent speakers of the language so they could get jobs in call centers and also acquire upward mobility. These youth wanted the financial and social advantages associated with being like the hi-fi class.

The aspiration to learn English was then tied to the larger cultural aspirations and beliefs about social mobility in a neoliberal economy—prestige, honor, and good salaries. Within the context of the hi-fi class, the aspiration to learn English was intimately tied to their beliefs about good schools, academic preparation, studying abroad, hanging out with peers who speak English, watching English films, reading English books, traveling abroad, and making English "integral" to one's identity. The English language divide, similar to the caste category, plays a vital role in determining whom the youth will marry, which friends they will have, where they will work and shop, what schools they will attend, what books they will read, where they will travel, how much they will earn, and what media they will consume. The way in which the English language was tied to class identities forces us to think about aspirations and capacities as *intertwined* with larger language-based communicative practices.

When parents from these upper- and middle-class families are teaching their children English, they are also socializing them to acquire a hybrid mix of global, postcolonial Indian identity. Language socialization researchers have argued that the impact of language on our everyday, mundane, routine communication can be seen in two important ways. First, we learn language in the process of becoming culturally competent members of society. Second, in the process of learning language, we learn about the cultural stories and practices of our communities (Miller et al., 1992; Schieffelin & Ochs, 1986). Caregivers' input not only plays an important role in children's language acquisition but also provides an important basis for caregivers and children to construct shared narrative *meanings* about the social order. Caregivers' narrative practices, through particular use of language, foreground certain situational meanings or epistemic qualities about their family's or community's way of life.

The language-based practices create particular narratives and stories of cultural capacities and maps of aspirations, economic pathways, and collective meanings about family, work, and marriage. The language practices of the urban youth living in the *basti*—their ways of speaking in Marathi and Hindi—are often viewed as markers of a low-income lifestyle, being "vernacular" and not part of the "mainstream discourse." It is through these language socialization discourses about self and others that narratives about whom to marry, where to work, and with whom to mingle become consolidated as identities.

CASTE AND CLASS IDENTITIES: BABASAHEB IS OUR GOD

Most of the *basti* youth that I spoke to identified themselves as *kaam karne wale log* (working class) or as *garib log* (poor people). A few of them, such as Ravi and Priyanka, referred to their family having "middle-class values." Here, they separated their socioeconomic status from the values and norms that they espouse. In other words, they may be located in a lower economic strata and did not enjoy the social or economic privileges that came with being middle class, but they identified with what they viewed as middle-class values. Some of the youth who referred to themselves as *garib* or *kaam karne wale log* alternatively referred to themselves as *Dalit*. Dudley Jenkins (2003) argues that the so-called "untouchable" castes or Dalits are at the "bottom of the caste system." The term Dalit means oppressed or "ground down." Some of the *basti* youth I interviewed employed the discourse of being working class and Dalit interchangeably when they resisted and protested against the inequities that surrounded them.

Despite the regional diversity in present-day caste practices, Jenkins (2003) writes that "caste continues to play a major role in the lives of many Indians, often having a profound effect on opportunities in terms of residence, education, occupations, social interaction and marriage" (p. 13). The leadership of Babasaheb Ambedkar, who championed the cause of Dalit equality, provided the structural impetus to declare caste and casteism as illegal in the constitution of India. A mixture of colonial legacy, postcolonial policies, electoral politics, and the powers of the state had led to the creation of the Scheduled Caste Order in the Indian constitution in 1950. The Scheduled Caste Order of 1950 gave special allotment of seats to Dalits in the electoral legislative process and also created affirmative action programs for jobs in the public sector and reserved seats for admission in universities and in most educational fields.

What are the origins of the caste categories in India? How do these inform identity? It is important to contextualize how stories and interpretations of caste and class identities are connected to how youth think about collective mobilization and social change. One of the earliest Aryan texts, the *Rig Veda*, provides the rationale for the four ranks of social categories that form the framework of the original caste system in India. According to Milner (1994), ancient Indian society was divided into four social categories or *varnas*. The *Brahmans*, perched at the highest rank, belong to the priest class; the *Kshatriyas* below them are described as warriors; the third-ranked *Vashiyas* are the farmers and merchants; and the *Shudras*, placed in the lowest category, are described as laborers and servants (Milner, 1994). Those individuals who are born in the first three categories are designated as "twice born" (*divijas*). They are considered to be reborn when they take the vows at the initiation ceremony to devote the first stages of their lives to studying the classical Hindu texts. Those who are born in the *Shudra* caste are fated to be servants to the first three castes and unable to study such texts. The yoking of caste categories with professions and work is a unique feature of the Indian caste system. Khilnani (1997) argues that the roots of the *varna* system are not fully clear, but they seem to be derived from one of the hymns of *Rig Veda*, which identifies a cosmic giant named *Purusha*, who is known as a primeval male and whose sacrifice created the world.

The maiming of the *Purusha* is recorded in the hymns through a rhetorical question: "When they divided the Man, how many parts were made out of him? How do they describe his mouth, his two arms and thighs and feet?" (Khilnani, 1997, p. 18). The answer to this question in the hymn is that the *Purusha's* mouth represents the Brahman caste, the arms symbolize the *Kshatriya* (warrior) caste, his thigh is identified as the *Vaishysa* caste (merchant), and his feet represent the *Sudras* (servants). The *Manusmriti* (The Laws of Manu) codified and consolidated the caste system, and it is dated to around 100 CE. According to the *Manusmriti*, "one occupation only the lord prescribed to the *Sudra*, to serve meekly even these other three castes" (Milner, 1994, p. 47).

In *Annihilation of Caste*, Ambedkar (1971) reminds us about how "status power" was used to create specific social rules that were necessary for creating and regulating the identity of what was referred to in pre-independent India as "depressed" classes or "untouchables." He writes that "untouchables," during the *Peshwa* rule of the Maratha Kingdom in the 16th century, were prevented from using public streets. Even if the shadow of an "untouchable" touched a Brahmin, it was considered to have the power of polluting the Hindu Brahmin. He points out that specific practices were enacted to consolidate the separation of the pure from the impure and the sacred from the profane. Ambedkar observes,

> The untouchable was required to have a black thread either on his wrist or on his neck as a sign or a mark to prevent Hindus from getting themselves polluted by his touch through mistake. In Poona, the capital of Peshwa, the untouchable was required to carry, strung from his waist, a broom to sweep away from behind the dust he treaded on lest a Hindu walking on the same should be polluted. In Poona, the untouchable was required to carry an earthen pot, hung in his neck wherever he went, for holding his spit lest his spit falling on earth should pollute a Hindu who might unknowingly happen to tread on it. (p. 39)

Gandhi, who coined the term *Harijan* (children of god) to refer to untouchables, believed in the abolition of caste and the removal of untouchability, but his proposed reforms were radically different from that of Ambedkar (1971). For instance, he replied to Ambedkar's ideas in *Annihilation of Caste* by stating that Dr. Ambedkar had challenged the core principles of Hinduism and that caste had nothing to do with religion. In a response to Ambedkar's speech on caste, Gandhi wrote (as cited in Ambedkar, 1971),

> It is a custom whose origin I do not know and do not need to know for the satisfaction of my spiritual hunger. But I do know that it is harmful both to spiritual and national growth. . . . The law of *Varna* teaches us that we have each one of us to earn our bread by following the ancestral calling. It defines not our rights but our duties. . . . The calling of a Brahmin-spiritual teacher—and a scavenger are equal, and their due performances carries equal merit before God and at one time seems to have carried identical reward before man. (p. 119)

Gandhi's letter directly stated that Ambedkar was engaging in a selective misreading of the classic texts, and he also insinuated that the texts that Ambedkar had used in his speech were not authentic. He also faulted Ambedkar for judging the Hindu religion by its worst specimen and not its ideal representative. Gandhi's foundation of radical social reform and his critique of modernity and industrial society were based on a village-based, self-sustainable society. His vision for India was very much tied to the *Brahminical* vision of Hinduism, in which technology and sexuality were viewed as entrapping human beings in desire (Omvedt, 2011). Gandhi found caste to be an immoral position, but he could not go along with Ambedkar's suggestions of demolishing the structural foundations of Hinduism that had in the first place given birth to caste categories.

Ambedkar (1971) argued that in order for caste to be abolished in India, the sacredness of the social order on which the caste system was founded had to be destroyed. He took aim at the destruction of the core classical texts that provided the initial basis of caste and thus wrote, "You must therefore destroy the sacredness and divinity with which Caste has become invested. In the last analysis, this means you must destroy the authority of the *Shastras* and the *Vedas*" (p. 93).

It would take many chapters to chart Ambedkar's biography and political influence, so suffice it to say here that he was born into a poor family of the Mahar caste, and growing up he suffered the indignities of being an "untouchable." Ambedkar studied in an army cantonment school and then moved to Bombay to study at Elphinstone College in 1912. His educational achievements drew the attention of the Maharaja Gaekwad of Baroda, who then gave him scholarship money to travel to the United States to obtain a PhD in political science from Columbia University and later to obtain law degrees from the London School of Economics and the London Bar (Dirks, 2001). Despite his brilliant educational achievements, he could not practice law in Baroda because he was subjected to continuous caste insults and discrimination; thus, he moved to Bombay to become a lecturer at a college and to practice law (Dirks, 2001).

Ambedkar's foray into social reform began by taking up the cause of educational access for "untouchables," and he worked to address three other issues: (1) the abolition of work and labor associated with being a Mahar, (2) the reform for having equal access to water for "untouchables," and (3) the campaign for granting untouchables permission to enter the temple premises (Dirks, 2001). Ambedkar critiqued the foundation of caste by attacking the Brahminical aspects of Hinduism and described Brahmanism as a poison that had destroyed Hinduism. According to him, caste was based on the sacred rules of Hinduism and, thus, the foundations of the religion had to be destroyed. Ambedkar (1971) stated, "I have therefore, no hesitation in saying that such a religion must be destroyed and I say, there is nothing irreligious in working for the destruction of such a religion" (p. 105). Ambedkar is known as the architect of the Indian constitution, and in 1956 he announced his conversion to Buddhism; at approximately that time, he also converted more than a half million Dalit supporters to Buddhism or Buddha–dharma thorough a mass conversion ceremony in which his followers took 22 sacred vows.

In many slums across Pune city, photographs and statues of Ambedkar are a common sight. Gauri, whose story I discussed previously, was a fervent follower of Dr. Ambedkar. One afternoon, I sat with Gauri and her friend for a conversation about her life in Panchsheel *basti*. She told me that her caste is from the backward classes and that she does not believe in God but, rather, in the teachings of Dr. Babasaheb Ambedkar:

> Now see, in our faith we don't believe in God as such. We believe in Dr. Babasaheb
> Ambedkar. Our Baba has said all of you come together and study and do

something. We live by his words and thoughts. We don't feel that there is anything like this, though we think that there is God. But mostly we don't believe in God. We don't believe in God at all. We live by his principles. . . . All of us are from him only. There was discrimination against us, but we are here today because of him only. In our caste, he's the only one who is so learned and has become a barrister. Only because of him today you and I are talking. Otherwise these people wouldn't have spoken to us.

Gauri said that Babasaheb had told the Dalits that "don't make me a God, but use my teachings to fight against oppression and brutality." Her friend, Seema, who was also part of the conversation, commented that in the past the backward classes and the Dalits experienced systematic injustices, and it was only due to Dr. Ambedkar that they feel they have some dignity today:

> As in first our religion was called Mahar Jat. Now it's not Mahar, he (Ambedkar) gave us Bo Dharma/DIKSHA on the 14th of October 1956. Since then we don't believe in our caste, we don't say that it's Mahar . . . it's Bo Dharma. We have done a great deal of study on it, no need to even say anything about it. Lot of study! We read their books and from those books we gain a little bit of knowledge. We've studied those books a lot. We had gone for Vipassana course one or two months back. Vipassana is part of Bo Dharma.

Gauri believed that Babasaheb's story had given them the cultural narrative to resist the upper classes and the injustice that surrounded them. She also believed that many *basti* folk were capable of mobilizing to bring about change on both structural and psychological levels.

In other words, Babasaheb's story not only induced aspirations in them but also gave them the tools to think about a better future for the families in the *basti*. Both Seema and Gauri had attended a free 10-day course in Vipassana meditation in Pune (which is now offered in centers throughout the world). They emphasized that meditation does not take them out of poverty, but it allows them to cope with the stress of daily life. Both of them believed that Ambedkar was responsible for fighting for equal rights for the Dalits and the backward classes, and he gained all his "knowledge about the world" by studying abroad. Here is an instance in which Gauri applies her narrative capacity through Ambedkar's story and her own spiritual development as a counterstory to her oppressive conditions. However, while Gauri and Seema can recognize and can articulate social injustice through the lens of Ambedkar's philosophy, they are unable to realize its revolutionary potential due to the prevailing economic and social structural constraints. In contrast to Gauri's narrative, most of the *basti* youth were reluctant to discuss caste. They saw themselves less through caste narratives and more through class-based hierarchies. Part of this reluctance stems from the fact that many of the *basti* dwellers would not necessarily be from Scheduled Caste categories but, rather, from the broader "Other Backward Classes" category.

To recognize and ameliorate the social and economic inequalities that continued to persist despite the protective categories of Scheduled Castes and Scheduled Tribes, the Indian government developed the category of Other Backward Classes (OBC) in 1980. The category of OBC recognizes groups who have been systematically disadvantaged socially and economically. Consequently, religious minorities and various working-class and artisanal groups were included in this broader category. By employing the designation of OBC, a much larger swathe of the population is now recognized as being underprivileged in India.

The families in the Panchsheel *basti* labored in informal sectors. They worked in the construction and housing industries, service industry, or held jobs as security guards, garage mechanics, custodians, and janitors. Despite the changes in the caste system, social stratification continues to exist through the prism of caste and class in contemporary India. In urban India, many of the old caste-based occupations and professions have disappeared, and these populations have moved into doing degraded forms of modern labor. Some OBC farmers have become wealthy by selling their land and by modernizing the agricultural process. The OBC category, then, is dynamic and at times politicized, with groups being included and removed based on whether they qualify as being structurally oppressed and disadvantaged.[10]

Ram Mahalingam, a cultural psychologist, has conducted several studies (see Mahalingam, 2007) to show how marginalized caste groups in India create alternative cultural narratives to cope with their marginality. He argues that without access to structural power, it is difficult for Dalits to transform the dominant social hierarchies in India. He writes,

> Brahmin adults believed that caste identity would be transmitted from mother to offspring, whereas Dalit adults believed that caste identity would be acquired through socialization. Being the dominant group in the caste hierarchy, it was to Brahmins' advantage to believe in a caste identity fixed at birth, but Dalits resisted notions of caste identity as biologically transmitted. (p. 304)

Upper-caste groups such as Brahmins have used their power to selectively frame and shape their identity as normative, and thus privileged, while simultaneously framing the identity of the Dalits as lower caste and inferior. The Dalits do reinterpret and reframe the meanings of ethnicity that are assigned to them by the upper-caste Brahmins, but they do not have the power or the cultural capital to transform those meanings into social norms (Mahalingam, 2007). How do narratives of caste endure under neoliberal capitalism and practices of globalization? How does caste survive under neoliberal capitalism and globalized forms of multiculturalism? Natrajan (2012) notes that recent scholarship on caste suggests that there is decline in the application of the two central tenets of the caste system: There is a weakening in the practice of "ritual hierarchy" and in the practices of "occupational hereditary" (p. 10). The third tenet of caste refers to the mutual separation of caste identities. Natrajan notes that there are several reasons for the gradual erosion of the caste system. First, the British colonial rule undermined the economic foundation of a caste-based village economies. Second, there is a waning of religious notion of caste identity because of the implementation of law that emphasizes the non-legality of caste along with the passing of constitutional laws of reservation policies for reducing caste-based social inequalities. Third, increasly lower-caste communities have moved out of their traditional occupations that were assigned to them. This resistance has been fuelled by the spread of the message of the anti-caste movements and the active political engagement and mobilization from the Dalits. Natrajan writes that despite the caste system fading away,

> the declining power of the caste system has been noted to be matched by the rising significance of *caste identities* in social and political life where caste-based marital practices endure, caste associations and communities flourish, and caste has become by far the most fecund access of political mobilization for political parties in contemporary India. (p. 11, emphasis in original)

He reminds us that the new mechanisms of democracy, the language of liberal rights, and state-based protections given to minorities in contemporary India make it illegal to practice caste-based discrimination and stigmatization.

Although the hard forms of caste-based identities manifested through brutal forms of exploitation and ineradicable social inequality have weakened, there has been a continued expansion of the presence of caste in other spheres, such as labor markets, educational institutions, banking, housing, and marriage and family contexts. Therefore, Natrajan (2012) observes that a new paradox of identity with regard to caste has emerged, and now there is "castes without the caste system, casteism without traditional legitimacy" (p. 11). The process of culturalization is caste's last triumph that obliterates Ambedkar's vision of annihilating the structures of caste that were based in religious texts. Natrajan views the so-called "silent revolution" of the rise of the political power of marginalized groups as a democratization of caste rather than as a genuine structural makeover of the legacy of power and politics associated with casteism. Natrajan asserts that "culturalization of caste sustains a powerful illusion that caste can be tolerated by, accommodated within, or even facilitates the building of deep democracy, or that the annihilation of caste is no longer a necessary condition for democracy in India" (p. 8). When caste is constructed as culture through the process of culturalization, it promotes a type of multiculturalism where caste identities become part of a mosaic of other types of diverse identities that are organized along language, religion, region, and tribe, and it elevates caste to a benign category founded on difference rather than on discrimination, injustice, and inequality.

What I found in the narratives of youth and families in the *basti* was that caste categories were being mixed with class-based cultural identities. For instance, as mentioned previously, youth talked about themselves as *kaam karne wale log* (working-class people) and differentiated themselves from the hi-fi class. Vinod's narrative powerfully expresses the focus on class identity and lack of economic mobility as a discursive category.

VINOD: GLOBALIZATION IS A *KHOKLA* (EMPTY) TERM

I interviewed Vinod, a 24-year-old male, in July 2015, first in a focus group and then individually. He felt constrained in the focus group discussion and wanted to be able to speak freely, so he came to the interview with two of his trusted friends. Vinod began by telling me that one of the main problems in his life is that he did not receive a proper education. He and his three sisters lost their father when he was 7 years old. Vinod's mother worked as a maidservant, washing dishes and utensils at wealthy people's *banglas* (big houses) in Kalyani Nagar and Koregaon Park in Pune. She would cook food in their *bangla* and work as a *bai* (maidservant), and that is how she supported her four children and provided for the education of her three *didis* (sisters). She had spent 40 years of her life working as a maidservant in various houses nearby. One of Vinod's sisters, Sarika, also started working as a *bai* when she was 9 years old; she simultaneously went to school, returning home to visit her family once a month. Sarika's employers were abusive and controlling, but she still continued to work doing *jhadu-pocha* (sweeping and cleaning) until she was 17 years old.

Vinod lost interest in studying further and dropped out of school. He started doing odd jobs and worked in a low-end job at a catering business as a server at weddings. Later, he found a housekeeping job in Mira hospital making Rs. 5000 ($90) a month. He often worked three shifts in a row to get overtime pay. He mainly did patient care that involved cleaning, bathing, and feeding patients and taking orders from the management to do all kinds of menial and dirty jobs that no one else would do. The job of a "ward boy" is one of the lowest-level jobs in an Indian hospital and requires intense physical labor. After 2 years, Vinod left Mira hospital and joined the new Pemberton Asia Hospital, one of the largest hospitals in Pune, as a ward boy. His salary increased to Ra. 10,000 ($180), and Vinod believed that the presence of multinational companies was benefitting the *basti log*. There were new employment opportunities, but he added that the wages were relatively meager compared to what the management personnel made. The high cost of living and ever-increasing inflation canceled out any minor raises in salaries and wages of these unskilled labor jobs. Vinod had lived all his life in the *basti* and had seen the impact of neoliberal globalization around him as new call centers, restaurants, residential apartments, and deluxe housing were built around his neighborhood. He had a theory of how globalization worked in Pune:

> The real rich around here are not from proper Pune. These outsiders who come to Pune are wealthy people and they strike deals with local people, wealthy people and they look out for their mutual interests. So the local rich people are becoming richer as new financial capital is coming in. The difference between the rich families and the families living in the *basti* is that when a child is born in a rich and educated family, the first question the parents ask is: "What should I make him?" Should I make him an engineer or something else?" Then right from the beginning the upper class folks will make sure that the entire educational apparatus is put in place for their child so he is on the path to becoming an engineer. In our *basti*, we also start out with big ambitions for our children but then we realize that we don't have the resources. We want our children to be lawyers and doctors and then we tell them to start doing labor jobs or we ask them to scale down their ambitions due to lack of English education and good schooling.

Vinod argued that the government-sponsored, free Marathi Medium schools (vernacular schools run by the municipalities and taught in the local language Marathi) do not provide the right kind of education. The teachers in the non-English medium schools, according to Vinod, did not care whether students showed up to class or had done their homework. Many children from the *basti*, he observed, often told their parents that they went to school while they were really spending time in parks or other public spaces smoking or drinking alcohol. He explained,

> The educational system for *basti* kids is corrupt. . . . If there are 100 people serving in a particular government job, 75 of them are thieves. You just see the case of the government-sponsored Marathi schools. There is money allocated for free books, but the children never get any financial help. Bishop's school (a well-known English-speaking school for the upper class and elites), on the contrary, spends about 30,000 Rupees ($500) a year for a child only for transport. The curriculum is in English and the students are highly disciplined with their hair combed, ironed uniforms, and polished shoes. But if you go to Marathi school, you are not going to succeed, as there is no emphasis on education or discipline. These Bishop kids get all the facilities and a good package with teachers that care for their students. Once the child comes home from these good schools the parents speak in English and say "Hi, Baby."

Vinod noted that the class differences between the rich and middle-class youth versus the urban poor youth have always existed, but now the *basti* youth have aspirations and they are not willing to accommodate to their station in life. He stated that the youth from the *basti* today are exposed to television, media, and films and they want what the upper-class, hi-fi youth have. They have dreams about doing well and having a house and a car, but hi-fi people view the *basti* youth as *chota nazariya* (inferior people).

Vinod continued that their (the *basti* people) lives are full of *qurbani* (sacrifices) at every turn. Vinod and the two boys who accompanied him for the interview emphasized that one of the most difficult issues facing young men in the *basti* pertains to finding a "right girl" to marry. He said that young women from the *basti* want "to see" and marry a boy who has a good salary of Rupees 30,000 ($500) a month, a decent house and transportation, whereas most young men do not have any of these amenities. He laughed, "I had two girlfriends but I could not provide them with these amenities so they married other boys who were more well to do. I have the ability to *patao* (to court) girls for 2 to 3 years, but somehow they don't stay with me. Then they go with someone else."

Rajesh said that one difference between youth from the upper-class families and the *basti* youth is that *basti* youth do not have any privacy. Most of the homes in the *basti* are small single rooms with an attached small kitchen, and in some homes there is a toilet. He lamented that there are many homes in the *basti* that have two brothers living with their parents and often one brother will get married and the newly wedded husband and wife have to make adjustments. He asked me, "What do new couples want to do? They want to be intimate, but they don't have privacy here."

Rajesh elaborated that the couples are sharing a one-room space with so many others that they cannot have personal conversations freely. The couples cannot go outside and have sex, and they cannot have it easily at home either. If couples go out of their house to be intimate, there are closed-circuit TVs all over the place and they will get caught. He said that most people in the *basti* live in a 10 × 10-foot space, and sometimes there are more than five family members sleeping and living in such a small space so the young couples become frustrated. Rajesh argued that the urban poor struggle with basic needs of living, such as water, food, and education, but he also warned me not to overlook the privacy and psychological needs of families that live in crammed spaces:

> If the unmarried younger brother goes out for 15 minutes then the married brother may have a chance to be with his wife to be intimate, but if he comes back quickly then the young married couple cannot do anything. Sometimes parents understand and give the newly wedded couple privacy but other members don't understand so the couple becomes frustrated. The wives want

nail polish, a TV, and they make demands on the husband and then the older parents also make demands on their son to get groceries and their medicine. This one earning member feels the pressure and cannot satisfy everyone's demands. Often young newly married men find that they are not sexually satisfied and nor are they getting any family support. Even when husband and wife are sleeping next to each other in the night they have to whisper to each other. There is no privacy. We have to worry about a lot of things. Life is full of *qurbani* here and there is danger at every corner. . . . The young generation that are affluent don't have this problem. They have sex in their house and in cars and we have seen that their cars are dancing when they are having sex in the back of the car.

Rajesh told me that sociocultural changes in Indian society at large have lifted taboos about sex and sexuality in the *basti*. Unlike the older generation of the *basti*, Rajesh said sexual intimacy and privacy is given importance in the younger generation. He emphasized that it is not just married young men who do not have privacy for being intimate with their wives. Other young men from the *basti* also have to go through a major ordeal to be intimate with their girlfriends.

The young boys often have to organize an "encounter" with their respective girlfriends weeks in advance by calling six or seven of their friends, and they usually have to find a friend who works in an office on a Saturday and is willing to give them a room for about 30 minutes. Rajesh told me that the *basti* youth have to have "hurried sex" as the friend who has arranged for a room in the office is on the lookout for his or her boss and keeps shouting, "Hurry up, the boss might be coming soon."

Vinod stated that today's *yuva pidi* (younger generation) from the *basti* did not focus much on caste distinctions, but instead they believed that social class differences in urban Indian prevented the *basti* youth from achieving social mobility. He reiterated his aspirations to own an apartment and have a married life, but he believed that the path to achieving his goals was filled with challenges that were going to be difficult to overcome. The multinational companies, call centers, and large malls, Vinod observed, provided employment for the youth in *basti*, but the wages were low and the conditions were exploitative. He noted that "we are impacted by the lifestyle of the affluent youth and we copy their way of speaking and dressing but we are not like them." His generation, he commented, believes that globalization or progress is a *khokla* (empty and meaningless) term because not much has changed in their lives. He stated that the government, the politicians, and the elite and educated families are not going to assist the poor. The younger generation who live in urban *bastis* will have to rise up by themselves. Vinod believed that members of his generation were ready to take charge of their future but they will have to find their own ways to fulfill their dreams. He believed that the *basti* people had a shared bonding of *pyaar aur qurbani* (love and sacrifice) that the upper-class and the rich did not have. They—*basti* youth—faced hardships, he argued, but they knew how to maximize their happiness in conditions of scarcity. Vinod believed that the *basti* families' ability to cope with the misfortunes of their lives made them morally superior to their more affluent neighbors.

GLOBALIZATION, NARRATIVE, AND THE URBAN POOR: THE POLITICS OF RECOGNITION AND REDISTRIBUTION

The imagery and tone of the youth narratives presented I this chapter are radically different from those of the upper- and middle-class youth that I analyzed in Chapters 3 and 4. Panchsheel *basti*, as I noted previously, is located amid two of the most affluent neighborhoods in Pune.

I characterize the stories of the *basti* youth as *dispossessed* because they are shaped by and connected to the possessions of the dominant class who live nearby and the unequal structural conditions of their *basti*. These stories reveal that globalization, by and large, has exacerbated the structural inequality in the slum settlements in Pune. Structural inequality refers to a system that creates and perpetuates an unequal distribution of material and psychological privileges, such as access to health care, education, and employment; permanent housing; clean water and sanitation; environmentally safe spaces; leisure; recreation; and dignity. The system creates a societal condition in which the valuable material, symbolic, and psychological privileges are unequally distributed across nations, groups, abilities, categories, castes, classes, races, and gender.

The narratives of Aman, Zainab, Wasim, Ravi, Gauri, Vinod, and others show us their remarkable ability to plan, negotiate, aspire, and have voice, but they are unable to mobilize their capacities into objective advantage for themselves. The youth's stories in the *basti* are dialogically connected to economic and cultural global flows in surrounding neighborhoods and the structural realities of the slums—insufficiency of access to toilets, temporary housing, and lack of financial and cultural resources. Lack of power to make changes disproportionately impacts the stories and voices of the youth living in slums. The capacity to aspire is not just an individual trait or a psychological voice but, rather, a narrative capacity, which is unevenly distributed in society.

It is important to clarify that the "capacity to aspire" is based on the assumption that the poor have the capacity to wish, plan, aspire, and voice their needs. However, part of being in poverty is having reduced opportunities to implement these practices and create experiences of favorable outcomes. Taylor (1992) writes that the "crucial feature of human life is its fundamental *dialogical* character" (p. 32, emphasis in original)—we create and define our identity in dialogue and struggle with our significant others. He writes,

> Thus my discovering my identity doesn't mean that I work it out in isolation, but that I negotiate it through dialogue, partly overt, partly internal, with others. That is why the development of an ideal of inwardly generated identity gives a new importance to recognition. My own identity crucially depends on my dialogical relations with others. (p. 32)

Taylor's (1992) notion of the "politics of recognition" is based on the idea that we have an ethical obligation to give dignity and rights to others in both the private and the public sphere. If our identities are shaped by "recognition or its absence" from real and imagined others, dominant others, and familiar others, then "nonrecognition or misrecognition can inflict harm, can be a form of oppression, imprisoning someone in a false, distorted, and reduced mode of being" (p. 25).

This notion of recognition gives political and moral power to "psychological" concepts of tolerance, intercultural understanding, and dignity. If we conceive of the urban poor as a community of persons who are embedded in particular class and cultural practices through which they have been made invisible, erased, and marginalized, then we have to first begin by "recognizing" the conditions in which they have been placed. We need to recognize the historical and social sources that give their *stories and identities* meaning. However, giving "recognition" or giving equal dignity to the urban poor in the dialogical equation is only a partial step.

We must make sure that cultural recognition of their stories and lived experience can also guarantee them access to power, basic human rights, and equitable redistribution of resources. Beyond recognizing the urban poor, we have to find ways to strengthen the capacities to create conditions that cultivate their "voice" and their *narrative capacity* in political debates around poverty and welfare so they can shape their future (Appadurai, 2013; Sen, 1999). Appadurai writes that just as human beings use categories to describe themselves as belonging to a certain group or place, poor people also see themselves as belonging to a class or a group in their societies. He is not advocating the thesis that the urban poor youth live in a "culture of poverty" but, rather, that they have deep cultural and economic understanding of how their world works. The urban poor often have depleted sources and capital when it comes to negotiating their terms of recognition.

The *basti* youth are not just people who reflect the condition of poverty but, rather, they constitute a social group who are only partly defined by statistics and government/UN/official measures. They are self-reflexive and aware of how their narratives are shaped by belonging to a particular cultural group or class. What is the relationship between culture, narrative, and poverty?

First, members of poor communities can express their relationship to these norms through resistance, irony, distance, and cynicism. This ironic sense allows them to maintain some dignity despite their experiences of marginality and oppression. Second, the poor also demonstrate compliance by expressing "deep moral attachment" to the cultural narrative practices that directly "supports their degradation" (Appadurai, 2013, p. 185). Appadurai cites the example of lower-caste groups in India who comply by the demeaning rules and caste practices such as ideas about fate, caste duty, rebirth, and social hierarchy. The practices are shaped by their moral beliefs about their social order, and their narratives of personhood are also acquired from these practices. As a consequence, Appadurai notes that the poor frequently find themselves in a position in which they are prompted to follows norms, stories, and practices that diminish their dignity, exacerbate their inequality, and worsen their ability to access basic amenities and goods. Appadurai clarifies this point:

> When I refer to operating under adverse terms of recognition, I mean that in recognizing those who are wealthy, the poor permit the existing and corrupt standing of local and national elites to be further bolstered and reproduced. . . . The poor are recognized, but in ways that ensure minimum change in terms of redistribution. So, to that extent that poverty is indexed by weak terms of recognition for the poor, intervention to positively affect these terms is a crucial priority. (p. 187)

Narrative psychology has an important role to play in both understanding the stories of the *basti* youth and showing how they are embedded in the larger narratives of globalization and affluence. We can gain insights about youth identity formation in the *basti* by examining how both acts of recognition and acts of redistribution comingle in their narratives. That is, just having the narrative voice to express one's aspirations or desire is not enough. The poor have to be given the tools to transform their narrative voice into a cultural voice so they can mobilize change not just through individualized, abstract, universal democratic principles but also through their collective participation. Appadurai (2013) explains:

> Because for voice to take effect, it must engage in social, political, and economic issues in terms of ideologies, doctrines, and norms that are widely shared and credible, even by the rich and powerful. Furthermore, voice must be expressed in terms of actions and performances that have local force . . . as the poor seek to strengthen their voices as a cultural capacity, they will need to find those levelers of metaphor, rhetoric, organization, and public performance that will work best in their cultural world. And when they do work, as we have seen with various movements in the past, they change the terms of recognition, indeed the cultural framework itself. (p. 186)

Thus, for "empowerment" to take effect in Panchsheel *basti*, the youth's narrative voices must be imbued with local meanings of consensus building, implementation of policies, and grass-roots mobilization. What follows from the linking of culture and narrative with poverty is that the concept of aspiration gets removed from the individual cognitive realm and is created in relation to the larger collective life of self–other relationships.

NOTES

1. The 2012 United Nations' "Millennium Development Goals Report" (United Nations Development Programme, 2012) states that 626 million people in India do not have access to a toilet and practice what is called "open defecation." Every day, millions of women and girls in India experience teasing, sexual harassment, stalking, violent assault, and rape when they go out to defecate in open fields, in bushes, and in gutters on the road.
2. The young participants who were not well-versed with the English language were aware of the word "globalization" as a phenomenon and translated it as *naya zamana*, meaning a new era or new society, or *pragati*, which means progress.
3. Osho Rajneesh, a well-known Indian philosopher and guru, became famous throughout the world in the 1970s for his radical views on sexuality, marriage, God, and the purpose of life. By the 1980s, he had a strong following in the West. When I was growing up in Pune, he was called Acharaya Rajneesh or Bhagwan Rajneesh, and his disciples wore maroon- or orange-colored robes with a *mala* (beaded necklace) and were frequently seen near the "Rajneesh Ashram" that was located in Koregaon Park.
4. The city of Pune was much smaller when I was in college; it resembled a small town, and there were fewer affluent areas. Koregaon Park was typically associated with "old money" people, and the "camp area" was associated with the "nouveau riche." That distinction does not apply any longer because global investments in Pune and the residential boom have significantly altered the geography of the city, expanding zones of affluence of the super-rich.
5. The Pune Central Mall near Bund Garden, which I used to pass frequently when I was doing fieldwork in Pune, displayed a sign that read "Shop, Eat, Celebrate." There was a perpetual "Happiness Sale" on display near the entrance of the mall. Life-size photos of young—mostly Euro-American—models were displayed both in the interiors and on exteriors of the stores. Brands such as Calvin Klein, Adidas, Nike, Luis Phillips, Allen Solly, and Peter England were being marketed to the growing affluent and aspiring middle classes of India. The advertisements typically displayed mostly pictures of young Euro-American male and female models. One of my participants somewhat ironically asked me what would happen if all the US malls suddenly displayed only Indian models.
6. Much of urban planning and future development projects that are undertaken by the Municipal Corporation in Pune do not include the slum settlements. The local NGO, Shelter Associates, has undertaken extensive poverty mapping and has found that it is extremely rare for the slum settlements to be integrated in official planning discussions. Their projects have documented that even when the slums in questions are going to be impacted through the construction of bridges, roads, industries, and so on, the families from the *basti* are rarely included in discussions

or dialogue initiated by the local government. It is rare that the city's slum settlements are considered in major proposals, and the Municipal Corporation plans for slum settlements through haphazard, piecemeal projects. There is no integrated inclusive approach to planning for the whole city. A large part of the problem is inadequate information about the poor. Reliable and comprehensive information about slums, their locations, and their population is needed as a basis for ensuring that planning works for all citizens, not just those people who live outside slums.

7. Water logging was used to describe the frequent flooding that occurred near their houses during monsoons. The rainwater often flooded their dwellings because the government did not provide any services for water removal or for erecting barriers that would divert the flow of water to other areas.

8. As I was writing the first draft of this chapter in May 2014, the press in India reported the rape of two girls. The newspapers were reporting that two cousins, aged 14 and 15 years, from the Katra Sadatganj village in Badaun district of the state of Uttar Pradesh went out after dusk to the nearby fields. They were searching for a secluded spot to relieve themselves because they did not have a toilet at home. That evening, these two girls were gang raped and murdered. Their bodies were found hung to a mango tree, in a nearby field, by their pink and green headscarves. That same evening, Baburam, the father of one of the girls, had set out to inspect his crops, which were close to the mango tree, when he heard screams. He was carrying a flashlight because there was no electricity. The transformer in the village was malfunctioning and had not been repaired for 8 days. He reported to the newspaper, *Indian Express*, "I was walking back when I heard the screams of two girls. I flashed my torch around but couldn't see anything at first. Then I saw movement, and Pappu Yadav and three other men. They were dragging one of my nieces by the hair." Baburam intervened, but he retreated when the young men threatened to kill him with a handgun. Sohan Lal, the brother of Baburam and the father of one of the girls, went to the police, but they refused to investigate the matter. Several hours later, a policeman called Lal and told him, "Go to the mango trees, the body of your daughter is there." What the two teenagers encountered as they were searching for a place to defecate is an experience that many young women from the *basti* spoke about in their interviews.

9. The multiplex cinema halls began to be built in the mid-1990s in many cities, and these theaters show movies on 3–15 screens. These theaters have mall-style food courts, arcades, and stores. The ticket prices are usually very high, so only middle- and upper-class Indians can afford to watch movies in these multiplexes.

10. For instance, there is controversy about the *Jats* being considered an OBC group because they are viewed as a relatively prosperous community. Recently, the *Patel* community has agitated for being considered an OBC group, despite the fact that they are a relatively successful community of entrepreneurs.

CHAPTER 8

Toward a Transnational Cultural Psychology

Narrative and Social Justice in the Age
of Unequal Globalization

This book is intended to be much more than merely a discussion of how globalization as a discursive and material reality shapes urban Indian youth. It is my hope that the analyses presented in this book reveal how specific local psychologies assume a dominant position and become appropriated throughout the world. It shows that Euro-American psychology and identity are represented as perched on a branch that is high above the other psychologies of the world, resting comfortably outside all other people's histories. Euro-American psychology's power does not just reside in the fact that it can continue to exist by largely ignoring the histories of other nations and societies. Rather, like other imperial entities, it exudes power because it also provides the maps, guidelines, and profiles by which other individuals usually understand and determine their own psychological identities.

Urban Indian youth represent one of the largest segments of the youth population in the world, and their lives reveal to us the complex ways in which they engage with practices and discourses of globalization. Rather than conceiving of globalization as solely made up of a one-directed, Western external cultural flow that writes itself on the local canvas, this book has examined how youth strategically deploy narratives of globalization to negotiate, reimagine, and contest their "Indianness." I have discussed examples of Indian urban youth across three classes to show how the study of these shifting class identities within specific contexts of globalization is an important undertaking for psychology and human development. By focusing on these youth, my attempt was to also make visible those peripheral identities so often marginalized, even made invisible, within Euro-American psychology. The narratives of urban Indian youth give us a nuanced understanding of how both the local and the global are reworked to create new stories of identity and identification. These stories of Indianness are shaped by neoliberal structures and asymmetrical flows of capital and labor, and they are composed of uneasy collisions of cultures that point to what Kraidy (2005) refers to as "hybridity without guarantees" (p. xii).

The discourses of globalization or neoliberalism are not completely hegemonic, but instead they intersect with other material or cultural discourses to give us dynamic and multiple practices in which identities are embedded (Walkerdine & Bansel, 2010). I argue that one of the major gaps in contemporary cultural psychological research is related to understanding how "power and intracultural variation" and "cultural narratives" play critical roles in understanding how marginalized groups express their agency (Mahalingam, 2007, p. 15). Although there is a certain degree of convergence or class-based similarities among the social practices of Indian youth, I cannot underscore enough the significance of how regional variation and class shape the narratives of Indian youth (Lukose, 2009; Titus, 2015). As I conclude this book, I aim to articulate a vision for psychology that is made up of an uneasy combination of toilets and theories, cultures and stories. I say "uneasy combination" because I believe that for a very long time an unbridgeable cleavage has existed between psychology and principles of social justice. Psychology has not yet developed a meaningful theoretical vocabulary or a willingness to explore questions of social justice that are wrapped around qualitative methods and community-based practices because these are usually conducted in faraway places with marginalized populations that have had no history or recognition in American psychology or in the United States.

Psychology has a tendency to reframe problems related to structural inequality as individual problems, whereas I envision a psychology in which questions of social justice and the public good could become central to its mission—a mission that speaks to the lives of the majority of the world's population. I admit that crafting such a vision is daunting. Nevertheless, in concluding this work, I aim to build a psychology or a psychological perspective that is deeply *Other*-oriented.

NARRATIVE PSYCHOLOGY AND IDENTITY: ANOTHER WORLD IS POSSIBLE

Indian writer Arundhati Roy (2003) states that "we must tell stories that are different from the ones we're brainwashed to believe. . . . Remember this: Another world is not only possible, she is on her way. On a quiet day I can hear her breathing" (p. 127). If we were to embrace Roy's plea that we remain open to this other world, then we need to listen to different stories that have different themes, cadences, rhythms, and *breathing* patterns. Narrative psychology can play an important role in the efforts to decolonize psychology of its dominant emphasis on stories of variables, generalizations, meta-data, neuro-identities, and statistical manipulation. The focus on lived experience and realities on the ground does not mean that theories are not important; rather, a focus on stories provides different experiential vantage points from which we can understand the psychology of the marginalized (Bochner, 1997; Brockmeier, 2012).

There is an ongoing debate within narrative psychology about meaning-making that occurs in "big stories" and "small stories" (Bamberg, 2011; Freeman, 2011). The focus in the big-story approach is on first-person narrations of self that occur through self-reflection and retrospective meaning-making that one sees in memoirs, life-history narratives, and autobiographies. This "big story" of self is created through sustained acts of reflection and intro-spection, and it provides unity, purpose, and coherence to the fragmented experiences of an individual. In contrast to the big story framework, there are other scholars who study self and identity formation by examining the "way stories surface in everyday conversation (small stories), as the locus where identities are continuously practiced and tested out" (Bamberg, 2011, p. 15). The focus in the small story approach is on narration, "in contrast to *narrative* or *story*, in order to emphasize the activity of narrating, and to de-emphasize the final product of a text placing emphasis on small stories" (p. 17, emphasis in original). Thus, the small story perspective conceives of a person as "socially interactively constituted," such that the meanings of self and others emerge from social interaction. The small story approach is intended to move away from an emphasis on first-person biography as the "sole and privileged" narrative domain for identity construction (Bamberg, 2011).

Whether one studies narratives that are constructed by engaging in a "distanced mode of reflection" (Freeman, 2011, p. 118) or by examining the contextually situated, here-and-now aspects of narration, we are still faced with crucial questions about how individuals negotiate "otherness," "difference," and "injustices" in their everyday lives. If our meanings about self and other are drawn from a diverse array of cultural sources or practices (MacIntyre, 1984), then we need to (1) understand the varied stories that are narrated by Indian youth to make sense about their identity in contemporary cultural contexts and (2) examine how their narrative meanings emerge from conflicting and contested cultural sources and practices. This examination is critical if the discipline of narrative psychology is to understand how the biographical and self-reflective components of the life-story approach and the "here-and-now," dialogical aspects of "small stories" are shaped by larger sociocultural contexts. How exactly is the "cultural" constituted in the "life as reflected" and "life as lived" (Bamberg, 2011, p. 14) modes of sense-making?

In summary, both the "big story" and the "small story" frameworks have to account for how narratives are tied to what Bruner (1990) has called "cultural settings." If narrative inquiry is fundamentally rooted in a cultural psychology, then we must aim to understand how particular narratives are given meaning in contexts of cultural practices that are defined by migration, postcolonialism, neoliberalization, and globalization. The narrative dimension plays an important role in creating autobiographical meanings of an individual's past, present, and future. Thus, narrative imagination and autobiographical understanding are dialectically constituted. Freeman (2007) observes:

> Even in the midst of my present engagement with the past, I am moving into the future, giving form and meaning to the self-to-be. . . . Exploring the process of autobiographical understanding serves to underscore the idea that both the personal past and self whose past it is are indeed constructions, issuing from the narrative imagination. This is emphatically not to say, however, that these constructions are fictions or illusions or lies: The imagined is not be equated with the wholly imaginary, and *poiesis*, the act of making meaning, is not to be understood as one in which something is made *ex nihilo*, out of nothing. (p. 138)

Narrative imagination is thus crucial to understanding how individuals make meaning of their lives and how their social imagination is shaped by moments of sociocultural change. The concept of imagination is linked to the "narrative way of knowing" that Bruner (1990) distinguishes from a paradigmatic way of knowing that is so essential to understanding personhood. This narrative imagination is essentially made up of the stuff of psychology—in which emotions, memory, identity, and sense-making come together to create identities. These imaginations are what give us insights into identity, identification, subjectivity, and cultural transformations.

Molly Andrews (2014) argues that imagination can take an infinite number of forms, and narrative constitutes one of them. But when narrative and imagination are conjoined, we "encounter the balancing act of what defines us as human—living, breathing and interacting in the world even while our minds are full of memories and dreams" (p. 2). What needs to be noted, however, is that in the field of psychology, there are very few accounts about how non-Western populations living in urban areas are using their narrative imagination to come to terms with their changing conceptions of identity. If narrative imagination defines our humanity, as Andrews states, then we need more *narrations* of imaginative practices that depart from what is taken to be normal or natural in mainstream psychology.

My argument is that our "global" or "local" imagination about others comes alive through narratives—the stories we tell about others are created through how we imagine the other. A typical call center worker in India has hundreds of daily phone interactions with customers from the United Kingdom or the United States, but this worker will never be able to afford to take a trip to see the country and culture of the people to whom he or she is speaking on a daily basis. However, despite the physical distance, the call center worker imagines how his or her customers live—what they drive, eat, watch on TV, and how they spend their weekends. Vasavi (2008) writes that youth employed in call centers, business process outsourcing companies, and information technology (IT) firms are the "new brigade of global subjects/workers" (p. 212) who are threatening the ideology of the Indian family and are reimagining what it means to be an urban Indian living in times of globalization. She further states that the educated urban Indian youth "constitute an unanticipated category of workers–consumers who rupture many established and ascribed roles and norms, and signify the potential reordering of urban Indian family structures, inter-generational relations and the positioning of youth" (p. 212).

Many call center workers' imagined "America" is shaped by media—film, television, and the Internet—and by circulation of commodified images about the US and European culture, as well as the meaning of "cultural difference" they have encountered at work. Appadurai (1996) writes that these mythic images of others get incorporated in the stories one creates about oneself and others—imagination and actual physical mediation with global cultural flows becomes an integral part of one's cultural identity. Living in a globalized, imagined community (Anderson, 1991) does not mean that one's imagination is unreal. Rather, it means that imagining a world outside one's local culture gives one scripts for living other possible selves and thus ways of creating new identities. The focus on narration, telling, and storytelling then puts narrative into the realm of practices and compels us to think about narrative as action.

Refashioning Indianness

The stories of Indian youth that I sketched in Chapters 5–7 are deeply connected to the story of neoliberal forms of globalization that I analyzed throughout the book. One of the significant objectives of this book is to de-center American psychology by using a narrative approach to studying globalization. In particular, I argue that the growing field of narrative psychology is theoretically and conceptually well-equipped to explain how individuals make meaning of their lives in the face of cultural change. A narrative perspective pushes us to focus on how these new stories of self and others are being fashioned and refashioned in the context of cultural globalization. How do youth, living in the centers and peripheries of urban India use stories to make sense of their lives? How do their identity narratives reveal ambiguity, contradiction, and complexity? The phenomenon of globalization described in this book cannot be disconnected from the larger neoliberal apparatus that in the first place has created the modern market of global flows and intersecting scapes. It would be naive to assume that we live in a borderless world where people of all backgrounds can freely move across countries. Globalization has spawned new open markets and created a flow of new capital and goods but has simultaneously seen the rise of class barriers, tightening visa regulations, racial profiling, ethnic violence, suicide bombings, extreme political violence against civilians, and a clash of global ideologies and a new "civilization of clashes" (Appadurai, 2006). The idea that cultures are traveling across borders and are on the move, however, seems a very simplistic analysis of globalization. For large tracts of the world, where hunger, lack of education, and unsanitary conditions still persist, the concept of globalization is empty and has not reduced their daily hardships. As globalization has opened up borders and frontiers, we have also witnessed the simultaneous creation of new forms of class inequality, the rise of the privatization of public resources, and the asymmetrical construction of class and cultural privileges. It is against this backdrop of unequal practices and discourses of globalization that I have made an attempt to detail how "liberalization's children" in urban India are reconstructing their identity narratives. How does their story unfold as they interact with new practices of globalization?

The youth's diverse social imagination about self and others is shaped by a socially unequal society that is also connected to larger structural, cultural, and institutional frameworks of politics, governance, and economics and postcolonial forms of acculturation. Throughout the book, I have argued that, above all, narrative and "narrations" play an important role in ordering and giving meaning to our scattered, fragmented, and fleeting experience of our lives. The equipment of narrative also allows us to further investigate how Indian youth use cultural discourses about globalization to refashion their personal identity. As reviewed previously, this is what Brockmeier (2012) refers to as the hermeneutic circle that locks culture and narrative together and gives us the tool to understand human sense-making. This dynamic view of narrative shifts the idea from seeing narrative as cognitive instrument of the mind to what Hammack (2011) calls "narrative engagement" (p. 2).

Recall how Raj and Sunaina's personal narratives presented in Chapter 4 showed globalization as creating new imaginations of their lives. They are gripped by moments of certainty and ambiguity, and they are searching for new horizons and frames of meaning to understand and express their "Indianness." Raj's and Sunaina's narratives tell us how their self-reflective competing discourses about identity during a period of intense sociocultural change make narrative psychology an important theoretical framework in psychology. That is, as families and individuals in India are exposed to divergent cultural discourses about tradition and modernity, autonomy and connectedness, they are creating new "narrative demands" on the individual to negotiate the varied contradictory flows that are coming their way.

What are the implications of narrative research for decolonizing psychology? Where should we go with narrative? Schiff (2012) argues that as narrative scholars we should

> focus on the process of meaning-making—on what narrative does and how it accomplishes this—in the concrete circumstances in which meaning-making happens. How do persons, in time and space, make sense of life experience. . . . This is the unique contribution that narrative research can make to the advancement of psychology and social sciences. (p. 45)

From the perspective of the current study, I take Schiff's question and reframe it as follows: How do persons, who are located in varied, contradictory, and asymmetrical transnational cultural discourses and practices, make sense of their life experiences? What do their narratives tell us about how they are being "hailed" or "interpellated" by discourses, and what kinds of stories do they create in response to this "hailing"? The large body of knowledge that we describe as narrative psychology has been overwhelmingly created out of stories that are located in the Global North or have originated from a Eurocentric culture.

Narrative psychology, as I have shown, has provided us the tools to understand and analyze identities or counternarratives that are often overlooked in mainstream Euro-American psychology, including narrative psychology. We can further broaden the "landscape" of narrative inquiry (Clandinin & Rosiek, 2007) by creating a psychology that theorizes, analyzes, understands, legitimizes, validates, and listens to the stories and struggles that have often been ignored or suppressed in the past cannons of the Western "science of psychology." This is an important decolonizing move for both narrative and general psychology given that for too long Euro-American psychology has been creating ethnocentrically based Orientalist images of non-Western others. Narrative psychology, with its emphasis on meaning-making, has an opportunity to engage with and understand stories that are emerging from localities where both the West and non-West sit in a hybrid, dialogical, uneasy, and often exploitative, and even violent arrangement.

The urban Indian youth in contemporary India are at the center of the processes of change that are associated with globalization. They are coming of age in a culture in which they must negotiate and contend with contradictory stories, images, scripts, and sensibilities. Their values, social networks, aspirations, and symbols of a good life are shaped by the traditions of familial relations, hierarchy, and community; at the same time, however, they are also being shaped by ideologies of Western consumerism, individualism, and materialism. One of the implications associated with processes of globalization is that youth are responding to these uncertainties by creating new narratives of self and others—their narratives are negotiating both sides of the equation of traditions and modernity in ways that had been unprecedented in previous generations.

In his introduction to the *Oxford Handbook of Psychology in India*, Misra (2011) states that India is an ancient civilization that is fast moving toward technological advancements, and it offers a unique cultural setting to study the interplay between "tradition and modernity, especially with regard to the cultural mediation of the psychological processes" (p. 1). Contemporary urban Indian youth, as the book highlights, are moving in and out of different cultural worlds, and their identities display contradictory cultural sites of negotiations where family obligations, social networks, self-sacrifice, and religious values clash with individual desire, autonomy, pursuit of money, materialism, and consumption.

Unequal power structures and hierarchies of social class practices shape the hybrid youth narratives that were analyzed in Chapters 5–7. While the youth narratives were fashioned through the class locations and their encounters with complex, globalization discourses, their stories were not uniform. The elite youth were concerned with acquiring a global outlook—where cosmopolitan forms of "appropriate Indianness" were deployed for acquiring social mobility and to further their transnational privileges. A lifestyle based on consumption practices and the freedom to appropriate select Indian traditions was absolutely essential to the self-image of these transnational youth. This was not the hybridity of the margins—this was a *hegemonic hybridity* that was made at the center of Indian society, and their stories symbolized their class domination. The elite, transnational, and upper-class youth had the power and the financial and multicultural capital to construct mobile, culturally streamlined forms of global Indianness (Radhakrishnan, 2011). The Meridian youth had the financial and cultural capital and transnational privileges to define the characteristics of "global Indianness" into a singular cultural difference that was often produced not only for the Western gaze but also for constructing an identity of being world-class citizens, cosmopolitan Indians, or "ultimate global Indians." The idea that the West is superior—especially American colleges and universities, media, and brands—still has a strong hold on the imagination of parents living in the metropolitan cities of India. However, at the same time, they are becoming aware that their children do not have to go to England or America to experience modernity or what Appadurai (1996, p. 2) calls the "embodied sensations" of modernity. They can now create an Indian modernity through their exposure to the global images of American culture—through education, social media, travel, television, and their social imagination. For those urban Indian youth, who are similar to some of the Meridian students, the West as a globally valued signifier has been unhinged from its source and has now found a reincarnated life or new avatar in the local geographies of Asia. The sustained exposure to and consumption of global cultural flows and commodities is playing a powerful role in shaping the everyday lives of Indian youth: Their practices of work, romance, marriage, sex, and family are being reimagined and reinterpreted to suit their imagination.

The construction of "global youth" or "global Indianness" with all its crass materialism, delectable ironies, and paradoxes has taken root at home to produce what Pam Nilan and Carles Fexia (2006, p. 3) call new "youth landscapes," "youth stories," and "youth histories." The narratives of Indian youth who study in spaces such as Meridian are constructing a hybrid Indianness that is culturally commodified and based on neoliberal practices of consumption. These identities reinforce new forms of colonial hierarchies; foster a language of auto-Orientalism; idealize neoliberal practices; and tend to fetishize transnational mobility, Euro-American identities, and psychological discourses of self. Such transnationally "appropriate" forms of Indian hybridity tend to ignore the larger social and structural inequities and hierarchies in urban India and find their larger meaning in a consumption-based language of citizenship and identity. This small minority of upper-middle-class and elite youth was producing new and powerful narratives of "global Indianness" that also circulated as "master narratives" (Hammack, 2011) in the popular imagination and across other classes.

In contrast to the transitionally oriented youth, who had the cultural capital, financial wealth, and privileges of class and caste, the call center workers whom I spoke to were mostly from middle- and working-class families from Pune and other Indian cities. The workers I interviewed, especially women, had joined a call center to become financially independent and have a career that would enable them to strive for a middle-class lifestyle. The distinction between the transnational and middle-class youth in India is important because the latter lived in modest housing, rode scooters or motorcycles, and came from families where refrigerators, television sets, and other consumer durables were considered a luxury.

Most of the call center women I interviewed were working as call center agents because they wanted to become culturally and financially independent from their families, they had to support their families, and they liked working as "global employees" or were attracted to the Western lifestyle associated with the call center jobs. The young women who worked as call center agents were subjected to a mobility–morality narrative through which their presence in public space or during the night shift was constructed through a patriarchal discourse. These women were seen as "bad girls" with "immoral character," "promiscuous," and were often subjected to public surveillance and "shaming" by their families and friends. Undoubtedly, there were cultural similarities between call center workers and the upper-class Meridian youth. Both groups were exposed to American media, films, television shows, and traditional family practices, but the larger cultural and spatial contexts in which they were reconstructing their Indianness were quite different. Their particular intersection of class and gender locations played a pivotal role in how the call center workers were refiguring their identities.

The call center work also provided the youth with financial and cultural capital to "individualize" their identities so as to challenge traditional gender roles and question oppressive patriarchal discourses about divorced women. The call center workers did not have the privilege of "discovering their identities" in expensive college environments, but they were reimagining their identities in neoliberal work conditions that were often demanding and exploitative. Call center salaries gave them the financial push to maintain their middle-class-ness or to aspire to "becoming somebody" through the purchase of branded clothes and other socially valued goods.

The call center workers whom I interviewed for the project were already situated in wider cultural discourses about the "identity of call center youth" in urban India. The analysis of call center youth also points to how global corporations have provided young, upwardly mobile Indians with new forms of employment, social mobility, and psychological discourses of self that often clash with their local conceptions of Indianness. The transnational and middle-class narratives also demonstrate a vacillation between performing Western-style cosmopolitanism while still being true and authentic to one's traditions.

The stories, imagery, and tone of the transnational and middle-class youth narratives are radically different from those of youth who live in urban slums in Pune. The structural realities of the slums—lack of access to toilets, temporary housing, lack of financial and cultural resources, and a lack of power to make changes—disproportionately impact the stories and voices of the youth living in them. The youth of the *basti* have an asymmetrical dialogical relationship with the structures that symbolize inequality or the individuals who represent those power structures, such as politicians, police officers, local leaders, government officials, and the dominant classes. These organizational structures (lack of sanitation or impermanent housing) or representatives of those structures collectively create conditions of marginality and poverty for the youth.

The stories of youth from Panchsheel *basti* demonstrate linkages between class, caste, and new practices of globalization. An analysis of their narratives shows that youth enact their agencies and assert their will within the ecological contexts of their slums, but many find themselves struggling with conditions of poverty and without the cultural resources that are necessary to improve their lives in the future. By agency, I am not referring to a person working from outside the system who acts upon the world with a free will and as a rational agent. Rather, these are acts of assertion that are played out in the microcontext of everyday cultural practices in which the agent is both enabled and constrained by the larger political and cultural forces. Through the invocation of these and other strategies, the young participants from the slums are trying to take control of how they, and others, view their marginality. The youth mimicked the youth from the "hi-fi" class by buying inexpensive and cheap "locally made" foreign brands from Fashion Street or Lakshmi Road. They positioned themselves as being morally and spiritually superior to affluent youth—who were mostly seen as corrupted by money, sex, and power. The *basti* youth's stories represent more than just their condition of poverty; they point to practices of consumption that Srivastava (2015, p. 62) describes as "subaltern consumerism." The stories of the urban poor also reveal "the promises of redemption held out by forms of consumerism that directly address them as consumers" (p. 263).

The interviews make clear that low-income, working-class, and poor youth do have aspirations and dreams, but the structural and cultural pathways for reaching those dreams and goals are limited or absent. Effort alone is not a guarantee of realizing one's outcomes. The condition of being dispossessed is about lacking the cultural, structural, and narrative capacity to create conditions in which the youth can realize their aspirations successfully. Thus, I argue that the capacity to aspire then provides an "ethical horizon" through which concrete human capabilities can be shaped, made sustainable, and given meaning and expression in local contexts. The practice and exercise of these capabilities, according to Appadurai (2013), "verifies and authorizes the capacity to aspire and moves it away from wishful thinking to thoughtful wishing" (p. 193). Thus, the concept of "freedom" that is linked to capabilities and development cannot have a sustainable impact unless it is connected to the narrative practices and collective web of social meaning through which the horizons of hope and wants, aspirations, and capacity find their expression.

The refashioning of Indianness in contemporary India and in Euro-American psychology reveals a preoccupation with elite, affluent, and middle-class identities and a larger neglect of identities that live and form in the margin. Decolonizing psychology then means asking questions about whose narratives represent India and whose stories are visible and included in the structure of opportunity and advancement. It means asking questions that are fundamental to social justice and identity formation. Boo (2012) notes, "Whose capabilities are given wing by the market and a government's economic and social policy? Whose capabilities are squandered?" (p. 248).

Globalization, mostly rooted in corporate capitalism and the logic of Western modernity, has inserted a new set of subjectivities, world views, and rhythms of everyday living that are reconstructing and reframing at least two "ideals" of Indian culture (Mohan, 2011). The two ideals that define Indian culture are (1) the communitarian and family ideal and (2) creativity and the spirit of accommodation (Mohan, 2011). One of the most unique features of the "Indian self" or "Indian psyche" is that it is shaped by community-based relationships of family, kinship, and caste, as well as through socialization in religious practices. The familial self in India has an inner world that is composed of a hierarchically created set of intimate relationships, and it also contains several groups from family to friends and neighbors. This familial self, according to Roland (1988), is made of small subselves that thrive on symbiotic reciprocity and emotionally resonant social interactions. The emotional bonds with others are fostered by cultivating a high degree of empathy with others; the Indian self is always embedded in an atmosphere of evolving relationships.

Chaudhary (2004) argues that the multiple hierarchical relationships in India, within the family context, are expressed through very fluid interpersonal bonds, ritual conversations that flow through permeable boundaries between the private and the public space, and through a language of kinship terms that are highly localized. She notes that the individual's discursive creation of social worlds creates a "we–self" representation in which the relational identity of "our" and "us" becomes much greater than any "I." In a dynamic combination, autonomy and interdependence mutually feed each other and maintain cultural stability; Chaudhary explains that "if this were not the case, globalization would have broken the social architecture of Indian society" (p. 179).

Second, Madan (1989) argues that one of the strengths of Indian culture has been the spirit of accommodating multiple faiths, religions, and world views. The traditions associated with the religions and philosophies of Sikhism, Jainism, Hinduism, Buddhism, Santism, and Islam comprise important elements of what can be loosely described as Indian culture (Madan, 1989). Mohan (2011) describes a dynamic and evolving sense of culture by using the word *ravayaat* (i.e., flowing or constantly in motion). Despite India's "terrible record" of social inequality, the cultural notion of *ravayaat* has fostered a spirit of inclusiveness and "pluralist toleration" (Sen, 2005, p. 34).

This spirit of tolerance has largely embraced the ideological diversity of groups, personal beliefs systems of individuals, and the religious and moral frameworks that underpin the various world views co-present in many groups at any given time in India. In principle, the postcolonial Indian independent state embodies a notion of secularism that is very much tied to the philosophies and religious practices that emphasize religious tolerance and acceptance.[1] Instead of adopting the word "recognition" to imply an acceptance of plural culture, Sen (2005) writes that Indian culture's regard for diversity is captured much more clearly in the Sanskrit word *Swikriti*, which means "the acknowledgement that the people involved are entitled to lead their own lives" (p. 35). This term, while underscoring the significance of acknowledging plurality in cultural practices, does not convey any declaration or upholding of the principle of equality between groups.

The component of plurality that has defined ideals of Indian culture should not blind us to the fact that Indians have deployed the vocabulary of identity, whether it is based on religion or caste, to wage wars and engage in riots, mass killings, uprisings, and rebellions. We can point to several examples in history where this impulse to flow or be in motion that has tended to protect the pluralist principle of *Swikriti* has cut both ways: It has brought about communal amity and also created deep social division unleashing untold suffering, grief, and carnage. The Partition of India in 1947 has been called an "unspeakable sadness" and the "*memento mori*" that gave birth to India and Pakistan (Khilnani, 1997). India's experiment with secularism and democracy has led Khilnani to assert that Indian history after 1947 can be construed as an adventure that hinges on a single idea of democracy. He describes the postcolonial phase of independent India as a third moment in the democratic experiments that were spurred by American and French Revolutions in the concluding decades of the 18th century. Each of these moments, he says, represented and rediscovered the classical ideas of democracy in very different cultural contexts, in which concepts of nationhood, freedom, community, public good, and social equality were highly contested and vigorously debated. Each of these experiments, Khilnani writes, has

> released immense energies; each raised towering expectations; and each has suffered tragic disappointments. The Indian experiment is still in its early stage, and its outcome may well turn out to be the most significant of them all. Partly because of the sheer human scale, and partly because of its location, a substantial bridgehead of effervescent liberty on the Asian continent. (p. 4)

The idea of Indian democracy as a bridge to liberty has always built on the assumption that "Indianness" has to be essentially conceived through "unity in diversity," giving recognition to others, and by incorporating the principles of plurality and morality. Kapur and Misra (2011) note that Indian social identity is largely shaped by forces of religion, culture, and tradition, and such forces also tend to create social exclusion and sectarian identification in the plural Indian democracy. They also note that in contemporary India, the dominant representation of Hindu identity as "we" is usually complex, whereas the minority groups—the "they"—are viewed primarily through their Muslimness, Sikhness, or Christianness. Thus, Kapur and Misra argue that the anti-Muslim violence in Gujarat in 2002 was normalized in the name of "personal, communal, national, and even international security" (p. 154).

The two principles that make up "Indian ideals" should be regarded as "ideals" that reflect collective cultural aspirations alongside other simultaneous cultural forces of communal division, hatred, materialism, Americanization, and individualism that also play a role in shaping contemporary stories of an "Indian self." Globalization, however, does not signify absolute personal freedom and internalization of Western values, nor does it signify an absolute loss of Indian values of *dharma*, traditional notions of hierarchy, marriage, and the joint family system. Rather, globalization, as Nadeem (2011) argues, creates identities that are based on an "Indian morality play where the pleasure principle clashes with demands of custom and obligation, where *kama* (pleasure) and *dharma* (duty) meet in uneasy suspension" (p. 52). The cultural mediation of youth identities discussed in previous chapters reveals an interplay between *kama* and *dharma*, between modernity and tradition. Despite the fact that the present context of globalization and the transnational cultural flows are destabilizing old notions of joint family and old traditions in urban India, the family and relationships continue to play important roles.

Globalization, with its symbols of malls, new work styles, advertisements, consumerist culture, Western lifestyle, and emphasis on individualism and travel, has given new meanings to the sensibilities, values, narratives, and reference points associated with the traditional conceptions of "Indianness." Indian families are *reimagining Indianness* through rearticulating new hybrid meanings of modernity and tradition via each other as they come into contact with global rituals of consumerism, sociality, and work (Misra, 2011; Nadeem, 2011; Ramesh, 2008; Saraswathi & Larson, 2002; Shome, 2006). It is this process of individual and collective *hybrid reimagining* that makes the concept of cultural, narrative, and identity so central to psychology.

Hybrid Narratives and Power

The concept of hybridity that I am proposing gives us one way of understanding how youth reimagine their Indianness within new cultural contexts of power, mobility of labor and capital, and discourses of class, consumerism, and transnational mobility. It gives us the tools to examine how power and agency are expressed within particular constructions of these social identities (Kraidy, 2005).

Adding an analysis of power asymmetry to the hybridity of Indian youth narratives allows us to go beyond conceptualizing identity through simple explanations of cultural differences or positing homogeneous national identities. It is quite another thing to theorize about how young Indian intercultural identities are shaped by labor conditions, social inequalities, neoliberal economies, and colonial legacies. Obviously, these cross-cultural experiences do indicate that we are not merely moving toward cultural homogenization or standardization. It is quite common to dismiss the position that globalization does not equate to cultural imperialism and to assert that people in the "non-Western" countries do not passively accept Western or external cultural flows. It is also conventional wisdom in academic circles to argue that globalization produces cultural reframing, contestation, and resistance. I argue, however, that cultural imperialism and heterogeneity, sameness and difference, and mimicry and resistance all play an important part in shaping Indian youth narratives.

Thus, it is not surprising that Nadeem (2011), whose book examines how global outsourcing is changing the way Indians reimagine themselves, asks whether discourses of globalization are similar to colonialism in some of its cultural dynamics and effects. He calls Indian call center workers "Lord Macaulay's (Cyber) Children" in describing how their hybridity moves between sameness and difference and between homogeneity and heterogeneity.

The West as a locus of modernity is now being imagined by Indian youth through the lens of postcolonial culture and the new symbols of globalization: American cultural flows of television, films, commodities, and lifestyles. The concept of postcolonial identity then plays an important role in producing contemporary cultural narratives of identity in urban India—they are one layer of history among others that give us an analytic framework to understand how young, urban, "global Indian" identities are tied to both postcolonial and transnational contexts. Thus, we need to be cautious about being overly utopian about using benign forms of cultural fragmentation and hybridity as manifestations of resistance.

The many IT workers and call center agents whom I interviewed for this book mostly used Western notions of modernity as a metric for measuring their progress. The elite students were enacting a transnational hybridity that reinforced their privilege and dominance through their social class standing, whereas American media, fashion, and music played an important role in their hybrid imaginations. Examining heterogeneous and complex narratives of hybridity that come into play as a result of sociocultural, material, and economic transformations is crucial, as argued by Kraidy (2005), who writes that "hybridity as a sociocultural condition at large, disconnected from its political and economic contexts and from its constitutive processes, is conceptually untenable and ethnographically problematical" (p. 75). The discussion of agency in these debates is imbued with an emancipatory rhetoric that is filled with optimism (Khan, 2007, p. 654). This "teleological optimism," according to Khan, turns into a self-fulfilling prophecy and as "a consequence our understanding of power, processes of change, and the work of culture are skewed" (p. 654). When we study hybridity or hybrid psychologies, we have to be careful not to create a psychology of otherness that celebrates the strange as exotic. We must refrain from depicting romantic representations of agency in the discourse of hybridity and globalization—especially discourses that contradict the various ways in which agents of hybridity can themselves be ambivalent in their identity and identification processes (Khan, 2007).

CULTURE, TRANSNATIONAL CONNECTIONS, AND NEOLIBERALISM

As culture travels from "here" to "there," through diverse transnational circuits, we get new configurations of identity not just in "First World" spaces but also in the cultures of the "Global South" and developing countries. Today's world is then characterized by movement of transnational cultural flows; migrations of individuals, refugees, tourists, students, corporations, neoliberal economic circuits, expatriates, and international experts; as well as circulation of common images in popular culture, television shows, music, and magazines. Also, through the intensification of social media, there are new constellations and dynamics and constellations of identity.

The youth, who are at the center of globalization, frequently become the ideological battleground for debates about the transnational global flows and how they shape tradition, modernity, cosmopolitanism, and consumerism. Even when youth are not crossing borders and are located in their homes, they are becoming integral parts of transnational systems through their work in multinational production facilities (e.g., Nike, Gap, and Apple), the IT sector (e.g., software industries, billing, accounting, and medical transcription), and mechanisms of outsourcing of customer services (e.g., call centers). The concept of transnational movement also implies that the category of youth is not just a geographic and temporal site but also a place that is connected to movement of labor, social and cultural flows, and colonial and postcolonial histories that traverse borders and boundaries (Maira & Soep, 2005).

Decentering Culture

Much of psychology has presented a conception of identity as decontextualized because explanations of culture are largely removed from the dynamics of power, privilege, and conflict (Dixon, Tropp, Durrheim, & Tredoux, 2010; Hammack, 2011). The concept of culture in much of psychology is described as a static and essentialized entity that has implicit properties (Valsiner, 2007). This definition of culture simultaneously indicates the "commonality of such belonging (the descriptive or classificatory role of the use of the term), and some, usually unspecified, causal system that guarantees the relative similarity of all the persons who 'belong to' the given culture" (Valsiner, 2007, p. 20). There is an assumption in psychology that every person who "belongs to" a given culture shares similar qualities and traits with (nearly) every other member of that culture. It is assumed in psychology that "discontinuity forms the starting point from which to theorize contact, conflict and contradictions between cultures and societies" (Gupta & Ferguson, 1992, p. 6). As a result of this assumption, we have a world that is neatly divided into nations and countries, each representing its own culture; thus, the colors and lines on a world map are intended to reflects nations as disjointed, self-contained, and bounded by their own territory and space.

In order to understand how culture becomes decentered and takes on new meaning across borders and transnational spaces, we need to delink the concept of culture as rooted in a fixed space of a "nation," or as a "variable," or designate it as equal to a "population sample." Many mainstream social, developmental, and cross-cultural psychologists define culture primarily as a variable. For example, cross-cultural psychologists Segall, Lonner, and Berry (1998) define culture as "comprising a set of independent or contextual variables affecting various aspects of individual behavior" (p. 1102). Furthermore, the universalist assumptions about culture are based on the idea that there are "basic characteristics common to all members of the species (i.e., constituting a set of psychological givens) and that culture influences the development and display of them (i.e., culture plays different variations on these underlying themes called 'variform universals')" (p. 1104). The reluctance to situate human interaction in politicized and messy contexts of cultural discourses is partly a result of wanting to formulate a psychology that is neutral, nonaligned, and without reference to racial, sexual, or gender politics. This reluctance to directly engage in a contested conception of culture also allows psychologists to continue to reproduce a dominant positivistic conception of psychological science.

The transnational cultural perspective that I am articulating, in contrast, is highly attuned to contexts of power, coloniality of psychology, marginality, transnational cultural flows, human agency, and the epistemic violence (Teo, 2011) that is often caused by certain psychological frameworks. It transcends the dualisms permeating much of mainstream psychological discourse that separates the individual and society, cognition and culture, self and community, and host and home society. Similarly, Hermans and Kempen (1998) have made a call for alternative ways of thinking about identity in the field of psychology. They argue that in a period of increasing globalization, the rapid creation of multinationals, the formation of diasporic communities, and massive flows of transmigration and border crossings, we should think of the relationship between culture and identity as contested and mixing and moving. Mark Freeman (2010), in arguing that we need a vastly spacious concept of selfhood in narrative psychology, states that understanding "my story" or the trajectory of "I" in one's individual biography is created by "secondhand sources" and essentially mediated by a wide range of cultural practices. Acknowledging and studying the self as intersubjective or distributed does not take away the subjective grounding of the story. Rather, Freeman writes that "what is 'mine' is, at one and the same time, permeated by what is 'other' and, in turn, that any and all attempts to separate selfhood from its sociocultural surround must fail" (p. 137). The idea of locating subjectivities in discourses of global flows is not tantamount to denying the importance of our bodies, brains, or our psychological capacities, but it serves to remind us that one of the main goals of psychological inquiry is to study persons acting in their biophysical and sociocultural worlds (Kirschner & Martin, 2010).

The task of poetically constructing an identity also means that we do not reduce the vastness and complexity of the sociocultural space to quantitative variables and mean differences within and between groups. Cultural meanings and representations are not controlling variables or isolated, politically neutral external "factors," but instead they are tied to the contested power hierarchies in which dominant groups show their superiority by constructing particular stories and images of those who are marginalized. These cultural meanings also provide insights into what Jerome Bruner (1990) has described as folk psychology. In contrast to rational, predictive, evidence-based, and rigorous scientific thought, folk psychology refers to a set of loosely connected "normative descriptions about how human beings 'tick,' what our own and other minds are like, what one can expect situated actions to be like, what are possible modes of life, how one commits oneself to them, and so on" (p. 35). Underlying folk psychologies are implicit and explicit assumptions about how persons act; what meanings people draw on to support their actions; how they form their world views; and presuppositions about the meanings and function of collective norms about health, well-being, and quality of life (Geertz, 1973). Embedded within folk psychologies are what Christopher, Wendt, Marecek, and Goodman (2014) call moral visions about how a person is and how he or she ought to be or ought to act in a given situation. Moral visions point to underlying values and meanings about how persons ought to carry out their duties and obligations to their family and society and prescriptive rules as to how they ought to behave, think, and relate to others. Moral visions are rooted in cultural practices; shape how academic disciplines ought to study children and define development; and provide the basis for how people demarcate certain rituals as abhorrent, as taboo, or as norms.

Culture provides guidance about moral visions surrounding practices such as young children co-sleeping with their parents, making pilgrimages to cleanse oneself, the importance of respecting kinship, committing suicide as a form of protest, believing in myths or superstition, expressing love through arranged marriages, and upholding principles of self-sacrifice at the cost of self-harm. The asymmetrical power differentials between the culture of majority and minority groups determine very different "moral visions" about the meaning of development for their respective individual members.

A transnational psychological approach to culture alerts us to not only the varied folk psychologies and the moral visions implicit within them but also how these folk psychologies are being revised and reinterpreted in the face of engaging with discourses of globalization. Such an approach to culture then prompts us to define identity not in terms of fixed, absolute essences but, rather, as creations of cultural discourses, history, and power. Human agency and meaning is simultaneously shaped by evolving historical and cultural practices and by an individual's reflective engagements and mediations with the given sociocultural practices. Agency from a sociocultural view is both "determined and self-determining" (Sugarman & Martin, 2010, p. 162). Transnationalism does not make the nation state irrelevant but, rather, highlights its continued significance and the ways in which it enacts certain policies, regulations, and discourses that enable the creation of specific trajectories or circuits of movement (Fine & Ruglis, 2009) across spaces and boundaries for certain classes of people. Transnational connections and relations are specific to postcolonial societies given their unique colonial histories.

Thus, call center work shifted to India, as Patel (2010) argues, due to access to cheap labor, differential time zones, and the availability of millions of educated youth who were fluent in English. The call center worker is now part of a transnational service economy due to India's colonial history and because of the neoliberal forms of policies that were enacted by the Indian government in the 1990s. For example, the Meridian youth analyzed in Chapter 5 were constructing a type of hybrid global Indianness that was based on their transnational class privileges, their postcolonial class locations, and their ability to have access to a type of "mobile Indianness" that was considered as having multicultural capital. As communication scholar Angharad Valdivia (2011) states, some "hybridities demonstrate that while mixture is endemic, certain mixtures are more powerful, commodifiable, and therefore transnationally circulated" (p. 64). The transnational cultural processes are therefore different for Indian call center workers as opposed to upper-class software engineers who can make quick sojourns to the United States or Germany for work, travel, or leisure. Thus, the growth of gated communities, call centers, high-tech parks, exclusive residential areas, and mall spaces and the Indo-German Urban *Mela* that I analyzed in Chapter 2 are enabled by the new transnational flows and scapes, and these connections then create the conditions of contemporary forms of globalization.

It is important to note that the word "transnational" does not mean that every individual or community that is impacted by global flows somehow has a transnational identity or identifies with that term. There are others whose lives in India are impacted by transnational flows, but they may reject or resist such practices. Chhabria (2016) reminds us that "when discussing relations and connections across spaces, we ought to be attentive to the dynamics of power in those connections so as not to render the connection natural

(p. 11)." Thus, any analysis of culture or cultural practices in the contemporary world has to be able to speak to the ways in which identity and subjectivity are embedded in the asymmetrical power matrix created by these transnational connections and flows. The prefix "trans" in "transnational," as Ong (1999) states,

> denotes both moving through space or across lines, as well as changing the nature of something. Besides suggesting new relations between nation states and capital, transnationality alludes to the *trans*versal, the *trans*actional, the *trans*national, the *trans*lational, and the *trans*gressive aspects of contemporary behavior and imagination that are incited, enabled, and regulated by the changing logics of state and capitalism. (p. 4, emphasis in original)

Similarly, Arjun Appadurai (1996) uses five broad analytical units—ethnoscapes, technoscapes, financescapes, mediascapes, and ideoscapes—to analyze the various transnational relationships that exist between five key cultural dimensions of globalization. *Ethnoscape* refers to the landscape of persons who are moving through multiple global circuits, such as tourists, immigrants, refugees, exiles, guest workers, and other groups. *Technoscape* refers to computer-mediated processes such as Internet and satellite technologies that connect previously distant and distinct territories. *Financescape* covers the informal and formal circuits that generate and dispose new forms of global capital. *Mediascape* encompasses the distribution and dispersal of media texts and images such as movies, advertisements, television, and new media to large and small audiences throughout the world. *Ideoscape* refers to ideas and terms such as freedom, socialism, welfare, rights, democracy, and tradition. All these scapes overlap with each other such that individuals in the modern world are shaped by the various configurations of cultural scapes and practices. The transnational scapes and their accompanying cultural practices signify power and authority, and they play an important role in reshaping taken-for-granted concepts in psychology, such as culture and nation.

The contemporary cultural psychology movement came into being as a result of the dissatisfaction with the way the concept of culture was incorporated in both cross-cultural and mainstream psychological research (Cole, 1996). Cultural psychology, according to Shweder (1990), is the study of "the way cultural traditions and social practices regulate, express, transform, and permute the human psyche, resulting less in psychic unity for human kind than in ethnic divergences in mind, self, and emotion" (p. 1). This vision of cultural psychology has been reconstituted and expanded upon by cultural psychologists who adopt a sociocultural approach to study human action (Rogoff, 1990; Shweder, 1990; Valsiner, 2007; Wertsch, 1991). Culture in a sociocultural approach is no longer taken to be a core, integrated whole that is disconnected from issues of gender, race, power, struggle, and contestation

(Gjerde, 2004). Cultural psychology opens up the theoretical space to discuss issues related to how individuals who inhabit multiple cultural worlds negotiate their selves and identities.

The transnational elasticity of culture provides us with a point of departure as we reconsider how the concept of culture is undergoing change as it travels to new places and lodges itself in new geographies. How are ideals of "Indian culture" being reconfigured under neoliberal forms of globalization? What new forms of identity are being negotiated in contexts of IT industries, exposure to media, call center practices, and international mobility? Globalization is a dual phenomenon. It refers to the rapid formation of connections and disruptions in the world through media; movement of people and goods; and interlocking systems of finance, politics, and economics. It also refers to the ways in which globalization has become a discourse with its attendant values, language, and vocabulary, and it serves as a guide for individuals to process the cultural change that they encounter. These discourses shape an individual's lived experiences and his or her imagination, family, nation, and folk psychologies of what it means to be a global Indian or a modern person.

Neoliberalism and Narratives of Self

Neoliberal governmentality (Foucault, 2008) is essentially a mode of "governing through freedom" (Rose, 1996) that requires people to be master of their abilities, goals, choices, and accomplishments. Foucault (2008) coined the term "governmentality" to refer to varied ways in which the state regulates and exercises power over its citizens. Neoliberal governmentality fosters particular regimes of corporate culture that often expect employees to find the resources within themselves or their self-narrative to deal with larger structural problems of low wages, cost-cutting, and the proliferation of contract jobs without access to health care and retirement benefits. Psychology is complicit in creating an ideology of neoliberalism that is now accepted as common sense (Rose, 1996; Sugarman, 2015). In this model, the self-narratives are fashioned through neoliberal discourses about happiness, optimism, well-being, creativity, and corporate forms of globalization that often encourage employees to embrace the tenets of "positive psychology" for maximizing their productivity and efficiency. Thus, neoliberal globalization creates specific processes of "psychologization," and it raises questions about whether or not psychologists are making responsible ethical decisions by reinforcing the neoliberal political order (Sugarman, 2015).

The American psychological discourses of self-discipline and management of self through the vocabulary of self-enterprise, self-actualization, happiness, teamwork, and "re-engineering the self" have become a mainstay in Indian corporations, as detailed in Chapters 1 and 5. Large numbers of global businesses are disseminating Western "corporate power, knowledge, and rules" to cities around the world as representing best neoliberal practices (Ong, 2006, p. 219). There are now experts, human resource managers and cross-cultural trainers, who are using scholarship from cross-cultural psychology and other fields to control, shape, and mold Indian employees to the ideology of a global/Western work culture. Upadhya (2008) argues that in workshops and training seminars, Indian workers are often constructed as having a "feudal" or "hierarchical" mindset (p. 122). The employees do indeed reframe and resist these stereotypes, but given the structural nature of the corporate work conditions, many Indian employees have to work within the power structure of their organizations. The call center workers were part of a neoliberal economy through which they were subjected to accent-reduction training, de-Indianization, and were expected to remove their mother tongue-influenced speech. These agents received cultural training through diversity workshops so they could "auto-Orientalize" their Indian culture and deconstruct "American" and "Australian" psychology in 20 minutes. This is why call center agents have been described as "phone clones," "cyber coolies," and "modern mimics" (Basi, 2009; Mirchandani, 2012; Nadeem, 2011).

Drawing on Beck and Beck-Gernshiem's (2002) work, Brodie (2007) argues that "individualization is a disciplinary and dividing practice that places steeply rising demands on people to find personal causes and responses to what are, in effect, collective social problems" (p. 103). Individualization is a process in which we all have to walk alone and find a biographic answer to systemic problems of structural inequality. Thus, a transnational cultural psychology that is anchored in a social justice orientation shows how neoliberal forms of globalization play a role in reframing social problems through the illusion of choice and free market economics. Such a transnational perspective highlights how social problems resulting from globalization of production, environmental displacement, racism, and poverty are now shifted to the entrepreneurial self, who has to take personal responsibility for his or her success and failures. It is this neoliberal discourse of consumer choice, transnational mobility, and the pursuit of branded goods that is now part of the new discourses of "appropriate Indianness" that shape elite and upper-class identities (Radhakrishnan, 2011).

As global capitalism spreads to developing countries such as India, we must pay attention to how Euro-centered forms of knowledge in psychology and its subdisciplines, such as cross-cultural, counseling, personality, cognitive, and developmental psychology, are being used across the Indian educational system and in Indian workplaces to create particular subjects of the global order. Undoubtedly, these knowledge instruments are customized to the local realities, but overall there is a heavy emphasis on Euro-American psychological approaches. It is not just India; as Ahiwa Ong (2006) suggests, global business practices now rely on American and Chinese American managers to teach Chinese employees "corporate norms of self-initiative, self-responsibility and self-engineering" (p. 222). She argues that tensions arise when Western rational conceptions of work and personhood are applied to the Chinese understanding of *guanxi*. Ong explains:

> A narrow Western view of production worth blinds Western managers to the kind of benefits gained from paying attention to the social values of workers as well. While there is recognition that some kinds of guanxi practice has been used for kickbacks and other corrupt behavior, the corporate system cannot ignore the importance of how Chinese people define social worth, based on Confucian ethics, specifically the value of being accountable to coworkers and to relatives and friends. (pp. 237–238)

We usually tend to think of "host cultures" as traditionally being in the United States and Europe and the migrants as being from different homelands and nations who arrive via border crossings, boats, and planes in these "host cultures" or "receiving societies." However, through various neoliberal reforms, new knowledge frameworks, and transnational flows of capital, globalization has changed the equation. Today, we are witnessing large numbers of people in the world who are rooted in their societies but have experiences that are similar to those of migrants and transnational communities. As they encounter new cultural and work practices, they often feel psychologically displaced or dislocated from their familiar environments of work and home. Understanding the narratives that speak to the experience of "dislocation at home" is an important part of the goal of a transnational cultural psychology. This is why Sugarman (2015) argues that we need new psychological ethics in the age of globalization. It is up to psychologists to interrogate the ideology of neoliberalism and how it impacts our society and ultimately ask what it means for questions of identity and personhood.

TOWARD A TRANSNATIONAL CULTURAL PSYCHOLOGY: THE OTHER HALF OF THE STORY HAS NOT BEEN TOLD

As noted in Chapter 1, much of what is characterized as the legitimate field of psychology or "the psychology" throughout the world is still grounded in studies done on WEIRD populations. How do we create a psychology that speaks to the experiences of what Kagitçibasi (1996) has called the "Majority World"; Arnett (2002) has described as the "neglected 95%"; Gergen, Gulerce, Lock, and Misra (1996) have called "psychologies of non-Western societies"; Smith (2012) has called "indigenous communities"; and Spivak (1988) has termed "subaltern" groups. Even researchers who are from the "Majority World" or the developing world tend too often to uncritically embrace the scientific frameworks of psychology and often address their research goals in such a way that their scholarship is mostly relevant to the intellectual debates in the academic centers of the Global North. Gergen et al. describe the dominant voice of what they call a "Western mode of thinking":

> The current Western thinking of the science of psychology in its prototypi-
> cal form, despite being local and indigenous, assumes a global relevance and
> is treated as a universal mode of generating knowledge. Its dominant voice
> subscribes to a decontextualized vision with an extraordinary emphasis on
> individualism, mechanism, and objectivity. This peculiarly Western mode of
> thinking is fabricated, projected, and institutionalized through represen-
> tation technologies and scientific rituals and transported on a large scale
> to the non-Western societies under political–economic domination. As a
> result, Western psychology tends to maintain an independent stance at the
> cost of ignoring other substantive possibilities from disparate cultural tra-
> ditions. Mapping reality through Western constructs has offered a pseudo-
> understanding of the people of alien cultures and has had debilitating effects
> in terms of misconstruing the special realities of other people and exoticizing
> or disregarding psychologies that are non-Western. Consequently, when peo-
> ple from other cultures are exposed to Western psychology, they find their
> identities placed in question and their conceptual repertoires rendered obso-
> lete. (pp. 497–498)

We have to acknowledge the witting or unwitting imperialism embedded in the Euro-American power structure and the ways in which its flows of psychology, symbols, and popular culture insert themselves in non-Western spaces, while we also make room for how individuals living in non-Western spaces imagine, appropriate, and reframe these flows. We need to pursue the question of decolonization and empowerment not only through modern Euro-American power structures but also in reference to the growing social inequalities that exist within the developing postcolonial nations. The strug-gle for decolonizing psychology in the age of globalization is multi-sited, fluid, and contested, and it involves understanding how power shapes inter-secting spaces, stories, identities, subjectivities, histories, languages, and resistances.

One of the goals of this book is to interrupt the steady, self-important, and sedimented narrative of the discipline of psychology. Next, I articulate a vision of a psychology that takes into account how the co-mingling of colo-nial, modern, traditional, postcolonial, and global contexts creates new coun-ternarratives of identity that go beyond the binary logic of East versus West, traditional versus modern, and collectivist versus individualist.

Cultural Humility and Moral Visions

One of the central aims of decolonizing research is not to theorize in a way that rejects or minimizes Western or Euro-American psychological theory, research, and knowledge. Rather, the aim is to question and interrogate its universality and canonical legitimacy while simultaneously re-centering other lives, psychologies, world views, indigenous ideas, and thoughts. Second, I am not advocating a psychology that "rescues" people from their plight or frames the oppressed as having no voice or agency, such that they need outsiders to come and teach them how to live their lives. As we contemplate envisioning psychology in the contexts of global social inequality, we need to make sure that we engage in research without resorting to some type of epistemological violence that actually harms those whose oppression we wish to understand and highlight (Teo, 2011). My call for a renewed psychology invites us to be self-reflexive about its dominant status and induces us to urgently take steps to be accountable and answerable to those whose lives it has minimized and overlooked. It is a call for creating a psychology that focuses on cultivating cultural humility and a self-reflexive awareness about its own moral vision, power, and privilege. Third, I want to be clear that a decolonial approach to psychology via the stories of urban Indian youth is not intended to merely "add on" yet another fragment of knowledge to the formidable archive of Euro-American psychology or psychological science. The turn to understanding Indian youth stories is not based on a tourist or explorer model to studying cultural and racial others (Mohanty, 2003).

In the *psychology-as-tourist model*, the *Other* is given token recognition while basic core assumptions of psychological science remain untouched. It is also not based on creating a *psychology-as-explorer* model that ventures out to study other groups and cultures through cross-cultural research that is essentially grounded in the dominant framework of Euro-American scientific psychology. Such a psychology appears to be progressive and emancipatory, but in the end, it reifies the "us and them" relationship and creates concepts that frame entire populations as collectivistic or as individualistic. Thus, Chaudhary (2011) argues that much of Western psychology is shaped by the European philosophical understanding of the concepts of individualism and collectivism. This means that any definition of individualism that does not fit into the larger Eurocentric tradition is "instantly labelled as 'collectivistic,' or 'relational,' or 'interdependent,' without accessing the subtleties of human social understanding and cultural tradition" (p. 173). This way of understanding social issues leaves the hierarchies of "us versus them" intact and creates a knowledge system that keeps the older order of Euro-American psychology well settled and complacent (Mohanty, 2003).

The radical psychologist, Frantz Fanon (1963), has provided one the most revolutionary model for decolonizing dominant frameworks that were mainly grounded in the European colonial thinking and imperial actions (see Desai, 2013). Fanon describes the process of decolonization and the message of an anticolonial stance as follows:

> Decolonization never takes places unnoticed for it influences individuals and modifies them fundamentally. It transforms spectators crushed with their ines-sentiality into privileged actors, with the grandiose glare of history's floodlight upon them. It brings a natural rhythm into existence, introduced by new men, and with a new language and a new humanity. Decolonization is the veritable creation of new men. . . . The "thing" which has become colonized becomes man during the same process by which it frees itself. In decolonization, there is there-fore the need of a complete calling into question of the colonial situation. (p. 36)

Fanon's (1963) anticolonial language was meant to interrogate the European hegemonic structures of thinking that had become the absolute intellectual yardstick by which progress of all civilizations was measured and quantified. Fanon's (1967) call to dismantle the aftereffects of the colonial apparatus still holds relevance in times of globalization as we witness ongoing forms of inequity in the world: dire poverty; gender violence; and economic, social, racial, and caste injustices. How do we create a psychology that creates a new language, a new humanity, and a new psychology?

One phenomenon or social condition that has preoccupied postcolonial theorists is how to understand the varied ways the colonizer and the colo-nized were shaped by a mutually evolving psychology (Bhabha, 1994; Fanon, 1967; Gandhi, 1998). The eviscerating tentacles of colonization do not end with the colonial period but, rather, they reform themselves in the postco-lonial period to ravage the mind, psyche, body, and the nation (Desai, 2013; Hook, 2012). The psychological resistance to colonialism began when coloni-zation took root in the colonies, and it took another "psychopolitical" form when the colonial occupation had ended. Fanon (1967), for example, argues that in colonial contexts blackness or black identity was essentially defined in relation to the superiority of Whiteness. He analyzes the psychological trauma that was experienced by Black subjects in the face of sustained, irre-versible, and violent colonial encounters with apartheid regimes of Whiteness over centuries. Fanon (1963) thus believes that for the black native or the colonized, decolonization of self means "total liberation" in which the heavy darkness of the colonial past must be left behind (p. 310). However, there is an inherent paradox in the postcolonial imperative because the colonized has to study how the postcolonial "psychological" condition arises out of the brutal and militaristic colonial apparatus while reinventing and reframing the inau-gural moment of independence as separate from that long-oppressive duress of colonization. What many key colonial and postcolonial thinkers and leaders have argued is that the postcolonial project was essentially a psychological project that entailed a "recovery of self" (Nandy, 1983), initiated dialogue on a "new humanity" and renewed "humanism" (Fanon, 1963, p. 246), and then moved toward creating the conditions for "autonomous dignity" (Memmi, 1965, p. 128).

The task of psychology then becomes to take seriously not only theorizing about the terror of colonization and orientalism but also "the idea of a psychological resistance to colonialism's civilizing mission" (Gandhi, 1998, p. 17). The mantle of resistance in different disguises and in different eras had been a core pursuit of postcolonial theory. Decolonizing psychology, as a liberatory move, would mean introducing a justice orientation so it can directly address the populations whose lives are on the margins, both by bringing attention to their lives and by embedding their lives in the larger social psychological contexts. By that token, it would be incorrect to lump the struggles of the *basti* youth or their *identity narratives* with those of the youth from the call centers and Meridian College. The middle- and upper-class youth in urban India are still a minority compared to the large number of poor youth who make up the majority of the population in so many Indian cities. The *basti* youth whom I analyzed in Chapter 7 are left out of the larger narrative of progress, but their consumption practices, desires, and aspirations are shaped by the lifestyle of the affluent hi-fi class that surrounds their neighborhood.

Psychology and Stories of Social Justice

In her book *Listening to Grasshoppers*, Arundhati Roy (2009) writes that many of the upper- and middle-class Indians have waged a secessionist struggle to create a country of their own so they can merge with the elite of the world. The era of neoliberalization, she says, has reinforced and recalibrated some of the deep hierarchies of ancient India. This old society, Roy writes,

> has curdled and separated into a layer of thick cream—and a lot of water. The cream is "India's market" of many millions of consumers (of cars, cell phones, computers, Valentine's Day greeting cards), the envy of international business. The water is of little consequence. (pp. 8–9)

How can the marginalized and invisible subjects, whom Roy describes as discarded, leftover "water," be considered as relevant to the field of psychology?

The urban youth growing up in slums such as Panchsheel *basti* are exposed to malnutrition, lack of education, lack of sanitation and clean water, uncovered landfill, and congested areas. The latest report from the IRIS Foundation and UN Habitat, titled "State of Urban Youth, India 2012: Employments, Livelihoods and Skills," states that every third person in an Indian city is a youth. There are 430 million young Indians between the ages of 14 and

34 years. One of the most telling numbers in this report highlights that a large number of youth growing up in cities see stark inequalities, urban sprawl, and deteriorating conditions in the slums. The report further mentions that approximately one-fifth of the Indian urban population lives below the poverty line—that is, lives on less than $2 per day. The report highlights that large segments of the Indian youth are unemployed, and 90% of those who have jobs are employed in the informal sector. These statistics mirror the reality of slums such as Panchsheel *basti* in Pune and urban slums throughout much of India. The report also emphasizes that the youth who are growing up in Indian cities are confronted with the reality of gated communities and luxurious residences residing next to slums that are in danger of being demolished or the occupants are in danger of being evicted. Indian working-class youth who live in slums have not been the beneficiaries of globalization, and the pattern of inequitable urbanization has created a world of haves and have-nots.

The *basti* youth whose hybrid stories I analyzed in Chapter 7 are left out of the larger narrative of progress, but their consumption practices, desires, and aspirations are shaped by the lifestyle of the affluent hi-fi class that surrounds their neighborhood. While there is a rising middle class in the slums that has relatively more means to consume, and some of them now have access to basic amenities and are living far better lives than in the past, the overall rate of families living in poverty in slums throughout India is still staggering (Dreze & Sen, 2013). As stated previously, the middle- and upper-class youth in urban India are still a minority compared to the large number of poor youth who comprise the majority of the population in most Indian cities. In 2009, the World Bank published a report that estimated that by 2015, almost 34% of the world's population living on less that $2 per day would be living in India. Mander (2015) notes,

> If one uses the median developing-country line of $2 per day on purchasing parity, 80 percent of India's rural inhabitants and just under 70 percent of India's urban residents would be recognized as being poor. The big story which these figures tell is that whichever way you define poverty, the largest proportion of the world's poor live in India—a situation that is likely to persist in the near future. (p. xxxii)

What needs to be highlighted in these numbers is that one of the large majorities that make up India's poor are India's youth. He further writes that half of India's population is younger than age 25 years, making it home to the largest population of young people in the world, and he predicts that the majority of them will not be able to meet their aspirations and dreams. It is worth mentioning that only about 7% of India's youth are able to get a college degree, and the percentages of educated youth are even less for historically disadvantaged populations such as young women, Dalits, tribal populations, and Muslims (Mander, 2015).

The unique dimension of Indian inequality—which includes the rising concentrations of wealth and power in the hands of the affluent, elite, and upper class, along with huge disparities in education, health care, social facilities, environmental support, sanitation, and employment—is well documented in Dreze and Sen's (2013) book, *An Uncertain Glory*. This book also paints a positive picture of India's progress in confronting the challenges of poverty since India's independence and its efforts at reducing social inequality. Despite the social and economic gains in India since independence, Dreze and Sen argue that there still exists a huge disparity between the social classes and that the gulf between the "lives of the privileged and the rest" has widened. The neoliberal policies, according to Dreze and Sen, have been advantageous to the Indian elites. Writings by well-known Indian journalist P. Sainath on the state of rural India and deepening social inequality reveal that since the neoliberal policies of the Indian state were put in place, 300,000 Indian farmers have committed suicide, thus creating an agrarian crisis. The agriculture crisis for farmers is a result of heavy indebtedness, increasing production costs, a drastic decline in the prices of farm crops, corporate globalization, and monopoly over seed supply and copyright issues.

It is against this history of the gulf between the classes that we need to understand the stories that I have analyzed in this book. Amartya Sen (2005) argues that class represents itself in many guises and expresses itself in many voices in India, but "it has a very special role in the establishment and reach of social inequality, and it can make the influence of other sources of disparity (such as gender inequality) much sharper" (p. 205). Neoliberal reforms have accentuated the economic and class-based inequalities across much of the world (Harvey, 2000; Tabb, 2002).

In contrast to the neoliberal version of globalization, Tabb (2002, p. 2) notes that those who "privilege social justice" conceive of globalization from below. This alternative form of globalization increasingly puts pressure on the nation state to provide basic public goods to citizens, such as food, water, and housing; access to public services of health care and education; enforcement of regulation of capital and equitable distribution of profits; a collective sense of a global society that promotes environmental regulation, equal wages across borders, and labor rights; and a society that is based on equity, democracy, and shared risk for all of its members. The Indian urban youth in Pune or Mumbai are creative, resourceful, and find ways to implement their dreams and desires, but the governance structures are stacked against them. Thus, a social justice orientation is needed in psychology to understand how neoliberal policies have shaped their life stories and identity narratives.

There are several theories of social justice, including the feminist social justice offered by Fraser (2009), the virtue ethics about the good life espoused by MacIntyre (1984), Ambedkar's (1971) constitutionally driven social justice movement, Marxist notions of class struggle (Marx, 1906), and the human capabilities approach (Nussbaum, 2000). Typically, social psychological approaches to justice are anchored in three fundamental questions:

> Distributive justice: What types of resources are allocated?
> Procedural justice: How is justice administered and delivered?
> Inclusionary justice: Who participates, gets respected, and is represented in the decision-making process?

Going beyond these three dimensions of justice, Opotow (1997) suggests that we need a social justice orientation of *how, what, who, when*, and *where*. She claims that alternative possibilities to the status quo can be discovered in specific places and by historicizing our questions so the normal concepts of justice are disturbed, collecting evidence, and then complicating our view of the present (Opotow, 2010, p. 7). The concept of "social" in psychology needs to be linked to the historicized and politicized notions of "social" in social justice.

A social justice orientation in psychology can begin by examining conceptions of justice that emerge from the central and peripheral sections of the society, from dominant and marginalized communities, and probing how institutions, organizations, and the larger civil society adopt principles of justice and examine the contexts in which justice is served. Lee Ann Bell (2007) describes social justice as both a process and a goal. The broader goal of social justice is to ensure that all groups are given opportunities for full and equal participation. She explains:

> Social justice includes a vision of society in which the distribution of resources is equitable and all members are physically and psychologically safe and secure. We envision a society in which individuals are both self determining (able to develop their full capacities) and interdependent (capable of interacting democratically with others). Social justice involves social actors who have a sense of their own agency as well as a sense of responsibility toward and with others, their society, and the broader world in which we live. These are conditions we wish not only for our own society but also for every society in an interdependent community. (pp. 1–2)

Social justice is based on a theory of oppression in which power and practice combine to form a liberating moment of praxis. It becomes a theory that specifically addresses the various ways in which we interrogate established truths, one-dimensional histories, and hegemonic narratives so we can understand the social conditions that give rise to processes of cooptation, exploitation, resistance, and ignorance.

The term *oppression* highlights the omnipresent and inescapable social inequality that permeates throughout all spheres of our society—it combines oppression that arises from structural and systemic forces, historical disparities and inequities, with oppression that emerges from social prejudices, personal bias, bigotry, and individual acts of discrimination. The mechanisms that fuel oppression move through the circuits of institutions and normative traditions, but they are also appropriated within our psychology and our bodies, thus causing immeasurable psychological and physical harm (Bell, 2007).

Brodie (2007) points to a paradox about social justice when she writes that the social justice rhetoric and discourse about equality have increased while actual support for social justice policies backed by the state has declined. There is more talk of social justice while the house of social justice—the State that is supposed to deliver social justice—is burning. In many areas of the world, the liberal conception of the social is now reconfigured through the neoliberal language of erasing social programs, privatizing and subjugating public goods to market forces, narrowing or downsizing social programs that are labeled at-risk, and fiscalizing social policies into tax credits and deductions, thereby creating a language of individualization. Individualization is different from individualism and is at the heart of the neoliberal conception of social justice; it is broadly understood as self-actualization or self-seeking behavior.

The "social" in a socially just psychology should be about power and contestation and should refer to contexts in which racist and class-based ideologies are born. It needs to analyze the eviscerating impact of colonization and postcolonization that lives in bodies and minds, and it needs to focus on the creation of uneven geographies of poverty and stories connected to asymmetrical flows of globalization. In *Spaces of Hope*, David Harvey (2000) writes,

> As we collectively produce our cities, so we collectively produce ourselves. Projects concerning what we want our cities to be are, therefore, projects concerning human possibilities, who we want, or, perhaps even more pertinently, who we do not want to become. (p. 159)

A social justice perspective in psychology is about imagining alternative human possibilities and alternative stories of who we may become.

The larger project of decolonization, from an indigenous perspective, involves claiming history, giving indigenous testimonies, making spaces for storytelling and oral histories as valid knowledge, celebrating survival, engaging in collective remembrance for healing and transformation, indigenizing the world views and images of settler communities, intervening through action research, revitalizing indigenous languages and arts, offering critical rereading of Western history, researching back, writing and theory making, renaming the lost world of the indigenous people, negotiating self-determination and sovereignty, and so on (Smith, 2012).

Decolonizing involves understanding the present situation of colonialism and its devastating consequences in settler communities, and it requires what Richards (2014) calls "epistemological decolonization" (p. 14)—showing how marginalizing particular ways of knowing, thinking, and researching is rooted in both epistemic and material inequalities. She further elaborates on this concept:

> Colonialism rests on the notion that colonizing settlers are the "knowers" and the indigenous that which is to be known. And it is colonial knowledge on which the dominant system comes to be built—so European/Northern knowledge about everything from how to set up a state and legal system to property ownership, the relationship between humans and the environment, religion, language, cultural practices, education, and health care are privileged as correct and legitimate ways of knowing, while indigenous knowledge in these same areas is marginalized, annihilated, or viewed as suspect and subjective. This epistemic aspect of the ongoing colonial relationship justifies dispossession to this day. (p. 145)

From a transnational psychological perspective, decolonizing psychology means paying attention to how the dominant epistemic system erases and undermines the goals of several indigenous psychologies. It also entails focusing on creating psychology that is tied to asymmetrical transnational flows of globalization and a psychology that goes beyond the cultural essentialism of Euro-centrism or Asian-centrism. The transnational cultural psychology that I conceive of not only focuses on hybridity in terms of cultural mixing and free-floating intercultural encounters but also focuses on how power, sovereignty, mythology, cultural relevance, land rights, and dynamics of settler colonialism shape hybrid imaginations in various geographies and communities. Hybridity, as I have previously argued, is not a postmodern play of cultural invention; rather, it is connected to larger global forms of labor markets and other transnational capitalist projects.

Many marginalized indigenous communities throughout the world are locked in a struggle to reclaim their land rights from their settler colonial states or federal governments. In essence, these communities are already situated in an *anticolonial position*, and there are instances where it is appropriate to employ strategic forms of essentialism as a transformative tool to resist hegemonic discourses that violate indigenous rights (Dudgeon & Walker, 2015). Similarly, Grande (2015) states that

> American Indians are not like other subjugated groups struggling to define their place within the larger democratic project. Specifically, they do not seek greater "inclusion"; rather they are engaged in a perpetual struggle to have their legal and moral claims to sovereignty recognized. The duration and severity of

this struggle for American Indians removes the question of identity from the superficial realm of cultural politics to the more profound arena of cultural survival (p. 153).

The indigenous struggles of American Indians are thus of a different order than the attempts to define an indigenous psychology, say, in India, Bangladesh or Pakistan, South Africa or Philippines.

Let us take the example of India, where indigenous psychology or philosophy was largely neglected in favor of adopting Western psychological frameworks since independence. The Indian psychologists from the post-independence era were disillusioned by their indigenous traditional psychological therapies such as meditation, yoga, and tantric healing practices and questioned the scientific validity of these various ancient practices (Bhatia, 2002). The first prime minister of independent India was Jawaharlal Nehru, and his vision of India as a secular, modern nation free from poverty and disease was anchored in the promise of science and technology. Like their counterparts in science, medicine, and economics, the first generation of foreign-trained Indian psychologists genuinely believed that Euro-American psychology, as an empirical science, with its claims to cultural neutrality, had the power to provide insight into the religious and superstitious worlds of the Indian population. If the dependence of Indian psychology on Euro-American psychology was a part of a narrative of the past, then Indian psychologists in the present would have much about which to rejoice. However, Nandy's (1974) comment that "if it rains in the metropolitan centers of psychology, we of course have to open our umbrellas" (p. 2) still holds true for Indian psychology. Under these circumstances, Nandy made a plea to Indian psychologists to "rediscover" themselves as professional psychologists (Bhatia, 2002). He acknowledged that he felt "strange" asking Indian psychologists to be reflective, because self-discovery has been the "quintessence of all knowledge" in much of ancient Indian psychological traditions (Nandy, 1974, p. 12). Nandy was not asking Indian psychologists to abandon the psychological frameworks that are derived from Euro-American societies; instead, he was appealing to Indian psychologists to re-examine how compatible Western psychological frameworks are with a society that is traditional, multireligious, multilingual, secular, and modern (Bhatia, 2002).

For several decades, prominent Indian psychologists made repeated pleas and also took constructive steps toward "indigenizing" modern psychology to make it more relevant to their local and cultural practices (for a review, see D. Sinha, 1986). However, the move toward indigenization of psychology in India and other countries in the "Third World" refers to what some Indian psychologists have described as cosmetic, superficial, and outward. The bulk of indigenization, for example, within Indian psychology has been mainly carried out within the overall core structure and principles of Euro-American

psychology (Naidu, 1994; Verma, 1995). Naidu notes that "one may indige-
nize some peripheral aspect of research by, say, giving local color to the items
of an imported questionnaire or insisting that the use of a native sample
alone renders the study indigenous!" (p. 78). What Naidu was highlights in
this excerpt holds true for much of the emerging psychology in developing
nations as well. Indigenization in psychology departments in developing
nations, for the most part, means transporting and using the core aspects of
Euro-American psychology—empiricism, experimentation, and quantitative
measurements—in regard to a certain set of cultural issues (Enriquez, 1992;
Moghaddam, 1987).

The indigenous psychology movement within India, for example, has
grown rapidly, but it has been fraught with contested claims and debates
about what indigenous psychology means in postcolonial, modern, and global
contexts. In contrast to the scientific indigenous psychology movement proposed by Kim, Yang, and Hwang (2006), 160 Indian psychologists gathered in
Pondicherry in 2002 to create a new manifesto for Indian psychology. Their
manifesto boldly declared that psychology in India has played almost no role
in national development. This manifesto, titled the "Pondicherry Manifesto
of Indian Psychology" (2002), further states that Indian psychology is in an
unfortunate state of decline because psychology in India is

> essentially a Western transplant, unable to connect with the Indian ethos
> and concurrent community conditions. Therefore, it has been said repeat-
> edly that psychological studies in India are by and large imitative and replica-
> tive of Western studies, lacking in originality and unable to cover or break any
> ground. . . . What we have now in India is a psychology of sorts, but not Indian
> psychology (http://www.indianpsychology.net/about_pmip.php)

The vision of an Indian psychology that is proposed is not primarily based
on scientific principles or universals but instead is grounded in an "Indian
ethos" of Indian classical thought and practice and Indian philosophy of yoga,
meditation, and introspection. The foundations of Indian psychology are
seen as emerging from a 2,500-year-old Indian civilization and through the
religious texts of Vedas and Upanishads (shastras). This psychology is based
on the principles of vigorous refection, observation, experimentation that is
achieved through training with a Guru, and engaging in contemplative practices of inner experiences (Dalal & Misra, 2010).

An important dimension of Hindu psychology and philosophy is the
attempt to understand both self and community through religious symbolism
and through the postulation of a single God or multiple divine Gods. These
Gods are honored and emulated through practices of devotion, pilgrimage,
prayer, yoga, and meditation, as well as through modern variations on these
forms of religious practices. There is a dual emphasis on being in the world

of material things and human relationships while simultaneously pursuing transcendent goals of self-realization, equanimity, non-attachment, and an inward spiritual orientation. The attempt to create the bridge between the self-affirming world of activity such as jobs, money, family, and wealth and the pursuit of other-worldly activities of spiritual connectedness to a guru, a religion, or through a set of devotional practices begins with the acknowledgment of the concept of *dharma* in the Indian context. The notion of personhood, for example, in the Hindu context is based on the idea that a person who abides by the moral practices and traditions as embedded in social contexts and relations puts the principles of *dharma* into play and comes one step closer to achieving the *moksha* or "liberation" self. *Moksha* is a release from the endless cycle of birth and death, and it signals an end to suffering that is inherent in human existence.

The classic Hindu text, *Upanishad*, describes the self as *atman*, which provides coherence, continuity, and permanence to human experiences. K. Ramakrishna Rao (2011), an Indian psychologist, argues that the Indian self (within the Hindu tradition) can be understood through a *Trisula* (Trident) model of personhood that proposes the concept of self as having overlapping connections between body, mind, and consciousness. He argues that one significant aspect of the Indian model of person is that mind and consciousness are conceived as qualitatively different, and this distinction has meaningful implications for the psychological conceptions of personhood. Mind in the classical Indian texts is taken to be an instrument of awareness and a mechanism that connects us to the reality of the world. When this instrument connects and comprehends the physical world through the sensory system, we have transactional awareness, and when the mind makes connection with the psychological realm, we experience "transcendental realization" (p. 20).

In the Yoga metaphysics, consciousness is called *purusa*, and it has no beginning and ending and does not develop or decay—it has no form or appearance and it is indescribable and non-material. Consciousness is *Sattva*, where knowing, feeling, and being are fused and inseparable. Rao (2011) argues that in Western psychology, the person's consciousness is described as subjective awareness that is localized in the brain. In contrast, Indian psychology is concerned with the study of the person (*jiva*), which is embodied through consciousness. This notion of consciousness is different from brain and the mind. Mind acts as a mediator and facilitator between consciousness and processes of the brain. Consciousness becomes conditioned and shaped by the connections between the mind and the body, and this conditioning gives rise to unique individual thought, ego, mental states, action, and a person's worldly identity. The ego reacts to the world with attachment, craving, and aversion and thus experiences anxiety and suffering (*dukkha*). Therefore, the highest form of human development in the *dharmic* tradition is for individuals to liberate themselves from ignorance and suffering to attain *moksha* by meditation, entering transcognitive states, and practicing various form of yoga, such as *jnana* yoga (knowledge focused), *bhakti* yoga (devotion focused), and *karma yoga* (action focused) (Rao, 2011).

In contrast to Indian psychology, Western and modern psychology's conception of knowledge is created to predict and control the external and observable behavior of others (Paranjape, 2011). Indian psychology from the beginning has focused on introspection, understanding human experience, and self-knowledge that helps in liberation. In contrast, in Western psychology,

> the psychologists' gaze is totally outward bound or extraspective. . . . When the "value free" stance of science is added to the mix, psychology is a mere tool; qua scientist, a psychologist need not bother whether knowledge is used for peace or war, for benign goals or nefarious ones. (p. 137)

The notion of personhood in the Hindu context is based on the idea that a person who abides by the moral practices and traditions as embedded in social contexts and relations puts the principles of *dharma* into play and comes one step closer to achieving the liberation of self.

The concept of *dharma* is commonly translated as duty, righteousness, or truth. *Dharma* is the basic foundation of all the major Indian religions, such as Hinduism, Jainism, Buddhism, and Sikhism, and it refers to the moral rules that regulate social contexts and relationships for all people in the society and their social status (*varna*), the specific stage and season of their life (*ashrama*), and innate predispositions and qualities that they have (*guna*). *Dharma* as the foundation of a good life requires individuals to engage in economic and political activity (*artha*) along with pursuing pleasure (*kama*). These goals combined together constitute the goals of life (*purushartha*) (Madan, 1989).

The creation of an Indian psychology based on indigenous systems is an important decolonizing move, but the conceptions of personhood are largely derived from Hindu texts and do not include core concepts from Islam, Sufism, Buddhism, and Sikhism. Decolonizing psychology also means building bridges with critical perspectives from Indian and Euro-American psychology and creating a psychology that also speaks to the contemporary hybrid cultural realities of people who are living in a neoliberalized society.

One of the problems with recovering culturally essentialized ideas for a group or nation from precolonized or ancient times is the ways that it might be used to create pure identities or collective group identities that can be dangerous and exclusionary. The creation of the Pondicherry Manifesto is an important decolonizing move—it straightforwardly points out the psychological imperialism of Euro-American psychology. This is a laudable goal and movement, but we must also be cautious about how we define the counternarrative of an Indian psychology.

The Pondicherry Manifesto, for example, does not define what it means by "Indian psychological studies." How does it differentiate between secular and religious modes of psychology? Does it include in a meaningful way Islamic, Jain, and Sikh psychological and religious principles? How is *Indianness* defined—given that Indianness is multitemporal and embedded in layers of history of the ancient, precolonial, colonial, postcolonial, global, regional, local, modern, traditional, and secular and further wrapped in an entrenched caste and class-based system. Does decolonizing means emptying out all Western psychological ideas and replacing them with Indian psychological principles? The Pondicherry Manifesto is indeed a landmark moment, but it must find ways to speak to the current Indian society that is shaped by transnational forces of neoliberal globalization, and it has to tackle questions about intersecting cultural flows, colonialism, global capitalism, social inequality, and boundary crossing of ideas and systems of thinking. Indian psychology can build bridges with a transnational cultural psychology that includes engaging with "cultural history, pedagogy, philosophy, post-coloniality and sociology" (Kumar, 2006, p. 248). The concept of "culture" within Indian psychology can also expand and move beyond its core canonical references to dominant Hindu texts, and it can also directly engage with communities and the marginalized voices of the population.

There are several conceptual and political problems with making appeals to specific aspects of a dominant and pure culture. First, the problem of appealing to some reified Indian culture or Bangladeshi culture is that the self-appointed purveyors of cultural truths and protectors of traditions may squelch dissent and engage what is called "authenticity policing" as I described in Chapter 4 in relation to the Valentine's Day example in India. Cultural essentialism can also lead to a tendency to romanticize the local or local practices as pure and uncontaminated, and such essentialism itself can lead to an oppressive system of control and regulation by the elite members of the society or the religious figureheads.

Particular groups of powerful people can use local cultural practices to redefine the meaning of the nation that leaves out the psychology of minority and marginalized populations. Kumar (2006) writes that if the future of Indian psychology is connected to its colonial past, then the

> psychology of the oppressed has to be pursued with more rigor and commitment. It is important in this sense to invite those who are thrown off to the margins because of politics of elitism and exclusion that the discipline of psychology plays in its entrenchment in Euro-American cultural–psychic structures and explanations.... Inclusion of the voices of women, children, dalits, marginalized communities and alternative paradigms that survive on the edge of the psychological discourse have to be actively pursued. (p. 252)

The imagined community of Indian psychology, then, cannot be equated solely with the majority Hindu nation. Thus, it would have to broaden its scope to create a hybrid cultural psychology that analyzes core concepts and texts from diverse religions and pays attention to how these religious and social practices shape identity formation in contexts that are at once global, local, modern, traditional, and neoliberal.

Anderson (1991, p. 3) has famously argued that nation, culture, nationality, and nationalism are notoriously difficult to define, let alone analyze. To posit that the "nation" can be understood as a durable, ontological, material, geopolitical concept ignores the counternarratives, the contested identities, and the historical inventions that continuously challenge any unified understanding of a nation. A nation is more than a geographically identified space; rather, it is what Anderson terms an "imagined community," what Renan (1990, p. 19) calls a "spiritual principle" constituted by memories that swallow up discordant details, and what Bhabha (1990, p. 297) refers to as a series of narrations constructed by "scraps, patches and rags" (Bhatia & Ram, 2002) The issue of indigenous psychology should be tackled through a cultural standpoint as well as from a decolonizing and a social justice perspective. What we need to avoid, in any case, is a rigid essentialism; instead, we need to focus on the emancipatory potential of strategic essentialism (Spivak, 1988) and strategic hybridity (Bhabha, 1990).

As we etch out a narrative psychology of *strategic hybridity*, it is imperative that we formulate critical definitions of the identity and subjectivity within contexts of globalization. Ella Sohat (1992) reminds us that if we engage in a mere celebration of syncretism, hybridity, and mixing and not ask difficult questions of how race, class, and neocolonial power relations are refigured in the construction of hybridity, we "run the risk of appearing to sanctify the fait accompli of colonial violence" (p. 109). My point is that adding the analysis of power and asymmetry to the theories of identity allows us to go beyond conceptualizing identity through the metaphors of "mixing" and "melting pot."

Dudgeon and Walker (2015) write about the need to deploy various forms of strategic essentialism and hybridity in the development of an indigenous Australian psychology. They state,

> social transformation and decolonization depend on both a strategic essentialism . . . and strategic hybridity . . . that allow the individual not only to claim their distinctive cultural elements but also to assert, negotiate, and situate their evolving identity in contemporary society without being assimilated by the dominant culture. These arguments have an important place in decolonizing psychology. They require psychologists to acknowledge and respect the role of identities and culture and the intentionality of Indigenous Australians to reassert their spiritual and ontological connections as both a counter hegemonic strategy and a cultural reconnection. (p. 284)

If we were to adopt a transnational cultural psychology perspective as part of the decolonizing project, then it is important for Euro-American psychologists to acknowledge and highlight the historical role of psychology in unconsciously perpetuating Orientalist representations about non-Western others (Bhatia, 2002). Similarly, psychologists from developing nations need to recognize that the Euro-American brand of indigenous psychology has had a long history within the academic universities of postcolonial nations, and it cannot be simply replaced by new "indigenous" or "traditional" psychologies. What needs to be undertaken by postcolonial, indigenous, and Western psychologists is a systematic transnational historical investigation of the meaning of the role of Euro-American psychology in directly or indirectly providing justification for the Orientalist agenda in both colonial and postcolonial contexts. Crafting a transnational cultural psychology also means engaging in a struggle to "refuse, reimagine, and rearticulate" (Grande, 2015, p. 7) the assimilating logic of Euro-American psychology. Drawing on the work of indigenous scholar Taiaiake Alfred (1999), Grande argues that we need to rearticulate the meanings of tradition and practice a "self-conscious traditionalism" to suit the present realities of the community. She also argues that a self-conscious traditionalism is an intellectual, social, and political movement that is intended to "reinvigorate indigenous values, principles, and other cultural elements best suited to the larger contemporary and political and economic reality" (p. 234). Thus, traditionalism does not mean an invocation of essentialized and pure cultural myths and stories but, rather, a revitalization project that is informed by indigenous knowledge beliefs and systems and also knowledge derived from critical, cultural, and narrative psychology.

The second issue concerns the meaning of the term *indigenous psychologies*, which needs to be clarified. Just as there is no singular monolithic, homogeneous Euro-American psychology, it would similarly be a mistake to conceptualize indigenous psychology as referring to one dominant set of psychological beliefs and practices. For example, there is an explicit assumption in Euro-American psychological science that it is a universal psychology and that other cultures should use the model of psychology that is practiced in the West (Berry, Poortinga, Segall, & Dasen, 1992; Gergen et al., 1996). Such an assumption overlooks the point that this brand of Euro-American psychology is based on certain a priori cultural assumptions about the construction of personhood (Sampson, 1988). Furthermore, there are multiple forms of indigenous psychologies within Euro-American psychology, and many of these psychologies (e.g., experimental, feminist, narrative, and discursive) operate with their own distinct underlying set of assumptions about how personhood is constructed.

Third, we have to create a transnational cultural psychology that focuses on theoretical and epistemological pluralism. In such a pluralism, several indigenous psychologies can maintain their distinctive and traditional world views, but they also need to form coalitions, solidarities, cross-cultural exchanges, and transnational connections through questions of justice, equity, and democratic participation. The model of theoretical pluralism cannot be based on benign multiculturalism or simplistic theory of cultural difference, essentialism, and inclusion; it has to work toward a fundamental move to a decolonization of psychological science. In such a model, there is much value to including Western psychological frameworks that are based on a critical, cultural, narrative, feminist, hermeneutic, and postcolonial psychology along with other indigenous frameworks to create psychological perspective that is deeply transnational. I envision that such a psychology need not be Western-centric, Indian-centric, or Asian-centric but instead, as I have argued in this book, it would focus on how individuals who are located in diverse geographies are creating new stories of their selves and others as they imagine new psychological modernities. Such a perspective would include and recognize the influence of power and assymetrical cultural flows of the East, West, local, and global. This remapping of an alternative psychology through a transnational cultural focus needs to be undertaken "in order to draw attention to the tensions between the simultaneous plurality and narrowness of borders and the emancipatory potential of crossing through, with and over these borders in our everyday lives" (Mohanty, 2003, p. 2). Such a psychology, however, needs to be inherently attentive to questions of identity, justice, power, history, culture, marginalization, and exclusion.

A transnational cultural psychology also forces us to ask what it means to teach globalization in an increasingly socially unequal world—especially when students from North America are encouraged to become "global citizens" or engage in "global learning." Chhabria (2016) reminds us that when we teach courses on globalization or engage in globalization talk or incorporate globalization studies in our curricula, we need to ask ourselves whose stories and experiences are included in the narrative of globalization and whose stories are being left out. She argues that by reading and discussing critical accounts of globalization along with the more dominant cultural theories of globalization, students can then "de-center myopic accounts of globalization which re-enlist Eurocentric arguments about process and change. They can overcome the impasses between conceptualizing North Atlantic *ways of life* in opposition to Asian *ways of life* or other such generalizing binaries" (p. 14, emphasis in original).

In summary, we need a psychology that is anchored in theoretical and epistemological pluralism. The model of theoretical pluralism cannot be based on benign multiculturalism or some simplistic theory of cultural difference, essentialism, and inclusion; rather, it has to work fundamentally toward a decolonization of psychological science. I propose that such a vision of psychology need not be Western-centric, Indian-centric, or Asian-centric. Instead, as

I have argued throughout this book, it would focus on how individuals who are located in diverse geographies are creating new stories of themselves and others as they imagine new psychological modernities that include cultural fragments of the East, West, national, local, global, modern, and other intersecting sociocultural realities. Our angles, questions, research inquires, and practices can draw on diverse frameworks of psychological knowledge.

NOTE

1. India's postcolonial embrace of the divergent and mutually incompatible religious world views and local identities ensued through an Indian secularism that contained both the dreadful elements of division and some sparkling moments of democratic coherence. Under conditions of Western modernity and Christianity, secularism becomes the dominant interpretive framework for reading and interpreting religious identities. Secularism, through the device of the nation state, makes citizenship the primarily principle of identity and thus transcends the principles of race, religion, ethnicity, and gender. Secularism in India, however, is constituted within the fragmented "imagined communities" of the religious sphere. In other words, the concept of Western secularism was artificially imposed on India via colonialism. As a result, unlike the Western notions of a civil society, the Indian secular state maintains its impartiality "not by abstinence from religious affairs but by its 'fair' involvement on India's multi-religious terrain" (Vanaik, 1997, p. 67). However, Indian political history and practice remind us that the state has, to quote Vanaik again, too often indulged in an "active balancing of favors to various religious communities" (p. 67). Such a partial and biased involvement toward a single or several religious groups is quite contrary to the fundamental principles of "impartiality" implemented in the Western secular state.

CHAPTER 9

Studying Globalization at Home

Reflections on Method, Self-Reflexivity,

and Narrative Inquiry

My aim in this book was to understand how young urban Indians, who occupy different social worlds, construct meanings about their identities as they engage with contradictory cultural flows of globalization. This project was rooted in cultural and narrative psychology in the sense that I traced how British colonization, postcolonial modes of acculturation in urban India, neoliberal practices, American media, as well as global images of lifestyles of youth become inflected in these young adults' personal narratives.

There is significant interest in the adoption of interpretive methods or qualitative research in psychology. The epistemological and ontological assumptions undergirding qualitative research reflect multiple "practices of inquiry" and methodologies that have different orientations, assumptions, values, ideologies, and criterion of excellence (Gergen, 2014a). Similarly, Wertz (2011) describes the blossoming of contemporary qualitative research as a qualitative movement that does not have a unified, overarching paradigm. This movement, he notes, "includes constructivism, critical theory, feminist theory, critical race theory, cultural studies, semiotics, phenomenology, hermeneutics, deconstruction, narrative theory and psychoanalysis" (p. 84). Until recently, psychology's preoccupation with quantification and experimentation required psychologists to think about their scientific activity as based on the 19th-century model of science consisting of hypothesis generation, measurement through instrumentation, and confirmation based on an accumulated body of findings. What was missing from psychology's narrative of scientific progress was the recognition that all psychological knowledge was essentially socially and historically grounded (Danzinger, 1990). The conventional and mainstream view of psychology, according to Danzinger, is derived from a model of science that is similar to the tale of Sleeping Beauty. He writes,

> The objects with which psychological science deals are all present in nature fully formed, and all the prince–investigator has to do is find them and awaken them with the magic kiss of his research. But in truth scientific psychology does not deal with natural objects. It deals in test scores, rating scales, response distributions, serial lists, and innumerable other items that the investigator does not just find but constructs with great care. (p. 2)

Although the mainstream scientific approach continues to dominate much of American psychology, there is a growing recognition about the limits of positivistic psychology that is built on quantitative data and controlled experimental or quasi-experimental designs (Willig & Stainton-Rogers, 2008). The waning influence of the foundationalist perspective in philosophy of science, logical positivism, standardized testing, and cognitive–experimental psychology and the rise of interpretive and linguistic turn with its emphasis on multiplicity and cultural, textual, and discursive meanings have created an impetus for embracing qualitative research (Gergen, 2014a; Madill & Gough, 2008). Furthermore, the rise of qualitative research has been coupled with the gradual increase in the presence and participation of scholars from historically underrepresented marginalized groups in the social sciences, and the declining ability of experimental methods to speak to social issues has contributed to the multiple practices and forms of inquiry (Gergen, 2014a). On the social and cultural front, the anti-war movement, the civil rights and feminist movements, along with an increased awareness that the production of knowledge is shaped by one's cultural social location have been instrumental in the flowering of qualitative psychology (Gergen, Josselson, & Freeman, 2015).

QUALITATIVE INQUIRY AND WRITING CULTURE

Anthropological writings during the past three decades have contributed to qualitative psychology by showing how cultural meanings are produced through contested social codes, power relationships, and one's politics of location (Bhatia, 2007; Macleod & Bhatia, 2008). These writings have analyzed how the concept of culture is made up of conflicting representations of gender, race, class, and sexuality; concepts of self-reflexivity, accountability, and voice are integral to the relationship between the researcher and the researched, and descriptions about culture are connected to the act of writing (Amit, 2000; Appadurai, 1996; Behar, 1995; Clifford & Marcus, 1986; Rosaldo, 1993).

The reluctance to view creative writing as separate from critical writing is an important shift in feminist writings of culture and has served as a reminder to social scientists about the power of constructing knowledge through contested linguistic, social, and historical practices and through multiple modes of writing and genres. Ruth Behar (1996) states that "when you write vulnerably, others respond vulnerably" (p. 16). To write vulnerably implies paying attention to how life histories, emotions, personal experiences, autobiography, witnessing, travels, and journeys shape our research questions, inquiries, and ultimately the entire framework of constructing knowledge. Behar argues that the rise of "first-person" narratives from scholars who come from underrepresented groups has challenged established truths and canonical theories and has also deconstructed the inherent Orientalism present in many classic texts in social sciences.

One of the most important forces that have contributed to the field of qualitative research in social sciences is the publication of *The Sage Handbook of Qualitative Research* in 1994 by Norman Denzin and Yvonna Lincoln. This handbook, which has gone through four editions, has played a significant role in laying the foundations of qualitative research in the social sciences (Gergen, 2014a). In the introduction to the 2005 edition of the handbook, Denzin and Lincoln summarize important moments that have defined and framed the conceptual issues of qualitative research. They outline "eight moments" or "phases" that have defined the history of qualitative research in North America. One of their most important contributions has been to locate the researcher and his or her personal biography of class, race, gender, and ethnicity at the center of the research process.

The collection of articles in the various editions of *The Sage Handbook of Qualitative Research* show how self-reflexivity plays a crucial role in bringing the ideologies, assumptions, interpretations, and background knowledge of the researcher to the research setting. There is no longer any meaningful separation between the knower and the known or the observer and the observed. Some of the traditions associated with qualitative research are postcolonial theories of class, nationality, gender, and culture, as well as postmodern theories such as critical and feminist epistemologies. The individual's lived experience is articulated through novel genres such as "literary, poetic, autobiographical, multivoiced conversational, critical, visual performative, and co-constructed representations" (Denzin & Lincoln, 2005, p. 20). One of the key contributions of the four editions of the *The Sage Handbook of Qualitative Research* is displaying the legacy of the various historical moments as they remain alive in the contemporary field of qualitative inquiry.

DECOLONIZING METHOD: THE STRUGGLE AT THE MARGINS

Skeptical of the imperialism shrouded in Western knowledge claims about Others, Linda Tuhiwai Smith (2012) writes that when indigenous activists look at research from an insider perspective, they ask the following questions: Whose research is it? Who own its? Whose interest does it serve? Who will benefit from it? Who has designed its questions and framed its scope? How will its results be disseminated? She then goes on to state that from an indigenous perspective, what may appear to be the right answer, the most desirable answer, may still be judged incorrect. Smith shakes and interrupts the legacy of the Western research framework in her book *Decolonizing Methodologies*. She demonstrates how Europeans used science not only to construct knowledge about indigenous groups but also to colonize and conquer them. She argues that the term "research" is one of the dirtiest terms in the indigenous world because it brought forth devastating consequences for the indigenous people. Smith explains that when the word "research" is used in indigenous contexts, it invokes silence, brings up disturbing memories, and produces a knowing and distrustful smile. Science, she argues, has been "implicated in the worst excesses of colonialism" and carries a "history that still offends the deepest sense of our humanity" (p. 1). Furthermore, Smith reminds us that any metaphor that designates marginality such as "borders, boundaries, bridges, center–periphery, and insider–outsider sheds light on not only how people are demarcated in spatial terms but also in socioeconomic, political and cultural terms" (p. 204). Similarly, postcolonial theorists have used a "liminal" perspective to describe the conditions of those living in the margins (Bhabha, 1994). Gloria Ladson-Billings (2000) argues that "the work of the liminal perspective is to reveal the way the dominant perspectives distort the realities of other in an effort to maintain power relations that continue to disadvantage those who are locked out of the mainstream" (p. 259). The question for me, as a qualitative researcher, is how do I reveal my methods in such a way as to not only bring to the surface the liminality of the group I am studying but also how do I reveal the hierarchy, heterogeneity, and internal conflicts and politics, as well as the betrayals, that define the group's marginality. Without understanding the spaces of periphery and the collusions, betrayals, and conspiracies that occur there, it is difficult to know what questions I will ask, how I will probe, why a particular story of oppression comes to the foreground, who speaks for the group, and what is not being told to me as a researcher (Bhatia, 2015). Thinking about marginality requires a situated analysis of the shifting power relationship of the marginalized persons/culture to four intersecting relationships of power. I have elsewhere described these as *entangled marginality* (Bhatia, 2015), which consists of the following:

1. Hierarchy: What is the hierarchical relationship between different members of the marginalized groups?
2. Equivalence: How do they position their marginality in relation to the dominant class and race?
3. Solidarity: What is the social and historical pattern of the marginalized group's relation with other marginalized groups?

4. Language: What language is deployed by the dominant group to articulate the social psychology of the marginalized group?

Entangled marginality builds on intersectionality theory (Crenshaw, 1994) but also specifically focuses on articulating what Michelle Fine (2013) has called the "grammar of participation," where collaborating with insiders as an insider can be rich and insightful but simultaneously messy and full of contradictions. The grammar of participation is then inherently linked to the grammar of methods. My understanding and inside knowledge of the tension and paradoxes of these four elements of marginality are then prerequisite to constructing innovative methods and creating a credible social–psychological account of the marginalized group in question.

Participatory action research, critical race theory, social justice research, community action research, and indigenous and indigenous psychology research have wrestled with the politics of location and relocation that shape marginalized groups. Understanding such entangled relationships on the margins reveals what bell hooks (1990) describes as the radical possibility of choosing the margins both as a site of belonging and as a site for struggle and resistance. Unraveling the entangled marginalities within the US context of race and racial formations, for example, is thus different from the spaces of marginality and oppression that exist in urban India, where the current project is situated.

The narratives of urban youth and families who live in *basti* settlements are defined by what Appadurai (2013) has called "bare citizenship"—their agency is asserted within the ecological chronic shortages of food, housing, medicine, education, sanitation, permanent unemployment, and threats of eviction from their dwellings. In India, "where distance from one's own excrement can be seen as the virtual marker of class distinction, the poor, for too long, having literally lived in their own shit, are finding ways to place some distance between their waste and themselves" (p. 170). The experience of marginality involved in defecating in public for men, women, and children who live in *bastis* or *jhopad-pattis* (shacks or temporary dwellings in slums) is tied up with issues of dignity, the body, and privacy.

Entangled marginality is a relational concept and requires teasing apart how social groups experience the burden of marginality and oppression in similar and distinct ways. For example, the politics of defecating in public for the urban poor in India speaks of a bare marginality that is radically different from the marginality experienced by the Indian diaspora in the United States. Despite their location in the First World and the fact that a large number of Indians in the diaspora are affluent, they continue to experience marginality as they are positioned as racialized others in relation to the dominant White majority. The concept of "entangled marginality" thus focuses on vocabularies, terms, and concepts that attempt to link together various sociopolitical structures of oppression or marginality that occur in the peripheries of both the Global North and the Global South.

Michelle Fine (2006) and colleagues (Fine & Torre, 2006; Fine & Weis, 2005) have, for example, significantly contributed to the archive of knowledge in psychology and qualitative research by contextualizing knowledge as a sociopolitical project. In their work, Fine and colleagues interrupt and dismantle long-held scientistic assumptions about generalizability, validity, expertise, and objectivity in psychology. They ground their knowledge in participatory action research through which their subjects become their collaborators and marginalized youth, youth of color, and youth in prisons become co-constructors and co-articulators of knowledge.

Fine and colleagues have introduced new ways of thinking about research in which generalizability is not just about extrapolating a set of findings from research but instead becomes a call to provocative thinking or "provocative generalizability" about everyday injustices. The term "construct validity" that assumes a natural unity and group consensus becomes an object to be challenged by counterstories, outliers, and other muted voices (Fine, 2006). Drawing on Harding's (1987) work, Fine argues for deeply questioning the "God's eye view" of the meaning of objectivity in psychology—a notion that seems illusionary and allows researchers to exclude themselves from the messiness of the social domains that are the primary repositories of acts of injustices and inequities. Instead, Fine proposes a notion of strong objectivity where researchers strive hard to incorporate their own social positionality, vulnerability, values, and predispositions by forming arguments and collecting evidence from many distinct standpoints. Fine's scholarship then "recuperates the notion of *objectivity* through flickering debates in social psychology about researchers delicately exploring—rather than denying—researchers' subjective interests, biases and perspectives" (p. 89, emphasis in original).

The present qualitative moment offers multiple frames and theories in which there is a constant emphasis on new ways of inquiring, arguing, interpreting, reframing, and validating qualitative knowledge. While Denzin and Lincoln's (2005) *Handbook* has set important foundations for the field of qualitative research, additional books, articles, and handbooks have also contributed to the creation of a qualitative psychological methodology (Behar, 1996; Clandinin & Rosiek, 2007; Clifford & Marcus, 1986; Creswell, 2013; Daiute, 2014; Gubrium & Holstein, 2007; Josselson, 2013; Van Maanen, 1988).

In summary, qualitative approaches in psychology present us with a provocative and complex vision of how the key concepts related to describing and interpreting cultural codes, social practices, and lived experience of others are suffused with both the poetical and political elements of culture. The new ways of doing ethnography and writing and making interpretations about culture no longer involve only an analysis of the historical, linguistic, and cultural practices that shape and give meaning to everyday cultural routines and events. Rather, the new critical ethnography looks at cultures "as composed of seriously contested codes and representations" in which the poetic and the political, the literary, and the social scientific genres of writing are mutually constituted (Clifford, 1986, p. 2). This book is grounded in the idea that qualitative researchers "stress the socially constructed nature of reality, the intimate relationship between the researcher and what is studied, and the situational constraints that shape inquiry" (Denzin & Lincoln, 2005, p. 11). Furthermore, the project is also anchored in the belief that qualitative research methodology offers "rich descriptions" of the cultural worlds and can bring us "closer to the actor's perspective through detailed interviewing and observation" (Denzin & Lincoln, 2005, p. 12).

PARTICIPANTS AND INTERVIEWS: FIELDWORK, STORIES, AND RELATIONSHIPS

During the past 10 years, I have conducted approximately 62 formal and 25 informal interviews and completed several hundred hours of participant observation. The formal interviews were recorded, and when the participants were not comfortable with having their conversations recorded, I took down notes and reconstructed the interview. The informal interviews were not recorded, and they took the form of spontaneous conversations I had with the participants whom I had met in the field. I provide more information and contextualize the interviewing process later in this chapter. I also conducted six focus groups consisting of various class and community groups. These included (1) youth belonging to the affluent and elite class, (2) middle- and upper-class youth enrolled in college, (3) middle-class youth working for call centers, (4) middle managers and information technology (IT) workers at call centers and business process outsourcing companies (BPOs), and (5) two focus groups with youth from working-class groups located in *bastis* (slums).

My interviews included many middle-aged adults who were born in the 1960s and raised in pre-globalized, pre-liberalized India. For many in this generation, they are witnessing their world change rapidly around them. They are the parents of the youth whom I interviewed. I needed to listen to their stories to make sense of and give context to my interviews with Indian youth. I analyze how these interview narratives are embedded within other stories and how their self-making was connected to neoliberal practices that were enacted in everyday life in bazaars, call centers, slums, workplaces, streets, cafes, bars, pubs, malls, and colleges. In particular, the youth's social class locations played a critical role in shaping their identity narratives and their level of engagement and exposure to discourses about globalization.

Defining Social Class in India

The current class formations and hierarchies in urban India are deeply tied to India's colonial and postcolonial history. I contextualize the social class locations of young people in Pune so their stories can be better understood. There are several historical origins of the construction of class identities in India, especially middle-class identities. The term "middle class" is a contested and elusive category within contemporary Indian society, and scholars have noted that there is no single Indian middle class but, rather, "middle classes" that encompass a wide range of identities, professions, salaries, and income levels. The concept of being "middle class" is deeply tied to cultural values of family, honor, morality, respectability, gendered identities, consumerism, and modernity (Donner & Neve, 2011). The modern origins of middle-class identities emerged out of the creation of a "salaried class" that was primarily the outcome of industrialization and bureaucratization of the state apparatus (Jafferlot & van der Veer, 2008).

Writing in 1961, B. B. Misra set out to find the sociological and historical origins of the middle-class identity in India at that time. He wrote that in contrast to the West, the idea of the middle class in India was tied to the British Raj and its accompanying set of practices. The middle-class way of life was practiced and created through specific bureaucratic and civil institutions that came into being during the British Raj. The middle class, Misra wrote, arose as a result of the changes in the "law and public administration," and the people who were considered middle class were mainly in the "learned professions" (p. 5). He argued that the imperialist economic structure of the British Raj combined with preexisting Indian values for higher learning to create the dominant middle class.

These English-speaking Indians who were well versed in the ways of the British and were primarily socialized in their traditions went to Britain to study law and medicine. These men came back as "England Return" *babus* (government workers and bureaucrats) and held middle-class values that were largely based on the framework of the British middle class. Misra (1961) explains:

> The idea and institutions of middle class social order were imported into India. They did not grow from within. . . . The middle class which the British aimed at creating was to be a class of imitators, not the originators of new values and methods. (p. 11)

In post-independence India, the middle class then comprised an elite segment of the society—the educated civil servants, doctors, officers, and accountants—who knew how to live with their traditions, interrogate their burdens, and yet navigate through the culture of modernity (Jafferlot & van der Veer, 2008). This colonial middle class comes into being during the late 19th and early 20th centuries as the struggle for India's independence movement reaches its apex and the calls for identity based on Indian nationalism gain mass traction. The involvement of the middle class in the nationalist movement led to the "the creation of professions, social reform with a special emphasis on the status of women, regional literature and, of course, the anticolonial struggles" (Baviskar & Ray, 2011, p. 4).

Middle class in post-independent India was not just a reference to a socioeconomic entity but also stood for specific values and a way of being in the world. Baviskar and Ray (2011) note that Jawaharlal Nehru, the first prime minister of India, was educated in a private school at Harrow in the United Kingdom and was the son of a prominent and wealthy Brahmin, who lived in one of the most palatial and grand mansions of Allahabad. They further remind us that Nehru once said, "I am, of course, a middle-class person." In declaring that he was a middle-class person, Nehru was pointing to the creation of a specific mindset. What did this mindset mean within the Indian urban context? To be middle class within the context of postcolonial India meant being

> open minded and egalitarian; following the rule of law and not being driven by private motive or particularistic agenda; being fiscally prudent and living within one's own means, and embracing science and rationality in the public sphere. It demanded setting aside primordial loyalties of caste and kinship and opening oneself to new affinities and association based on merit, and to identities forged in the work. (pp. 5–6)

The prominent leaders of the Indian independence movement, such as Gandhi and Nehru, also utilized and embraced a specific model of "Indianness" in post-independence India that then became fused with class identities. Their visions of Indianness was fashioned through their scrupulous and often slanted historical and religious understanding of India and through cultivating specific personas and identities. Nandy (1983) argues that with the advent of modernity, the rise of the West in general, and the British colonization of India in particular, was considered a natural development of progress and modernity's outward movement from its so-called birthplace in the West to the non-West. However, for Gandhi, the arrival of modernity through colonization was an opportunity to critique the immorality of both colonization and modernity. Gandhi (1909/1997) thought that modernity could be thwarted by drawing not on the contemporary history of India but, rather, by going very far back to the classical principles of *dharma, karma, artha, ahimsa,* and *satyagraha*; he conceived the core ideals of Indian self by going inward. This interior move implied that the ideal of Indian identity with its body and mind was to find both foundation and meaning in a set of spiritual practices that advocated self-control, self-realization, and a renunciation of superfluous materialism. Spirituality was Gandhi's principled rejoinder to the avocations of modernity.

In *Hind Swaraj*, Gandhi (1909/1997) provides the clearest explanation for the foundations of a middle-class Indianness. He writes,

> Civilization is that mode of conduct which points out to man the path of duty. Performance of duty and observance of morality are convertible terms. To observe morality is to attain mastery over our mind. So doing, we know ourselves. (p. 67)

Later in *Hind Swaraj*, Gandhi elaborates:

> The tendency of Indian civilization is to elevate the moral being, that of the Western civilization is to propagate immorality. The latter is godless, the former is based on a belief in God. So understanding and so believing, every lover of India is to cling to the old Indian civilization even as a child clings to its mother's breast. (p. 71)

In his chapter on civilization, Gandhi (1909/1997) writes that British and European civilization are founded on a religion that is essentially an irreligion, and the citizens of Europe have embraced the immorality of their culture and have lost their sanity. He describes Europeans as half-mad, lacking physical courage or strength, and as deriving their energy not through spirituality but by imbibing alcohol. Their pursuit of spreading their civilization by conquest and colonization is a disease, and that incurable disease afflicts all European people. Thus, *Swaraj* (independence and home rule), for Gandhi, was not based on physical acts of decolonization; rather, it was primarily a process of psychological decolonization from the contaminating attachments of modernity and material progress. Gandhi stated clearly, "Real home rule is self–rule or self-control" (p. 118). This was the vision of self-identity that Gandhi had in mind for all Indians.

Both Gandhi and Nehru provided the ideological materials for constructing a middle-class identity—an Indian orientation to everyday practices of living in post-independence India. Gandhi's ideals of personhood and the values it symbolized were difficult to apply and sustain for the larger middle classes. In contrast, the middle-class identity formation in post-independence was primarily carried out through the "Nehruvian developmental regime" (Upadhya, 2011, p. 259). This regime created a class of people who were given the task of running the higher education system and scientific and research labs, and it also included civil servants who were entrusted with governing the burgeoning public sector in India. These technical and professionally competent knowledge workers were imbued with the ideologies of nationalism and were simultaneously exhorted to live through the Gandhian message of "high thinking and simple living" (Upadhya, 2011, p. 59).

The middle class in the 1970s symbolized the *aam adami* (common man), and the politics of the middle class were organized around the demands of survival: *roti* (food), *kapda* (clothes), and *makaan* (shelter). The demands of the *aam adami* in urban India have undergone transformation and have been replaced by the new needs of *bijli* (electricity), *sadak* (roads), and *pani* (water) (Baviskar & Ray, 2011). The figure of the *aam adami* as reflection of the quintessential middle-class values and outlook has a long history in India, but it invited deep attention and focus after the economic liberal reforms that India undertook in the early 1990s. The onset of liberal reforms in India at that time largely represented the arrival of foreign brands, luxury goods, and new forms of transnational media.

To be middle class in India is to signal an affiliation and a belonging to a social group and appropriating a specific set of practices that are sanctified and recommended by the group. The new subjectivities of the Indian middle class, however, emerge from a hierarchical structure of class that is shaped by old forms of caste inequalities; dominant social and religious identities; and inequities in how social, educational, linguistic, and economic capital is distributed throughout the society.

One problem of defining the class structure in India is that the "middle class" is an open category that refers to many social groups with diverse social backgrounds, incomes, and occupations. Even the elite and the upper class are frequently included in the middle-class category because it is a class that symbolizes financial status, values, and aspiration. Given the economic and cultural capital of the middle class in India, it is also commonly referred to as the ruling class. The category of the middle class in India is often assumed to be universal and having shared values because it often speaks on behalf of the nation (Deshpande, 2003).

Even by the most general definition, the middle class in India is approximately 26% of the population. Approximately 70% of Indian families live on incomes that are lower than middle-class incomes, and approximately 40% of that population earns below poverty levels (Baviskar & Ray, 2011). One of the most reliable indexes of estimating the size and variation in social classes in India is the data collected by the Market Information Survey of Households (MISH; Sridharan, 2011). In 1998–1999, the elite middle class was approximately 6% of the population, the expanded middle class was 12% of the population, and the broadest middle class that consists of the elite and upper-class categories was approximately 26% of the population. The actual middle class was only approximately 8% of the population. Sridharan (2011) elaborates:

> In other words, depending on how expansively the middle class is conceived, it consisted of 55 million people (the elite definition), 115 million people (the

expanded definition), or 248 million people (the broadest definition) out of almost a billion people in 1998–99. (p. 40)

Although the MISH data reported here are more than 15 years old, they provide a reliable heuristic of how the categories of social class are constructed in India. In 2007, the McKinsey Global Institute issued a report titled "The 'Bird of Gold': The Rise of India's Consumer Market" (Ablett et al., 2007) that forecasted India's future economic growth. After using the government-based MISH data and other data sets such as that of the National Sample Survey Organization, it created an econometric model to predict economic growth in India from 2006 to 2025.

A key finding of the McKinsey Global Institute's report (Ablett et al., 2007) that has been circulated widely is that the Indian economy will grow at a compound rate of 7.3% over two decades and the middle class will expand from 50 million to 583 million by 2025; much of India's wealth is expected to be created in urban areas. This forecast of economic growth is rather optimistic, based as it is on the assumption that India will modernize its economy, thereby addressing severe gaps in education, poverty levels, and infrastructure. In any case, Ablett et al. reframe the traditional social class categories described previously by MISH by creating five categories based on real *annual income* and social characteristics:

Global Indians (Rs. 1,000,000+; $21,882+)
Strivers (Rs. 500,000–1,000,000; $10,941–$21, 882)
Seekers (Rs. 200,000–500,000; $4,376–$10,941)
Aspirers (Rs. 90,000–200,000; $1,969–$4,376)
Deprived (less than Rs. 90,000; less than $1,969)

What the numbers and social categories in the report do not fully illustrate is that opening up of the Indian economy in 1991 not only led to an increase in the culture of consumption in the middle class but also refashioned the middle class as a class of consumers (Fernandes, 2011; Upadhya, 2011). Not only does this neoliberal moment represent the middle-class family's obsession with consumption but also the larger discourses about consumption itself become central to the identity of the elite and middle-class Indians. Thus, public discourses about dining out, living in gated communities, hiring servants, traveling abroad, consuming foreign brands, cars and pursuing a certain lifestyle have also added a transnational or global dimension to middle-class identities.

The new Indian middle class is a culturally constructed category that is mainly shaped by practices of consumption related to goods, brands, and luxuries and by access to spaces such as malls, restaurants, pubs, and multiplex cinemas (Fernandes, 2011; Varma, 2010). This is why Fernandes observes that "the new middle class represents the political construction of a social group that operates as a proponent of economic liberalization" (p. 68). The social classes that have benefited from a globalized economy are likely to hold traditional cultural and nationalist values, they are oriented toward consumption of brands and goods, and they want India to be perceived as a world power (Varma, 2010). These practices have created new narratives that position India as having a new middle class of 200 million individuals who are different from the "old" middle class that was primarily constrained by the Gandhian ideals of austere living and Nehru's state-driven socialism.

Locating Fieldwork in Sites of Social Class

I used a "multi-sited ethnography" (Marcus, 1998) to explore connections and contrasts between different social classes. A multi-sited approach offers the researcher "an opportunity to dislocate the ethnographer from the traditional strong filiation to just one group of subjects among whom fieldwork is done and instead to place her within and between groups in direct, or even indirect and blind, opposition" (Marcus, 1998, p. 20). A multi-sited approach to research produces local knowledge that is based on a network of relationships between how cultural symbols and structures of power are revealed in everyday practices through an analysis of hierarchies and multi-sited social and cultural formations. Burawoy and colleagues (2000) similarly argue that global ethnography involves understanding the links between local sites and global processes and the transnational forces, connections, and imaginations that mark and make these sites. Thus, the global processes or cultural dynamics become accessible from the local spaces, and ethnographers who study others in space and time can capture this lived experience of globalization.

I collapsed the previously mentioned McKinsey Global Institute report's classification (Ablett et al., 2007) of five social class groupings into three broad social class categories. The income levels, as mentioned in the McKinsey report, were used as a guide to determine the socioeconomic status of the participants of the study. The first category consists of elite and upper-class Indians who are senior corporate executives, management consultants, CEOs of corporations, politicians, industry owners, big land owners, top-tier professionals and upwardly mobile mid-level executives, Bollywood actors or celebrities, and well-known professionals such as doctors, engineers, designers, and architects. The elite and upper-class Indians have wealth, lifestyles, and tastes similar to those of their Western counterparts; these are the two groups referred to in the McKinsey report as "strivers" and "global Indians." The strivers represent the upper classes, and they are senior government officials, well-established professionals, traders, merchants, and farmers. The second category that I use in the study refers to the middle class, which represents the "seekers" and "aspirers" in the McKinsey report. The seekers are medium-scale business traders, merchants, and young graduate students as well as call center workers, mid-level government employees, BPO employees, and entry-level workers. The third category in my study is the urban poor or the working class. In contrast to the McKinsey report, I consider the "aspirers" to be part of the working class because many of them also live in conditions of degradation and in a state of dissatisfied basic needs. The people who fall into this group are mostly lower-income earners who struggle to make ends meet. They are usually considered "toilers" because they often work in temporary jobs as construction workers, unskilled laborers, custodians, janitors, waiters, mechanics, and in the industrial and service industries. A large portion of the third category of urban poor represents what the Mckinsey report describes as the "deprived" class. People in this group comprise the majority of India's population; their income is below poverty levels, and they often live on less than $2 per day. This population often experiences starvation, disease, and chronic hunger. However, there are many aspirers who also live in slums and have working-class or lower-middle-class salaries but live in a semi "deprived" state without having access to basic necessities such as clean sanitation, education, and employment. Many of the youth and families whom I interviewed in the slums of Pune could be described as belonging to the aspirers and deprived class, and that is why I placed them in the third category.

My choice to collapse the Mckinsey report's (Ablett et al., 2007) five social class groups into three groups was based on cultural similarities and social patterns, financial status, income, occupation, education, access to cultural capital, and their aspiration levels. Rather than describing the Indian social class system through categories such as "global Indians" or "aspirers," I prefer to use the traditional social class categories of elite/upper class, middle class, and low income/poor. Although categories such as "global Indians" and "strivers" are extremely useful as a heuristic device, they are fairly reductive and do not capture the fluidity, porousness, and messiness of Indian social class positions. The call center youth are not rich or elite Indians, so they would not be classified as "global Indians" in the McKinsey report. However, as my study revealed, the call center youth also imagine themselves to be global Indians as they interface with their customers abroad; speak in global accents; and deploy global management discourses about happiness, individualism, and creativity. The call center youth imagine a kind of global Indianness that is different from that of the rich and elite Indians and thus both can lay claim to creating their *own* versions of global Indianness.

I place the elite and upper class in the same category because the students I interviewed had similar backgrounds in terms of their access to education, ability to travel abroad, and their accumulation of financial and cultural capital. Although the elite students were definitely wealthier and had lived a more privileged life than the upper-class students, both groups had similar levels of exposure to discourses of globalization, opportunities to travel abroad, influential social networks, and access to high-quality private education.

I consider the youth working in call centers and BPOs to be middle class because they belong to families with constrained financial resources. Some of the call center youth have a college education, fluency in English, and earn good money, whereas others who work in domestic call centers make meager salaries. Many of the call center youth who worked for multinational corporations had high disposable income, but they drove scooters or motorbikes and lived in rented apartments or in small apartments that belonged to their families. Several of the call center youth in the study were migrants from other states and had moved out of their states to get jobs so they could support their families. By focusing on social class location, one of the main aims of the study was to understand the individual stories that were embedded in the three respective social class worlds. In addition, I also wanted to analyze how these stories from different social classes were fundamentally separate yet connected to each other.

My first fieldwork site was composed of youth who mainly worked for call centers, BPOs, the IT industry, and other ancillary units that had emerged in the urban landscape as a result of outsourcing (e.g., nightclubs, restaurants, and coffee shops). In 2005, and 2008, and 2010 I interviewed trainers, consultants, and adults who were associated with the growing call center industry and the BPOs. I conducted a focus group with another set of 10 youth who were mostly local college students to get different perspectives on the impact of call centers on youth identities and urban culture in Pune. I also interviewed a CEO of a call center and a BPO, several parents of call center workers, and other adults who were older and belonged to a different generation than that of the call center workers. I interviewed these individuals to get their perspectives and stories as to how call centers and BPOs were refashioning urban Indian youth's imagination about "Indianness," "globalization," and "American culture." The middle-class Indian youth spoke about how the upper-class and elite youth—who they called the *hi-fi class*[1]—had the cultural power to define "Indianness" through their social background, consumer lifestyle, and displays of luxury possessions that became fetishized by other youth.

Therefore, I added another dimension to this research project in 2008, when I began interviewing elite and upper-class youth attending a liberal arts management college so that I could understand how they were imagining "Indianness" through the discourses of globalization. I expanded in this way to learn how their identities differed from those of the call center workers. The elite and upper-class youth in Pune largely tended to dismiss the call center workers as middle-class Indians who could not make it into a professional world. They framed these workers as living a life on debt that was financed by their disposable income and their lifestyle.

The liberal arts management college called Meridian College became the second site for my fieldwork. I conducted a series of individual and group interviews with affluent, upper-class Indian students at Meridian College in Pune. In 2008, I spent several weeks with students, talking to them about their education; how they viewed the sociocultural changes in urban India; their understanding of globalization; and how they were reimagining Indianness in the context of new media, brands, increasing materialism, and greater exposure to Western cultures. I conducted narrative interviews with 20 students, one focus group with 8 students, three interviews with faculty, and one interview with a non-teaching staff member. Both the elite and the middle-class Indian youth seemed sympathetic to the plight of the poor youth, but they remained largely segregated from the poor youth and lived in their own social universe. The stories I heard from the middle-class and elite youth compelled me to connect them to stories that I had not yet heard but suspected must exist and that were largely invisible to much of Indian society.

I therefore decided to add a third component to this project in 2011 by interviewing youth living in a slum called Panchsheel *basti*.[2] This slum is situated between Kalyani Nagar and Koregaon Park areas, where a large number of multinational call centers have been built. I was interested in finding out how the large majority of Indian urban youth—who are mostly working class and poor—were being impacted by the cultural forces of globalization. What was their engagement with practices of globalization? How did the worlds of consumption, fashion, social media, and dating that surrounded them influence the lives of the youth from the slums?

As mentioned previously, Panchsheel *basti* is located near Kalyani Nagar and Koregaon Park, which are considered to be two of the most affluent and "rich" localities of Pune. These neighborhoods had been directly transformed as a result of new flows of capital and outsourcing centers. Pune's wealthiest class lived in these areas, and these spaces had seen a dramatic increase in the building of malls, restaurants, upscale apartment buildings, IT parks, call centers, and nightclubs. I interviewed approximately 15 youth who lived in Panchsheel *basti* to hear their stories, with the goal of examining their relationship to new practices of globalization and how their lives were being shaped by their proximity to these centers of wealth.

During my visits to Pune, I recognized that the lives of the urban poor and working-class Indian youth were invisible and completely erased out of India's narrative of an emerging global power. The youth's stories about their lives in the *basti* and their struggles with unemployment, poverty, and lack of access to housing and sanitation facilities were threatening a clean narrative of "India shining." The elite and middle-class youth had become the representatives of the "new India." The stories of urban youth that were circulating in the media were about the consumerist lifestyles of Indian call center workers, young software engineers succeeding in the United States, elite young businessmen creating a Silicon Valley culture in Bangalore, the nightlife of the young urban Indians, Indian beauty pageants, and portrayals of young Bollywood actors and cricket players drinking Pepsi and Coke and selling branded goods in advertisements. The new globalized youth of India, as depicted in one of the widely read mainstream publication, defined the contemporary Indian youth as "zippies" (Lukose, 2009):

> A young city or a suburban resident, between 15 and 25 years of age, with a zip in their stride. Belongs to Generation Z. Can be male or female, studying or working. Oozes attitude, ambition and aspiration. Cool, confident and creative. Seeks challenges, loves risks and shuns fear. Succeeds Generation X and Generation Y, but carries the social, political, economic, cultural or ideological baggage of neither. Personal and professional life marked by vim, vigor and vitality (origin Indian). (pp. 5–6)

This narrative of Indian youth as being "zippies" was in public circulation in media and popular discourses. These youth were further described as having grown up in a globalized India that has "transcended its colonial and postcolonial histories" (Lukose, 2009, p. 7). The youth I interviewed in the *basti* gave me a chance to listen to their stories of globalization; how they articulated their aspirations, dreams, and ambitions; how they experienced the cultural changes around them; and how they made sense of their lives in the *basti* and their encounters with new India.

The research at Panchsheel *basti* allowed me to compare the stories of middle- and upper-class/elite youth with those of the working class and youth who were located among the urban poor. My multi-sited research project developed organically during the decade from 2005 to 2015. This book became centered around the narratives of youth from these three worlds and their stories about their class; how they imagined the youth from other classes to be; and about family, relationships, work, media, sexuality, globalization, and marginalization. The elite upper-, middle-, and working-class worlds mostly remained socially secluded and segregated from each other. When youth from the three class groupings described interactions with each other, these were mostly limited to their work lives. The urban youth from the slums worked as servants, janitors, security guards, cleaners, cooks, and ward attendants in hospitals, while many of their mothers worked as *bais* (maids or "maid servants") doing *jhadu and pocha* (sweeping and cleaning) in the homes of the upper-class folks. As expected, there was more interaction between the middle- and upper-class youth, but by and large that contact was still limited to professional work settings. Going back and forth between the stories of these three class groupings allowed me to gain insights about how their subjectivities were formed and how their lives were separate yet connected with each other.

These social class groups and the stories I analyze in the book are heterogeneous and are not intended to in any way represent a reified, fixed, coherent, essentializing "class psychology." Rather, these narratives reveal "competing stories" and "counterstories" about how Indian urban youth are relationally connected to each other through the axes of power, privilege, mobility, and status. These narratives reflect stories that show dominant and marginalized ways of engaging with practices of globalization and creating shifting meanings of Indianness. I draw on Weis and Fine's (2004) notion of "compositional studies" to argue that these multi-sited social class groups work through each other as companion projects. Insights about one group are refracted through other groups and are understood relationally and partly derive their identities by being positioned *against* and with *each* other. One of the core principles underpinning the "compositional method" is the reliance on simultaneously approaching social categories as formed by plural, porous, shifting, and multiple intersecting *social* and *material* locations (Weis & Fine, 2004). Although these categories may be fluid, for many urban Indian youth they are also foundational in ways their family history circumscribes their life in particular trajectories. The urban Indian youth do creatively reframe their identities, but there is only so much reassertion and reframing some youth can take on given their limited power and resources.

The shifting yet materially grounded nature of the social class categories gives us insights into how urban Indian youth identity formation and social relationships is sutured through stories that bring together threads from global, national, and local formations.

A NARRATIVE APPROACH TO INTERVIEWS

Narrative research is one the most extensively embraced forms of qualitative inquiry (Gergen et al., 2015). The narrative approach, as described by Gergen et al.,

> assumes that one of the major ways in which we understand our lives and center our actions is through stories. We live our lives in terms of dramas of achievement, love, conflict, and so on. To understand others, then, is to comprehend (or "feel with") the stories by which they live. (p. 4)

There are various approaches to using narrative methods in psychology. Some scholars use a life-history perspective to understand personality and identity, other scholars use a discursive and textual analysis for studying how narrative reflects cultural meanings, and several other scholars use conversational and linguistic analysis for making meaning of everyday narratives (Daiute, 2014).

I chose to use participation observation and in-depth narrative interviewing as my main methodological tools to study the patterns of identity construction in Pune city and to collect narratives of selves and identities that were told and retold by the participants. Some stories seemed fully formed, coherent, and had neat beginnings, middles, and ends, whereas other stories seemed to mimic fragmented stories in which the participants had many pauses and the conversations stumbled along. However, both "fragmentary" and "fully formed" narratives, big and small stories, were useful in shedding light on the interlinkages between culture, narrative, and self.

Scholars for whom meaning-making and interpretation are central goals of their research often use a narrative approach (Bruner, 1990; Sarbin, 1986). Thus, narrative inquiry "aims to understand life as it is lived and interpreted in the participant's own words. . . . Narrative inquiry takes meaning to be inherently personal, social, and political . . . and is therefore a particularly strong method for investigating issues of social justice" (Toolis & Hammack, 2015, p. 53).

Researchers who use "narrative as a method" usually embrace the assumption that one's story is one of the most fundamental ways of understanding an individual's experiences as "constituted, shaped, expressed, and enacted" by social and cultural forces (Clandinin & Rosiek, 2007). Thus, in narrative research, "data" and "theory," stories and concepts, experience and systems are not separate variables but, rather, mutually inform and shape each other. The aim of using narrative interviews is to capture the dynamic and contradictory experiences of participants. The conversation produced through interviews is co-constructed, relational, and depends on how the interviewer and the interviewee position each other. This narrative method shares some similarities with a grounded theory approach to interviews. Charmaz (2001) explains that "a grounded theory interview can be viewed as an unfolding story. . . . This unfolding story arises as interviewer and participant together explore the topic and imprint a human face on it" (p. 690). I conducted interviews not just to obtain "information" about my participants' lives but also to uncover and understand what language they used to describe their self and others, how they reframed and interpreted stories, and how they described their experience of cultural change and globalization.

The interview context then follows, as Josselson (2013, p. 6) notes, the "hermeneutic circle." The idea that the whole must be understood through its relationships with the parts and the meaning of the parts only becomes evident through their relationship with the whole is the basis of this principle. Thus, the act of interpretation in narrative research is based on the mutually constituted relationship of meaning between the whole and the parts. As Josselson writes,

> When we enter the interview situation, we know about neither the whole nor
> the parts, but our understanding of both will be building simultaneously—and

our understanding will grow when we take the text back to our workspaces to analyze it. (p. 6)

Thus, an interview builds on an intersubjective process that temporally unfolds over time and provides us with conversations that are often fragmentary, incomplete, and partial; narrative interviews as conversations are always in the process of being retold and remembered (Jackson & Mazzei, 2013).

Interviewing in the field implies that we view knowledge as relational, such that who said what to whom is important in understanding how cultural knowledge is produced (Denzin, 1997; Gubrium & Holstein, 2004, Mishler, 1986). From this perspective, power plays an important role in structuring the relationships between those who write about culture and narrative and those whose lives are "lived in" culture. Mishler reminds us that interviews are not made sensible through a stimulus–response paradigm but are instead interactional accomplishments created through discourse and speech events coordinated between speakers. Cultural knowledge is produced at the overlapping points of the relationship between participants and the researcher's individual relationship with those participants. I used concepts, theories, and questions to make meaning of the narrative interviews, but the narrative material was often co-produced through our joint deflections, pauses, turn-taking, misunderstandings, and clarifications (Bhatia, 2007, 2008b, 2010b, 2015; Bhatia & Ram, 2009).

I used both structured and unstructured interviews to create "conversations" between the participants and myself. I often probed for stories; identified contradictory claims in the interviewees' responses; and also asked for deep reflections, comments, and clarification. I often went further, asking my participants to explain why their particular narration was important to them. My interviews reflected an intertextual collage of meanings. When a call center worker, for example, mentioned his or her parents or the manager of the company or his or her accent trainer, I followed up and interviewed the trainer, the manager, and/or the parents to understand how their individual stories were connected to other stories. I often had to "chase" one story to give meaning to another story and draw the conceptual and thematic links between those stories.

DOCUMENTING OURSELVES: REFLEXIVITY AND SUBJECTIVITY IN THE CONDUCT OF QUALITATIVE RESEARCH

A qualitative psychology that pays acute attention to the "subjects" who are living in the current postcolonial condition requires being aware of how both the *politics of location* and the *politics of representation* shape the research process (Behar, 1996; Bhatia, 2007; Macleod & Bhatia, 2008). The stories and struggles of Indian youth have often been neglected because of their invisibility in the "First World" and the demands of Indian psychology to conform to the holy trinity of empiricism, positivism, and objectivity in psychology. These studies often have unwittingly transformed their personhood and subjectivity into decontextualized cultural variables.

My colleague Catriona Macleod and I (Macleod & Bhatia, 2008) have argued that research conducted in postcolonial cultures needs to be vigilant and reflexive about how the axes of race, class, and gender inform the theory and research process. Postcolonial researchers, however, have to add another dimension to this self-reflexive process and become aware of (1) the epistemic privilege involved in using academic discourse, (2) the multiple and conflicting accounts of insiders or local people, and (3) the intellectual and political locations through which we discuss and analyze our research. The way the politics of location shapes how we produce knowledge is a complex process, however. Paying attention to the politics of location involves not just being aware of our social position as a researcher, an anti-colonialist, or an anti-racist. Rather, we need to make clear how our privileged location as researchers shapes what psychological research we study, how we study the phenomenon, with whom we create research, where we study, how we move between fields, where we publish, and who benefits from our research.

Such a politics of representation demands that we remain self-reflexive and vigilant about how we capture the voices of our participants—how we interview, record, approach, and frame them in our studies. In subaltern studies, for example, Guha (1988) and others raise questions about how the colonized, muted subject's small voice is represented in history, how the subaltern's identity is constructed, and through what channels or medium the identity of the subaltern gains expression. In Spivak's (1988) famous essay, "Can the Subaltern Speak?" the young Bengali widow, Bhubaneswari Bhaduri, did not speak not because she was silenced or muted but, rather, because she was depicted as someone who was not capable of being in a dialogically constituted speaker–listener relationship. The question for Spivak was not whether the subaltern can speak but whether she has been given the space, the privilege, and the status of an equal communicator in the dialogical relationship. The terms of representation, the channels of communication, and the language that she can use to express her agency are decided by either the colonizer or the ones who come to rescue her oppressed subjectivity. Thus, the politics of location and representation inform each other; speak to each other; and raise questions about the mechanisms we employ in understanding others, the language we deploy to frame others—where representation refers to an act of production and not a mirror reflection of reality. This process also means "researching back" (Smith, 2012) and correcting how postcolonial subjects have been framed, theorized, and articulated in Euro-American research (Macleod & Bhatia, 2008).

Critical forms of qualitative inquiry that are conducted in postcolonial locations have to be especially attuned to how the researchers position themselves in the field, how they move in their own communities in the field, and how they are positioned by others in their "home." Thus, doing fieldwork transforms into "homework" for many of us who return to our homes, hometowns, home communities, and homelands to do research. Home and field become blurred boundaries where the personal becomes closely intertwined with the research process and in fact becomes a site of negotiation (Visweswaran, 1994). Van Maanen's (2010) definition of fieldwork is perhaps unassuming and yet one of the most apt and profound summaries of this process. He writes,

> Fieldwork is a technique of gathering research materials by subjecting the self—body, belief, personality, emotions, cognitions—to a set of contingencies that play on others such that over time, usually a long time, one can more or less see, hear, feel and come to understand the kinds of responses others display (and withhold) in particular social situations. (p. 219)

There is a clear recognition that the ethnographic research process involves one's body, culture, politics, thoughts, and emotions. My self-narrative was deeply intertwined with the research process of using a qualitative inquiry framework at home in Pune. In particular, my ethnographic observations about the social field generally, and about my participants in particular, were framed through my status as a postcolonial researcher who was both an insider and an outsider. Ethnography involves what Granek (2013) has called "putting ourselves on the line"—where a researcher's self is not just shaped by the participant through intersubjective exchange but also the researcher makes emotional investments in his or her participant's stories and their cultural worlds.

I had lived, grown up, and studied in Pune but had never thought that its cultural space would one day be a legitimate object of inquiry for me. Home is to be lived in and not studied. Home is a natural space where objects and people do not stand out but, rather, draw you to settle in. I was an insider and an outsider, a native of my hometown and also, according to my mother, a "son who is successfully settled in America." I had the privilege and the resources of being faculty from an American college, yet I could easily cross boundaries at home by speaking the local language and code switching (Delpit, 1995) my ways of talking and being across the social class spectrum.

While I formed connections with the young urban participants in Pune, I was also aware of my privileges of mobility, social class standing, and status. I felt my privileged location most acutely when talking to the youth in the slum settlements of Pune. The working-class urban youth often talked about living in a slum as being a life full of *qurbani* (sacrifices) where they had lack of access to sanitation, education, employment, housing, and means to learn

English. I recall one incident during a humid day in July 2015 when I had conducted interviews with the youth in a tiny 10 × 10-foot house in the *basti*. The room had a tin roof, and the heat and humidity were oppressive. There was no fan to relieve the heat, and the family that lived in the house had six members, all of whom lived and slept in the main room. I could enter and leave this space as I desired, but the young families in the *basti* had to permanently coexist with heat, garbage and sewage smells, overflowing drains, malfunctioning public toilets, the loud disruptive sounds of trains passing by, and the constant insecurity about being evicted from their houses.

After my interview, I could leave the *basti* and move across multiple classes and boundaries with a certain ease, whereas these youth continually experienced the daily indignity of living a life without access to basic amenities and facilities. I could "look away," as Harsh Mander (2015) reminds us, at the huge pile of rotten garbage and dried up excreta that greeted me at the entrance of *basti*, but the youth and families who passed this area daily considered it a feature of their neighborhood. My identity and "structural positioning" (Dutta, 2015) as an insider and outsider, local and alien, from "here" and "there," spurred me to ask deeper questions about the research process itself: How do you produce knowledge of self and others when a familiar home is transformed into a subject of study and becomes a field site? How do I make sure I am accountable to my participants? How do I make sure my self-reflexivity and interpretations reflect the "faithfulness" (Freeman, 2013) of the participants' narrative accounts?

My fieldwork became *transnational* when the traveling back and forth from Barrington, Rhode Island, to Pune, Maharashtra, India, to conduct research provided me with contrasting images, grating scenes, and a perpetual feeling of dislocation. These contrasting experiences of note taking and recording my observations were an important part of the overall research process. Rather than dismissing these reflections in the field as extraneous and irrelevant, they became a source of knowledge that added to my cultural comprehension about globalization and identity formation of urban Indian youth. Next, I use a series of first-person "ethnographic vignettes" to illustrate how cultural knowledge about my field was created at the awkward and often uneasy intersections of being both a researcher and a native, a migrant and a local, a foreigner and a familiar other.

Blurring the Boundaries of Homework and Fieldwork

In January 2011, I arrived at Boston Logan International Airport from Pune, India. I had just completed an intense and busy 6-week fieldwork trip to study how the uneven forces of globalization were shaping the psychological worlds of the urban, middle-class Indians. My flight arrived in Boston in the evening.

A driver from "Big Daddy" taxi service picked up me and my family from the airport. I had been at this airport more than 20 times and yet it seemed unfamiliar. I was exhausted from the journey. I noticed many "foreigners" sitting in rows of chairs with their backs facing each other. I noticed how public space at the airport was orderly and hyperclean, and there was no jostling, nudging, or pushing that are typical outside Indian airports. As the car entered the ramp toward Interstate 95, the familiar became stranger. I complained to my ever-patient wife, "Why so many cars?" "Where are the people?" "Why so, so clean?"

The temperature gauge at my house read 15° F outside (–9°C), and I bundled up to go to the local Stop and Shop grocery store to buy milk and bread. The clean roads, open unobstructed sky, neatly arranged houses on the Barrington river, the towering, narrow, white steeple of the church, and the brick paved streets seemed bizarrely coordinated and unusually well organized to me. My home in Barrington seemed curiously antiseptic, and I was disturbed by the apparent lack of disorder in my town.

I ran into a friend at the grocery store. She greeted me enthusiastically, "Welcome home! How was your trip?" I replied, "Going home was great! I am still there." Her American accent sounded loud and harsh to me. We talked some more, but our conversation seemed as though it had occurred in a dream. Her body language, tone, and words appeared noncontextual. I resorted to an inner dialogue: "How do I know these people? Where am I? Is this real?" I was missing my home. I was missing being in India, where I could be invisible yet connected in a thriving public space. Field and home had become blurred and distorted for me.

The images of "back home" were still present with me even as I settled back in at my other home in the United States. The First World public space "here" appeared too still, too calm to me. It seemed that this space had acquired a sudden pathology or a disorder that caused excessive silence. I yearned to be back in Pune and immersed in fieldwork—to be in the public space, abuzz with life. The public space in India is indeed that—it is *public*. The teeming millions live in public spaces, their bodies rubbing against each other, and their vehicles just missing each other by inches. The edges of the streets are buzzing with activity—shops, merchants, *chai* vendors, *paan-wallahs* (places that sell beetle leaf, tobacco, and cigarettes), gas stations, and pedestrians gesturing drivers to stop as they make heroic attempts to cross the road.

Driving my car in the spare, orderly streets of Barrington, I recalled the rickshaw stop located at a major intersection before the Yerwada bridge in Pune from where one of the central national highway begins. At this traffic signal, young men and women make furniture from wicker on the road. There is a crematorium on one side of the road. Food stalls, small houses, *thele wallas*, garage repair shops, and rows of small general stores hug each other on both flanks of the road. There are hordes of people on one side of the street waiting for the municipal bus. There are as many people outside as inside the bus stop. At the various *chowks* (intersections), I would see children playing cricket on the roadside and throngs of men and women sitting down aimlessly, sleeping, biding their time, some perched on mango crates and plastic chairs reading the newspaper or just looking at the traffic. The infrastructure on the road may be in the advanced stages of decline and deterioration, but the living spaces on the streets appeared energetic and vibrant. Life is vigorously animated on the roads in India. Traffic stops and paved roads are not just spaces for transportation of people and goods. The roadside spaces are made of interdependent ecological communities in which a multitude of families reside and engage in commerce and cooking. Men and women live out their everyday lives in the small nooks and crannies alongside the roads.

It is in the city of Pune that I became a teenager, an undergraduate student, and a postgraduate student. In short, the city marked the evolution of my self in various phases and initiated my transition from childhood to youth and then to young adult. However, throughout the years, the city was gradually acquiring an element of familiar foreignness. The very street that I roamed when I was growing up in Pune now stood out in new frames. I was re-reading my "Pune" home via my other "Barrington" home in the United States. Pune was undergoing a radical change when, during every visit, I was confronted with the erasure of recognizable old landmarks—bungalows, shops, sites, playgrounds, theaters, and cafés. My participant observation involved capturing the dynamic spatial and social changes that were occurring around me. The various visual representations of the city became the text through which I was deciphering the impact of globalization on the urban culture in Pune. The public space, with its cluttered hoardings, advertisements, and signs, was a very live narrative: There was a story to be told about how the new urban culture was being represented and transformed under the guise of globalization, outsourcing, and symbols of "hypercapitalism."

In December 2012, I visited Pune to conduct interviews and to capture how layers of modernity, tradition, and neoliberal globalization were creating new individual and collective identities. I struggled with how the public space felt alien and foreign to me. I recall walking on the streets of Pune just before the 2013 New Year was going to be celebrated across Pune. I had started my walk on North Main Road in Koregaon Park, one of the high-class residential areas that is considered a "posh locality." I passed the famous German Bakery that, in 2010, was the site of a terrorist bombing that killed 17 people and injured 60. Foreign students, local call center youth, and devotees from the nearby Osho Ashram frequented this café; it was now cordoned off and under construction. Opposite the bakery stood the swanky and "modern chic" five-star O Hotel. As I turned left, I saw a huge plum-colored advertising board that caught my attention. Right in front of a building there was a colossal board with bold capital letters, "POISON." The letter "I" was red, and the others were black. Under this word, the following was written: "ANTI AGINIG CLINIC PVT. LTD: For Removing Obstacles to Beauty." There were two headshots of models—both looked White and one had black hair and the other brown. Under the photo of the woman with black hair, the caption read, "Advanced Skin: Whitening Treatments." Next to the picture of the White woman's face, the shot read, "Anti-Wrinkle Treatments: Botox, fillers, skin tightening."

I walked past the Poona Blind Men's Association, past the bus stop, and saw a cluster of colorful posters for the New Year's Eve celebrations, each one trying to draw attention to itself by its flamboyant language and imagery. The first post I saw read, "Frozen Night: The Biggest New Year Blast." This poster showed a picture of a DJ standing tall with his hands up and looking down at the throngs of crowd below the stage. On the poster were the names "DJ Ravi (King of Bollywood and Punjabi)," "DJ Shane (King of Hip Hop)," and "DJ Big Daddy (King of Commercial and House)."

Another poster screamed, "Pune's Biggest New Year Bash at Forest Valley: Ecstasy 2013." An image of a young, well-toned, bikini-clad White woman with angel wings was placed in the center of the poster. Across the breasts of this woman were the following words: "Free Your Angels and Demons." I was not sure what that meant. I paused and reflected. I was not sure why somebody had to free their angels as well as their demons. I thought demons were what we had to get rid of or conquer and angels stayed.

In any case, the poster that drew my attention and that was plastered all over the urban areas of the city stated, "New Year's Party at Mulik Grounds, Kalyani Nagar: Strictly Couples Entry and Stag with Groups." The poster showed six White women dressed in colorful costumes that were inspired by the wardrobe designs of *Moulin Rouge*, the Rockettes, and other Broadway musical cabaret shows of New York City. The women were dressed in either red or blue silk lingerie, and they were wearing elaborate samba and cabaret headgear with feathers.

I was both puzzled and dismayed by the insertion of images of Whiteness in local advertising. I bemoaned, "What is happening to my home?" The America from which I had escaped to come home was now here in my intimate space, and my place of refuge was under assault. What I was witnessing in Pune, Mumbai, and Delhi was a carving out of visual and geographic spaces that were marked as global or transnational to be mostly consumed by the upper-class youth. These posters symbolized the dreams and aspirations of the urban youth, where images of White women in ostentatious costumes symbolized permission to have fun, drink, and break rules. The DJ music scene was quite popular in Pune's bars and nightclubs, and some DJs attracted much bigger crowds that others. The sociocultural trajectory of globalization had reorganized the cultural activities in urban Pune and had created a segmented visual culture and an uneven social geography. Through its spatially expansive networks, globalization was carving out new visual images of hip-ness, happi-ness, and coolness to "interpellate" the urban youth.

Loss of Culture and Home

The concept of home, as Shelley Mallet (2004) notes,

> raises the question whether or not home is (a) place(s), (a) space(s), feeling(s), practices, and/or an active state of being in the world? Home is variously described in the literature as conflated with or related to house, family, haven, self, gender, and journeying. (p. 62)

While capturing the visual landscape of Pune, I felt I was journeying into an unfamiliar public culture but a very familiar geography. I lamented to my friends that the familiar signposts and landmarks in Pune were being torn down with every passing year. For some of my participants and friends, India was coming out of its old traditional shell. What caused an interior consterna-tion was that some Indians who were also witness to these remarkable changes seemed defiantly buoyant and did not grumble much about the new Pune. To them and many others who had stayed, Pune was bubbling with future pros-pects, brilliantly shining in the afterglow of IT sectors, high-class restaurants, and slick Bollywood films.

Where I saw erasures of my old life in India, many of my participants saw progress and told me repeatedly that India was a different place now and in some way it had "arrived." Their positive outlook was reflected in the idea that globalization and modernity had come to them. They did not have to go any-where to feel modern. I was the one who had left India to discover Western modernity, but they just stayed and now they have access to Indian moder-nity. My young participants told me stories not only about how their lives were changing but also how they were negotiating this contact with Western and American culture. On other occasions, most parents with whom I spoke blamed the American media for loss of culture in India and the corruption of Indian youth.

America was admired by many for its world-class facilities and as a country that was seen as "highly advanced" while it was simultaneously dismissed as highly materialistic, arrogant, and war hungry. America was often viewed as a country in which most marriages resulted in divorce, the elderly were impris-oned in assisted facilities, parents encouraged their children to leave home after they had graduated from college, racism was rampant, and Indians lived as successful model minorities and as second-class citizens. These imagina-tions about American culture played an important role in shaping their ideas of Indianness.

The fundamental self-reflexive question in doing classical, colonial ethnography from mainly a Western perspective was guided by the following questions: "How do I capture cultural difference?" and "How do I describe the other?" When fieldwork becomes homework (Visweswaran, 1994), the self-reflexive question changes. Clifford (1986) argues that ethnography in the current context is akin to "alliance building" with participants and with the culture in which the ethnography is being done. The question then becomes, How can the context of alliance with the local networks be managed, negotiated, and articulated without claiming complete objective distance or complete intimacy? Clifford also writes that ethnography in the moment of blurred genres and the self-reflexive turn signals a shift from rapport to alliance and from *representation* to *articulation*.

Questions about self-reflexivity and articulation become far more complicated when postcolonial scholars such as myself return to study and do fieldwork in the places they were raised and return to it as both insiders and outsiders and from both "here" and "there." Vamsee Juluri (1998) notes that postcolonial scholars share the "burden and privilege of certain kinds of colonized and racialized subjectivities" that allow them to speak as "both insiders and outsiders and as transnational intellectuals and as representatives of specific national and/or local constituencies" (p. 86). Following Voloder (2008), I argue that the insights gleaned from doing insider research at home do not necessarily have to

rely on assumptions of shared experiences and identifications between oneself and participants, but rather that it is in the exploration of the convergences and divergences in these experiences and identification that the researcher's experiential self can be used as a key heuristic source. (p. 28)

In particular, it is through my different forms of positions in the field and through the various intersections between my personal story and the stories of my participants that I was able to produce qualitative forms of cultural knowledge about how the global, national, and local cultures were interacting together to create new narratives of self and other in urban India. Instead of attempting neutrality and distancing myself from my research observations, I did as Cohen (1992) has suggested: I exploited "the intrusive self as an ethnographic resource rather than suffer it as a methodological hindrance" (p. 226). If narrative psychology is about the investigation of self and other relationships, then I think it is legitimate to integrate one's experiential, self-reflexive knowledge in the process of understanding how others make sense of the world. This is not a self-reflexivity that becomes narcissistic but, instead, it shows how narrative theory and method can productively investigate the paradoxes and tensions between the personal and cultural worlds of the research subjects and the researcher.

NOTES

1. This was a vernacular term used by most working-class youth to define youth from upper and middle classes. Hifi youth have come to symbolize ostentatious displays of material wealth, riding in a car with a well-dressed girlfriend or boyfriend, going out to pubs, drinking alchohol, having a carefree attitude, and speaking English.
2. The term *basti* is used in Hindi to refer to a settlement. Following Srivastava (2015), I adopt this term "in preference to 'slum' in order to avoid spurious judgments regarding illegality, criminality, and lack of industriousness inherent within such spaces" (p. 5).

REFERENCES

Ablett, J., Baijal, A., Beinhocker, E., Bose, A., Farrell, D., Gersch, U., ... Gupta, S. (2007, March). *The "bird of gold": The rise of India's consumer market*. San Francisco, CA: McKinsey Global Institute. Retrieved from http://www.mckinsey.com/global-themes/asia-pacific/the-bird-of-gold

Abraham, L. (2004). Redrawing the Laxman Rekha: Gender differences and cultural constructions in youth sexuality in urban India. In S. Srivastava (Ed.), *Sexual sites, seminal attitudes: Sexualities, masculinities and culture in South Asia* (pp. 2011–2041). New Delhi, India: Sage.

Adams, G., Dobles, I., Gómez, L. H., Kurtis, T., & Molina, L. E. (2015). Decolonizing psychological science. *Journal of Political and Social Psychology, 3*, 213–238.

Ambedkar, B. (1971). *Annihilation of caste*. Jullundur, Punjab, India: Bheem Patrika.

Amit, V. (2000). Introduction: Constructing the field. In V. Amit (Ed.), *Constructing the field: Ethnographic fieldwork in the contemporary world* (pp. 1–18). London, UK: Routledge.

Anderson, B. (1991). *Imagined communities*. London, UK: Verso.

Andrews, M. (2014). *Narrative imagination and everyday life*. New York, NY: Oxford University Press.

Anzaldua, G. (1987). *Borderlands/la frontera*. San Francisco, CA: Spinsters/Aunt Lute Press.

Appadurai, A. (1996). *Modernity at large: Cultural dimensions of globalization*. Minneapolis, MN: University of Minnesota Press.

Appadurai, A. (2006). *Fear of small numbers. An essay on the geography of anger*. Durham, NC: Duke University Press.

Appadurai, A. (2013). *The future as a cultural fact: Essays on the global condition*. New York, NY: Verso.

Arnett, J. J. (2002). The psychology of globalization. *American Psychologist, 57*, 774–783.

Arnett, J. J. (2008). The neglected 95%: Why American psychology needs to be less American. *American Psychologist, 63*, 602–614.

Ashmore, R. D., & Jussim, L. (1997). Toward a second century of the scientific analysis of self and identity. In R. D. Ashmore & L. Jussim (Eds.), *Self and identity: Fundamental issues* (pp. 1–22). New York, NY: Oxford University Press.

Auge, M. (2008). *Non-places: Introduction to an anthropology of supermodernity*. London, UK: Verso.

Bakhtin, M. M. (1981). *The dialogic imagination*. Austin, TX: University of Texas Press.

Bamberg, M. (2006). Big or small, why do we care? *Narrative Inquiry, 16*, 139–147.

Bamberg, M. (2011). Who am I: Narration and its contribution to self and identity. *Theory and Psychology, 21,* 3–24.

Banerjee-Guha, S. (2010). Transformative cities in a new global order. In S. Banerjee-Guha (Ed.), *Accumulation by dispossession: Transformative cities in a new global order* (pp. 1–16). New York, NY: Sage.

Banerji, A., & Duflo, E. (2011). *Poor economics: A radical rethinking of the way to fight global poverty.* New York, NY: Public Affairs.

Barthes, R. (1975). *The pleasure of the text* (R. Miller, Trans.). New York, NY: Hill & Wang.

Basi, T. J. K. (2009). *Women, identity and India's call center industry.* London, UK: Routledge.

Bauemister, R. F., & Tierney, J. (2011). *Willpower: Rediscovering the greatest human strength.* London, UK: Allen Lane.

Baviskar, A., & Ray, R. (2011). Introduction. In A. Baviskar & R. Ray (Eds.), *Elite and everyman: The cultural politics of Indian middle classes* (pp. 1–26). New Delhi, India: Routledge.

Beasley-Murray, J. (2000). Value and capital in Bourdieu and Marx. In N. Brown & I. Szeman (Eds.), *Pierre Bourdieu: Field work in culture* (pp. 100–122). Boston, MA: Rowman & Littlefield.

Behar, R. (1995). Introduction: Out of exile. In R. Behar & D. A. Gordon (Eds.), *Women: Writing culture* (pp. 1–29). Los Angeles, CA: University of California Press.

Behar, R. (1996). *The vulnerable observer: Anthropology that breaks your heart.* Boston, MA: Beacon.

Beck, U., & Beck-Gernsheim, E. (2002). *Individualization: Institutionalized individualism and its social and political consequences.* London, UK: Sage.

Bell, L. (2007). Theoretical foundations for social justice education. In M. Adams & L. Bell (Eds.), *Teaching for diversity and social justice* (pp. 1–14). New York, NY: Routledge.

Benham, M. K. P. (2007). Mo'olelo: On culturally relevant story making from an indigenous perspective. In D. J. Clandinin (Ed.), *Handbook of narrative inquiry: Mapping a methodology* (pp. 512–534). Thousand Oaks, CA: Sage.

Berry, J., Poortinga, Y., Segall, M., & Dasen, P. (1992). *Cross-cultural psychology: Research and applications.* Cambridge, UK: Cambridge University Press.

Bhabha, H. (1990). DissemiNation: Time, narrative, and the margins of modern nation. In H. K. Bhabha (Ed.), *Nation and narration* (pp. 291–322). London, UK: Oxford University Press.

Bhabha, H. (1994). *The location of culture.* New York, NY: Routledge.

Bhatia, S. (2002). Orientalism in Euro-American and Indian psychology: Historical representation of "natives" in colonial and postcolonial contexts. *History of Psychology, 5,* 376–398.

Bhatia, S. (2006). Reinterpreting the inner self in global India: "Malevolent mothers," "distant fathers," and the development of children's identity. *Culture and Psychology, 12,* 378–392.

Bhatia, S. (2007). *American karma: Race, culture, and identity in the Indian diaspora.* New York, NY: New York University Press.

Bhatia, S. (2008a). Rethinking culture and identity in psychology: Towards a transnational cultural Psychology. *Journal of Theoretical and Philosophical Psychology, 28,* 301–321.

Bhatia, S. (2008b). 9/11 and the Indian diaspora: Narratives of race, place and immigrant identity. *Journal of Intercultural Studies, 29,* 31–39.

Bhatia, S. (2010a). Theorizing cultural psychology in transnational contexts. In S. Kirschner & J. Martin (Eds.), *The sociocultural turn in psychology: Emergence of mind and self in context* (pp. 204–227). New York, NY: Columbia University Press.

Bhatia, S. (2010b). Interpreting the meanings of schooling, hybridity, and multicultural citizenship in diaspora communities. *Teachers College Record, 112*(13), 66–81.

Bhatia, S. (2011). Narrative inquiry as cultural psychology: Meaning-making in a contested global world. *Narrative Inquiry, 21*, 345–352.

Bhatia, S. (2013). Religious identity on the peripheries: The dialogical self in a global world. In H. Zock & M. Buitelaar (Eds.), *Religious voices in self-narratives: Making sense of life in times of transitions* (pp. 215–240). Berlin, Germany: De Gruyter.

Bhatia, S. (2014a). Orientalism. In T. Teo (Ed.), *Encyclopedia of critical psychology* (pp. 1294–1300). New York, NY: Springer.

Bhatia, S. (2014b). *Critical psychology: Can knowledge become power?* Invited paper presented at the launch of the *Encyclopedia of Critical Psychology*, City University of New York, New York, NY, September.

Bhatia, S. (2015). *Entangled marginality and qualitative inquiry.* Invited talk presented at the annual meeting of the Society for Qualitative Inquiry in Psychology, New York, NY.

Bhatia, S., & Ram, A. (2001). Rethinking "acculturation" in relation to diasporic cultures and postcolonial identities. *Human Development, 44*, 1–17.

Bhatia, S., & Ram, A. (2004). Culture, hybridity and the dialogical self: Cases from the South-Asian diaspora. *Mind, Culture and Activity, 11*, 224–240.

Bhatia, S., & Ram, A. (2009). Theorizing identity in transnational and diaspora: A critical approach to acculturation. *International Journal for Intercultural Research, 33*, 14–149.

Bhatia, S., & Stam, H. (2005). Editorial: Critical engagements with culture and self. *Theory and Psychology, 15*, 419–430.

Binkley, S. (2014). *Happiness as enterprise: An essay on neoliberal life.* Albany, NY: State University of New York Press.

Bochner, A. (1997). It's about time: Narrative and the divided self. *Qualitative Inquiry, 3*, 418–439.

Bochner, A. (2014). *Coming to narrative: A personal history if paradigm change in the human sciences.* Walnut Creek, CA: Left Coast Press.

Boo, K. (2012). *Behind the beautiful forevers: Life, death, and hope in a Mumbai undercity.* New York, NY: Random House.

Bourdieu, P. (1994). *Language and symbolic power* (G. Raymond & M. Adamson, Trans.). Cambridge, MA: Harvard University Press.

Boussebaa, M., Sinha, S., & Gabriel, Y. (2014). Englishization in offshore call centers: A postcolonial perspective. *Journal of International Business Studies, 45*, 1152–1169.

Brock, A. C. (Ed.). (2006). *Internationalizing the history of psychology.* New York, NY: New York University Press.

Brockmeier, J. (2009). Reaching for meaning: Human agency and the narrative imagination. *Theory and Psychology, 19*, 213–233.

Brockmeier, J. (2012). Narrative scenarios: Toward a culturally thick notion of narrative. In J. Valsiner (Ed.), *The Oxford handbook of culture and psychology* (pp. 439–467). New York, NY: Oxford University Press.

Brockmeier, J. (2014). Narrative psychology. In T. Teo (Ed.), *Encyclopedia of critical psychology* (pp. 1218–1220). New York, NY: Springer.

Brodie, J. (2007). Reforming social justice in neoliberal times. *Studies in Social Justice*, *1*, 93–107.

Bruner, J. (1986). *Actual minds, possible worlds*. Cambridge, MA: Harvard University Press.

Bruner, J. (1990). *Acts of meaning*. Cambridge, MA: Harvard University Press.

Bruner, J. (1991). The narrative construction of reality. *Critical Inquiry*, *18*, 1–21.

Bulhan, H. A. (1985). *Frantz Fanon and the psychology of oppression*. New York, NY: Plenum.

Bulhan, H. A. (2015). Stages of colonialism in Africa: From occupation of land to occupation of being. *Journal of Social and Political Psychology*, *3*, 239–256.

Burawoy, M., Blum, J. A., George, S., Gille, Z., Teresa, G., Lynne, H., Klawiter, M., Lopez, S., O'Riaian and Thayer, M. (2000). *Global ethnography: Forces, connection, and imaginations in a postmodern world*. Berkeley, CA: University of California Press.

Burke, K. (1969). *A rhetoric of motives*. Berkeley, CA: University of California Press.

Burman, E. (1994). *Deconstructing developmental psychology*. East Sussex, UK: Psychology Press.

Burman, E. (2007). Between orientalism and normalization: Cross-cultural lessons from Japan for a critical history of psychology. *History of Psychology*, *10*, 179–198.

Cancilini, N. G. (1995). *Strategies for entering and leaving modernity*. Minneapolis, MN: University of Minnesota Press.

Carr, D. (1986). *Time, narrative, and history*. Bloomington, IN: Indiana University Press.

Castells, M. (1996). *The rise of the network society*. Oxford, UK: Blackwell.

Chacko, E., & Varghese, P. (2009). Identity and representation of gated communities in Bangalore, India. *Open House International*, *34*(3), 57–64.

Chadha, N. (2011). Social–emotional development in the cultural context. In G. Misra (Ed.), *Oxford handbook of psychology in India* (pp. 181–192). New Delhi, India: Oxford University Press.

Chakrabarty, D. (2000). *Provincializing Europe: Postcolonial thought and historical difference*. Princeton, NJ: Princeton University Press.

Chambers, L. (2007, October). If India were a woman, how would you dress her? *Vogue*, p. 53.

Charmaz, K. (2001). Qualitative interviewing and grounded theory analysis. In J. F. Gubrium & J. A. Holstein (Eds.), *Handbook of interview research: context & method* (pp. 675–694). Thousand Oaks, CA: Sage.

Chatterjee, P. (1993). *The nation and its fragments: Colonial and postcolonial histories*. Princeton, NJ: Princeton University Press.

Chaudhary, N. (2004). *Listening to culture: Constructing reality from everyday talk*. New Delhi, India: Sage.

Chaudhary, N. (2011). Rethinking human development research and theory in contemporary Indian society. In G. Misra (Ed.), *Oxford handbook of psychology in India* (pp. 165–180). New Delhi, India: Oxford University Press.

Chaudhary, N. (2012). Negotiating with autonomy and relatedness: Dialogical processes in everyday lives of Indians. In H. J. M. Hermans & T. Gieser (Eds.), *Handbook of dialogical self theory* (pp. 169–184). Cambridge, UK: Cambridge University Press.

Chhabria, S. (2016). Inequality in the era of convergence. Using global histories to challenge globalization discourse, 13. http://worldhistoryconnected.press.illinois.edu/13.2/

Christopher, J. C., Wendt, D. C., Marecek, J., & Goodman, D. M. (2014). Critical cultural awareness: Contributions to a globalizing psychology. *American Psychologist*, *69*, 645–655.

Clandinin, D. J. (2007) (ed.). *Handbook of narrative inquiry: Mapping a methodology*. Thousand Oaks, CA: Sage Publications.

Clandinin, J. D., & Rosiek, J. (2007). Mapping a landscape of narrative inquiry: Borderland spaces and tensions. In D. J. Clandinin (Ed.), *Handbook of narrative inquiry: Mapping a methodology* (pp. 35–75). Thousand Oaks, CA: Sage.

Clifford, J. (1986). Introduction: Partial truths. In J. Clifford & G. E. Marcus (Eds.), *Writing culture: The poetics of ethnography* (pp. 1–26). Berkeley, CA: University of California Press.

Clifford, J., & Marcus, G. E. (Eds.). (1986). *Writing culture: The poetics of ethnography*. Berkeley, CA: University of California Press.

Cohen, A. (1992). Self-conscious anthropology. In J. Okely & H. Callaway (Eds.), *Anthropology and autobiography* (pp. 221–241). New York, NY: Routledge.

Cohler, B. (1982). Personal narrative and life course. In P. Baltes & O. G. Brim (Eds.), *Lifespan development and behavior* (Vol. 4, pp. 205–241). New York, NY: Academic Press.

Cole, E. (2009). Intersectionality and research in psychology. *American Psychologist, 64,* 170–180.

Cole, M. (1996). *Cultural psychology: A once and future discipline*. Cambridge, MA: Belknap.

Coulthard, S. G. (2014). *Red Skin, white Masks: Rejecting the colonial politics of recognition*. Minneapolis, MN: University of Minnesota Press.

Crenshaw, K. W. (1994). Mapping the margins: Intersectionality, identity politics, and violence against women of color. In M. A. Fineman & R. Mykitiuk (Eds.), *The public nature of private violence* (pp. 93–118). New York, NY: Routledge.

Creswell, J. (2013). *Qualitative inquiry and research design: Choosing among five approaches*. Thousand Oaks, CA: Sage.

Cushman, P. (1990). Why the self is empty. *American Psychologist, 45,* 599–611.

Daiute, C. (2014). *Narrative inquiry: A dynamic Approach*. Thousand Oaks, CA: Sage.

Dalal, A. K., & Misra, G. (2010). The core and context of Indian psychology. *Psychology & Developing Societies, 22,* 121–155.

Danzinger, K. (1990). *Constructing the subject: Historical origins of psychological research*. Cambridge, UK: Cambridge University Press.

Darwin, C. (1888). *The descent of man and selection in relation to sex* (Vol. 1). London, UK: John Murray. (Original work published 1871)

Darwin, C. (1958). *The origin of species*. New York: Penguin. (Original work published 1859)

Das, G. (2002). *India unbound*. New York, NY: Anchor Books.

Dasgupta, P. (2007, October). If India were a woman, how would you dress her? *Vogue*, p. 52.

Dasra. (2012). *Squatting rights: Access to toilets in urban India*. Mumbai, India: Author.

David, E. J. R. (2011). *Filipino-American postcolonial psychology: Oppression, colonial mentality, and decolonization*. Bloomington, IN: Author House.

Davis, M. (2007). *Planet of the slums*. New York, NY: Verso.

Day, J., & Tappan, M. B. (1996). The narrative approach to moral development: From the epistemic subject to dialogical selves. *Human Development, 39,* 67–82.

De, S. (2007, October). If India were a woman, how would you dress her? *Vogue*, p. 52.

De Vos, J. (2012). *Psychologisation in times of globalisation*. London, UK: Routledge.

Delpit, L. (1995). *Other people's children*. New York, NY: The New Press.

Denzin, N. K. (1997). *Interpretive ethnography: Ethnographic practices for the 21st century*. Thousand Oaks, CA: Sage.

Denzin, N., & Lincoln, Y. (Eds.). (1994). *The Sage handbook of qualitative research*. Thousand Oaks, CA: Sage.

Denzin, N. K., & Lincoln, Y. (2005). Introduction: The discipline and practice of qualitative research. In N. Denzin & Y. Lincoln (Eds.), *The Sage handbook of qualitative research* (3rd ed., pp. 1–32). Thousand Oaks, CA: Sage.

Derne, S. (2008). *Globalization on the ground: New media and the transformation of culture, class, and gender in India*. New Delhi, India: Sage.

Desai, M. (2013). Psychology, the psychological, and critical praxis: A phenomenologist reads Frantz Fanon. *Theory and Psychology, 24*(1), 58–75.

Deshpande, S. (2003). *Contemporary India: A sociological view*. New Delhi, India: Viking.

Dirks, N. (2001). *Castes of mind: Colonialism and the making of modern India*. Princeton, NJ: Princeton University Press.

Dixon, J., Tropp, L. R., Durrheim, K., & Tredoux, C. G. (2010). "Let them eat harmony": Prejudice-reduction strategies and attitudes of historically disadvantaged groups. *Current Directions in Psychological Science, 19*, 76–80.

Donner, H., & Neve, D. G. (2011). Introduction. In H. Donner (Ed.), *Being middle class in India: A way of life* (pp. 1–22). Oxon, UK: Routledge.

Dreze, J., & Sen, A. (2013). *An uncertain glory: India and its contradictions*. Princeton, NJ: Princeton University Press.

Driscoll, C. (2002). *Girls: Feminine adolescence in popular culture and cultural theory*. New York, NY: Columbia University Press.

Dudgeon, P., & Walker, R. (2015). Decolonizing Australian psychology: Discourses, strategies, and practice. *Journal of Social and Political Psychology, 3*, 276–297.

Dutt, G. (1959). *Kagaz Ke Phool*. India. Guru Dutt Films Private.

Dutta, U. (2015). The long way home: The vicissitudes of belonging and otherness in northeast India. *Qualitative Inquiry, 21*, 161–172.

Ehrenreich, B., & Hochschild, R. A. (2002). *Global woman: Nannies, maids, and sex workers in the new economy*. New York, NY: Holt.

Enriquez, V. G. (1992). *From colonial to liberation psychology: The Philippine experience*. Diliman, Quezon City, the Philippines: University of the Philippines Press.

Erikson, E. (1963). *Childhood and society*. New York, NY: Norton.

Erikson, E. (1968). *Identity: Youth and crisis*. New York, NY: Norton.

Fanon, F. (1963). *The wretched of the earth* (C. Farrington, Trans.). New York, NY: Grove Press. (Original work published 1961)

Fanon, F. (1967). *Black skin, white masks* (C. L. Markmann, Trans.). New York, NY: Pluto Press. (Original work published 1952)

Fernandes, L. (2011). Hegemony and inequality: Theoretical reflections on India's "new" middle class. In A. Baviskar & R. Ray (Eds.), *Elite and everyman: The cultural politics of Indian middle classes* (pp. 58–82). New Delhi, India: Routledge.

Fine, M. (2006). Bearing witness: Methods for researching oppression and resistance—A textbook for critical research. *Social Justice Research, 19*, 83–108.

Fine, M. (2013). Echoes of Bedford: A 20-year social psychology memoir on participatory action research hatched behind bars. *American Psychologist, 68*, 687–698.

Fine, M., & Ruglis, J. (2009). Circuits and consequences of dispossession: The racialized realignment of the public sphere for US youth. *Transforming Anthropology, 17*, 20–33.

Fine, M., & Sirin, K. (2007). Theorizing hyphenated selves: Researching youth development in and across contentious political contexts. *Social and Personality Psychology Compass, 1*(1), 16–38.

Fine, M., & Torre, M. E. (2006). Intimate details: Action research in prison. *Action Research, 4,* 253–269.

Fine, M., & Weis, L. (2005). Compositional studies, in two parts. In N. Denzin & Y. Lincoln (Eds.), *Handbook of qualitative research* (3rd ed., pp. 65–84). Thousand Oaks, CA: Sage.

Fivush, R., & Nelson, K. (2004). Culture and language in the emergence of autobiographical memory. *Psychological Science, 15,* 586–590.

Flew, T. (2014). Six theories of neoliberalism. *Thesis Eleven, 122,* 49–71.

Foucault, M. (1982). *The archaeology of knowledge and the discourse on language.* New York, NY: Vintage.

Foucault, M. (1988). *Technologies of the self.* Boston, MA: University of Massachusetts Press.

Foucault, M. (2008). *The birth of biopolitics: Lectures at the Collège de France 1978–1979.* Basingstoke, UK: Palgrave Macmillan.

Fox, D., & Prilleltensky, I. (Eds.). (1997). *Critical psychology: An introduction.* London, UK: Sage.

Frank, A. (2012). Practicing dialogical narrative analysis. In J. A. Holstein & J. F. Gubrium (Eds.), *Varieties of narrative analysis.* Thousand Oaks, CA: Sage.

Fraser, N. (2009). *Scales of justice: Reimagining justice in a globalizing world.* New York, NY: Columbia University Press.

Freeman, M. (1993). *Rewriting the self: History, memory, narrative.* London, UK: Routledge.

Freeman, M. (1997). Why narrative? Hermeneutics, historical understanding, and the significance of stories. *Journal of Narrative and Life History, 7,* 169–176.

Freeman, M. (2007). Autobiographical understanding and narrative inquiry. In D. J. Clandinin (Ed.), *Handbook of narrative inquiry: Mapping a methodology* (pp. 489–511). Thousand Oaks, CA: Sage.

Freeman, M. (2010). *Hindsight: The promise and peril of looking backward.* New York, NY: Oxford University Press.

Freeman, M. (2011). Stories, big and small: Toward a synthesis. *Theory and Psychology, 21,* 114–121.

Freeman, M. (2013). Qualitative inquiry and the self-realization of psychological science. *Qualitative Inquiry, 20,* 1–8.

Freeman, M. (2014). *The priority of the other. Thinking and living beyond the self.* New York, NY: Oxford University Press.

Friedman, T. (2004, June 24). Doing our homework. *The New York Times.* Retrieved from http://www.nytimes.com/2004/06/24/opinion/doing-our-homework.html?_r=0

Galton, F. (1883). *Hereditary genius: An inquiry into its law and consequences.* New York, NY: Appleton.

Gandhi, L. (1998). *Postcolonial theory: A critical introduction.* New York, NY: Columbia University Press.

Gandhi, M. (1997). *Hind Swaraj and other writings* (A. J. Parel, Ed.). Cambridge, UK: Cambridge University Press. (Original work published 1909)

Gaonkar, D. P. (2001). On alternative modernities. In D. P. Gaonkar (Ed.), *Alternative modernities* (pp. 1–23). Durham, NC: Duke University Press.

Gee, J. (1992). *The social mind: Language, ideology, and practice.* Westport, CT: Bergin & Gravey.

Gee, J. P. (1999). *An introduction to discourse analysis: Theory and method.* New York, NY: Routledge.

Geertz, C. (1973). *The interpretation of cultures*. New York, NY: Basic Books.

Georgakopoulou, A. (2007). *Small stories, interaction, and identities*. Amsterdam, the Netherlands: Benjamins.

Gergen, K. J. (1999). *Invitation to social constructionism*. London, UK: Sage.

Gergen, K. J. (2014a). Pursuing excellence in qualitative inquiry. *Qualitative Psychology, 1*, 49–60.

Gergen, K. J. (2014b). From mirroring to world-making: Research as future forming. *Journal for the Theory of Social Behaviour, 45*, 287–310.

Gergen, K. J., Gulerce, A., Lock, A., & Misra, G. (1996). Psychological science in cultural context. *American Psychologist, 51*, 496–503.

Gergen, K. J., Josselson, R., & Freeman, M. (2015). The promise of qualitative inquiry. *American Psychologist, 70*, 1–9.

Gergen, M. M., & Gergen, K. J. (1984). The social construction of narrative accounts. In K. Gergen & M. Gergen (Eds.), *Historical social psychology* (pp. 173–190). Hillsdale, NJ: Erlbaum.

Giddens, A. (1991). *Modernity and self-identity: Self and society in late modern age*. Stanford, CA: Stanford University Press.

Gjerde, P. F. (2004). Culture, power, and experience: Toward a person-centered cultural psychology. *Human Development, 47*, 138–157.

Gjerde, P. F., & Onishi, M. (2000). Selves, cultures and nations: The psychological imagination of "the Japanese" in the era of globalization. *Human Development, 43*, 216–226.

Goffman, E. (1959). *The presentation of self in everyday life*. New York, NY: Random House.

Good, M. J. D., Hyde, S. T., Pinto, S., & Good, B. (Eds.). (2008). *Postcolonial disorders*. Berkeley, CA: University of California Press.

Gough, B., McFadden, M., & McDonald, M. (2013). *Critical social psychology: An introduction* (2nd ed.). Houndmills, UK: Palgrave Macmillan.

Gould, S. (1981). *The mismeasure of man*. New York, NY: Norton.

Gramsci, A. (1971). *Selections from the Prison Notebook* (Q. Hoare & G. N. Smith, Eds. & Trans.). London, UK: Lawrence & Wishart.

Grande, S. (2015). *Red Pedagogy: Native American Political and Social Thought* (2nd Edition). Lanham, MD: Rowman and Littlefield.

Granek, L. (2013). Putting ourselves on the line: The epistemology of the hyphen, intersubjectivity and social responsibility in qualitative research. *International Journal of Qualitative Studies in Education, 26*(2), 178–197.

Greene, M. (1995). *Releasing the imagination: Essays on education, arts, and social change*. San Francisco: Josey-Bass Publishers.

Gregg, G. (2005). *The Middle-East: A cultural psychology*. New York: NY, Oxford University Press.

Grosfoguel, R. (2007). The epistemic decolonial turn. *Cultural Studies, 21*, 211–223.

Gubrium, J. F., & Holstein, J. A. (2004). From the individual interview to the interview society. In J. F. Gubrium & J. A. Holstein (Eds.), *Handbook of interview research: Context & method* (pp. 3–32). Thousand Oaks, CA: Sage.

Gubrium, J. F., & Holstein, J. A. (2007). The construction mosaic. In J. F. Gubrium & J. A. Holstein (Eds.), *Handbook of constructionist research*. New York, NY: Guilford.

Gudykunst, W., & Kim, Y. Y. (1997). *Communicating with strangers: An approach to intercultural communication* (3rd ed.). New York, NY: McGraw-Hill.

Guha, R. (1998). *Subaltern studies VI*. Delhi, India: Oxford University Press.

Gupta, A., & Ferguson, J. (1992). Beyond "culture": Space, identity, and the politics of difference. *Cultural Anthropology, 7*, 6–23.

Haddi, M. (2007, October). If India were a woman, how would you dress her? *Vogue*, p. 53.

Hall, G. S. (1904). *Adolescence: Its psychology and its relations to physiology, anthropology, sociology, sex, crime, religion, and education.* New York, NY: Appleton.

Hall, S. (1991a). Old and new identities, old and new ethnicities. In A. D. King (Ed.), *Culture, globalization, and the world-system: Contemporary conditions for the representation of identity* (pp. 41–68). Binghamton, NY: State University of New York Press.

Hall, S. (1991b). The local and the global: Globalization and ethnicity. In A. D. King (Ed.), *Culture, globalization, and the world-system: Contemporary conditions for the representation of identity* (pp. 19–39). Binghamton, NY: State University of New York Press.

Hall, S. (1993). Culture, community, nation. *Cultural Studies, 7*(3), 349–363.

Hall, S. (1996). "New ethnicities." In D. Morley & K Chen (Eds.), *Critical dialogues in cultural studies* (pp. 441–449). London, UK: Routledge.

Hammack, P. L. (2008). Narrative and the cultural psychology of identity. *Personality and Social Psychology Review, 12,* 222–247.

Hammack, P. L. (2011). *Narrative and the politics of identity: The cultural psychology of Israeli and Palestinian youth.* New York, NY: Oxford University Press.

Harding, S. (1987). Introduction: Is there a feminist method? In S. Harding (Ed.), *Feminism and methodology* (pp. 1–14). Bloomington, IN: Indiana University Press

Harré, R., & Gillett, G. (1994). *The discursive mind.* Thousand Oaks, CA: Sage.

Harvey, D. (1990). *The condition of postmodernity.* Oxford, UK: Blackwell.

Harvey, D. (2000). *Spaces of hope.* Berkeley, CA: University of California Press.

Harvey, D. (2005). *A brief history of neoliberalism.* New York, NY: Oxford University Press.

Hayden, M. E. (2013, January). Home space. *The Open Magazine,* pp. 60–62.

Hegde, R. (2011). Introduction. In R. Hegde (Ed.), *Circuits of visibility: Gender and transnational media cultures* (pp. 1–20). New York, NY: New York University Press.

Henrich, J., Heine, S. J., & Norenzayan, A. (2010). The weirdest people in the world? *Behavioral and Brain Sciences, 33,* 61–83.

Hermans, H. J. M. (1996). Voicing the self: From information processing to dialogical interchange. *Psychological Bulletin, 119,* 31–50.

Hermans, H. J. M., & Dimaggio, G. (2007). Self, identity, and globalization in times of uncertainty: A dialogical analysis. *Review of General Psychology, 11,* 31–61.

Hermans, H. J. M., & Hermans-Konopka, A. (2010). *Positioning and counter-positioning in a globalizing society.* Cambridge, UK: Cambridge University Press.

Hermans, H. J. M., & Kempen, H. J. G. (1993). *The dialogical self: Meaning as movement.* San Diego, CA: Academic Press.

Hermans, H. J. M., & Kempen, H. J. G. (1998). Moving cultures: The perilous problems of cultural dichotomies in a globalizing society. *American Psychologist, 53,* 1111–1120.

Hirschman, A. O. (1970). *Exit, voice, and loyalty: Responses to decline in firms, organizations, and states.* Cambridge, MA. Harvard University Press.

Hochschild, A. R. (1983). *The managed heart.* Berkeley, CA: University of California Press.

Hofstede, G. (1980). *Culture's consequences: International differences in work-related values.* Beverly Hills, CA: Sage.

Hofstede G. (1997). *Cultures and organizations: Software of the mind.* New York, NY: McGraw-Hill.

Hook, D. (2012). *A critical psychology of the postcolonial: The mind of apartheid.* New York, NY: Routledge.

hooks, b. (1990). *Yearning: Race, gender, and cultural politics.* Boston, MA: South End Press.

Hyvärinen, M. (2012). Prototypes, genres, and concepts: Traveling with narratives. *Narrative Works: Issues, Investigations, & Interventions, 2,* 10–32.

Inda, X. J., & Rosaldo, R. (2002). A world in motion. In J. X. Inda & R. Rosaldo (Eds.), *The anthropology of globalization: A reader* (pp. 1–35). Oxford, UK: Blackwell.

Jackson, M. (2002). *The politics of story telling: Violence, transgressing, and intersubjectivity.* Copenhagen, Denmark: Museum Tusculanum Press.

Jackson, Y. A., & Mazzei, L. A. (2013). Plugging one text into another: Thinking with theory in qualitative research. *Qualitative Inquiry, 19,* 261–271.

Jafferlot, C., & van der Veer, P. (Eds.). (2008). *Patterns of middle class consumption in India and China.* New Delhi, India: Sage.

James, W. (1890). *Principles of psychology.* New York, NY: Holt.

Jenkins, D. L. (2003). *Identity and identification in India: Defining the disadvantaged.* London, UK: Routledge.

Jensen, L. (2003). Coming of age in a multicultural world: Globalization and adolescent identity formation. *Applied Developmental Science, 3,* 189–196.

Johnson, R. (1993). Editor's introduction: Pierre Bourdieu on art, literature and culture. In P. Bourdieu (Ed.), *The field of cultural production* (pp. 1–25). New York, NY: Columbia University Press.

Joshi, H. (2011, September). Pune becomes a hot spot for German companies. *Business Standard.* Retrieved from http://www.business-standard.com/article/companies/pune-becomes-hot-spot-for-german-companies-111092700037_1.html

Joshi, P., Sen, S., & Hobson, J. (2002). Experiences with surveying and mapping Pune and Sangli slums on a geographical information system (GIS). *Environment and Urbanization, 2,* 225–240.

Josselson, R. (2013). *Interviewing for qualitative inquiry: A relational approach.* New York, NY: Guilford.

Josselson, R., & Lieblich, A. (Eds.). (1993). *The narrative study of lives* (Vol. 1). Thousand Oaks, CA: Sage.

Juluri, V. (1998). Globalizing audience studies: The audience and its landscape and living room wars. *Critical Studies in Mass Communication, 15,* 85–90.

Kagitçibasi, C. (1996). *Family and human development across cultures: A view from the other side.* Hillsdale, NJ: Erlbaum.

Kakar, S. (1996). *The Indian psyche.* New Delhi, India: Oxford University Press.

Kapur, P., & Misra, G. (2011). Social identity in India: Continuities and fractures. In G. Misra (Ed.), *Oxford handbook of psychology in India* (pp. 149–164). New Delhi, India: Oxford University Press.

Katz, C. (2004). *Growing up global: Economic restructuring and everyday lives.* Minneapolis, MN: University of Minnesota Press.

Khan, A. (2007). Good to think? Creolization, optimism, and agency. *Current Anthropology, 48,* 653–673.

Khilnani, S. (1997). *The idea of India.* New York, NY: Farrar, Strauss, & Giroux.

Kim, U., Yang, K. S., & Hwang, K. K. (Eds.). (2006). *456 Indigenous and cultural psychology: Understanding 457 people in context.* New York, NY: Springer.

Kinnvall, C. (2004). Globalization and religious nationalism: Self, identity, and the search for ontological security. *Political Psychology, 25,* 741–767.

Kirschner, S. (2015). Subjectivity as socioculturally constituted. In J. Martin, J. Sugarman, & K. Slaney (Eds.), *The Wiley handbook of theoretical and philosophical psychology: Methods, approaches, and new directions* (pp. 294–307). Oxford, UK: Wiley.

Kirschner, S. R., & Martin, J. (2010). The sociocultural turn in psychology: An introduction and invitation. In S. Kirschner & J. Martin (Eds.), *The sociocultural turn in psychology: The contextual emergence of mind and self* (pp. 1–27). New York: Columbia University Press.

Kraidy, M. (2005). *Hybridity or the cultural logic of globalization.* Philadelphia, PA: Temple University Press.

Kreiswirth, M. (1992). Trusting the tale: The narrative turn in human sciences. *New Literary History, 23,* 629–657.

Kumar, M. (2006). Rethinking psychology in India: Debating pasts and futures. *Annual Review of Critical Psychology, 5,* 236–256.

Kuruvilla, A. (2007, October). The burden of wealth. *Vogue,* pp. 148–150.

Ladson-Billings, G. (2000). Racialized discourses and ethnic epistemologies. In N. Denzin & Y. Lincoln (Eds.), *Handbook of qualitative research* (2nd ed., pp. 257–277). Thousand Oaks, CA: Sage.

Larson, R. (2002). Globalization, societal change, and new technologies: What they mean for the future of adolescence. *Journal of Research on Adolescence, 12,* 1–30.

Leiblich, A., & Josselson, R. (2012). Identity and narrative as root metaphors of personhood. In J. Martin & M. Bickhard (Eds.), *The psychology of personhood: Philosophical, historical, social-developmental, and narrative perspective* (pp. 203–222). Cambridge, UK: Cambridge University Press.

Lesko, N. (2012). *Act your age! A cultural construction of adolescence.* New York, NY: Routledge.

Liu, W. (2015). The embodied crises of neoliberal globalization: The lives and narratives of Filipina migrant domestic workers. *Women's Studies International Forum, 50,* 80–88.

Lukose, R. (2009). *Liberalization's children.* Durham, NC: Duke University Press.

Lykes, M. B., & Moane, G. (2009). Editors' introduction: Whither feminist liberation psychology? Critical explorations of feminist and liberation psychologies for a globalizing world. *Feminism & Psychology, 19,* 283–297.

Macaulay, T. B. (1972). Minute on Indian education. In J. Clive (Ed.), *Selected writings* (pp. 237–251). Chicago, IL: University of Chicago Press. (Original work published 1835)

MacIntyre, A. (1984). *After virtue: A study in moral theory* (2nd ed.). Notre Dame, IN: Notre Dame University Press.

Macleod, C. (2011). *"Adolescence," pregnancy and abortion: Constructing a threat of degeneration.* London, UK: Routledge.

Macleod, C., & Bhatia, S. (2008). Postcolonialism and psychology. In L. Willig & W. Stainton-Rogers (Eds.), *Qualitative research in psychology* (pp. 576–589). Thousand Oaks, CA: Sage.

Madan, T. N. (1989). Religion in India. *Daedalus, 118*(4), 114–146.

Madill, A., & Gough, B. (2008). Qualitative psychology and its place in psychological science. *Psychological Methods, 3,* 254–271.

Mahalingam, R. (2007). Essentialism, power, and the representation of social categories: A folk sociology perspective. *Human Development, 50,* 300–319.

Mahalingam, R. (2012). Misidentification, misembodiment and the paradox of being a model minority. *Sikh Formations: Religion, Culture, Theory, 8*(3), 299–304.

Maira, S., & Soep, E. (2004). United States of adolescence? Reconsidering youth culture studies. *Young: Nordic Journal of Youth Research, 3*, 245–269.

Maira, S., & Soep, E. (2005). Introduction. In S. Maira & E. Soep (Eds.), *Youthscapes: The popular, the national, the global* (pp. xv–xxxv). Philadelphia, PA: University of Pennsylvania Press.

Maldonado-Torres, N. (2007). On the coloniality of being: Contributions to the development of a concept. *Cultural Studies, 21*, 240–270.

Mallet, S. (2004). Understanding home: A critical review of the literature. *Sociological Review, 52*, 62–89.

Mander, H. (2015). *Looking away: Inequality, prejudice and indifference in new India*. New Delhi, India: Speaking Tiger.

Marantz, A. (2011, July/August). My summer at an Indian call center. *Mother Jones Magazine*, 1–4. Retrieved from http://www.motherjones.com/politics/2011/05/indian-call-center-americanization

Marcus, G. E. (1998). *Ethnography through thick & thin*. Princeton, NJ: Princeton University Press.

Marsella, A. J. (1985). Culture, self, and mental disorder. In A. J. Marsella, G. DeVos, & F. Hsu (Eds.), *Culture and self: Asian and Western perspectives* (pp. 281–308). London, UK: Tavistock.

Marsella, A. J. (1998). Toward a global-community psychology: Meeting the needs of changing world. *American Psychologist, 53*, 1282–1291.

Martin, J., Sugarman, J., & Hickinbottom, S. (2010). *Persons: Understanding psychological selfhood and agency*. New York, NY: Springer.

Martín-Baró, I. (1994). *Writings for a liberation psychology* (A. Aron & S. Corne, Trans.). Cambridge, MA: Harvard University Press.

Marx, K. (1906). *Capital: A critique of political economy, Volume I*. New York, NY: The Modern Library.

Mathur, N. (2010). Shopping malls, credit cards and global brands: Consumer culture and lifestyle of India's new middle class. *South Asia Research, 30*, 211–231.

Mazzarella, W. (2003). *Shoveling smoke: Advertising and globalization in contemporary India*. Durham, NC: Duke University Press.

McAdams, D. P. (1993). *The stories we live by: Personal myths and the making of the self*. New York, NY: Guilford.

McAdams, D. P. (1997). The case for unity in the (post)modern self: A modest proposal. In R. D. Ashmore & L. Jussim (Eds.), *Self and identity: Fundamental issues* (pp. 46–80). New York, NY: Oxford University Press.

McAdams, D. P. (2001). The psychology of life stories. *Review of General Psychology, 5*(2), 100–122.

McAdams, D. P. (2006). *The redemptive self: Stories Americans live by*. New York, NY: Oxford University Press.

McLean, K. C., & Pasupathi, M. (Eds.). (2013). *Narrative development in adolescence: Creating the storied self*. New York, NY: Springer.

Memmi, A. (1965). *The colonizer and the colonized*. Boston, MA: Beacon.

Mignolo, W. D. (2007). Introduction: Coloniality of power and de-colonial thinking. *Cultural Studies, 21*, 155–167.

Mignolo, W. D. (2010). Introduction: Coloniality of power and de-colonial thinking. In W. Mignolo & A. Escobar (Eds.), *Globalization and the decolonial option* (pp. 1–21). London, UK: Routledge.

Miller, J. H. (1990). Narrative. In F. Lentricchia & T. McLaughlin (Eds.), *Critical terms for literary study* (pp. 64–69). Chicago, IL: University of Chicago Press.

Miller, P., Mintz, J., Hoogstra, L., Fung, H., & Potts, R. (1992). The narrated self: Young children's construction of self in relation to others in conversational stories of personal experience. *Merrill Palmer Quarterly, 38*, 45–67.

Milner, M. (1994). *Status and sacredness: A general theory of status relations and an analysis of Indian culture.* New York, NY: Oxford University Press.

Mirchandani, K. (2012). *Phone clones: Authenticity work in the transnational service economy.* Ithaca, NY: Cornell University Press.

Mishler, E. (1986). *Research interviewing: Context and narrative.* Cambridge, MA: Harvard University Press.

Misra, B. B. (1961). *The Indian middle classes: Their growth in modern times.* Delhi, India: Oxford University Press.

Misra, G. (2003). Implications of culture for psychological knowledge. In J. W. Berry, R. C. Mishra, & R. C. Tripathi (Eds.), *Psychology in human and social development* (pp. 31–67). New Delhi, India: Sage.

Misra, G. (2011). Introduction. In G. Misra (Ed.), *Oxford handbook of psychology in India* (pp. 1–13). New Delhi, India: Oxford University Press.

Mitter, S., Fernandez, G., & Varghese, S. (2004). On the threshold of informalization: Women call center workers in India. In M. Carr (Ed.), *Chains of fortune: Linking women producers and workers with global markets* (pp. 165–183). London, UK: Commonwealth Secretariat.

Moane, G., & Sonn, C. (2015). Postcolonial psychology. In T. Teo (Ed.), *Encyclopedia of critical psychology.* New York, NY: Springer.

Moghaddam, F. (1987). Psychology in the three worlds: As reflected by the crisis in social psychology and the move towards indigenous Third World psychology. *American Psychologist, 42*, 912–920.

Mohan, K. (2011). Cultural values and globalization: India's dilemma. *Current Sociology, 59*, 214–228.

Mohanty, C. T. (1991). Under Western eyes: Feminist scholarship and colonial discourses. In C. T. Mohanty, A. Russo, & L. Torres (Eds.), *Third World women and the politics of feminism* (pp. 51–80). Bloomington, IN: Indiana University Press.

Mohanty, C. T. (2003). *Feminism without borders.* Durham, NC: Duke University Press.

Morawski, J. G. (1994). *Practicing feminisms, reconstructing psychology: Notes on a liminal science.* Ann Arbor, MI: University of Michigan Press.

Mothiar, J. (2008, June). *Get shorty: Simply Mumbai.* Retrieved from http://indiatoday.intoday.in/story/Get+shorty/1/9686.html

Nadeem, S. (2011). *Dead ringers: How outsourcing is changing the way Indians understand themselves.* Princeton, NJ: Princeton University Press.

Nandy, A. (1974). Non-paradigmatic crisis psychology: Reflections on a recipient culture of science. *Indian Journal of Psychology, 49*, 1–20.

Nandy, A. (1983). *The intimate enemy: Loss and recovery of self under colonialism.* Calcutta, India: Oxford University Press.

Natrajan, B. (2012). *The culturalization of caste in India: Identity and inequality in a multicultural age.* London, UK: Routledge.

The new India. (2006, March). *Newsweek.*

Naidu, R. (1994). Traditional Indian personality concepts and the unrealized potential for paradigm shift. *Psychology and Developing Societies, 6*, 70–85.

Nilan, P., & Feixa, C. (2006). Introduction: Youth hybridity and plural worlds. In P. Nilan & C. Feixa (Eds.), *Global youth? Hybrid identities, plural worlds* (pp. 1–13). London, UK: Routledge.

Nilekani, N. (2008). *Imagining India: The idea of a renewed nation*. New Delhi, India: Penguin.

Nsamenang, B. (2002). Adolescence in sub-Saharan Africa: An image constructed from Africa's triple inheritance. In B. B. Brown, R. W. Larson, & T. S. Saraswathi (Eds.), *The world's youth: Adolescence in eight regions of the globe* (pp. 344–362). Cambridge, UK: Cambridge University Press.

Nsamenang, B., & Dawes, A. (1998). Developmental psychology as political psychology in sub-Saharan Africa: The challenge of Africanisation. *Applied Psychology, 47*, 73–87.

Nussbaum, M. (2000). *Women and human development: The capabilities approach*. New York, NY: Cambridge University Press.

Ochs, E., & Capps, L. (2001). *Living narrative: Creating lives in everyday storytelling*. Cambridge, MA: Harvard University Press.

Omvedt, G. (2011). *Understanding caste: From Buddha to Ambedkar and beyond*. New Delhi, India: Orient Blackswan.

Ong, A. (1999). *Flexible citizenship*. Durham, NC: Duke University Press.

Ong, A. (2006). *Neoliberalism as exception: Mutations in citizenship and sovereignty*. Durham, NC: Duke University Press.

Opotow, S. (2010). *Forgotten alternatives and the inclusionary trajectory*. Paper presented at the conference on Forgotten Alternatives: Denaturalizing Conditions of Injustice, City University of New York, New York, NY.

Opotow, S. (1997). What's fair? Justice issues in the affirmative action debate. *American Behavioral Scientist, 41*(2), 232–245.

Owusu-Bempah, K., & Howitt, D. (2000). *Psychology beyond Western perspectives*. Leicester, UK: British Psychological Society Books.

Painter, D. (2015). Postcolonial theory: Towards a worlding of critical psychology. In I. Parker (Ed.), *Handbook of critical psychology* (pp. 366–375). New York, NY: Routledge.

Paranjape, A. (1984). *Theoretical psychology: The meeting of East and West*. New York, NY: Plenum.

Paranjape, A. (2011). The psychology of self and identity: Perspectives from the Indian and Western traditions. In G. Misra (Ed.), *Oxford handbook of psychology in India* (pp. 127–138). New Delhi, India: Oxford University Press.

Parker, I. (2005). *Qualitative psychology: Introducing radical research*. Buckingham, UK: Open University Press.

Parker, I. (2012). Postcolonial psychology. *Postcolonial Studies, 15*(4), 499–505.

Patel, R. (2010). *Working the night shift: Women in India's call center industry*. Stanford, CA: Stanford University Press.

Phinney, J. (1989). Stages of ethnic identity development in minority group adolescents. *Journal of Early Adolescence, 9*, 34–39.

Pickren, W., & Rutherford, A. (2010). *A history of modern psychology in context*. New York, NY: Wiley.

Pieterse, J. N. (2004). *Globalization and culture: Global mélange*. Lanham, MD: Rowman & Littlefield.

Polkinghorne, D. E. (1988). *Narrative knowing and the human sciences*. Albany, NY: State University of New York Press.

Prashad, V. (2012). *The poorer nations: A possible history of the global South*. New York, NY: Verso.

Puri, A. (2008, March). The English speaking curse. *Outlook*. Retrieved from http://www.outlookindia.com/article/english-speaking-curse/237015

Radhakrishnan, S. (2011). *Appropriately Indian: Gender and culture in a new transnational class.* Durham, NC: Duke University Press.

Radway, J. (1984). *Reading the romance.* Chapel Hill, NC: University of North Carolina Press.

Raggatt, P. (2012). Positioning in the dialogical self. In H. J. M. Hermans & T. Gieser (Eds.), *Handbook of dialogical self theory* (pp. 29–45). Cambridge, UK: Cambridge University Press.

Rajan, N. (2012, December). Love at first site. *Business Today.* Retrieved from http://www.businesstoday.in/magazine/features/india-new-love-interest-is-online-dating/story/190332.html

Ram, A. (2014). *Consuming Bollywood. Gender, globalization and media in the Indian diaspora.* New York, NY: Lang.

Ramesh, B. P. (2004). "Cybercoolies "in BPO: Insecurities and vulnerabilities of non-standard work. *Economic and Political Weekly, 39,* 492–497.

Ramesh, B. P. (2008). Work organization, control and empowerment: Managing the contradictions of call centre work. In C. Upadhya & A. R. Vasavi (Eds.), *In an outpost of the global economy: Work and workers in India's information technology industry* (pp. 136–161). New Delhi, India: Routledge.

Rao, K. R. (2011). Trisula: Trident model of person in Indian psychology. In G. Misra (Ed.), *Oxford handbook of psychology in India* (pp. 17–35). New Delhi, India: Oxford University Press.

Rao, M. A., Berry, R., Gonsalves, A., Hastak, Y., Shah, M., & Roeser, R. W. (2013). Globalization and the identity remix among urban adolescents in India. *Journal of Research on Adolescence, 23,* 9–24.

Renan, E. (1990). What is a nation. In H. Bhabha (Ed.), *Nation and narration* (pp. 9–22). New York, NY: Routledge.

Richards, G. (1997). *"Race," racism and psychology: Towards a reflexive history.* London, UK: Routledge.

Richards, P. (2014). The Global South and/in the Global North: Interdisciplinary investigations. *The Global South, 8,* 139–154.

Ricouer, P. (1981). *Hermeneutics and the human sciences.* Cambridge, UK: Cambridge University Press.

Riessman, K. C. (2008). *Narrative methods for the human sciences.* Thousand Oaks, CA: Sage.

Robertson, R. (1992). *Globalization: Social theory and global culture.* Thousand Oaks, CA: Sage.

Rogoff, B. (1990). *Apprenticeship in thinking: Cognitive development in sociocultural activity.* New York, NY: Oxford University Press.

Rogoff, B. (2003). *The cultural nature of human development.* New York, NY: Oxford University Press.

Roland, A. (1988). *In search of self in India and Japan.* Princeton, NJ: Princeton University Press.

Rosaldo, R. (1993). *Culture and truth: Remaking of social analysis.* Boston, MA: Beacon.

Rose, N. (1996). *Inventing our selves: Psychology, power, and personhood.* Cambridge, UK: Cambridge University Press.

Roy, A. (2003). *War talk.* Boston, MA: South End Press.

Roy, A. (2009). *Listening to grasshoppers: Fieldnotes on democracy.* New Delhi, India: Penguin.

Rushdie, S. (1981). *Midnight's children.* New York, NY: Knopf.

Said, E. W. (1979). *Orientalism.* New York, NY: Vintage.

Said, E. W. (1993). *Culture and imperialism*. New York, NY: Vintage.

Sampson, E. (1988). The debate on individualism: Indigenous psychologies of the individual and their role in personal and societal functioning. *American Psychologist, 43*, 15–22.

Sampson, E. (1993). *Celebrating the other: A dialogic account of human nature*. Boulder, CO: Westview.

Saraswathi, T. S., & Larson, R. (2002). Adolescence in global perspective: An agenda for social policy. In B. B. Brown, R. W. Larson, & T. S. Saraswathi (Eds.), *The world's youth: Adolescence in eight regions of the globe* (pp. 344–362). Cambridge, UK: Cambridge University Press.

Sarbin, T. R. (Ed.). (1986). *Narrative psychology: The storied nature of human conduct*. New York, NY: Praeger.

Saldhana, A. (2002). Music, space, identity: Geographies of youth culture in Bangalore. *Cultural Studies, 16*, 337–350.

Sathaye, S. (2008). The scientific imperative to be positive: Self reliance and success in the modern workplace. In C. Upadhya & A. R. Vasavi (Eds.), *In an outpost of the global economy: Work and workers in India's information technology industry* (pp. 136–161). New Delhi, India: Routledge.

Schieffelin, B. B., & Ochs, E. (Eds.). (1986). *Language socialization across cultures*. London, UK: Cambridge University Press.

Schiff, B. (2012). The function of narrative: Toward a narrative psychology of meaning. *Narrative works: Issues, investigations, & interventions, 2*, 33–47.

Schiff, B. (2013). Fractured narratives: Psychology's fragmented narrative psychology. In M. Hyvärinen, M. Hatavara, & H. Lars-Christer (Eds.), *The travelling concepts of narrative* (pp. 245–264). Amsterdam, the Netherlands: Benjamin.

Segall, M. H., Kagitçibasi, C., & Berry, J. W. (Eds.). (1997). *Handbook of cross-cultural psychology: Vol. 3. Social behavior and applications* (2nd ed.). Needham Heights, MA: Allyn & Bacon.

Segall, M. H., Lonner, W. J., & Berry, J. W. (1998). Cross-cultural psychology as a scholarly discipline: On the flowering of culture in behavioral research. *American Psychologist, 53*, 1101–1110.

Segalo, P., Manoff, E., & Fine, M. (2015). Working with embroideries and counter-maps: Engaging memory and imagination within decolonizing frameworks. *Journal of Social and Political Psychology, 3*, 342–364.

Seligson, H. (2011, February 19). Jilted in the U.S., a site finds love in India. *The New York Times*. Retrieved from http://www.nytimes.com/2011/02/20/business/20ignite.html

Sen, A. (1999). *Development as freedom*. New York, NY: Random House.

Sen, A. (2005). *The argumentative Indian: Writings on Indian history, culture, and identity*. New York, NY: Farrar, Straus & Giroux.

Seymour, S. (2004). Multiple caretaking of infants and young children: An area in critical need of a feminist psychological anthropology. *Ethos, 32*, 539–556.

Sharma, D. (2003). Infancy and childhood in India. In D. Sharma (Ed.), *Childhood, family, and sociocultural change in India: Reinterpreting the inner world* (pp. 13–47). New Delhi, India: Oxford University Press.

Sheller, M., & Urry, J. (2006). The new mobilities paradigm. *Environment and Planning, 38*, 207–226.

Shields, S., & Bhatia, S. (2009). Darwin on race, gender and culture. *American Psychologist, 4*, 111–119.

Shohat, E. (). Notes on the "Post-Colonial." *Social text, 31*, 99–113.

Shome, R. (2006). Thinking through the diaspora: Call centers, India, and a new politics of hybridity. *International Journal of Cultural Studies, 9*, 105–124.

Shome, R. (2012). Asian modernities: Culture, politics and media. *Global Media and Communication, 8*, 199–214.

Shweder, R. A. (1990). Cultural psychology: What is it? In J. W. Stigler, R. A. Shweder, & G. Herdt (Eds.), *Cultural psychology: Essays on comparative human development* (pp. 1–43). Cambridge, UK: Cambridge University Press.

Singer, J. A. (2004). Narrative identity and meaning making across the adult lifespan: An introduction. *Journal of Personality, 72*(3), 437–459.

Sinha, D. (1984). Psychology in the context of Third World development. *International Journal of Psychology, 9*, 17–29.

Sinha, D. (1986). *Psychology in the Third World country: The Indian experience.* New Delhi, India: Sage.

Sklair, L. (2009). The transnational capitalist class and the politics of capitalist globalization. In S. Dasgupta, J. N. Pieterse, & J. Nederveen (Eds.), *Politics of globalization* (pp. 82–97). London, UK: Sage.

Smith, B., & Sparkes, A. C. (2008). Contrasting perspectives on narrating selves and identities: An invitation to dialogue. *Qualitative Research, 8*(1), 5–35.

Smith, L. T. (2012). *Decolonizing methodologies: Research and indigenous peoples* (2nd ed.). London, UK: Zed Books.

Sparkes, A. C., & Smith, B. (2008). Narrative constructionist inquiry. In J. A. Holstein & J. F. Gubrium (Eds.), *Handbook of constructionist research* (pp. 295–314). New York, NY: Guildford.

Spencer, H. (1969). *Social statics or the conditions essential to human happiness specified and the first of them developed.* New York, NY: Lelley. (Original work published 1851)

Spivak, G. C. (1988). Can the subaltern speak? In N. Cary & L. Grossberg (Eds.), *Marxism and the interpretation of culture* (pp. 271–313). Urbana, IL: University of Illinois Press.

Spivak, C. G. (1993). *Outside in the teaching machine.* New York, NY: Routledge.

Squire, C., Andrews, M., & Tamboukou, M. (2008). Introduction: What is narrative research? In M. Andrews, C. Squire, & M. Tamboukou (Eds.), *Doing narrative research* (pp. 1–20). Thousand Oaks, CA: Sage.

Sridharan, E. (2011). The growth and sectoral composition of India's middle classes: Their impact on the politics of economic liberalization. In A. Baviskar & R. Ray (Eds.), *Elite and everyman: The cultural politics of Indian middle classes* (pp. 27–57). New Delhi, India: Routledge.

Srivastava, S. (2015). *Entangled urbanism: Slum, gated community and shopping mall in Delhi and Gurgaon.* New Delhi, India: Oxford University Press.

Staeuble, I. (2005). The international expansion of psychology: Cultural imperialism or chances for alternative cultures of knowledge? In A. Gülerce, A. Hofmeister, I. Staeuble, G. Saunders, & J. Kaye (Eds.), *Contemporary theorizing in psychology: Global perspectives* (pp. 88–96). Concord, MA: Captus Press.

Stetsenko, A. (2015). Theory for and as social practice of realizing the future: Implications from a transformative activist stance. In J. Martin, J. Sugarman, & K. L. Slaney (Eds.), *The Wiley handbook of theoretical and philosophical psychology: Methods, approaches, and new directions for social sciences* (pp. 102–116). New York, NY: Wiley-Blackwell.

Stiglitz, J. (2002). *Globalization and its discontents.* New York, NY: Norton.

Sugarman, J. (2015). Neoliberalism and psychological ethics. *Journal of Theoretical and Philosophical Psychology, 35*, 103–116.

Sugarman, J., & Martin, J. (2010). Agentive hermeneutics. In S. Kirschner & J. Martin (Eds.), *The sociocultural turn in psychology: Emergence of mind and self in context* (pp. 159–182). New York, NY: Columbia University Press.

Sundararjan, L. (2015). *Understanding emotion in Chinese culture: Thinking through psychology*. New York, NY: Springer.

Swartz, S. (2005). Can the clinical subject speak? Some thoughts on subaltern psychology. *Theory and Psychology, 15*(4), 505–526.

Tabb, W. (2002). *Unequal partners: A primer on globalization*. New York, NY: New Press.

Taiaiake, A. (1999). *Peace, power, righteousness; An Indigenous manifesto*. Oxford, NY: Oxford University Press.

Taylor, C. (1985). *Philosophy and the human sciences: Philosophical papers*. New York, NY: Cambridge University Press.

Taylor, C. (1989). *Sources of the self: The making of the modern identity*. Cambridge, UK: Cambridge University Press.

Taylor, C. (1992). *Multiculturalism and the politics of recognition*. Princeton, NJ: Princeton University Press.

Taylor, C. (2004). *Modern social imaginaries*. Durham, NC: Duke University Press.

Taylor, P., & Bain, P. (1999). "An assembly line in the head": Work and employee relations in the call center. *Industrial Relations Journal, 30*, 101–117.

Teo, T. (2011). Empirical race psychology and the hermeneutics of epistemological violence. *Human Studies, 34*, 237–255.

Teo, T. (2015). Critical psychology: A geography of intellectual engagement and resistance. *American Psychologist, 70*, 243–254.

Tharoor, S. (2007). *The elephant, the tiger, and the cell phone: Reflections on India, the emerging 21st-century power*. New Delhi, India: Penguin.

Titus, R. (2015). *Yuva India: Consumption and lifestyle choices of a young India*. New Delhi, India: Random House India.

Tomlinson, T. (1999). *Globalization and culture*. Chicago; IL: University of Chicago Press.

Toolis, E. E., & Hammack, P. L. (2015). The lived experience of homeless youth: A narrative approach. *Qualitative Psychology, 2*, 50–68.

Tripathi, R. C. (2011). In search of a "glocal" psychology. In G. Misra (Ed.), *Oxford handbook of psychology in India* (pp. 370–373). New Delhi, India: Oxford University Press.

Trivedi, I. (2014). *India in love: Marriage and sexuality in the 21st century*. New Delhi, India: Aleph.

Tuck, E., & Yang, K. W. (2012). Decolonization is not a metaphor. *Decolonization: Indigeneity, Education & Society, 1*, 1–40.

United Nations Development Programme. (2012). *The millennium development goals report 2012*. New York, NY: United Nations.

United Nations Population Fund. (2014). Annual report—2014. New York, NY: United Nations.

UN-Water. (2008). *Sanitation contributes to international year of dignity and social development*. New York, NY: UNICEF.

Upadhya, C. (2008). Management of culture and managing through culture in the Indian software outsourcing industry. In C. Upadhya & A. R. Vasavi (Eds.), *In an outpost of the global economy: Work and workers in India's information technology industry* (pp. 101–135). New Delhi, India: Routledge.

Upadhya, C. (2011). Software and the "new" middle class in the "new India." In A. Baviskar & R. Ray (Eds.), *Elite and everyman: The cultural politics of Indian middle classes* (pp. 167–192). New Delhi, India: Routledge.

Urry, J. (2010). Mobile sociology. *The British Journal of Sociology, 61,* 347–366.

Valdivia, A. N. (2011). The gendered face of Latinidad: Global circulation of hybridity. In R. Hegde (Ed.), *Circuits of visibility: Gender and transnational media cultures* (pp. 52–67). New York, NY: New York University Press.

Valsiner, J. (2000, June). *Making meaning out of mind: Self-less and self-ful dialogicality*. Paper presented at the First International Conference of the Dialogical Self, University of Nijmegen, the Netherlands.

Valsiner, J. (2007). *Culture in minds and societies: Foundations of cultural psychology*. New Delhi, India: Sage.

Valsiner, J., & Rosa, A. (2007). Contemporary social–cultural research: Uniting culture, society, psychology. In J. Valsiner & A. Rosa (Eds.), *The Cambridge handbook of sociocultural psychology* (pp. 1–22). Cambridge, UK: Cambridge University Press.

Van Maanen, J. (1988). *Tales of the field: On writing ethnography*. Chicago, IL: University of Chicago Press.

Van Maanen, J. (2010). Ethnography as work: Some rules of engagement. *Journal of Management Studies, 48,* 218–234.

Vanaik, A. (1997). *The furies of Indian communalism: Religion, modernity and secularization*. New York, NY: Verso.

Varma, P. K. (2010). *Becoming Indian: The unfinished revolution of culture and identity*. New Delhi, India: Penguin.

Vasavi, A. R. (2008). "Service from India": The making of India's global youth workforce. In C. Upadhya & A. R. Vasavi (Eds.), *In an outpost of the global economy: Work and workers in India's information technology industry* (pp. 210–234). New Delhi, India: Routledge.

Verma, S. (1995). The social constructionist framework: An alternative paradigm for psychology in India. *Indian Journal of Social Science, 8,* 33–57.

Visweswaran, K. (1994). *Fictions of feminist ethnography*. Minneapolis, MN: University of Minnesota Press.

Voloder, L. (2008) Autoethnographic challenges: Confronting self, field and home (Bosnians in Australia). *Australian Journal of Anthropology, 19,* 27–40.

Wade, M. (2009, February 18). Hindus in Valentine's Day attack on lovers. *Sydney Morning Herald*. Retrieved from http://www.smh.com.au/world/hindus-in-valentines-day-attack-on-lovers-20090215-884e.html

Walkerdine, V. (Ed.). (2002). *Challenging subjects: Critical psychology for a new millennium*. New York, NY: Palgrave.

Walkerdine, V., & Bansel, P. (2010). Neoliberalism, work and subjectivity: Towards a more complex account. In M. Wetherell & C. T. Mohanty (Eds.), *The Sage handbook of identity studies* (pp. 492–507). London, UK: Sage.

Watkins, M. (2015). Psychosocial accompaniment. *Journal of Social and Political Psychology, 3,* 324–341.

Weis, L., & Fine, M. (2004). *Working method: Research and social justice*. New York, NY: Routledge.

Wertsch, J. V. (1991). *Voices of the mind: A sociocultural approach to mediated action*. Cambridge, MA: Harvard University Press.

Wertz, F. J. (2011). The qualitative revolution in psychology. *The Humanistic Psychologist*, *39*, 77–104.

White, H. (1978). *Metahistory: The historical imagination in nineteenth century Europe*. Baltimore, MD: Johns Hopkins University Press.

Williams, R. (1977). *Marxism and literature*. Oxford, UK: Oxford University Press.

Willig, C., & Stainton-Rogers, W. (2008). Introduction. In C. Willig & W. Stainton-Rogers (Eds.), *The Sage handbook of qualitative research in psychology* (pp. 1–12). London, UK: Sage.

Wolfe, P. (1999). *Settler colonialism and the transformation of anthropology*. New York, NY: Bloomsbury Academic.

INDEX

best practices, global
  training, India, 41–42
  WASP culture as, 43–45
Bhabha, H., 15, 16, 158, 252
bhakti yoga, 250
Bharamshi, Anita, 58
Bhatia, S., 37, 39, 41, 50, 51, 78, 90, 277, 294, 296
big stories, 217–218
black identity, 66
Boo, K., 225
borderlands, culture, 15
Bourdieu, P., 114, 115, 116, 194
Boussebaa, M., 158
BPOs. *see* business processing
  offices (BPOs)
Brahmans (Brahmins), 199, 203
Brockmeier, J., 85, 220
Brodie, J., 236, 245
Bruner, Jerome, 69–71, 74, 82, 188, 218, 232
Burawoy, M., 269
Burke, K., 86n4
burnout, call center workers, 132, 159
business processing offices (BPOs), 130–132, 131, 195, 271. *see also specific topics*
  on economy, 138
  employees, socioeconomic groups, 194
  English language skills for, 195
  evolution, 134
  fieldwork, 271
  individualization, 161
  on marriages, 134
  on youth, 140

call centers. *see also specific topics*
  defined, 131
  fieldwork sites, 271
  history and economics, 131–132
call center workers, India, 13
  attrition and burnout rates, 132, 159
  authenticity, 158–159
  demographic dividend, 24–26, 130–132
  English language
    skills, 51, 136
    training, 50–51
  identities, 143–144
  individualism, 143

mimicry and identity, 15, 156–162, 236 (*see also* mimicry, identity and)
mother tongue influence, 51, 136, 157–158
pink-collar, 152
psychological freedom, 135
racism, 136–138
salaries and class, 130–131, 132
stigma, 143
stress, 46–47
call center workers' stories, 132–152
  gender, agency, and "good money," 132–138
  individualized Indianness, 143–155 (*see also* Indianness, individualized)
  Madhu, 142–144
  Madhuri, 138–141, 147–148, 151
  marriage and divorce stigma, 139
  Namrata, 141–142
  racism, 136–138
  Vijay, 132–138, 148, 150
Cancilini, Nestor Garcia, 16, 113
capacity to aspire, 166, 186, 187–188, 197, 209, 225
capital
  cultural, 114–115
  landed, 23–24
  law, regulation, 24
  linguistic, 114–115
capitalism, neoliberal, 173–174
caste system. *see also* class
  Babsaheb Ambedkar on, 198–205
  class identities, 198–205
  Gandhi on, 200
  on identity, 199–200
  new, English language fluency as, 193–194
  origins, 199
  "Other Backward Classes," 203
  weakening, 203–204
Chacko, E., 170–171
Chakrabarty, D., 83
Charmaz, K., 275
Chaudhary, Nandita, 118, 119, 226, 239
Chhabria, S., 233–234, 254
children
  of globalization, 88
  liberalization's, 88, 101–102, 220

Dudgeon, P., 252
Duflo, Esther, 187
dukkha, 249

education
    caste, 198
    colonialism, 245
    for elites, 189, 191, 270–271 (*see also*
        Meridian College students)
    liberal arts, 88–91, 92,
        113–114, 125n3
    psychology, India, 69
    self-help courses, on Indian values,
        159–160
    on slum dwellers, 175, 183–185,
        190–198, 205–206, 209, 278
    structural inequalities, 209, 241, 243
    urban youth, 79
    urban youth, poor, 35, 243 (*see also*
        slum dwellers)
    women's access, 60, 177
ego synthesis, 66
elite consumption, 100–101
emic concepts, 81–82
emotional labor, 159
empowerment
    gainful employment, 143
    illusionary sense, 159
    slum dwellers, 212
    women's, call center work, 143, 155
English language fluency
    aspiration, 196–197
    capital access, symbolic, 194
    caste, new, 193–194
    curse, global economy, 194–196
    hi-fi class, 192–193
English language skills
    British, 132–138, 147, 157, 162–
        163n1, 196–198
    corporate Englishization, 158
    mother tongue influence, 51, 136,
        157–158
    neutral English, 51–52, 115, 136, 147,
        157–158, 180
    slum dwellers, 190–198
English language training, 156–158
    accent, 156–159
    access, unequal, 195
    colonial subjects , new, 50–51
    Indianisms, 51–52

necessity, 195
    western global speech and deficient
        Indian worker, 51–52
entangled marginality, 260–262
entrapment, temporal, 131
epistemological decolonization, 246
epistemological pluralism, 253–255
Erikson, Erik, 65–68, 75
Ethnicity store, 29–30
ethnography
    global, 269
    multi-sited, 269–270
ethnoscape, 234
Euro-American psychology, 1, 5–9
eviction anxiety, slum dwellers, 181–183
ex-centric, 190
experience, narrative, culture,
        and, 74–77
experience-near concepts, 81

familism, 118–119
family, Indian, 5
    American-style values, 62
    changing, 143, 145
    divorce and shame, 139
    expectations, *vs.* work, 129
    extended family cultures,
        43–44, 226
    globalization on, 12, 92, 110
    vs. individualism, 42
    Namrata's story, 142
    orientation and traditions, 106,
        111–112, 118–119, 120, 149
    psychological discourses, 46
    psychological freedom, 135
    status, car ownership on, 134, 150
    women
        honor, 143
        independence, financial, 93,
            144–146, 152–153, 223
        independence, psychological and
            cultural, 142, 152–153, 223
        traditional role, 60
Fanon, Frantz, 239–241
Femina, 99, 125n5
Fexia, Carles, 223
fieldwork. *see also specific work*
    definition, 278
    homework and, blurred boundaries,
        279–283

fieldwork (*cont.*)
  location, at sites of social class,
    269–274
  research positioning, 278
financescape, 234
Fine, M., 174, 261, 262, 274
First World, 20n1
Flutch, Michael, 32
folk psychology, 232–233
foreign ways of being, 106
Foucault, M., 54, 235
Frank, Arthur, 104
Fraser, N., 243–244
freedom
  of agency, 190
  psychological, 135
Freeman, M., 74, 81, 190, 218, 231–232
Friedman, Thomas, 130
Friends, 102–104, 109, 123

Gabriel, Y., 158
Gandhi, 266
Ganon, Frantz, 239–241
Gaonkar, D. P., 83
gazes, 161–162
Geertz, C., 84
gender. *see also* women
  bias, slums, 184–185
  roles and identities, 153–155
gendered rules, 153–155
geographical development, uneven, 174
Gergen, K. J., 72, 237, 257–258, 274
Gergen, M. M., 72
Germany, 32–36, 34
Giddens, A., 64
global citizens, 94
Global Desi store, 30–31
global governance, 24
global Indian, 50, 87. *see also*
    Indianness, global
  Americanized, 93–96
  cosmopolitan cultural centers, 92
  culture, 118
  elite Indian youth on, 99, 105, 106
  Indian youth on, 93
  polyphonic narratives, 104–108
  "ultimate," 97–104, 124
globalization. *see also specific topics*
  accumulation by dispossession, 23–24
  agency and personhood
    reconstruction, 146–149

from below, 243
children of, 92
college students on, 91
countertopographies, 166
on culture, 91–92
definitions, 22
as dual phenomenon, 235
elite Indian youth on, 99, 105
on family life, 92
hybridity, 124
imagined American cultural practices,
    108–109
individualism, 143
as *khokla* (empty) term, 205–209
lure, 104–108
narrative and urban poor, 209–212
neoliberal capitalism, 173–174
neoliberalism, 23–25, 39, 219–220
on slum dwellers, 179–180
teaching, in socially unequal
    world, 254
globalization, cultural psychology,
    21–36. *see also specific topics*
  concept, 21–22
  current, 23
  definitions, 21
  desi, 37n2
  desi, global, Phoenix Mall, 26–32, 37n2
    (*see also* Phoenix Mall, Pune)
  neoliberalism, 23–25, 39
    Indo-German urban *Mela,*
      32–36, 37n3
  time–space compression, 21–22
globalization, studying at home,
    257–285
  decolonizing as struggle at margins,
    259–263
  fieldwork, stories, and relationships,
    263–274
  interviews, 263
  location, sites of social class,
    269–274
  social class in India, 264–269
  interviews, narrative approach,
    274–276
  qualitative inquiry and writing
    culture, 258–259
  reflexivity and subjectivity, qualitative
    research, 276–284
  culture loss and home, 283–284
  fieldwork, research positioning, 278

Murray, Henry, 75
Myers-Briggs Type Indicator
(MBTI), 45–46

Nadeem, S., 124, 143, 156, 228, 229
Naidu, R., 247–248
Namrata's story, 141–142
Nandy, A., 247, 265
narration, 77
narrative, 57–85
  agency, 78
  American culture, perceptions and
    permissiveness, 61–63
  approach, interviews, 274–276
  capacity, 189, 209, 210
  cognitive and personality
    approaches, 74–75
  as communicative, 74
  culture, meaning-making, and, 68–70,
    71, 78, 158, 197–198
  culture-thick, 81–82
  demands, 221
  emic, 81–82
  empathetic, 74
  engagement, 220
  experience, culture, and, 74–77
  identity
    conflicts, webs of meaning and,
      79–88, 86n6, 189 (see also
      Valentine's Day narrative)
    psychology and, 64–65
  identity crisis, 58–61
    Erikson and, 65–68
  Ignighter.com (Step Out), 57–58,
    85–86n1
  imagination, 17–19, 218
  interpretive approaches, 75–76
  knowing the world, ways of, 70–71, 188
  method, 275
  narrative psychology
    as identity in cultural practices, 77–79
    theories, 71–73
  polyphonic, 104–108
  self, neoliberalism and, 235–237
  social imagination, 17–19
  sociocultural approach, 76–77
narrative psychology, 72, 221
  Bruner 's, 70
  cultural practices, identity, 77–79
  theories, 71–73

narrative way of knowing, 218
nation, 252
national cultures, 42
nationalism, 252
Natrajan, B., 203–204
navigational capacity, 186, 189–190, 192
Nehru, Jawaharlal, 265
neoliberal capitalism, globalization and,
  173–174
neoliberal governmentality, 235
neoliberalism. see also specific topics
  globalization, 23–25, 39, 219–220
  identities, Indian, 122
  Indo-German urban Mela,
    32–36, 37n3
  labor, 39–40
  psychology, 39 (see also neoliberal self)
  specialized transnational
    economy, 40
neoliberal self, 39–55
  cross-cultural psychology
    training, 41–42
  cultural difference and identity, 40
  English language and new colonial
    subjects, 50–51
  globalization, 39
  labor growth, offshore, 39–40
  narratives, 235–237
  personality tests, 45–46
  positive, scientific imperative to
    be, 46–50
  psychological science coloniality and
    global culture, 41–52 (see also
    coloniality, psychological science,
    global culture and)
  psychology as "global psy" discipline,
    53–55, 160
  specialized transnational
    economy, 40
  WASP culture as "global best
    practices," 43–45
  western global speech and deficient
    Indian worker, 51–52
night shift work
  independence and new gender roles
    and identities, 153–155
  women, 131, 138, 143, 152–153, 155,
    162, 224
Nilan, Pam, 223
non-places, 27–28

social justice, 216, 241–254 (*see also* cultural psychology, transnational)
psychology-as-explorer model, 239
psychology-as-tourist model, 239
psychosocial development theory, 65–68, 75
Psy complex, 64
psy discipline, global, 53–55, 160
Pune. *see also specific topics*
    expansion, 26–27
    geography, 166–167, 212nn4–5
    multiplex cinemas, 181, 213n9
    Phoenix Mall, 27–28
    urban planning and future developments, 212–213n6
    water logging, 175, 213n7
Puri, A., 195–196
purusa, 249
purusha, 199

qualitative approaches
    decolonizing psychology, struggle at margins, 259–263
    reflexivity and subjectivity, 276–284 (*see also* reflexivity and subjectivity, qualitative research)
    writing culture and, 258–259

racism, call centers, 136–138
Radhakrishnan, S., 118, 119–120, 122
Radway, Janice, 104
Raggatt, P., 105
Rajesh's story, 207–208
Rajneesh, Osho, 166, 212n3
Ram, Anjali, 120–121
Ramesh, B. P., 159, 161
Rao, K. Ramakrishna, 249–250
Rao, P. V. Narasimha, 22, 102
rational choice model, 187, 188
Ravi's story, 178–183
Ray, R., 265
recognition, politics of, 209–210
redefining psychology, 2–3
redistribution, politics of, 211
reflexive project, 64
reflexivity and subjectivity, qualitative research, 276–284
    culture loss and home, 283–284
    fieldwork, research positioning, 278

homework and fieldwork, blurred boundaries, 279–283
    politics of location and representation, 276–277
    self-narrative, 278–279
    self-reflexive process, 277, 283–284
    subjects, 276–277
refraction, ventriloquation, 149–150
Renan, E., 252
representation, politics of, 276–277
research
    as dirty term, 260
    participatory action, 262
    positioning, fieldwork, 278
    postcolonial cultures, 277–278
    qualitative, reflexivity and subjectivity, 276–284 (*see also* reflexivity and subjectivity, qualitative research)
Richards, P., 246
Ricouer, P., 77
Robertson, Roland, 22
Roland, A., 226
Rosa, A., 68
Rosaldo, R., 21
Rose, N., 54, 160
Roy, Arundhati, 216–217, 241
Ruglis, J., 174
rural-to-urban migration, 173

Sachs, Adam, 57
Said, E. W., 1
Sainath, P., 243
Saldhana, A., 97
sanitation, lack of, 177, 213n8. *see also* toilets, private, lack of
Sarbin, T. R., 72
Sathaye, S., 47–48, 160
sathyagraha, 265
Sawai Gandharva Bhimsen Mahotsav, 59–60, 86n3
Schiff, B., 73, 74, 75–76, 221
Scrubs, 102
Segall, M. H., 42, 230
self
    American, 47–48, 235–236
    concept of, promotion, 47–48
    consumerist, 100–102
    dialogical, 105, 129
    discourses, 115–117
    global, transnational class, 113–117

self (*cont.*)
global psy, 54
"happy selves," 159–162
new interior, 88
polyphonic, 104–105
positive psychology, 45–50, 235
self, outsourcing, 127–164
call center worker stories, 132–152
(*see also* call center workers'
stories)
human resources manager, 139–141
individualized Indianness,
143–155, 224 (*see also*
Indianness, individualized)
mimicry and identity, 15,
156–162, 236 (*see also* mimicry,
identity and)
self-conscious traditionalism, 253
self-control, 187
self-discovery, 117
liberal arts, 88–91, 125n2
self-help courses, on Indian values,
159–160
self-narrative, 278–279
self-reflexive process, 277, 283–284
Sen, A., 190, 226–227, 243
Sen, S., 171
sex, romance and arranged marriages,
108–112
Sex and the City, 100, 103–104,
109, 123
Shaadi.com, 85–86n1
Shome, R., 157, 161–162
shudras, 199
Shweder, R. A., 234
silent revolution, 204
Sinha, S., 158
Sklair, Leslie, 114
slum dwellers, 241–242
slum dwellers, Pune, 165–212, 205. *see
also specific topics*
Aman's story, 176–177
aspirations, identity, and structural
practices, 186–190
aspire, capacity to, 166, 186, 187–188,
197, 209
caste and class identities, 198–205
class inequalities and dangerous
living, 178–183 (*see also*
Ravi's story)

class struggles and eviction anxieties,
178–183
cultural practices and maps of
aspiration, 183–186 (*see also*
Priyanka's story)
gender bias, 184–185
globalization, narrative and urban
poor, 209–212
hi-fi identity, education, and English
language skills, 190–198 (*see also*
hi-fi class)
Panchsheel *basti* (Pune slums),
165–166, 241–242, 272–273
locating, 167, 171–177
poor, India's, 165, 212n1
Rajesh, 207–208
topographies and structural realities,
166–171, 224
Vinod, globalization as *khokla* (empty)
term, 205–209
willpower and self-control, 187
Zainab's story, 175–176
slums
definition, 171
megacities and exponential growth,
172–173
mega-slums, 174
population growth, 172
small stories, 217–218
Smith, L. T., 74, 75, 237, 259–260
social class, India, 264–269
social imagination, 17–19
India's youth, 26
narrative and, 17–19
socialization, indulgent, 118
social justice psychology, 216, 241–254.
see also cultural psychology,
transnational
class, 243
decolonization, 245–246
distributive justice, 244
globalization from below, 243
Hindu psychology and philosophy,
248–250
how, what, who, when, and where, 244
inclusionary justice, 244
indigenizing modern psychology,
247–248
indigenous communities, anticolonial
position, 246–247